MELANCHOLY ACTS

Melancholy Acts

DEFEAT AND CULTURAL CRITIQUE IN THE ARAB WORLD

Nouri Gana

FORDHAM UNIVERSITY PRESS   NEW YORK   2023

Copyright © 2023 Fordham University Press

All rights reserved. No part of this publication may be reproduced, stored in a retrieval system, or transmitted in any form or by any means—electronic, mechanical, photocopy, recording, or any other—except for brief quotations in printed reviews, without the prior permission of the publisher.

Fordham University Press has no responsibility for the persistence or accuracy of URLs for external or third-party Internet websites referred to in this publication and does not guarantee that any content on such websites is, or will remain, accurate or appropriate.

Fordham University Press also publishes its books in a variety of electronic formats. Some content that appears in print may not be available in electronic books.

Visit us online at www.fordhampress.com.

Library of Congress Cataloging-in-Publication Data available online at https://catalog.loc.gov.

Printed in the United States of America

25 24 23   5 4 3 2 1

First edition

In loving memory of my beloved mother, Fatma Jedīdī
(February 6, 1932 — January 31, 2013)

وَما انسَدَّت الدُنيا عَلَيَّ لِضيقِها
وَلَكِنَّ طَرفاً لا أَراكِ بِهِ أَعمى

Contents

NOTE ON TRANSLATION AND TRANSLITERATION ix

Introduction: Melancholy Acts 1

1 Melancholy Formations: From Nakba to
   Naksa and Beyond 45

2 Melancholy Forms: Poetry in the Aftermath of Catastrophe 89

3 Enduring Left Melancholy: Recasting the Crisis
   of the Nasserite Intellectual 123

4 Melancholy Manhood: Modernity and Neopatriarchy
   in Tunisian Cinema 158

5 Melancholy Ends: Palestinian Film and
   Narrative Martyrdom 195

6 Melancholy Islam: Jihad, Jouissance, and
   Female Clairvoyance 234

Epilogue: Melancholy Critique 277

ACKNOWLEDGMENTS 293

THE UNSHELTERING SKY: A NOTE ON THE COVER ART 297

BIBLIOGRAPHY 299

INDEX 313

Note on Translation and Transliteration

All translations from Arabic and French are my own, unless otherwise indicated. All transliterations are either from Arabic or dialect. I have adopted the IJMES transliteration system, except for proper names.

لو يذكرُ الزيتون غارسهُ
لصار الزيت دمعا!
—محمود درويش

Introduction
Melancholy Acts

> If the ultimate message of psychoanalysis amounts to the contention that we must manage to mourn what we have lost forever, this means it is a normalizing and adaptive discourse preaching the consensual virtues of renunciation and confession: the very thing priests have always advised, quite successfully, with no need for recourse to psychoanalytic theory.
>
> — PIERRE MACHEREY

On December 17, 2010, the Tunisian public was gripped by a horrific incident that I will qualify as a melancholy act. A young street vendor, Mohamed Bouazizi, set himself ablaze in front of the governorate headquarters of Sidi Bouzid, central Tunisia, following his humiliation by a municipal policewoman who not only fined him and confiscated his fruit cart but allegedly slapped him, spat in his face, and insulted his dead father. While terribly tragic, Bouazizi's act proved, retrospectively at least, quite empowering: it initially sparked small-scale gatherings, marches, and protests in Sidi Bouzid; soon, however, and thanks to local activist coordination and social media mobilization, the low-key airing of sociopolitical grievances spawned a nationwide wave of contention and protest whose ripple effects would afterward reach Egypt, Libya, Yemen, and Syria as well as Sudan and Algeria at later stages, along with, of course, the many other countries across the globe where demonstrations against dictatorships and/or the neoliberal dispensations took place.[1]

---

1. For more details on this incident and on the mass uprising that followed, see Nouri Gana, ed., The *Making of the Tunisian Revolution: Contexts, Architects, Prospects* (Edinburgh: Edinburgh

Bouazizi's act, which also gave rise to several copycat self-immolations across North Africa, is reminiscent of many instances in the Arab world where suicide has served for some as the only means left for communicating discontent, indignation, and disgust and for protesting against insufferable oppression and reprehensible injustices of various kinds. These instances have ranged from the infamous suicide bombings and martyrdom operations in Palestine, Iraq, Syria, and elsewhere in the Arab world to the shocking suicide of the modernist Lebanese poet Khalil Hawi, who shot himself to death on June 6, 1982, to protest the Israeli invasion of Beirut that same day.[2]

While the immediate catalysts and longstanding ideological motives, or "honorable considerations,"[3] as well as the empowering or disempowering effects, of these suicides remain debatable and will at any rate differ and vary from case to case, there is ample evidence, I argue, that, broadly speaking, they are individual materializations of a more collective disposition toward melancholy as, on the one hand, a psychoaffective response to the ever-deepening crisis of the postcolonial project of national liberation and social transformation, and as, on the other, a desperate or despairing response to the unyielding hegemony of the joined-up forces of local despotism, apartheid Zionism, and global neoliberal imperialism. Regardless of their variably distinct individual or ideological character, these suicide protests are precipitated by the affect that occasions them, ranging from the offensive shaming of a single person to the collective humiliation of an entire people, which is what authoritarian or colonial aggression constitutes from a deep or surface psychic and cognitive perspective. The intertwined dynamics between individual and collective responses to acts of shaming cannot be overstressed: while Bouazizi's case illustrates how personal indignation results in demonstrations of collective compassion

---

University Press, 2013). It has become clear that much of the backstory to Bouazizi's suicide was invented to maximize mobilization and effectiveness, yet there is no gainsaying the fact that it drew attention away from the everyday stories of rural agitation and dissent by farmers, peasants, and syndicalists. See Habib Ayeb and Ray Bush, *Food Insecurity and Revolution in the Middle East and North Africa* (London: Anthem Press, 2019), 70–72.

2. Cases of what may loosely be called suicide protests are too numerous to enumerate here. Suffice it to mention a few others about which I will speak in this book. The Syrian playwright Saadallah Wannous unsuccessfully tried to take his own life in protest against Anwar Sadat's visit to Israel on November 19, 1977, while the Jordanian writer and poet Tayseer al-Sboul took his own on November 15, 1973, after witnessing the meeting between the Egyptians and the Israelis in the wake of the Yom Kippur War of 1973. On June 7, 1997, the Egyptian communist and feminist activist Arwa Salih jumped from the tenth floor of an apartment balcony in what appears to be a belated epitaph-cum-condemnation of a co-opted leftist movement and a failed project of national liberation.

3. Albert Camus, *The Myth of Sisyphus*, trans. Justin O'Brien (New York: Penguin, 1979), 13.

and plebian solidarity that gradually gathered momentum and transformed into a nationwide movement of insurrection and revolt, Hawi's case demonstrates how the Israeli invasion of Lebanon as an act of colonial offense and gratuitous muscle-flexing is arrestingly apprehended and decried at the individual level of an Arab poet with a keen sensitivity.

Given the intimate collision/collusion between settler colonialism, neocolonialism, and authoritarianism in the Arab world, Hawi's and Bouazizi's suicides must be seen in a continuum of endogenous, fragmented, and dispersed micronarratives of resistance. Both are embodiments or graphic materializations of a morbid affective disposition that is equally aggravated and revolted by domestic as much as by foreign acts of aggression and shaming. It may be the case that both suicides, from a Lacanian perspective, are the tragic testaments to the conscious assumptions of the unconscious death drive—really, alternative modes of self-realization in the face of the "subjective impasses" generated by the collusion of authoritarianism and colonialism in Tunisia and Lebanon respectively—except that they are, from a plain historical perspective, unequivocal indictments of both Arab despotism and settler colonial Zionism.[4] As Jean-Paul Sartre puts it, "in attempting to get rid of my life I affirm that I live and assume this life as bad."[5] Insofar as they crystallize the enduring spirit of emancipatory revolutionism, much like the six Palestinian prisoners who miraculously tunneled their way out of a high-security Israeli prison, Hawi's and Bouazizi's suicides constitute geotemporal, discrete, and transgenerational acts of collaborative revolutionism, not in the sense of highly organized and rigorously implemented revolutionary strategies but in the sense of the generative, cumulative, and "collective actions of non-collective actors," as Asef Bayat puts in his astute analysis of the quotidian politics of everyday life.[6] All the more so given that shame is variably embedded in colonial

---

4. See Jacques Lacan, "The Mirror Stage as Formative of the *I* Function as Revealed in Psychoanalytic Experience," in *Écrits*, trans. Bruce Fink (New York: Norton, 2006), 80. Lacan speaks of the phenomenon of suicide in relation to an overall critique of existentialism, which according to him "can be judged on the basis of the justification it provides for the subjective impasses that do, indeed, result therefrom: a freedom that is never so authentically affirmed as when it is within the walls of a prison; a demand for commitment that expresses the inability of pure consciousness to overcome any situation; a voyeuristic-sadistic idealization of sexual relationships; a personality that achieves self-realization only in suicide; and a consciousness of the other that can only be satisfied by Hegelian murder" (80).

5. Jean-Paul Sartre, *Being and Nothingness: A Phenomenological Essay on Ontology*, trans. Hazel Barnes (New York: Washington Square Press, 1956), 556.

6. Asef Bayat, *Life as Politics: How Ordinary People Change the Middle East* (Stanford, CA: Stanford University Press, 2010), 14. See also Nouri Gana, "Introduction: Collaborative Revolutionism," in Gana, *The Making of the Tunisian Revolution*, 2.

and postcolonial societies—instilled and felt at both the individual and collective levels—in such a way that it continuously demands sublimation or psychoaffective release.

Postcolonial shame in the Arab world foments a tangle of psychoaffective and psychosomatic responses that range from self-impoverishment and visceral rage to regressive, depressive, or assertive narcissism and compensatory pride. All these psychoaffective responses are part and parcel of a generalized psychopolitical disposition toward melancholy or, as will become clear, the differential spectrum of melancholy. Melancholy unsettles and makes legible a series of seemingly contradictory proclivities in Arab contemporaneity, namely the unsuspecting divides between speech and praxis, illness and insight, suicide and protest, grief and grievance, defeat and defiance, compliance and critique, creativity and stasis, and commitment and detachment, as well as the recurrent aesthetic schism in Arab literary and cultural representation between the world of affect and the world of politics, or the world of ideality and that of reality, and so on. I should make it clear at the outset that I have no intention to stretch or overburden the concept of melancholy beyond its saturnine recognition; I contend, though, that the particular fluidity and fecundity of melancholy, as both a metapsychological concept and a dominant psychoaffective complex in the Arab world, offers a much-needed corrective to resilient orientalist, atavistic, and nativist approaches to Arab literary and cultural production. Much of the misprision and misconstrual of Arab literary and cultural production stems not simply from the sedimented allegories of reception that still dominate approaches to anything foreign in the Euro-American academy, but also from the particular rhetorical fecundity, indirectness, ambivalence, ambiguity, and opacity of Arab literary and cultural expression, all the more so as Arabs find themselves caught between the tragedies of settler colonial dispossession and the farcical narcissisms, albeit no less tragic, of everyday sectarianism and civil wars along ethnic and religious lines.

Melancholizing over Losses

It may not be surprising that modern Arab history has been marked by the experience of (settler) colonialism, but what is surprising is that (settler) colonial permutations should continue apace into the postcolonial phase. From the settler colonial occupation of Palestine before and after 1948 to the military invasion of Iraq in 2003 and beyond, settler colonial and imperial encroachments have cast a long shadow on the nationalist and socialist achievements of several Arab countries during the decolonization era, including the successful Egyptian and Algerian revolutions in the 1950s. There is no gainsaying the

INTRODUCTION: MELANCHOLY ACTS   5

fact that the more firmly entrenched the twin projects of settler colonialism and Euro-American imperialism become, the more insouciant Arab regimes get about democracy and human rights, especially in the wake of the 1967 defeat, which had de facto fermented the duel between autocratic and theocratic ideologies even while it initially spawned a good deal of ideological incredulity and intellectual self-critique. Ever since, it became clear that the loss of national sovereignty and individual self-regard can no longer be embodied or substituted by an ideology like Arab nationalism, communism, or Islamism or by a charismatic leader like Egyptian president Gamal Abdel Nasser (1918–1970). Could it be farfetched to suggest then that Hawi's and Bouazizi's suicides are desublimations of the aggression that would have been contained by either a proper process of grief and grievance or by the protective and consolatory shields of religion and national sovereignty?[7]

Hawi's and Bouazizi's suicides constitute in this sense less a melancholy *turn* than a *return* to the hauntingly traumatic legacy of the Naksa or setback—the June 1967 Six Day War, in which Israel decisively defeated and humiliated the Arab armies of Egypt, Syria, and Jordan and expanded its territory to the West Bank and East Jerusalem, the Golan Heights, and the Sinai Desert (later returned to Egypt following the 1978 Camp David Accords). While the Naksa has routinely been used in the social sciences as an analytical lens through and against which to read the Arab Muslim world (in the very same manner that notions of Islam, "Oriental despotism," or "the Arab woman" have previously offered generations of Orientalists indispensable categories of analysis), it has rarely been studied as an object of analysis *per se*, much less through the triptych of postcolonialism, deconstruction, and psychoanalysis. In this respect, George Tarabishi's 1991 book *Al-Muthaqqafūn al-Arab wat-Turāth* (Arab Intellectuals and Tradition) is a solitary and salutary undertaking—really, an exception to the generalized indisposition, if not resistance altogether, by Arab critics and intellectuals at the time to discern the psychoaffective legacy of the Naksa through the productive lenses of psychoanalysis and deconstruction (in favor of generally Marxist materialist or structuralist historicist methodologies).

For Tarabishi, the 1967 defeat spawned "a psychic epidemic or *wabā' nafsī*" that poisoned the affective map of the Arab psyche, and resulted in a "pathological effect on Arab subjectivity" (*maf'ūl mumriḍ 'alā al-shakhsiyya*

---

7. I am deliberately extending to the colonial and postcolonial setting Freud's engagement with the topic of loss at a more or less individual level in his influential essay, "Mourning and Melancholia." See Sigmund Freud, "Mourning and Melancholia," in *On Metapsychology: The Theory of Psychoanalysis*, ed. Angela Richards (London: Penguin, 1991), 245–69.

al-'arabiyya).[8] The subtitle of Tarabishi's book is *Al-taḥlīl al-nafsī li'usāb jamā'ī* (the psychoanalysis of a collective neurosis); as such, it offers a symptomatic reading of Arab thought in the aftermath of the 1967 military defeat, deliberately foregrounding the psychoaffective dynamics of which it was a product. For Tarabishi, while the sudden 1798 colonial encounter with European modernity (Napoleon in Egypt) had resulted in a productive shock that impelled Arabs to start the process of modernization (the *nahḍa* or rise, awakening and renaissance), the 1967 defeat resulted in a counterproductive trauma. This trauma compelled Arabs to look backward to the protective shield of tradition, a move that ran against the openness to European modernity which the *nahḍa* movement had for years strived to bring about. In other words, the 1967 defeat compelled Arab intellectuals to turn away from the *nahḍa* rather than return to it. Disowning the *nahḍa*, which had encouraged a critical embrace of European modernity, and seeking in its stead to reclaim early Islamic tradition became synonymous with a painful longing for belonging in the aftermath of defeat and humiliation. Slogans such as "Islam is the solution" gained traction even outside the circles of the Muslim Brotherhood and fostered the fantasy of a transcendental origin whose recovery would guarantee the recovery from the devastating effects of 1967, as well as the reinstatement of cultural identity and the reestablishment of sovereignty on a solid basis.

The longing for authenticity became, according to Tarabishi, all the more pronounced as Israel's phallic omnipotence (symbolized by the superiority of its Air Force) was seen to neutralize Nasser and his power as a transnational protective father figure for all Arabs. With the demise of that towering father figure, Arabs, according to Tarabishi, found in the return to *turāth* (tradition or heritage) an alternative or compensatory symbolic father. While the *nahḍa* was dominated by the searing sense of belatedness and the critical urgency to catch up with Europe, the Naksa was dominated by the shame of castration and the impulse to act out, react, repair, or compensate for the traumatic losses incurred by Israel's preemptive strikes. The 1967 defeat was traumatizing, according to Tarabishi, not only because of its utter unexpectedness (at a time when victory over Israel was thought to be only a matter of time), but also because of its humiliating swiftness and recursive aftereffects—aftereffects that still reverberate in Arab contemporaneity and that can best be illustrated by the dawning realization that victory over Israel has become as impossible as exemption from its expansionist aggression, much less from its routine settler racist and apartheid practices. It is as if the defeat had catapulted or expelled

---

8. George Tarabishi, *Al-Muthaqqafūn al-'Arab wa al-Turāth* (Arab Intellectuals and Tradition) (London: Riad El-Rayyes Books Ltd, 1991), 10.

Arabs out of history at the very moment when they were reentering it with the decolonial ideology of Arab nationalism and the successful anticolonial and revolutionary struggles (especially in Algeria). These nationalist and anticolonial movements and struggles have become exemplars of third-worldist and nonalignment imagination. The symbolic victory of Nasser in 1956, which had engendered feelings of euphoria and good omens at the time, must have made it even harder to stomach the subsequent trauma of the 1967 defeat. It may be the case, in hindsight, that Arabs must have overestimated their military might and underestimated the military prowess of their enemy.[9] The defeat's crushing impact and untimeliness were too much to bear at a time of high expectations for renewed Arab glory, which is why, for Tarabishi, it resulted in an excess of regressive psychopathological practices, namely the *returns of* forms of orthodoxy which the *naḥḍa* either surpassed or repressed.

The defeat of 1967 was, then, a beginning of an end that would later be gradually but steadily hammered home by a series of events ranging from the Camp David Accords to those in Oslo up to the annexation and normalization plans that were spearheaded by the Trump administration, not to mention the routine Israeli onslaughts on Gaza with complete impunity. (Since the al-Aqsa Intifada in 2000, Israel bombed Gaza in 2006, 2008, 2009, 2010, 2011, 2014, 2018, 2019, and 2021.) The finality of the defeat was such that it foreclosed the possibility of a second round. What is traumatizing is not so much the defeat in itself as the *afteraffect* in which it was and continues to be experienced and relived again and again as an irreversible destiny, a continually retraumatizing rememory—really, "an aftermath without end," to borrow David Scott's felicitous expression.[10] In other words, the defeat has left Arabs bereft of a dignified, let alone promissory, future, and, what is even more damaging, it has left Arabs with a sense that their past achievements (Arab Islamic glory and high nationalism) are actually the best they could have ever aspired to achieve. And this partly explains the Salafi and Islamist logic that professes and longs for a future for Arabs worthy of their past, a future past. Arab contemporaneity has become from this perspective unlivable without the imaginary fetishization of a glorious Arab Muslim past, a time of centralized caliphate rule and military omnipotence, but while the inspirational and compensatory psychic potencies

---

9. "Fantasies of omnipotence had been mistaken for real power and had accordingly led to a disregard of the adversary's superiority," see Alexander and Margarete Mitscherlich, *The Inability to Mourn: Principles of Collective Behavior*, trans. Beverley R. Placzek (New York: Grove Press, 1975), 12.

10. David Scott, *Omens of Adversity: Tragedy, Time, Memory, Justice* (Durham, NC: Duke University Press, 2014), 21.

of this fetishized past cannot be entirely discounted, it is largely a displaced expression of the post-Naksa crisis of the unfinished project of national liberation and social transformation.

Arab contemporaneity is then stranded, or suspended, in a present without potentiality, an impasse of individual dignity and national liberation or sovereignty. The severity of the defeat—its irrevocable verdict—matches only the cruelty with which it remained largely inassimilable to the collective Arab psyche. Notwithstanding the richness of his psychoanalytic reflections on the afteraffects of the Naksa, Tarabishi has uncritically *melancholized* Arab contemporaneity, reduced its complexity and compositeness to a corrosive and quasi-pathological regression that constitutes only one subcurrent of melancholy, but certainly not its most profound and generative current. Not that the defeat did not produce traumatic symptoms, but that the symptoms pertained to a heterogenous psychoaffective forcefield—a field of forces or force-feelings— that ranged from nonchalant soul-searching, feelings of guilt, anguished rage and collective shame to narcissistic refusal, defiance, and disavowal of or sheer indifference to defeat. The very fact that Nasser referred to the defeat in his famous resignation speech as a Naksa or setback speaks volumes about the ways in which its devastating effects had partly been euphemized, displaced, and disavowed rather than fully admitted, reckoned with, and apprehended. Yet, the issue may have less to do with the psychotherapeutic benefits of coming to terms with defeat and shame than with the obligation of maintaining the struggle against the joined forces of local despotism, imperial hegemony, and settler colonialism.

Accepting defeat in the Freudian teleological sense of overcoming mourning would amount to accepting the verdict of reality (Israeli superiority and invincibility) and the injunction to withdraw all psychoaffective investitures from the debris of broken ideals (national sovereignty, dignity, and freedom from injustice). It is in this sense that Pierre Macherey cautions in the epigraph against the reduction of psychoanalysis to the "normalizing and adaptive discourse" of mourning.[11] The reverse amounts to the unyielding determination, if not stubborn fixation in psychoanalytic terms, on recovering what is lost and redressing the colonial past of transgression, dispossession, and injustice. Commitment to such a colossal cause may seem hopeless, especially at the current historical juncture of increasingly brazen apartheid practices throughout historical Palestine, but, as György Lukács has taught us, the hopelessness of pro-

---

11. Pierre Macherey, "Out of Melancholia: Notes on Judith Butler's The Psychic Life of Power: Theories in Subjection," *Rethinking Marxism: A Journal of Economics, Culture and Society* 16, no. 1 (2004): 16.

active commitment to a lost cause pales in comparison to the hopelessness of abandoning commitment altogether. It would amount to nothing less than burying the lost cause for the second time. The commitment ought to be *melancholic* (self-reflexively principled, persistent, and proactive), but not, as is often the case, *melancholite* (uncritically reactionary, impulsive, and counterproductive).

Notwithstanding his groundbreaking insights, Tarabishi's mistake is that he presented—and therefore produced—the Arab intellectual as melancholite and left the melancholic dimension, which would in fact include his own highly critical contributions, entirely unaccounted for. His wholesale melancholization of post-Naksa Arab thought and culture has at least two negative political implications: on the one hand, his diagnosis seems to pathologize and delegitimize a legitimate condition of suffering in response to the colossal historical rupture of the 1967 military defeat; on the other, he inversely domesticates this very condition of melancholization which he repudiates: Tarabishi writes profusely on the structural belatedness of the Arabs, their fixation on the past, their regression to the narcissistic and hospitable realms of tradition, and their inability to deliver themselves from the defeatist position of stasis and paralysis even while he briefly acknowledges that "psychic dynamics [*al-dīnāmiyya al-nafsiyya*] contain forces that propel toward resistance, cure and progress."[12] Tarabishi does not linger on this other dimension of melancholy because he is actuated by the darker side of the psychic apparatus "so that it stops being a fertile epicenter for the ideology of obscurantism."[13]

Admittedly, Islamists have capitalized on the injuries of the Arab psyche and on the failures of secular nationalism as well as on the freshness of the colonial insult to spread their ideology and expand their clout, offering their followers the promise of salvation and the opportunity of self-realization. Yet, while fully aware of the regressive, reactionary and melancholite propensities of post-Naksa intellectual and ideological permutations, *Melancholy Acts* gives pride of place to the nuanced and scrupulous readings of the subtleties of psychoaffective operations against the grain of pathologization and melancholization. As will become clear throughout this book, what I find particularly compelling in Arab literary and cultural productions is the indirect, equivocal, and opaque undercurrent of resistance they elaborate, the loyalty to the remainder they demonstrate, and the capacity for vigilant hope they enunciate. There is indeed a measure of hope that is not mathematically calculable but that nonetheless resides in the steadfast commitment to lost causes,

12. Tarabishi, *Al-Muthaqqafūn al-'Arab wa al-Turāth* (Arab Intellectuals and Tradition), 12.
13. Ibid.

especially those challenging utopian or semi-utopian causes whose loss is, after all, too incomplete to be mourned. And while Slavoj Žižek contends that melancholy has become the norm that must be subverted, I argue that in the Arab world the priority is to subvert the colonial conditions of power relations of which melancholy is the product. All the more so given melancholy's tragic fidelity to lost objects, to lost ideals and human causes as a vantage point from which to unsettle the normative patterns of ritualistic and resilient mourning practices, which would at times take place not only at the expense of the irreparable and untreatable as such but also in alignment with the system of global imperialism and settler colonialism.[14]

As I will show, Žižek's observation is not only insensitive to the geopolitics of melancholy in non-Euro-American contexts but also insouciant about its complicity with the longstanding colonial proscription against the public mourning of the victims in whose death colonialism is implicated. Note, for instance, that the Israeli government passed a law in 2011 banning the public commemorations of the Nakba or Catastrophe (the 1948 dispossession of Palestinians and depopulation of historical Palestine preparatory to the establishment of the state of Israel). In the Arab world, to subvert melancholy without subverting the entrenched Israeli occupation and the continued Euro-American domination is to miss the mark and appropriate attention away from the underlying injustices of which melancholy is the product. Even the cessation of injustices would not necessarily result in the dissipation of melancholy, precisely because melancholy is a symptom of the living legacy of colonial pain and the method of reading, disseminating, and protesting the residual enormity of that pain.[15] There is a clear continuity between Hawi's and Bouazizi's suicides, just as there is a continuity between resisting authoritarianism nationally (Bouazizi) and colonialism transnationally (Hawi). The psychic economy and collective-connective symptomalogy of melancholy cannot be overstressed even while it generally remains critically unaddressed. The broad question that I grapple with in *Melancholy Acts* is not so much how suicide protests spark popular revolutions, or at least public contentions and acts of dissidence, as it is how popular revolutions sparked by suicide protests are

---

14. Slavoj Žižek, "Melancholy and the Act," *Critical Inquiry* 26, no. 4 (2000): 657–81.
15. I have in mind here the following observation by Frederic Jameson: "When a psychic structure is objectively determined by economic and political relationships, it cannot be dealt with by means of purely psychological therapies; yet it equally cannot be dealt with by means of purely objective transformations of the economic and political situation itself, since the habits remain and exercise a baleful and crippling residual effect." See "Third-World Literature in the Era of Multinational Capitalism," *Social Text* 15 (Fall 1986): 76.

materializations of a cultural and critical capital that has largely been determined by a collective disposition toward melancholy.

The Melancholization Pact

Bouazizi's suicidal protest and the various uprisings that ensued suggest that the 1967 defeat has not been assimilated by the Arab psyche precisely because it continues to be contested locally through the kinds of melancholy acts that followed suit from Hawi to Bouazizi, as well as the profuse literary and cultural melancholy acts I will be most concerned with throughout this book. Neither Hawi nor Bouazizi accepted defeat—neither to the colonial apparatus (Hawi) nor to the state apparatus (Bouazizi). It might, of course, be argued that the 1967 defeat far antedates Hawi's and especially Bouazizi's suicides and that each suicide had its own immediate triggering factors, but my contention is that without taking into consideration the loss of an entire worldview in which the 1967 defeat resulted—namely, the collapse of the foundational bearings of which that worldview is the product—it may be impossible to situate the suicides of Hawi and Bouazizi in their broad postcolonial historical context. As Jonathan Lear argues in *Radical Hope*, the collapse of a collective way of life that enables populations to thrive cannot be taken lightly: "we necessarily inhabit a way of life that is expressed in a culture. But our way of life— whatever it is—is vulnerable in various ways. And we, as participants in that way of life, thereby inherit a vulnerability. Should that way of life break down, that is *our* problem."[16]

The 1967 defeat decimated the conceptual foundation of the promissory project of a decolonized, united, and emancipated Arab nation and laid the basis for the disunited dictatorships and compromised national sovereignties of most Arab countries, including Lebanon and Tunisia, both of which were attacked by Israel with impunity in 1982 and 1985, respectively. Most of Tarabishi's diagnosis of the ailments that befell the Arab world, namely post-Naksa traumatization and melancholization, can be approached as profound and painstaking attempts to make sense of the confusion, uncertainty, and generalized paralysis in which 1967 resulted. All the more so given that the Naksa took place in the midst of the decolonization era (just five years after the

---

16. Jonathan Lear, *Radical Hope: Ethics in the Face of Cultural Devastation* (Cambridge, MA: Harvard University Press, 2006), 6, italics original. Likewise, Julia Kristeva argues in *Black Sun* that "if the meaning of life is lost, life can easily be lost: when meaning shatters, life no longer matters." See Julia Kristeva, *Black Sun: Depression and Melancholia*, trans. Leon S. Roudiez (New York: Columbia University Press, 1989), 6.

hard-won independence of Algeria, for instance), and therefore nipped in the bud the enchantments of a world tunneling its way out of colonial captivity and gathering its breath to forge ahead in future worldmaking projects on the pyre of colonialism. No wonder, then, that the social and psychological destruction of colonial violence would soon be reenacted internally and under different forms, ranging from recurring coups, riots, and insurrections to brutal power struggles, political assassinations, massacres, and lengthy civil wars along political, ethnic, or religious divides. Are postcolonial Arabs locked in a compulsion to repeat the atrocities of colonialism or were they oddly trying to understand them? Perhaps Eva Hoffman is not so off the mark in her musings in a different context: "Those who don't understand the past may be condemned to repeat it, but those who never repeat it are condemned not to understand it."[17]

Karima Lazali's more recent study of the psychic and political consequences of colonial oppression, *Le trauma colonial/Colonial Trauma*, is the latest and most important commentary on Arab culture through the lenses of psychoanalysis after Tarabishi's aforementioned *Al-Muthaqqafūn al-Arab wa-Turāth* and Fethi Benslama's 2002 book *La psychanalyse à l'épreuve de l'Islam/Psychoanalysis and the Challenge of Islam*. Lazali's *Le trauma colonial* is mostly devoted to postcolonial Algeria but, like Tarabishi's book, which is mostly focused on the Mashreq, it also melancholizes the postcolonial Algerian subject even while she shows an acute awareness of the still disavowed and unredressed losses Algerians incurred during the dark decades of French settler colonialism and its unspeakable crimes against humanity. Whether in her clinical practice in Paris and Algiers or in her cultural and historical research, Lazali discerns symptoms of a transgenerational *blocage* around the signifier "Algeria," a blackhole of colonial offense and obfuscation, parental silence, and survivor shame, as well as countless accounts of erasure (*effacements*), disfiguration or whitening (*blanchissement*), and invisible or invisibilized pain. She traces an uncanny continuity between the French colonial and Algerian postcolonial practices of oppression and disappearance, intransigent denialism and abnegation of responsibility.

The mimetic identification between former colonizers and colonized amounts, for Lazali, to a complicitous "colonial pact" that extends the condition of the coloniality of power into perpetuity.[18] Thus, in the very same man-

---

17. Eva Hoffman, *Lost in Translation: A Life in a New Language* (New York: Dutton, 1989), 278.

18. Karima Lazali, *Colonial Trauma: A Study of the Psychic and Political Consequences of Colonial Oppression in Algeria*, trans. Matthew B. Smith (Cambridge: Polity 2021), 212.

ner that the March 1962 Évian Accords granted the former colonizers amnesty for the crimes and atrocities they committed during the occupation of Algeria—especially since the massacres of May 8, 1945, in the provinces of Sétif, Guelma, and Constantine—"the political power in Algeria had also orchestrated its own impunity during the years of the Internal War."[19] The work of melancholization enables the integration of loss into the psychic structure of the subject, yet, in so doing, it risks offering state powers in both France and Algeria an alibi for the continued denial that the loss ever took place. As such, a tacit melancholization pact emerges between the victims and perpetrators of colonial and postcolonial violence in which the internalization of loss by the citizenry occurs in tandem with its dismissal from collective and public memory by state power. Melancholization becomes thus not only the symptom but also the mechanism of colonial and postcolonial state domination and sanctioned amnesia.

For Lazali, a thirteen-decade-long French colonial domination, during which almost one-third of the native Algerian population disappeared, "has plunged a number of post-Independence Algerian citizens into a state of melancholy [*mélancolisation*] that continues unabated today."[20] This morbid state of melancholization which is experienced at the level of individuals as an internecine conflict between the belligerent components of the psyche is amplified and exteriorized into a full-scale "internal war," waged by the postcolonial Algerian state against Islamists and its own people for well over a decade (since the protests and subsequent police repressions of 1988, *octobre noir*, and well over the 1990s, often referred to as *la décennie noire*, or the black decade).[21] No wonder the postcolonial subject is interpellated by the specter of a colonial legacy (including a language and a history) with which it identifies at the risk of losing its own legitimacy (independence). The civil war reduced Algeria to a postcolonial colonial state in which the warring entities resurrected and reenacted the colonial practices of erasure and disappearance in a panicked flight from illegitimacy and/or frantic scramble for legitimacy: "Jolted by a profound sense of insecurity, the subject, caught between paranoia and melancholy, faces two options: to kill the other or to kill itself."[22]

---

19. Ibid., 202.
20. Karima Lazali, *Le trauma colonial: Une enquête sur les effets psychiques et politiques contemporains de l'oppression coloniale en Algérie* (Paris: La Découverte, 2018), 263. See also Lazali, *Colonial Trauma*, 209.
21. Lazali, *Colonial Trauma*, 148.
22. Ibid.

In Lazali's dense construction of the ravages of the colonial rupture, namely its internalization and reenactment by postcolonial Algerians in a bitter internal war, melancholy receives a bad rap, not only because it embodies a miniature civil war at the level of the psyche but mostly because it seems to have externalized its psychic conflict, resulting in an auto- and hetero-destructive nationwide war. Little wonder that Lazali categorizes melancholy as a form of pathological complaint or grievance (*plainte*) rather than a psychocultural archive of losses and a potential pathway to freedom from colonial injustice and official amnesia.[23] Melancholy's refusal to turn the page on the colonial past may very well veer into the pathological abyss of civil war, yet the melancholic gesture is not antithetical to the vocation that Lazali accords to literature as a work of documentation, repair and reparation. Literary work is sustained, I would argue, by the kind of retrospective and introspective affective investitures that revolve in the saturnine orbit of melancholy. Literature emerges from and expresses the very melancholy that Lazali invalidates. Unquestionably, literature plays a crucial role not just as a record that "bears traces of bodily disfigurement," but also as a public "space for healing and repair."[24] It "strives to give expression to the blank spaces [*les blancs*] and the ideological blind spots present in the historical record. Above all, it alerts the reader to how a text is continuously shaped by its invisible margins."[25]

What Lazali leaves out of account is a theoretical reflection on the conditions of emergence of such a literature from within a space that is hostage to the impoverishing ravages of melancholy at the level of both individual and collective psyches. How can literature possibly escape from the melancholization pact that precedes, besieges, and inaugurates it? Is literature insulated from or in excess of the psychoaffective conditions of possibility of which it is a product? Furthermore, how is it that Algerians broke the obsolete melancholization pact in February 2019 and took to the streets in massive numbers (the Hirak movement), and eventually pushed President Abdelaziz Bouteflika to resign as soon as April 2019? Clearly, there is more to melancholy than predilection for tyranny, afflicted resignation, or despondency, and the 2019–2021 nationwide protests testify to a melancholy disposition toward insurrection and revolt that is reminiscent of the protracted resistance to the early French conquest mounted by Emir Abdelkader, a Sufi leader of the Qadari order, who succeeded in rousing and mobilizing the big tribes of Oran against the French. What I find quite puzzling is that Lazali describes in minute detail all the pre-

---

23. Ibid., 2; Lazali, *Le trauma colonial*, 7.
24. Ibid., 43.
25. Ibid., 7.

requisites for a massive onset of melancholy (including colonial and postcolonial practices of disappearance, disposability and destruction of entire tribes, lineages, languages and villages, as well as the early pillaging and depopulation of cities, confiscation or destruction of property, suppression of all forms of resistance, and the surrender of the otherwise uncatchable Emir Abdelkader in 1847), yet she still somehow approaches it as an illegitimate register of affective toil and turmoil. The suggestion that melancholization is an "abyss" erases the very injustices of which it is a symptom.[26] Melancholization without differentiation allows for historical injustices to disappear in the very same way that Lazali warns against. Given that mourning in such circumstances would amount to nothing but a betrayal of the disappeared—really, the disappearance of disappearance—I wonder whether apathy, affective detachment or affectless withdrawal would have possibly made for Lazali a more valid response to the colonial and postcolonial reenactments of violence. Not only would affectless withdrawal in this context boil down to the blind derealization of colonial atrocity, but it would also constitute de facto a defensive foreclosure of legitimate suffering (which is not without its own pathological implications, as Carl G. Jung and Alexander and Margarete Mitscherlich would argue).[27]

Melancholization in the embattled decolonial situation of Algeria is not a choice that Algerians could have made. It is the predictable, not to say inevitable, *affective correlative* of French settler colonial oppression, which massacred, erased, and disappeared without a trace and left postcolonial Algerian subjects with the injunction to offer an archaeological, philological, material, or concrete account of their losses. The refusal to comply to the neocolonial command to testify, to write an account of losses that are themselves lost—that refusal becomes de facto a disposition to melancholy. The blank spaces (*les blancs*) of which Lazali speaks are deliberate refusals to play the colonial game of archiving or documenting injustices, and not simply literal representations of the empty archive of memory. The dominant tenor of postcolonial Algerian and Arab literature is a testament to the refusal of the exhortation to testify or to play the role of the witness. "Khalil Hawi took a hunting rifle and hunted himself," asserts Mahmoud Darwish in his memorable account—*Memory for Forgetfulness*—of the Lebanese civil war and the Israeli invasion of Beirut, "not only because he wanted not to give evidence against anything

---

26. Ibid., 217.
27. Alexander Mitscherlich and Margarette Mitscherlich, *The Inability to Mourn: Principles of Collective Behavior*. Translated by Beverley R. Placzek and Robert Jay Lifton (New York: Grove Press, 1975).

but also because he wanted not to be a witness for or against anything."²⁸ This refusal marks the swerve of melancholy I am most concerned with in this book from a *colonial imposition* to a *decolonial disposition*.

The melancholy disposition in Arab contemporaneity bespeaks the necessity and precarity of the now stalled and unfinished project of decolonization with all its twists, turns, and detours. Accordingly, even the internal war that plagued Algeria's recent history is the *affective corollary* of its long colonial past, a past that still excites unsettled drives toward violence because it has neither been reckoned with nor redressed by the postcolonial political order in France and Algeria. Nominal independence with neither reconciliation nor reparation could have hardly reversed more than thirteen decades of colonial violence. Lazali's reductive pathologizing of melancholy and wholesale melancholization of Algerians may have grave implications for any elaboration of an affective politics of decolonization, all the more so given that the will to decolonize owes its buoyancy largely to the affective currents that sustain it. Ironically, though, the irreceivability of colonial history (*irrecevabilité de l'histoire coloniale*) by the current political order matches the irreceivability of melancholy by Lazali. Lazali's conclusions show the extent to which melancholization as a symptom of the colonial and postcolonial condition becomes naturalized as the defining pathological feature of Algerian contemporaneity and simultaneously repudiated for fostering a culture of defeat, complaint, and victimhood. By the same token, de-crying, lamenting, and blamestorming become the ontological truth of the Algerian subject today. In fact, Algerians are painted less as claimants of unsettled historical and political grievances than as self-pitying whiners who continually blame others for their inadequacies and abrogate their share of responsibility.

Taking responsibility for the colonial offense and its internalized violent legacies (including the internal war) is tantamount to accepting the thesis of "*colonisabilité*" that another Algerian, the social philosopher Malek Bennani, deployed to fault Arabs and Muslims for their amenability to colonialism by virtue of their civilizational stagnation and backwardness.²⁹ Bennabi states: "*On n'est colonisé que si l'on est colonisable. On cesse d'être colonisé lorsqu'on cesse d'être colonisable*" (We are colonized only because we are colonizable. We cease to be colonized when we cease to be colonizable).³⁰ It is as if Muslims and Arabs were screaming out to be colonized in the wake of their post-

---

28. Mahmoud Darwish, *Memory for Forgetfulness*, trans. Ibrahim Muhawi (Berkeley: University of California Press, 1995), 154.

29. Malek Bennabi, *Vocation de L'Islam* (Algiers: Edition ANEP, 2006), 33.

30. See Abdelkader Bouarfa, *Malek Bennabi: Une vie, une oeuvre, un combat* (Casablanca: Centre culturel du livre, 2019), 121.

Andalusian decadence, degeneration, arrested development, and subsequent descent into irrelevance. In other words, and as Octave Mannoni once claimed about the Malagasies, Arabs have only themselves to blame for their colonizability: "Not all peoples can be colonized: only those who experience this need."[31] While Mannoni's verdict absolves the French, at least by implication, from the colonial atrocities they committed in Madagascar, especially in the aftermath of the 1947 Malagasy revolt, Bennani's statement is addressed to Arabs and Muslims and is at best intended as an incitement to action, but it misses the opportunity to offer a humanistic critique of colonialism and its predatory tenets. One cannot but be reminded herein of Ghassan Kanafani's poignant humanist and humane lesson in *Returning to Haifa*: "the greatest crime any human being can commit, whoever he may be, is to believe even for one moment that the weakness and mistakes of others give him the right to exist at their expense and justify his own mistakes and crimes."[32]

Lazali and Bennani may be partially right about the melancholy state of postcolonial Algerians and the colonizable state of post-Andalusian Muslims, respectively, but the political implications of their diagnoses-cum-verdicts may in the end help feed rather than fight the protean coloniality of power relations and the intransigent refusal of former colonizers to admit their colonial crimes and make amends. But what breaks the hold of melancholization, on which the preservation of loss in the individual or collective psyche relies, except the affirmative identification and reclamation of the object whose loss the "colonial pact" embodies and yet denies?

Operation Melancholicization

Lazali and Bennani produce the Algerian Arab and Muslim subject as melancholized and colonizable. One need not look any further than the work of one of Bennani's contemporaries and Lazali's own hero, Frantz Fanon, to gauge the extent to which Bennani overlooks the violent colonial origins of colonizability and the fact that colonizability is the result of colonialism and not its instigator. Similarly, it will become amply clear the extent to which Lazali not only misreads the symptomology of melancholy but also depoliticizes its insurrectionary potential. Toward the end of *The Wretched of the Earth*, in the fifth and last chapter titled, "Colonial War and Mental Disorders," Frantz Fanon overturns Freud's conception of pathological and

---

31. Octave Mannoni, *Prospero and Caliban: The Psychology of Colonization*, trans. Pamela Powesland, 2nd ed. (Ann Arbor: Michigan University Press, 1990), 85.

32. Ghassan Kanafani, *Palestine's Children: Returning to Haifa and Other Stories*, trans. Barbara Harlow and Karen E. Riley (Boulder, CO: Lynne Rienner, 2000), 186.

autodestructive melancholy through a courteous and respectful yet incisive comparative cultural critique of the Eurocentric and racist ethnopsychiatry of the Algiers School of Psychiatry and of its founder, Antoine Porot, and his disciples. Cognizant of the complicity between European science and colonial domination, Fanon sets out to deconstruct and demystify the allegedly congenital aggressivity of the natives and "to explain the unorthodox behavior of the Algerian who is prey to melancholia":

> The French psychiatrists in Algeria found themselves faced with a difficult problem. They were accustomed when dealing with a patient subject to melancholia to fear that he would commit suicide. Now the melancholic Algerian takes to killing. The illness of the moral consciousness, which is always accompanied by auto-accusation and auto-destructive tendencies, took on in the case of Algerians hetero-destructive forms. The melancholic Algerian does not commit suicide. He kills. This is the homicidal melancholia which has been thoroughly studied by Professor Porot in the thesis of his pupil Monserrat.[33]

Fanon does not refute the validity of this hetero-destructive or homicidal dimension of Algerian melancholy; on the contrary, he capitalizes on Porot's thesis as some sort of a "teachable moment" in order to underscore two interrelated matters. First, that Algerian melancholy be understood as the byproduct of the colonial context even while it may still be, in the words of Edward Said, "a quite spectacular instance of a travelling theory gone tougher, harder, more recalcitrant."[34] Second, that the versatile role colonial affects play in the anticolonial struggle cannot be overestimated even while Algerian melancholy was given short shrift by French psychiatrists through sanctioned scientific disavowals (indeed, Porot ended up calling the Algerian typology of melancholy "pseudo-melancholia"). In the colonial context, Fanon argues unequivocally, everything, including psychic pathologies, ought to be mobilized for the purpose of decolonization in the very same manner that psychoanalysis, and more so psychiatry, were mobilized by the French colonial administration in the service of colonization. "Science depoliticized, science in the service of man, is often non-existent in the colonies," notes Fanon.[35]

---

33. Franz Fanon, *The Wretched of the Earth* (New York: Grove Press, 1963), 298–9.
34. Edward Said, *Reflections on Exile and Other Essays* (Cambridge, MA: Harvard University Press, 2003), 440.
35. Frantz Fanon, *A Dying Colonialism*, trans. Haakon Chevalier (New York: Grove Press, 1965), 140.

The nationalization of affect operates through incitements to militancy, through the internalization and politicization of aggressivity: "the objective of the native who fights against himself is to bring about the end of domination."³⁶ *Pace* Lazali, the internal war in Fanon is but a displaced longing for national liberation. This is the transformational generative movement from melancholizing to melancholicizing, the movement from the clinical and pharmaceutical to the analytical and political. "The universalization of aggressivity during the insurgency is the self's very liberating possibility; it is analytically what transforms melancholia, say, into resistance."³⁷ Fanon accords melancholia a revolutionary and political currency that I find of particular relevance today to a decolonial Arab critique of settler colonialism and its traumatic legacies in Algeria, Palestine and elsewhere across the Arab world. The capacity for critique in melancholia is, as Freud had long before concluded, its most distinct and defining feature. In "The Ego and the Id," the superego emerges as the kernel of a scrupulous critical agency that checks the movements of the ego and exacts punishments on it, driving it at times to the outbreak of mania or the impasse of suicide.³⁸ The suicidal bent of melancholy in Europe, however, took on a radically different path in the colonies and emerged in alignment with the incumbent task of national struggles for independence. The dynamic relationship between melancholy and revolutionary praxis in the decades following World War II were very much in the air, if not well articulated theoretically, such that Michel Foucault felt impelled to gibe in the preface to the American translation of Gilles Deleuze's and Félix Guattari's *Anti-Oedipus*, perhaps in a fit of impatience and frustration: "Do not think that one has to be sad in order to be militant."³⁹

---

36. Ibid., 309.

37. David Marriott, *Wither Fanon? Studies in the Blackness of Being* (Stanford, CA: Stanford University Press, 2018), 187. I thank Stefania Pandolfo for recommending this book.

38. "If we turn to melancholia first, we find that the excessively strong super-ego which has obtained a hold upon consciousness rages against the ego with merciless violence ... *we should say that the destructive component had entrenched itself in the super-ego* and turned against the ego. What is now holding sway in the super-ego is, as it were, a pure culture of the death instinct, and in fact it often enough succeeds in driving the ego into death, *if the latter does not fend off its tyrant in time by the change round into mania.*" See Sigmund Freud, "The Ego and the Id," in *On Metapsychology*, 394, italics mine.

39. Michel Foucault, preface to Gilles Deleuze and Felix Guattari, *Anti-Oedipus: Capitalism and Schizophrenia*, trans. Robert Hurley, Mark Seem, and Helen R. Lane (Minneapolis: University of Minnesota Press, 1983), xiii. Foucault states, *"n'imaginez pas qu'il faille être triste pour être militant,"* in Michel Foucault, *Dits et Ecrits II, 1976–1988* (Paris: Gallimard, 2001), 133–36.

In the wake of the 1982 Israeli invasion of Lebanon, the Lebanese Marxist intellectual Husayn Muruwwa wrote an op-ed in which he differentiated between "lethal sadness" (al-ḥuzn al-qātil, the sadness that paralyzes and immobilizes), and "militant sadness" (al-ḥuzn al-muqātil, the sadness that fights back), and argued, Fanon-like, that sadness becomes combative when it is anchored in an intellectual foundation that would facilitate its enlistment in the decolonial struggle.[40] In light of Muruwwa's argument, Foucault's equivocation may be read as a tacit disquiet about the emergent inextricability of sadness and militancy. It may, conversely, suggest that Foucault does not think that affect and political praxis should, much less ought to, be bundled together. Indeed, and as Ewa Ziarek has recently argued, one of the central legacies of European modernity is the constant oscillation it reproduces again and again between revolt and melancholy, as if the twain had never met, nor could they ever meet. This may partly explain Foucault's equivocation and even more so Porot's puzzlement over the homicidal twist of Algerian melancholy. Regardless, Ziarek's thesis about "the unresolved and endlessly replicated contradiction between 'revolutionary' and melancholic politics and art in Western modernity" is not particularly relevant in the colonies, where the contradictions between modernity and colonialism, between capitalism and humanism, or between civilization and barbarism gain pride of place.[41] Colonized peoples experienced both modernity and colonialism at one and the same time (for instance, Napoleon in Egypt); hence the continued and at times muted ambivalence that accompanies any use of the master's tools (modernity, technology, language) against those very masters' systems of oppression (colonialism, imperialism). Such an ambivalence may not be resolved psychically, much less intellectually, but forms, and continues to inform, the basis for the compatibility, if not the inseparability, between melancholy and revolutionary praxis.

Psychiatrists like Porot and his disciples failed to fully grasp the specific origins of Algerian melancholy and reduced its hetero-destructiveness to congenital and primitive sedimentations. French psychiatrists failed to read the compulsive aggressivity of Algerians against the iron fist of French settler colonialism and the everyday anger it excites in colonized Algerians; they failed to relate such compulsive aggressivity to a psychic grammar of compensatory jouissance or to a narcissistic expression of authentic virility, as Fanon himself suggests; they simply concluded that Algerians are incapable of experiencing

---

40. Hussein Mruwwa, *Kalimāt Ḥayya* (Beirut: Dar Al-Farabi, 2012), 29–30.
41. Ewa Plonowska Ziarek, *Feminist Aesthetics and the Politics of Modernism* (New York: Columbia University Press, 2012), 4.

INTRODUCTION: MELANCHOLY ACTS   21

the profound introspection that characterizes European melancholy and that can lead to personal and moral growth. They called Algerian melancholy a form of "pseudo-melancholia," not only because it was an unrecognized and unauthorized form of melancholy but also because the form of melancholy that the Western tradition legitimizes and universalizes is almost entirely associated with the white male creative genius. They hardly entertained the idea that the colonial situation is sufficiently original to allow for the emergence of a discrepant typology of melancholy (never mind the medieval Arab medical tradition of melancholy and the premodern elegiac tradition of *rithā'* or mourning). Fanon's insistence that Algerian melancholy be examined against the backdrop of colonialism serves not only as a corrective to the often unnuanced universalization of European knowledge, but also as a reminder of the decolonial valences of affects—namely, the shift that occurs in the aggressivity characteristic of Algerian melancholy from the *compulsive* in Porot to the *compulsory* in Fanon: "The national conflict seems to have canalized all anger, and nationalized all affective or emotional movements."[42] Once the mythic, fratricidal, and criminal canalization of violent impulses finds utterance in the decolonial struggle, not only do feuds and crimes decrease, but even psychopathologies such as melancholy become sites of, if not occasions for, resistance to colonialism.

Fanon discerns the psychoaffective swerve from the crushed state of melancholization and colonizability to the potent dynamic of melancholicization and decolonization. This is, in my view, Fanon's most daring theoretical venture: that the *compulsive* reenactment of aggressivity must, *pace* Porot, transform into a *compulsory* act of insurrection against colonization. Algerian melancholy becomes a geopolitically differentiated and accented psychocultural dynamic that cuts through the personal and the political, the individual and the collective, the psychoaffective and the epistemological. This shift in function is certainly a breakthrough in the understanding of the psychoaffective forces of decolonial movements, yet it has not benefited from the theoretical elaboration that it deserves, least of all in the context of the Arab world where its resonance cannot be overstated, especially since the Nakba and even more so since the Naksa.[43] In fact, Fanon's ardent contemporary, Ghassan

---

42. Fanon, *The Wretched of the Earth*, 306.

43. Ranjana Khanna's *Dark Continents* is in part an attempt to remedy this lack of theorization of the passage from Freud's pathological to Fanon's resistant or militant melancholia through her concept of "critical melancholia," which she sees as a symptom of colonialism and an energetic response to it. Ranjana Khanna, *Dark Continents: Psychoanalysis and Colonialism* (Durham, NC: Duke University Press, 2003), x.

Kanafani, understood the transformative potentialities of psychoaffective swerves at a very early age. In his 1956 "Letter from al-Ramla," Kanafani offers one of the earliest dramatizations of suicide martyrdom as a melancholy act of resistance to the 1948 Zionist atrocities in al-Ramla and Lydda, whose 60,000 inhabitants and refugees from Jaffa, both Muslims and Christians, including future PFLP leader George Habash, were driven out under escort on the orders of Ben-Gurion and Yitzhak Rabin in what constituted one of the largest expulsions that took place during the Nakba. The massive exodus became "a death march, with hundreds dying from thirst and hunger, trekking for days under a scorching sun."[44]

Kanafani tells the story of Abu Othman, Ramla's well-known barber and default doctor, through the eyes of a nine-year-old boy who witnesses Abu Othman's transformation from a gentle and loving man into a humiliated and grieving father and husband and finally into a murderer and a murdered victim. Even though Kanafani protects the young narrator from seeing the female soldier shoot Abu Othman's small daughter, Fatma, he makes him hear the three successive shots as well as see another soldier brutalize and shoot Abu Othman's wife and Fatma's inconsolable mother. The unspeakable brutality and cruelty of the Zionist militias—their callous slaughter of innocence with impunity—prompt Abu Othman to carry out the ultimate act of heterodestructive suicide that the deranged father in "The Land of Sad Oranges" only contemplates. Suicide in this case accents less the surrender of the body, or what is left of it, than the sovereign act of transforming powerlessness into power. Abu Othman's suicidal act resonates aptly with Fanon's aforementioned "homicidal melancholia," and instantiates the transformation of defeat and despair into defiance and self-sacrifice. The melancholic attachment to sovereignty in Kanafani's fiction almost always exceeds the pitiful failure to shield it from a crude reality. Consider the words of Shaddād, the protagonist of Kanafani's play, *Al-Bāb* (The Door), as he opts to risk his life rather than to surrender to the cruel will of the gods who forbid him from entering his own paradisical city: "The choice of death is the only real choice that could be made at the right time before it is imposed upon you at a wrong time or before you are pushed towards it for any reason beyond your own power to choose such as disease, defeat, fear or poverty. Death is the last place left for the only true free-

---

44. Ram Narayan Kumar, *Martyred but Not Tamed: The Politics of Resistance in the Middle East* (Los Angeles: Sage, 2012), 184.

dom that remains! [إنه المكان الوحيد الباقي للحرية الوحيدة والأخيرة والحقيقية!]"[45] Never before has Arabic literary expression been such a truly melancholicizing practice!

Kanafanni's poignantly lyrical epistolary short story, "Letter from Gaza," written when he was just and only twenty, is a laconic dramatization of the crucial swerve from settler colonial melancholization to decolonial melancholicization. The nameless speaker addresses his letter to his childhood friend, Mustafa, whom he is supposed to join in Sacramento, California. Mustafa seems to have made all the necessary arrangements for his friend's move to Sacramento to study Civil Engineering in the University of California. Both childhood friends had long ago vowed to carry on living together, to get out of Gaza and to become rich. Mustafa jumped on the first opportunity and left for California while the speaker moved to Kuwait to make enough money to pay for his trip. In Gaza, the speaker taught at UNRWA schools, but his meager salary was not enough for him to support his mother, his brother's widow, and her four children. He relied on the good sums of money remitted to him by Mustafa, and which he accepted in the dignified form of loans and not in the implied form of charity. The speaker wrote the letter to Mustafa between 1955 and 1956, at a time when Israel increased its crackdown on returnees to their homes and families (David Ben-Gurion's "war on infiltration") as well as on the paramilitary groups of fedayeen whose ultimate goal was to reclaim their rightful homeland. Israel launched several large-scale attacks on Gaza in the lead-up to the late October 1956 tripartite aggression on Egypt by Israel, France, and Britain. It was in between these brutal Israeli onslaughts on Gaza that the speaker returns home from Kuwait to prepare himself for his imminent trip to California.

Gaza's familiar scenes of wreckage, misery, and desolation, as well as the foul odor of defeat which had filled his nostrils since the Nakba, only intensified the speaker's urge to flee to green California and to sever all ties with Gaza, including self-limiting ties with his own family. Turning the page swiftly on the wretched homeland and running away from all the obstacles to his self-flourishing in a remote land of limitless opportunity is the only form of salvation that had eaten up the speaker's mind until he makes a visit to his beautiful thirteen-year-old niece, Nadia, in the Gaza hospital, and sees her completely amputated leg. Much to his own embarrassment, he discovers that "Nadia had lost her leg when she threw herself on top of her little brothers and sisters to

---

45. Ghassan Kanafani, *Al-Bāb* (The Door) (Nicosia, Cyprus: Dār Manshūrāt al-Rimāl, 2013), 33.

protect them from the bombs and flames that had fastened their claws into the house. Nadia could have saved herself. She could have run away, rescued her leg. But she didn't."⁴⁶ Nadia's tale of selfless sacrifice melancholized the speaker: his egocentric escapist schemes have, compared to Nadia's altruistic heroism, turned into sore points, fomenting in him feelings of ire and self-contempt. The "empathic unsettlement" of the speaker is such that he re-emerges from the hospital completely transformed and compelled to revise his plans and reverse his commitments.⁴⁷ Quite epiphanically, Nadia becomes the embodiment of that formerly "nebulous thing" ("الشيء الغامض"), or uncanny tug of gravity, that tethered him and Mustafa to Gaza and that had for so long "curbed [their] fervor to run away" to California, "the land where there is greenery, water and lovely faces."⁴⁸

Kanafani makes use of the epistolary convention not only to solicit the confidentiality and trust of the reader, but also to weave a story that wagers on the seductive reasoning of the Hegelian dialectical triplicity: a thesis (the desire to leave Gaza by which the speaker and his childhood friend Mustafa are consumed), an antithesis (the refusal to leave others behind that is best articulated by Nadia's bravery), and a synthesis (the announcement of a chiastic reversal and the pronouncement of a resolution to stay, making a rallying cry for *sumūd*, or steadfastness, resolve, and solidarity). The embedded speaker embarks on the epistolary effort of creating an overlapping communicative space from which to mentor and melancholicize not only his immediate addressee, Mustafa, but also the implied reader and audience at large. Through the dynamics of empathy and epiphany (or what I have elsewhere called "empiphany"),⁴⁹ the speaker suspends his preexisting norms of intelligibility, best exemplified by his melancholizing spree and his eagerness to flee war- and defeat-stricken Gaza; simultaneously, he opens up to the transformational generative force of Nadia's selfless act, an act that reveals a visceral commitment to collective salvation, which awakens in him the forgotten bond to the land and the people of Gaza and therefore completely obliterates his selfish pursuit of individual salvation. Not only does the pedagogical encounter with Nadia compel the speaker to reckon with the incumbent

---

46. Ghassan Kanafani, "Letter from Gaza," *Men in the Sun and Other Palestinian Stories*, trans. Hilary Kilpatrick (Boulder, CO: Lynne Rienner, 1999), 115.

47. Dominick LaCapra, *Writing History, Writing Trauma* (Baltimore, MD: Johns Hopkins University Press, 2014), 41.

48. Ghassan Kanafani, "Waraqa min Gaza," in *Arḍ al-burtuqāl al-ḥazīn* (Nicosia, Cyprus: Manshūrāt al-rimāl, 2013), 66, 63.

49. Nouri Gana, *Signifying Loss: Toward A Poetics of Narrative Mourning* (Lewisburg, PA: Bucknell University Press, 2014), 66.

task of solidarity with his own defeated yet unvanquished people and relinquish his wishful pursuit of the American dream, but it also propels him to seek to transform the alienating social norms of intelligibility that feed rather than fight the desire for flight. It is in this sense that we must understand his final exhortation to Mustafa: "I won't come to you. But you, return to us! Come back, to learn from Nadia's leg, amputated from the top of the thigh, what life is and what existence is worth. Come back, my friend! We are all waiting for you."[50]

Settler colonial power is never more successful than when it drives a wedge between Palestinians and their homeland. The speaker's belated melancholic turn is not a turn away from Gaza, but a return to that uncanny and repressed yet originary and incipient feeling that bound him and Mustafa to Gaza. The epistolary form of the story enacts a chiastic reversal whose transformative and generative effect has the merit of a political empiphany: the speaker's sudden recognition of his vocation at the moment of its phenomenological revelation. Nadia is the embodiment of both the vocation and the revelation. "Nadia" (ناديا), whose philological and onomatopoeic contiguity with "a call" (نداء) cannot be overstressed, is the name of that profoundly human call and calling for worldwide solidarity with Gaza. It is a call to Mustafa to get over their old melancholizing habits of mind and embark on the conscious decolonial task of melancholicization by *processing* Nadia's selfless ethics and enlisting in the "uprising of melancholy" (إنتفاضة الحزن): "Everything in this [new] Gaza rose up in sadness [ينتفض حزنا] over Nadia's amputated leg from the top of the thigh. It was not the kind of sadness that stopped at weeping. It was defiance; even more than that, it was something akin to the restoration of the amputated leg!"[51] This commentary betrays a melancholic strategy of reading in its own right: rather than only look *at* Nadia's amputated leg, and understand it, the speaker looks *through* it, and goes beyond it. It becomes the lens through which he scans the city afresh: he underscores its overall psychopolitical role in spawning a collective upsurge of grievance that is quite reminiscent of the militant sadness that Muruwwa called for almost three decades after Kanafani.

---

50. Kanafani, "Letter from Gaza," 115. Note that this final paragraph was not in the original version of the story published in 1956 but can be found in the second volume of his complete works published in 1973, one year after Kanafani's horrific assassination by the Israeli Mossad. This late addition further indicates the mobilizing force of political melancholicization that I am theorizing in this book. See "Waraqa min Gaza," *Al-Athār al-Kāmila: Al-qisas al-qasīra*, Volume II (Beirut: Mu'assasit al-Abḥāth al-'arabiyya, 1987), 351.

51. Kanafani, "Letter from Gaza," 115. Translation modified. See "Waraqa min Gaza," 70.

The speaker's melancholic reading practice is driven by the tacit fear that the loss of Nadia's leg could very well be lost to collective consciousness. Worse than loss is the loss of loss itself. The speaker is acutely aware that Nadia's loss is irrevocable, yet he ventures to liken the outbreak and obduracy of grief across Gaza to "the restoration of the amputated leg." Militant grief is restorative to the extent that it not only acknowledges and dignifies Nadia's loss, but also demystifies the brutality and cruelty of settler colonial Zionism and feeds the fight against it. Paradoxically, it is Nadia's amputated leg that propels forward the indefatigable pursuit of Palestinian liberation. The question is no longer about what is lost in Nadia's lost leg but rather about the range of possibilities opened up by the injustice of the loss, not least of which is the revitalization of the struggle to restore the heretofore compromised human dignity and national sovereignty. In his emotionally charged address to Mustafa, the speaker capitalizes on the spectral void created by the amputated leg as the *focus and locus of melancholicization*: a process of psychoaffective investiture that generates and sustains attachments to a sense of national consciousness, sovereignty and belonging, produced before, during, and after the Nakba and inculcated by a dizzying seriality of losses and unifying collective woes. In this sense, melancholicizing is not confined to the search for the concrete meaning of Nadia's loss but extends contiguously to the void created by the disappearance, erasure, and ethnic cleansing of historical Palestine and to the incumbent task of rescuing loss from loss into perpetuity. In fact, before closing his letter by calling on Mustafa to come back home, the speaker signals to him the urgent necessity to melancholicize, to recoup and retool the enigmatic feeling he experienced when he was leaving Gaza: "This obscure feeling that you had as you left Gaza, this small feeling must grow into a giant deep within you. It must expand, you must seek it in order to find yourself, here among the ugly debris of defeat."[52]

Kanafani institutes the process of melancholicization as the horizon of decolonial subjectivity; he wagers on the recuperation, cultivation, and amplification of an enigmatic originary affective tie as the conduit for the tangled processes of self-individuation, solidarity and decolonial resistance. Far from reenacting a melancholite or reactionary desire for flight, the melancholic disposition in Kanafani resuscitates a profoundly affirmative dialectic of self-discovery and becoming that is in part propelled by "a *strategic* use of positivist essentialism in a scrupulously visible political interest."[53] It elicits in the reader-

---

52. Kanafani, "Letter from Gaza," 115.
53. Gayatri C. Spivak, "Subaltern Studies: Deconstructing Historiography," in *Selected Subaltern Studies*, ed. Ranajit Guha and Gayatri C. Spivak (Delhi: Oxford University Press, 1988), 13.

cum-addressee a pedagogical reawakening to the ethical reading practices of "responsible literality," to the incumbent task of discerning the kernel of veridicality (Nadia's amputated leg) in the midst of overwhelming affective ambiguity and ambivalence (the "obscure feeling," the "debris of defeat," and so on).[54] Kanafani's story stresses the recuperative potencies of hermeneutic suspicion and incisive critique; it demands an attentiveness to detail of the sort that is never more to be desired than at a time when particular historical injustices keep sliding under the leveling chain of transhistorical and structural catastrophes and calamities, all the more so in an academic and intellectual climate in which the accelerated rates of disaster capitalist flows seem to have spawned consumerist and populist "surface reading" habits that cultivate aversion to in-depth analytical and theoretical reading endeavors.[55] Melancholicization is a nexus of generative energies, straddling symptomatic and close reading practices, coalescing ethical and contentious acts of agitation and reclamation, in which grief becomes grievance and solidarity becomes militant *sumūd*. Kanafani's "Letter from Gaza" exemplifies how the melancholia of the oppressed operates even from within extreme conditions of precarity and the way it sets alight in the speaker (and potentially in the addressee and in the reader writ large) an infectious longing for collectivity and solidarity that is in the final analysis indissociable from the intertwined and overlapping processes of decolonial subjectivization and national liberation.

The Ethics of Melancholicization

Melancholy Acts seeks to probe the concept of melancholy in psychoanalytic and postcolonial thought in order to illuminate its far-reaching relevance to an Arab cultural critique of postcolonial colonialism that stretches from the occupation of Palestine and the more recent occupation of Iraq to the Arab Uprisings and their disconcerting aftermaths. If, as Edward Said argues following Egyptian literary critic Ghali Shukri, Arabic literary writings became "a historical act" in the aftermath of 1948 and "an act of resistance" in the aftermath of 1967, my aim herein is to inquire about the psychoaffective dynamic, force, or disposition that must have sustained the production of literature as a

---

54. Gayatri C. Spivak, *Death of a Discipline* (New York: Columbia University Press, 2003), 72.

55. See Stephen Best and Sharon Marcus, "Surface Reading: An Introduction," *Representations* 108, no. 1 (2009): 1–21. See also Rita Felski, *The Limits of Critique* (Chicago: University of Chicago Press, 2015). For one of several engagements with the protagonists of the so-called "postcritique" movement, see Corey McEleney, "The Resistance to Overanalysis," *Differences* 32, no. 2 (2021): 1–38.

resistant, dissident, and decolonial act.[56] By "melancholy acts," I mean to describe the agentive double thrust of melancholy, its *recuperative* and *generative* dimensions—that is, the way it reclaims, seeds, and sustains an act that would be qualified, retrospectively at least, as a melancholy act. In other words, and insofar as the visual and literary scope of this book is concerned, I strive to examine the figuration or materialization in language, imagery, and form of the melancholic after-Naksa affect whose illocutionary and performative force registers a radical demand for justice and dignity that is in excess of any tokenisms or other perfunctory acts.

It is my contention that melancholia's underappreciated dissent from normative structures of mourning is a threshold moment of ethical, cultural, and psychopolitical empowerment in colonial and postcolonial societies, namely in the Arab world where the nexus between proxy and settler colonialisms continues to produce and reproduce almost all aspects of literature and culture. In this sense, Enzo Traverso's postulation that "melancholic critique is the condition of all critical thinking," is nowhere else more resonant than in the context of Arab contemporaneity in which this melancholy condition of critical thinking is compounded and confounded by the litany of military defeats against Israel and Euro-American invasions as well as by Arab-versus-Arab conflicts and infighting, not to mention the series of intranational wars that range from the Lebanese, Sudanese, and Algerian civil wars to the more recent ones in Iraq, Libya, Yemen, and Syria.[57] The diverse literary, theoretical, and cultural examples I make use of in the following chapters make legible at the level of language, imagery, and rhetoric the epistemic legitimacy of Arab political grievances and the continuity that Arab artists and intellectuals have established between resisting local authoritarianism and foreign imperialism.

The theoretical thrust of my argument hinges, first and foremost, on a generic understanding of "melancholy" as a symptom of an actual, imagined, or ideal loss that nonetheless remains the focus and locus of a spectrum of affective differentials that range—depending on the nature, cause, or perceived circumstances of the loss—from excessive grief, guilt, and militant inconsolability through identificatory ambivalence, regressive narcissism, and abject self-loathing to trauma, madness, suicide, and so forth. Second, while I use "melancholy" as an umbrella term to refer to an attachment complex, crisis, or

---

56. Edward Said, "Arabic Prose and Prose Fiction after 1948," in *Reflections on Exile and Other Essays* (Cambridge, MA: Harvard University Press, 2000), 48.

57. Enzo Traverso quoted in Jean Birnbaum, "The Lucidity of the Defeated: Enzo Traverso on Left Melancholy," trans. David Broder, December 29, 2016, Verso Books blog, https://www.versobooks.com/blogs/3026-the-lucidity-of-the-defeated-enzo-traverso-on-left-melancholy.

disorder that is produced by an actual, imagined, or ideal loss, aggravated by the negative dynamics of identification and self-flagellation, I make an important distinction between the *melancholite* (regressive, narcissistic, oppressive, and reactionary or phantasmagorical) and the *melancholic* (introspective, transformative, generative, and ethical or critical) responses to loss. Third, and as I have demonstrated through my sustained scrutiny of Kanafani's "Letter from Gaza," I make a key differentiation between *melancholizing* and *melancholicizing* discursive and sociopolitical practices. In a sense, I agree with Jonathan Flatley in his lucid reflections on Robert Burton's *Anatomy of Melancholy* that "melancholizing is something one *does*: longing for lost loves, brooding over absent objects and changed environment, reflecting on unmet desires, and lingering on events from the past. It is a practice that might, in fact, produce its own kind of knowledge."[58] Melancholizing, though, is not just what you do in a carefree way, or out of longing and ennui, much less so in an embattled sociocultural or ethnonational situation, but also what others subject you to, especially in structurally and cognitively overdetermined geopolitical contexts.

Under conditions of colonial domination and imperial hegemony, chances are you may find yourself being always already melancholized regardless of whether you are actually melancholizing or not. To be melancholized is to be privatized and produced as melancholite, emptied of political significance, and reduced to reactionary patterns of behavior that misconstrue any productive and agentive strategies of resistance you may be contemplating or actually undertaking. The melancholization of ethnic and racial identities in Euro-American societies oftentimes relies on publicly held images of, for instance, Arabs and Muslims and becomes therefore the manifestation of an underlying racist mode of intelligibility that insists on the validity of the stereotype and even incites Arabs and Muslims to conform to it. Recurrent incitements of this sort only further melancholize Arabs and Muslims, compelling them to hold on to their ethnocultural differentials, to take offense and to refuse, as Sara Ahmed succinctly puts it, "to let go of the pain of racism by letting go of racism as a way of understanding that pain."[59] Melancholization from this perspective becomes a psychopolitical power relation that is mutually reinforced by both aggressors and the victims of aggression (who oftentimes become reactive aggressors on their own). Throughout *Melancholy Acts*, I distinguish

---

58. Jonathan Flatley, *Affective Mapping: Melancholia and the Politics of Modernism* (Cambridge, MA: Harvard University Press, 2008), 2.

59. Sara Ahmed, "Happy Objects," in *The Affect Theory Reader*, ed. Melissa Gregg and Gregory J. Seigworth (Durham, NC: Duke University Press, 2010), 48.

between static, paralyzing, compulsive, impulsive, or reactionary melancholizing patterns of behavior—all of which have combined to give melancholy a bad reputation that ranges from its routine pathologization by its detractors to its instrumentalization by oppressive power systems—and self-reflective, patient, and productive as well as future-oriented melancholicizing practices operative in literary, cultural, and intellectual products or in grassroots sociopolitical movements of resistance to both authoritarianism and settler colonialism. Attending to the particularities of these melancholicizing practices as they come to be rhetorically embedded in specific theoretical, literary, or visual texts offers a key corrective to the melancholizing terms of reception of Arab culture in transnational contexts increasingly cast under the shadow of Euro-American soft-power dominance.

In a geopolitical battlefield that had for decades been the geostrategic target of orientalist locutions and epistemological violence, melancholicizing is a delicate pedagogical process of enhancing critical consciousness and cognitive demystification that includes as much sensitization and intellectual stimulation as dissection and unlearning of ideologically imbued modes of intelligibility. Kanafani's "Letter from Gaza," in which the epistolary form of the story makes possible an arresting chiastic reversal from melancholization to melancholicization, dramatizes the processes of ethical and empathic indignation in tandem with the speaker's cognitive reversal and revised remapping of Gaza in light of Nadia's story of supererogatory sacrifice. The ultimate goal of melancholicization is both politicization and mobilization; hence the dawning obligation under which the speaker felt compelled to raise awareness about the fierce urgency of political solidarity with the amputee, Nadia, and with her besieged and bombarded Gaza. Kanafani's story is the product and exemplum of the melancholia of the oppressed, in which melancholization emerges as the symptom of colonization while melancholicization as the midwife of decolonization.

This melancholia of the oppressed must be distinguished from what Paul Gilroy calls "postcolonial" or "postimperial melancholy" in his judicious and painstaking diagnosis of the imperial hangovers that permeate contemporary British society. The defeat of Hitlerism was quickly overshadowed by the demise of the British empire, which resulted in a generalized feeling of perplexity, shame, and discomfort; yet, rather than work through these feelings, Gilroy argues, "the nation has been dominated by an inability even to face, never mind actually mourn, the profound change in circumstances and moods that followed the end of the empire and the consequent loss of imperial prestige."[60]

---

60. See Paul Gilroy, *Postcolonial Melancholia* (New York: Columbia University Press, 2004), 90.

Worse, the persistent yet disavowed pathological attachment to the fantasy of imperial grandeur found release in runaway racist fears and xenophobic resentment of postwar newcomers from the former colonies, not least because they constitute further reminders of the loss of empire with all its attendant grandeur and disavowed guilt. Scapegoating the immigrant communities only deepened Britain's postcolonial melancholy such that the reinstatement of British self-esteem became synonymous, for some, with the fantasy of expelling or repatriating the new settlers to the countries they came from.

The melancholia of the oppressed is almost the exact reverse of Gilroy's postcolonial melancholy, since insofar as historical Palestine is concerned, it is the new settlers, and not the existing inhabitants, who have expropriated the land and carried out the expulsion and dispossession of the indigenous populations. The melancholia of the oppressed is precipitated by the Nakba and aggravated by the Naksa; its crippling psychopolitical *afteraffects* on Palestinians and Arabs far exceed the symptomatic and symbolic economies by which it is articulated. Insofar as it is animated by fantasies of colonial power and hegemony, British postcolonial melancholy is not so dissimilar to Zionist melancholy, which hinges squarely on an anachronistic yet narcissistic biblical nostalgia combined with a regressive longing for and hallucinatory fascination with ancient Israeli glory. Settler Zionism is melancholite and melancholizing while the Palestinian struggle for national liberation is melancholic and melancholicizing. The asymmetrical power-relations and the ethical differentials between the two melancholies (that of the oppressed and that of their oppressors) may have been discursively confounded or overshadowed by Israel's geostrategic alliance with Euro-American imperialism, but they remain of paramount importance to any intelligible conception of justice and equality. The aestheticization, romanticization, and normalization of Zionist melancholy never cease to banalize and perpetuate the settler colonial violence on which Israel is founded while Israel's pathologization and demonization of the melancholia of the oppressed Palestinians never cease to derealize, displace, and disperse the unspeakable crimes of which it is the product.

Arab culture, literature and film are bloated with ungrieved and ungrievable losses and corpses, staking, as it were, a claim to dignity and justice from beyond the grave. The extent to which we can identify and identify with such a near or remote claim will help chart the ethical contours of melancholicization. It may be instructive to recall that in Kanafani's "Letter from Gaza," the speaker ends up being impelled to stay in Gaza and to call on Mustafa to come back; Nadia's story of selfless sacrifice had jolted him wide awake to "what life is and what existence is worth."[61] The speaker's sudden course reversal signals

---

61. Kanafani, "Letter from Gaza," 115.

a radical awakening to the sacrificial ethics à la Nadia that give life its worth. His counterintuitive decision to let go of the opportunity to pursue a potentially happy life in California matches only his eagerness to hold on to a life of utter suffering and pain in wounded and bleeding Gaza. The speaker agrees to assume a position of compassion, exposure, and vulnerability—and to take the same risks that Nadia took when she intervened on behalf of her brothers—in an attempt to finally live a life worthy of its name, a life of self-less sacrifice, irreducible to the pursuit of happiness he would have experienced had he joined Mustafa in California. The belated fantasy of vulnerability as a condition of collectivity, of being with and for others, may very well serve as a corrective to the speaker's heretofore deflection and abnegation of responsibility and as a signal of an ethics of solidarity that does not stop at bearing witness to the pain and suffering of the victims of Zionism but further commits to being there among them in the midst of peril and precarity.

The speaker endorses an ethics of melancholicization that is marked as much by the urgency to hold a mirror up to Nadia's amputated leg, itself an index and indictment of Israel's ethical vacuum, as by the urgency to intervene on her behalf in what would constitute "something akin to the restoration of the amputated leg!"[62] To let go of the amputated leg would mean to let go of a limb whose ghostly void or phantomatic demarcation persists into the present of narration and into the present of writing. To hold on melancholically to the mutilated limb is to hold on to something that is gone but whose shadow lives on as an ethical demand for recognition and a political claim for justice. It may be argued that melancholia appropriates all attention toward the disoriented psyche of the survivor and further disappears the excised limb it is called up to preserve and restore but, to the extent that melancholic salvation threatens to clone the irrecoverably lost leg, this may be the perilous cost of the ethical imperative of remembering, signaling, and preempting historical injustices from sinking or dissolving into oblivion.

The speaker assumes a melancholic position that is simultaneously an ethical-political position and a corrective to his former pursuit of flight, of detachment and disengagement from Gaza. To the extent that he associates this position with a newly gained insight about the essence of life and the meaning of existence, and to the extent that the new ethical position is precipitated by the transformative discovery of Nadia's story of selfless sacrifice, I submit that the melancholic swerve, or the process of melancholicization instigated by Nadia's story, constitutes the inaugural datum of the ethics of the melancholia of the oppressed. I will say more about this melancholic swerve in chap-

62. Ibid.

ter 1. Suffice it to mention here that it is also a poetic and formal swerve, the product of the chiastic shuttle of the epistolary form of "Letter from Gaza" from individual to collective salvation. To read for the melancholic swerve is also to read for the poetic swerve, which is in turn to read for the ethical and political swerve to which the speaker ends up not only committing himself but also soliciting and urging others, namely his friend Mustafa and the implied readers, to make similar commitments. After all, the lesson of Kanafani's epistle is not just to pay tribute to Nadia's memory, but also to ensure that her originary commitment to collective salvation continues to inspire the struggle for national liberation. As I mentioned before, melancholia may itself constitute an epitaph to the very ungrieved losses it strives to resurrect and reckon with, but this risk may prove inevitable, if not palatable, in the effort to disinter and reinvigorate the lost causes, the foregone commitments or mundane dreams of the victims of settler colonial and authoritarian oppression from the Nakba to the Naksa and beyond.

In the writings of Kanafani, which emerged in the endless aftermath of the Nakba, melancholic attachments to home, land, and homeland must not be seen as attachments to complete losses but as attachments to losses that persist into the present, that is, to losses whose loss is far too incomplete to even warrant mourning. Melancholic attachments to incomplete losses are very taxing psychically yet highly affirmative politically insofar as they keep under close scrutiny the historical injustices of which these still unfolding losses are the product. In "Melancholy and the Act," however, Slavoj Žižek gives short shrift to losses produced by historical injustices. What matters for Žižek is not loss but Lacanian lack: given that every object is prefigured by its inevitable decay, it can never be fully possessed, and what can never be possessed can never be lost. "In short," Žižek claims, "what melancholy obfuscates is that the object is lacking from the very beginning, that its emergence coincides with its lack, that this object is *nothing but* the positivization of a void or lack, a purely anamorphic entity that does not exist in itself."[63] From this perspective, Nadia's amputated leg is lost only to the extent that the speaker's subjective and biased gaze distorts the objective features of reality. It has been lacking all along!

Žižek's dehistoricizing and derealizing logic may be tempting, especially for those who are not at the receiving end of historical injustices but are its beneficiaries; the fact remains, though, that the constitutive transience, structural decay or unavoidable mortality of any given object does not warrant the structural banalization of its loss before or after its occurrence, especially if

---

63. Žižek, "Melancholy and the Act," 660.

the loss is not the result of a natural process of decay, but of a gross act of injustice. Žižek's error is that he displaces and collapses historically specific experiences of loss into undifferentiated, transhistorical and constitutive instances of lack. Ironically, though, lack lacks dissonance with the very neoliberal consumerist society Žižek repudiates. Assuming that the object of desire is structured by lack and continually evades the grasp of the desiring subject, the demand for it could intensify and result in a relentlessly accelerating stampede of consumerism. All the more so, given that desire for Lacan as for Žižek "is neither the appetite for satisfaction nor the demand for love, but the difference that results from the subtraction of the first from the second, the very phenomenon of their splitting (*Spaltung*)."[64] Emerging and reemerging in the untraversable chasm between *demand* (love) and *need* (sex), the demand for love and the gratification of a sexual need, desire is a constant slide along the metonymic chain of signifiers. Capitalism, Todd McGowan suggests, "constantly seeks out and embraces what is new, because the new keeps desire going by helping to create a sense of lack."[65] Nothing is more emblematic of neoliberal consumer society than a psychic economy conditioned by the mythical idea that the new object holds the promise of satisfaction.

Žižek's insouciance about the affectual weight of actual historical losses is not inconsistent with his undifferentiated backlash on the "radical wing of today's academy," namely the practitioners of postcolonial studies, for elevating melancholy to the status of not only the "politically correct" but also the "hegemonic intellectual trend."[66] Insisting on what he perceives as the necessary "need to denounce the objective cynicism that such a rehabilitation of melancholy enacts," he posits that "what is wrong with the postcolonial nostalgia is not the utopian dream of a world they never had (such utopia can be thoroughly liberating) but the way this dream is used to legitimize the actuality of its vey opposite, of the full and unconstrained participation in global capitalism."[67]

Žižek's wholesale dismissal of postcolonial studies hinges on the assumption that postcolonial societies opted to participate in global capitalism, yet it never occurs to Žižek that postcolonial societies were never offered the choice

---

64. Jacques Lacan, "The Signification of the Phallus," in *Écrits*, trans. Bruce Fink (New York: Norton, 2006), 580.

65. Todd McGowan, *Enjoying What We Don't Have: The Political Project of Psychoanalysis* (Lincoln: University of Nebraska Press, 2013), 61.

66. Žižek, "Melancholy and the Act," 657, 658.

67. Ibid., 659.

to participate or not participate in global capitalism. They could not have possibly exercised, much less imposed, a choice they were never offered—on the contrary, their entry into the capitalist system is the inevitable outcome of European colonialism and now American imperialism, both of which produced and reproduced the global hegemony of capitalism. Blaming the victims, however, pales in comparison to Žižek's outright derealization of the historical injustices they incurred.

Žižek claims that postcolonial peoples make use of their melancholic attachments to their vanishing ethnic roots and traditions as an alibi to justify their full participation in the global capitalist game. My sense though is that postcolonial societies would have preferred not to participate in the capitalist game if it were up to them. I broach this particular issue in my discussion of left melancholy in chapter 3, but it won't be overhasty to say here that Žižek may be mistaking the actual policies of postcolonial authoritarian regimes with the affectual commitments of postcolonial writers and intellectuals. Žižek further claims that melancholy has been promoted by postcolonial studies to procure and protect the differential rights of ethnic minorities, on the one hand, and, on the other, that it has become a dominant intellectual paradigm almost vying with capitalism in its totalitarian ambitions.[68] The subversion of melancholy becomes therefore an ethical act, since "an ethical act is not only beyond the reality principle . . . it rather designates an intervention that changes the very coordinates of the reality principle. . . . And an act is not only a gesture that does the impossible but an intervention into social reality that changes the very coordinates of what is perceived to be possible; it is not simply beyond the good, it redefines what counts as good."[69]

Žižek propounds the "ethical act" as a performative subversion of normative Western melancholy but remains reticent about what comes after melancholy. I find his idealistic and quasi-revolutionary understanding of what constitutes an ethical act as an apt account of Kanafani's "Letter from Gaza," except that in Kanafani's case the ethical act is also a melancholy act. The epistolary story subverts the emigration fervor that had become the hegemonic norm in Palestinian society in view of the perilous and intolerable conditions of life under the constant threat of Israeli air raids. From the abject conditions of defeat in the beginning of the story, Gaza becomes toward the end "only

---

68. Note here that Žižek includes "Melancholy and the Act" in a later collection of essays titled *Did Somebody Say Totalitarianism? Five Interventions in the (Mis)use of a Notion* (London: Verso, 2001).

69. Žižek, "Melancholy and the Act," 671–72.

the beginning of a long, long road leading to Safad," to the camps of the fedayeen and to militant resistance.[70]

Through the speaker's ethical and epiphanic outburst at the sight of "Nadia's leg, amputated from the top of the thigh," not to mention the "grief which had molded her face and merged into its traits forever," Kanafani foregrounds the psycho-affectual inward revolt of the speaker that would eventually lead to his sociopolitical revolt against the normative hold of the fantasy of emigration on the social imaginary. The speaker and his friend Mustafa had themselves been infected by the germ of this fantasy since childhood. Nadia's generation, though, had been robbed of the very right to dream of an exit, let alone of a better life. As the speaker intimates to Mustafa: "I loved Nadia from habit, the same habit that made me love all that generation which had been so brought up on defeat and displacement that it had come to think that a happy life was a kind of social deviation."[71] The generational gap between the speaker and his niece, Nadia, who had imbibed only misery and defeat, sharpened his sense of ethical responsibility toward her and her generation. Having wondered throughout his address to Mustafa about the reasons why they couldn't just "leave this defeat with its wounds behind" and "move on to a brighter future," the speaker decides, through an epiphany of high resolve and at a moment of generative ethical insight, to let go of the possible dream of a better future in California and to hold on to the impossible, dreamless, futureless present of precarity.[72]

Such a counterintuitive decision is the exemplum of a radical melancholic sensibility: not only does it run against the dominant zeitgeist in Gaza, with all its attendant fantasies of escape and pursuit of a better life somewhere else, but also against the injustice of the settler colonial apparatus and its indiscriminate bombings of defenseless civilians and their homes. Above all, the speaker is actuated by an acute ethical responsibility that requires from him, to paraphrase Žižek, to intervene in social reality and to change the coordinates of what counts as the happy life. For the real crimes of the settler colonial regime are not confined to the number of deaths and material damages inflicted on Gazans but extend to the less visible yet no less damaging circuitous path whereby the likes of Nadia come "to think that a happy life was a kind of social deviation." The speaker's penetrating attention to the insidious encroachment of the settler colonial system upon Nadia's psyche helped crystalize the incumbent task he set himself, namely his commitment to the rescue of Na-

---

70. Kanafani, "Letter from Gaza," 115.
71. Ibid., 114.
72. Ibid., 113.

dia and her generation from the psychopolitical hegemony of colonialism. The speaker knows that he could have remained untouched by or indifferent to Nadia's predicament, but he became obligated and ethically bound to her because he realizes in the meanwhile that Nadia could have chosen not to rescue her brothers, but she didn't. The speaker learns from Nadia, that is, from the very generation for whom a happy life would be a kind of social deviation. Yet, it is to that very life that he commits his future, and not to a dream life in green California. "Each generation," Fanon pinpoints, "must out of relative obscurity discover its mission, fulfill it, or betray it."[73] Through the speaker's self-disclosure, self-exposure, and unconditional solidarity with his own people, not only does Kanafani point toward a melancholic path of self-reclamation but also toward an ethical-political commitment to the continuation of the struggle for Palestinian liberation.

Overview of the Book

It should have become clear by now that Žižek's sweeping condemnation of melancholia is not only untenable but clearly irrelevant to postcolonial colonial contexts in which attachments to individual and collective losses, or to compromised yet unalienable rights, constitute acts of survival, resistance, and decolonial agitation. In the geopolitical context of the Arab world, the ethical act along the lines that Žižek identifies would be a melancholy act par excellence not only because melancholia goes against the norms of the reality principle (and which are the norms of rudimentary Freudian mourning), and against the consumerist norms of global capitalism, but also because in the Arab world melancholia goes, above all, against the pacifying and appeasing norms of imperial and settler colonial dispossession. In its Arab sociocultural and political formation, melancholia is not just associated with the fall of self-esteem and the regression to infantile fantasies and primary narcissisms, not to mention the structural pathologies of gender and identity formations, but it is inextricably tied to the rise of self-reflexive critical subjectivities, decolonial dissent, and the Fanon-like rallying clamor for freedom from coercion and injustice. As such, the dispossessed Arab and Palestinian wagers, to the extent that it is possible, on melancholia to unsettle the coordinates of a reality principle produced by the intractable collusion of settler colonial Zionism, resilient authoritarianism, and Euro-American imperialism.

Moreover, the melancholy disposition at work in the cultural field permits us to make sense of the continued proliferation of Arabic literary production

---

73. Fanon, *The Wretched of the Earth*, 206.

in paradoxical conjunction with colonial and imperial wars, disastrous defeats and setbacks, civil wars, and the overall political impotence of Arab states from the dispossession of Palestine to the occupation of Iraq and beyond. The disunity of the Arab world today would make the thought of Nasser's 1950s ideology of Arab nationalism laughable. Yet, despite (or perhaps because of) the generalized paralysis of official political will and the gnawing sense of national malaise, the literary and cultural scene continued and continues to thrive at an unprecedented pace, all the more so after the Arab uprisings, which further sharpened the divide between the necessity and impossibility of revolutionary change. As Daniel Bensaïd argues, the commitment to revolutionary change becomes melancholy when "the necessary and the possible diverge."[74] The revolutionary euphoria that has taken the authoritarian Arab regimes by surprise soon devolved into civil wars (Syria, Libya, Yemen), or reproduced a variation of the military dictatorship of the ancien régime (Egypt), which further entrenched financial capitalism and the rentier economy on which most Arab nations variably rely. The near or complete failure of the Arab uprisings makes revolutionary change still very much a necessity in spite of its proven impossibility—really, in spite of the resilience of the triptych of authoritarianism, Zionism, and imperial hegemony.

Melancholia renders legible not only the predominant sense of malaise that characterizes Arab contemporaneity, or what Samir Kassir has called in a book of the same title *le malheur arabe* or "the Arab malaise," but also the explosion in literary and cultural activity since 1967.[75] While I would be remiss if I did not underscore the understandable compensatory valences of artistic productivity—which had amounted for several writers and artists to a substitute for direct political engagement—many of the post-Naksa literary and cultural works have struck out on a political path of their own and engaged with politics in their own terms by enacting or embodying at the level of language and rhetoric dissident acts of political empowerment. My sense is that these works, including the examples I will be studying in the different chapters of *Melancholy Acts*, have relied wittingly or unwittingly on melancholia as an ambient after-Naksa affect to sustain a commitment to freedom from injustice in a postcolonial colonial context of compromised dignity and lost sovereignty.

Chapter 1 fleshes out the notion of "melancholy acts" through a sustained reflection on the question of *iltizām* or commitment in the aftermath of the

---

74. Daniel Bensäid, *An Impatient Life: A Memoir*, trans. David Fernbach (London: Verso, 2014), 318.

75. Samir Kassir, *Considérations sur le malheur arabe* (Arles: Actes Sud, 2004), in English *Being Arab*, trans. Will Hobson (New York: Verso, 2006).

INTRODUCTION: MELANCHOLY ACTS 39

ongoing Nakba and Naksa. The argument will engage in targeted analyses of an eclectic number of plays, novels, poems, and films and cite short critical statements and dictums and at times even aphorisms in order to first hammer home what I mean by "melancholy acts" and then show how these "melancholy acts" do indeed serve as acts of decolonial cultural critique. The subsequent chapters embark on wide-ranging and detailed analyses of the psychoanalytical, literary, or cinematic examples I make use of as illustrations or case studies of the melancholy disposition of Arab contemporaneity.

Taking its cue from Theodor Adorno's by now infamous dictum, "To write poetry after Auschwitz is barbaric," chapter 2 examines its different configurations in contemporary Arabic poetry, which continues to fall irresistibly not so much under the shadow of the Holocaust as under the shadow of its proximate historical corollary, the Palestinian Nakba of 1948. Many Arab poets have made similar pronouncements to that of Adorno about the impossibility of poetry after every post-Nakba political onslaught on Arabland, starting from the devastating 1967 Israeli preemptive strike against Egypt, Jordan, and Syria up to the more recent "Operation Iraqi Freedom" orchestrated by the so-called Coalition of the Willing against Iraq. Studying an eclectic but substantial number of poems composed by such canonical contemporary figures as Nizār Qabbānī, Adonis, and especially Mahmoud Darwish, this chapter demonstrates how Arab poets strategically (and by now even routinely) conjure up the muse of impossibility of poetry (following every act of violence committed against Arab nations since the Nakba) in order to produce poetry. I inquire about the formal and political implications of this generative paradox.

Daniel Bensaïd's argument in *Le pari mélancolique*, "the impossible remains, despite everything, necessary," applies as much to the vocation of Arabic poetry as to the vocation of leftists in the aftermath of the serial Arab defeats.[76] Chapter 3 asks about what has become of the Arab left, and the Egyptian left in particular, in the wake of the 1948 catastrophe, the 1952 Nasserite revolution and the 1967 disaster. After having discussed the formation of a melancholy disposition in Arab contemporaneity from the encounter with settler colonialism (1948 and beyond) to American imperialism (2003 and beyond), this chapter zeroes in on national dynamics and on the frustrated hopes of bringing real change at the level of Arab nation and society. It is not for nothing that the focus here is on the Arab left which has historically been the harbinger of social transformation and national liberation. This chapter will focus on the psychodynamics of social change from below in Egypt while the

---

76. Daniel Bensaïd, *Le pari mélancolique: Métamorphoses de la politique, politique des métamorphoses* (Paris: Fayard, 1997), 255.

following chapter will focus on the modernist experiment in Tunisia and how social change is entered from above, by President Habib Bourguiba.

The Arab left was struck by the cruelty of what Benjamin once labeled "left-wing melancholy," at least three decades before the international left felt its harsh reality following the fall of the Berlin Wall and the collapse of the Soviet Union itself in 1989 and the early 1990s, respectively. This chapter draws on the general malaise that shook the Arab left by reading in tandem critical writings by Helmut Dubiel, Walter Benjamin, Wendy Brown, and Arwa Salih, among several others. The substantial portion of the chapter is devoted mostly to a reading of Naguib Mahfouz's 1965 novel *Al-Shahḥadh* (*The Beggar*). Published on the eve of the 1967 defeat, the novel uses the theme of the journey to allegorize the spiritual bankruptcy and political impotence of the Nasserite intellectual and presents Nasserism as both symptom and precipitating cause of the failure of the Arab left to apprehend the character of postrevolutionary Egypt and to create grassroots alternatives. The crisis that the main leftist character in the novel undergoes is, in turn, as much a symptom of as a melancholy response to the collapse of the Arab left writ large.

The failure of the Arab left to transform society and bring about democratic change must be understood dynamically in relation to Arab authoritarianism and settler colonialism whose duel at times has produced the effect of a conspiracy between corrupt Arab regimes and merciless imperialists. No wonder the legacy of colonial modernity fueled passionate attachments to tradition and impeded the kind of social transformation and modernization that Arab leftists wanted to implement. In this context, the case of Tunisia is exemplary, given that its first president wanted to implement the changes from above by changing Islamic laws in favor of civic laws. Chapter 4 focuses on the psychodynamics that these changes brought about on the system of patriarchy to which the anticolonial struggle adhered as part of its resistance to French colonialism. Bourguiba's rule over Tunisia (1956–1987) produced a breed of men that might be aptly called Bourguiba's sons. Suspended in a state of mutability that is simultaneously cultivated and frustrated, they have been able neither to come to terms with the challenges of modernity, of which gender equality is part and parcel, nor to relinquish fully the protective shelter of traditional patriarchy, in which male supremacy is the grantor of psychosocial stability.

Modern Tunisian cinema is abundantly invested in unraveling the ways in which Tunisian men are stranded in the pull of neopatriarchy, even while attempting timidly or defiantly to break free from its confines. Postcolonial films by, among others, Moufida Tlatli, Nadia Fares, Férid Boughedir, and Nouri Bouzid draw a markedly melancholy portrait of manhood. The challenges of modernity—to say nothing of gender and same-sex rights as well as the rights of sexual minorities writ large—have cast a grim shadow on traditional dimensions of manhood, masculinity, and sexuality. Melancholy manhood is born when a loss or crisis of old conceptions of manhood has taken place but has not been accompanied with the parallel and adequate psychosocial and hermeneutic readjustment necessary for its resolution.

The majority of the chapters of *Melancholy Acts* shed light on the psychodynamics of social transformation and national liberation by largely non-violent means. The systems of oppression (ranging from authoritarian regimes and settler colonial or imperial ones) remain violent though and have no qualms about using state violence against nonviolent protest as, for instance, Emad Burnat's and Guy Davidi's gripping documentary film *Five Broken Cameras* makes patently clear. In the remaining two chapters, the book moves on to examine the psychodynamics of resistance which resort to militant and/or suicidal violence. This chapter will focus on Palestine while the following one will open up to a discussion of religious radicalism in the Middle East and beyond; the stakes in the final chapter will be to understand the psychodynamics of suicidal protest at the crossroads of postcolonialism, Islamism and psychoanalysis.

Chapter 5 starts by exploring the aporias and dilemmas of representation that Arab writers and artists confront at a time when the Arab world has become overly mediatized and ideologically territorialized as a zone of sectarian violence and death. For all the reports on Iraq, Palestine, and Lebanon, the Arab world suffers from what might be called a collapse of witnessing. I focus mainly on the controversies over the humanization of terrorism in Hany Abu-Assad's film *Paradise Now* (*al-jannah-tul-ān*) and demonstrate the ways in which the film grapples with the construction of a narrative of terrorism that cannot be prediscursively (and on licensed grounds) discredited as a justification of terror. Oftentimes, narratives of terrorism are discredited not because they ostensibly raise ethical concerns over the aestheticization of terror but because they challenge the racial and geopolitical differentials on the grounds of which humanity is constructed, valued, allocated, or withheld. Almost readily convinced about suicide protest as a melancholy act par excellence, the film invests in a minimalist aesthetics of failure in order to hammer home this point. *Paradise Now* stages the collapse of the spectacle of terror (since it withholds the act of suicide bombing from view) and invests in, among others, "camera failure" and prolonged close-up scenes as well as in comic relief in order to reclaim and stage the right to narrate the tragedy of Palestine uninhibited by the criminalizing discourses attendant upon any attempt to understand the many competing and overlapping factors (ranging from the psychosocial dynamics of family history and economic disempowerment to the everyday humiliating existence under occupation) that precipitate martyrdom (arguably, suicidal) operations—the impasse of subjectivity.

The crisis of the Arab subject cannot be overstated—it is a subject that gives in to melancholy when it is no longer the agent of its own history. Suicide protests may be seen as attempts to regain agency and lost sovereignty and are therefore first and foremost symptoms of the aforementioned impasse of subjectivity. The closing chapter of *Melancholy Acts* connects this Lacanian understanding of suicide in relation to religious radicalism and Islamism in the work of the Tunisian psychoanalyst Fethi Benslama with a retrospective eye on the work of Freud's translator George Tarabishi. For Tarabishi, because Arabs have been stripped of their subjectivity, they were forced to find shelter in tradition; similarly, for Benslama the fantasy of return to origins that marks the Islamist project is spurred by the impasses of subjectivity brought about by the end of the Islamic caliphate. This concluding chapter examines how Benslama makes use of Lacanian vocabulary in order to deconstruct the myth of origin in Islam and the melancholite (i.e., reactionary and manic) economy of jouissance that sustains it. There is a tendency in Benslama to reduce what is historical to what is structural or endemic to Muslim societies; the effect is at times more demystifying than illuminating. While Oliver Roy distinguishes between "the radicalization of Islam" and "the Islamization of radicalism," there is hardly any such distinctions in Benslama's work. In his most recent book, entitled *Un furieux désir de sacrifice: Le surmusulman* (A Furious Desire for Sacrifice: The Super Muslim), Benslama expands his deconstruction of the Islamist obsession with the return to origins by constructing and deconstructing the figure of the *surmusulman*, the ultimate embodiment of *the despair of being oneself* and of the tormenting desire to return to pure Islamic origins as well as of the belief in the redemptive promise of the ethereal jouissance that lies in store.

Benslama is not unaware of the *external* socioeconomic and geopolitical circumstances that produce jihadist and surmusulman figures, but he refuses to give these factors pride of place, opting instead—in a more or less typical fashion since the publication of *Psychoanalysis and the Challenge of Islam* in 2002—to focus on the *internal* psycho-theological dimension of the jihadist spirit, that is, on the symptoms of the surmusulman, or, more precisely, on the surmusulman itself as a symptom of something gone awry in Islamic civilization from within. This chapter will engage with Benslama's alternatives to the Muslim impasses of subjectivity and will conclude by taking Benslama's own construction of a female Muslim itinerary of Islamic history as a salutary example of nonviolent melancholic critique that the book has tried to account for throughout the different literary and cultural examples discussed. Women, according to Benslama, are the unacknowledged midwives of monotheistic and Islamic origin par excellence. The conclusion will build on Benslama's pathologizing view of melancholy in order not only to expose his sanctioned displacements of historical reality into the structural determinacies of religion and language but also to further situate melancholy in a spectrum of affective differentials that range from melancholy pride to melancholy critique.

It will become clear throughout the different chapters of the book that melancholy is not just a symptom at times and a malady at others that seeps through the sociocultural fabric of Arab contemporaneity, but also an allegory of reading the political and intellectual legacy of which it is a product and a driving force. Given the divergent paths that melancholy can take, its incoherence and nonhomogeneity, it offers a postcontradictory and capacious approach, by no means hegemonic, to the concatenating and contentious currents of Arab contemporaneity.

1
Melancholy Formations
From Nakba to Naksa and Beyond

One of the most memorable scenes in Gillo Pontecorvo's 1966 film *The Battle of Algiers* is the press conference held by Colonel Mathieu (Jean Martin), the head of the paratroopers, after the capture of Larbi Ben M'Hidi, one of the six founding members of the Front de Libération Nationale (FLN) and, at the time of his arrest, the only remaining member of FLN's Comité de Coordination et d'Execution in Algiers (CCE). The press conference was cut short by Mathieu as soon as he realized that Ben M'Hidi's lightening repartees could backfire and take out much of the immediate sting of the soldiers' success in neutralizing the FLN. In one of the exchanges, a journalist asks Ben M'Hidi, "In your opinion, does the FLN still have some chance of defeating the French Army?" Ben M'Hidi administers a suave rebuff with disarming mildness: "The FLN has more of a chance to defeat the French Army than the French Army has of changing/arresting the course of history [*d'arrêter le cours de l'histoire*]." Ben M'Hidi's witticism debunks the mission-accomplished-rhetoric-cum-spectacle (that the press conference was called upon to serve) and contends that the irreversible forward flow of history far surpasses the obstructionist power of the French Army. Accordingly, the FLN is acting from within the imperative dynamics of history and must eventually prevail, while the French Army is clinging to a static posture of history and will gain only a transitory victory.[1] As it happened, the French Army won the Battle of Algiers (1954–57) but lost Algeria, while the FLN lost the Battle of Algiers but won the war of independence (1962).

---

1. This sentence is adapted from Julien Benda, *The Treason of the Intellectuals*, trans. Richard Aldington (New Brunswick, NJ: Transaction Publishers, 2009), 27–28.

The FLN's decolonial struggle seems from this perspective to have hinged squarely on historical necessity, more so than on the end result of revolutionary struggle. Ben M'Hidi's firm belief in the doctrine of historical progress along the exponential curve of decolonization is such that it risks attenuating the role of human agency and vitiating the outcomes of wars and battles. The tacit acknowledgment of the inadequacy of human agency to shoulder the burden of national liberation by itself fills Ben M'Hidi's wager on the emancipatory laws of historical development with cautious optimism. If mixed with theological and mythological notions of fate and destiny, this ambiguous nexus or schism between historical determinism and human agency becomes a fecund ground for the melancholy formation of postcolonial subjectivity in the Arab world. This is all the more so given that historical necessity is no longer in sync with the still necessary tasks of decolonization and national liberation. Assuming that the decolonial march of history did cast a ghastly shadow on France's settler colonial presence in Algeria, how come it has so far proven inconsequential with regard to Palestine? History may have vindicated Ben M'Hidi but has yet to replicate in Palestine the achievement of Algeria, not least because Palestine succumbed to the *retrograde* settler colonial Zionist project at the very same time that the *progressive* decolonial course of history was gaining momentum across the Global South.

The profound unrolling of history may hold open the promise of emancipation for colonized peoples, but the extent to which human agency is held at bay by the overriding course of historical dynamics remains as ambivalent and enigmatic as Marx's equivocation in *The Eighteenth Brumaire of Louis Bonaparte*: "Men make their own history, but they do not make it just as they please; they do not make it under circumstances chosen by themselves, but under circumstances directly encountered, given, and transmitted from the past."[2] Marx's ambivalent formulation lends itself to the possibility that men make history by being at its receiving end, or, as the melancholic Marxist and militant feminist Arwa Salih puts it, "Whoever said the masses make history was right! Unfortunately, they make history only insofar as they pay the price for making it."[3] "Historical materialists," Benjamin points out, "know what [this] means. Whoever emerged victorious participates to this day in the triumphal procession in which the present rulers step over those who are lying

---

2. Karl Marx, "The Eighteenth Brumaire of Louis Bonaparte" (1852), in *The Marx-Engels Reader*, edited by Robert C. Tucker (New York: Norton, 1978), 595.

3. Arwa Salih, *The Stillborn: Notes of a Woman from the Student-Movement Generation in Egypt*, trans. Samah Selim (New York: Seagull, 2017), 139, translation slightly modified.

prostrate."[4] There is no gainsaying the indelible imprint of decolonization on the course of post–World War II history, but its overall effect pales in comparison to the postcolonial resurgence of neocolonial hegemony. The Cold War Manichean tensions and rivalries weighed heavily on the prospects of decolonial futures throughout the Global South, but more cripplingly so in the Arab world where the creation of Israel swiftly reinscribed colonial power relations at the very moment of their unceremonious unraveling. According to Abdallah Laroui, "Israel by its very existence has checked the Arabs' progress and has been one of the determining causes in the process of continual traditionalization. All liberal, secularizing, and progressive thought appeared as a ruse of Zionist and imperialist propaganda."[5]

The promise of decolonization has not been fully achieved in the Arab world, not only because of the 1967 defeat to Israel—and the collapse of the 1950s and 1960s ideological vision of one united Arab nation—but also because of the Euro-American ceaseless imperial encroachments in the region, most recently in Iraq, Syria, and Libya. The unfathomable disasters brought on by the failed project of decolonization has become all the more pronounced as (settler) colonialism and Arab despotism have become mutually reinforcing. What makes the 1967 defeat, however, a large-scale threshold moment in contemporary Arab history is that it resulted in what Faisal Darraj aptly calls *al-hazīma al-mutawālida*, or "generative defeat," that is, the defeat which breeds or begets other defeats.[6] The macabre seriality of defeats that followed upon the Naksa prompted Darwish to decry, somewhat sarcastically, what he perceives as a lingering collective hangover from an overindulgence in self-inflicted defeats: "We like remembering June on its fortieth anniversary. If we don't find somebody to defeat us again, we'll defeat ourselves with our own hands so that we don't forget."[7] Darwish made this diagnosis in the bleak post-Oslo context of compromised aspirations for national liberation—really, a time when Ben M'Hidi's wager on the emancipatory valences of historical progress was eclipsed by the resiliency of the coercive continuum of colonial history. Raja Shehadeh articulates elegiacally what Darwish rebukes so derisively: "When the signing of the Oslo Accords dashed the hopes I had placed

---

4. Walter Benjamin, *Illuminations: Essays and Reflections*, trans. Harry Zohn (New York: Schocken Books, 1969), 256.

5. Abdallah Laroui, *The Crisis of the Arab Intellectual: Traditionalism or Historicism?* trans. Diarmid Cammell (Berkeley: University of California Press, 1976), 172.

6. Faisal Darraj, "The June War and the Foundation of Generative Defeat," *Majallat al-Dirasat al-Filastiniyya* 111 (2017): 47–50.

7. Mahmoud Darwish, *A River Dies of Thirst: Journals*, trans. Catherine Cobham (New York: Archipelago Books, 2009), 146.

in the Israeli-Palestinian negotiations, I experienced another crippling bout of despair. I could have suffered a spiritual death. . . . It was the writing of *Strangers in the House* that saved me."[8] In Darwish as in Shehadeh, the configuration of defeat is, it bears underscoring, indissociable from the melancholy act of overcoming it.

The aim of this inaugural chapter is to demonstrate the extent to which political and military defeats have spawned a psychoaffective disposition toward melancholy and become the recurring site of creative and critical inquiry, exacerbated even further by a predominant sense of unstoppable technoeconomic belatedness and existential precarity, as well as by the ever so pressing duels between the creative imagination and material history or between ideality and reality. Before I turn my attention in the rest of the book to extended meditations on specific topics in which the disposition to melancholy is most manifest, I attempt here to supplement the argument I laid out in the introduction with a set of reflections on an eclectic number of literary, cinematic, and philosophical works that best dramatize the cultural, political, and discursive gamut of the collective disposition toward melancholy. Of paramount importance are not only the intellectual inquiries about the role of literary and cultural practices in the wake of defeat, but also the future of the agonizing political projects of social transformation, national liberation, and freedom from injustice. It may not be entirely wrong to surmise that such decolonial pursuits have been severely crippled by the Naksa and relegated at best to the realm of mendacious sophistry, but there is no gainsaying the fact that much of contemporary Arab cultural production is still embroiled in such projects, if not variably compelled by their persistent impetus, irrespective of the cruel reality of Arab contemporaneity. "Simply to ignore the major change in the world and press on as before," Edward Said contends, "is one alternative and, ostrichlike, will continue to have its attractions, especially to someone like myself, who has written warmly about lost causes and has been congenitally involved with them for most of his life."[9]

"The condition of being [defeated] apparently contains," Reinhart Koselleck posits, "an inexhaustible [wellspring of intellectual] potential."[10] The

---

8. Raja Shehadeh, *Strangers in the House: Coming of Age in Occupied Palestine* (London: Profile Books, 2009), 238.

9. Edward W. Said, *Humanism and Democratic Criticism* (New York: Columbia University Press, 2004), 33.

10. Reinhart Koselleck, *The Practice of Conceptual History: Timing History, Spacing Concepts*, trans. Todd Presner, Kerstin Behnke, and Jobst Welge (Stanford, CA: Stanford University Press, 2002), 83. Translation slightly modified via Wolfgang Schivelbusch's *The Culture of De-*

commitment to lost causes matches only the belief that colonial injustice and conditions of unfreedom writ large are unsustainable, and that, as Ghassan Kanafani puts it, "Man, in the final analysis, is a cause," and is therefore, as Jean-Paul Sartre insists, "condemned to be free."[11] The melancholy formations I explore throughout this chapter are fomented by the Nakba and exacerbated by the Naksa as well as by the serial reenactment of defeats and setbacks that followed in the last half century but they reflect less a futile clinging to the past than an indignation at the desolation of the present and a longing for freedom from a living legacy of injustices of various kinds. I argue that Arab writers and artists have given pride of place not only to the delicate task of allegorizing defeated individual Arab subjects, proffering on them the dignity of recognition, but also to the incumbent task of inciting critical commitment and political engagement in the present.

Allegories of Defeat

The opening shot of Nouri Bouzid's 1986 debut film, *Riḥ Essed* (*Man of Ashes*), fastens our attention for a moment, while the opening credits start rolling, on a freshly slaughtered red rooster that is quietly succumbing to its wound, with blood dripping from its neck on the concrete surface before it starts flapping its wings spasmodically and drops dead. Surely, the slaughter of a red rooster in Islamic culture is part of various sacrificial rituals or rites of passage such as circumcision ceremonies, but the full significance of this epigraphic shot can only be discerned retrospectively, when we have watched the entire film, and reckoned with the particular trauma of Hachemi (Imad Maalal) and Farfat (Khaled Ksouri): two childhood friends who were not only routinely abused and beaten by their biological fathers but also molested at a tender age by their "initiation father" Ameur (Mustafa Adouani), a master carpenter who teaches them the trade. With nothing to rely on but their shared traumatic woes, they set out to negotiate their entry into adulthood in a society of men that has come, paradoxically, to blame them for their very victimhood and vulnerability. The scene of the bleeding red rooster that prefaces the film cannot then be just about the ritualistic initiation in blood of two children into manhood and then adulthood (as is commonly the case with circumcision, in which "the

---

feat: On National Trauma, Mourning and Recovery, trans. Jefferson Chase (New York: Picador, 2003), 4.

11. Ghassan Kanafani, *Returning to Haifa*, in *Palestine's Children*, trans. Barbara Harlow and Karen E. Riley (Boulder, CO: Lynne Rienner, 2000), 183; Jean-Paul Sartre, *Existentialism Is a Humanism*, trans. Carol Macomber (New Haven, CT: Yale University Press, 2007), 29.

sacrifice of the foreskin" anticipates marriage and the sacrifice of the hymen), nor can it just be about the retrospective-cum-proleptic evocation of the routine sacrifice of innocence on the altar of masculinity.[12] It is rather about a foreclosed initiation into manhood because of the traumatizing interference of rape. Rape—and not circumcision—has come to mark Hachemi and Farfat for life and to bind them together, albeit as outsiders to the society of men.

"A film is like a child," Bouzid points out, "the first page, the first idea contains the entire script, otherwise it's no good."[13] The wing-flapping, screeching red rooster gradually assumes in the context of *Man of Ashes* the shape of a subtle allegory of the après-coup world of the protagonists, Hachemi and Farfat, a world in which their childhood rape by the master carpenter is indelibly etched into their flesh, reducing it to ashes (which is why they are named "men of ashes" in the French and English titles of the film). The ashes represent the remains of their compromised manhood as well as the fire that still burns underneath those remains. In this sense, the allegory of the bleeding rooster sharpens rather than blunts the viewer's imagination of the trauma of child molestation; it reframes rather than replaces the real experience of rape; its reconstructive power hinges on its melancholic commitment: the desire to retain, preserve and approximate the primal horror of rape. Yet, as the story of the film develops and the two childhood friends become implicated in the heteronormative gender roles of society, their concrete individual experiences of rape transform in turn into an allegory of the broader story of postcolonial Tunisia and of the Arab world writ large in the wake of the Naksa or the 1967 defeat. The individual experience of rape segues seamlessly into an authoritative and all-encompassing allegory of defeat across the Arab world.

Bouzid's film presents the viewer with an extensive and dynamic allegory that keeps raising the threshold at which it stops appropriating the radical alterity and singularity of individual experience. The allegory of the après-coup generates, in mise-en-abîme style, other allegories out of the experiences it appropriates. Insofar as allegory poisons the grammar of rhetorical language, every allegorical encroachment entails the risk of abstracting and diminishing individual experiences. The collective Arab experience of defeat, however, remains in excess of allegorical appropriation, and therefore the object of the saturnine disposition in creative and artistic commitments. Allegory becomes therefore the unstable and slippery rhetorical ground through which Arab

---

12. Abdelwahab Bouhdiba, *Sexuality in Islam*, trans. Alan Sheridan (London: Saqi, 2004), 182.

13. Nouri Bouzid, "On Inspiration," in *African Experiences of Cinema*, ed. Imruh Bakari and Mbye B. Cham (London: British Film Institute, 1996), 50.

intellectuals, writers, and artists attempt to trope and reclaim both the singularity and collective resonance of the experience of defeat across the Arab world. Even while individual experience tends ever so pressingly toward the collective allegory of defeat in the aftermath of every historical convulsion in the Arab world, Bouzid's cinema allegorizes individual experiences (here the rape of Hachemi and Farfat) to foreground the critical edge of allegorical representation—really, its "disconcerting" "nature," as Walter Benjamin would put it.[14] "There is a tendency to dismiss the subject of the rape story on the ground that it is an allegory," notes Mieke Bal in her commentary on the rape of Lucretia.[15] It is in the interest of allegories of the collective Arab world to retain and remain melancholically committed to the particular experiences of every individual Arab.

Through its multilayered visual approach, Bouzid's *Man of Ashes* offers a genealogy of the Naksa that is rooted in the patriarchal continuum of the family unit, social norms, and state apparatus. Insofar as the master carpenter Ameur is their initiation father, the slaughtered red rooster is clearly an allegorical reenactment of the scene of paternal castration. In a postcolonial Tunisia under the rule of Habib Bourguiba (1956–1987), who in 1975 declared himself president for life and neutralized all forms of political opposition, the slaughtered red rooster assumes the form of a national allegory of the filicidal tendencies of the arch-patriarch Bourguiba. In other words, the après-coup world of Hachemi and Farfat becomes in turn of paramount allegorical significance to a vivid understanding of individual experience in the postcolony, all the more so given that Bouzid himself was arrested, tortured, and imprisoned for six years (1973–1979) by Bourguiba's regime for his participation in the political activities of a dissident left-wing socialist study and action group called *Āfāq* or *Perspectives*. In short, the slaughtered red rooster may be said to neatly condense Bouzid's endeavor to stage what Aziz Krichen calls "the drama of filiation/*le drame de la filiation*"—that is, the drama of paternal violence and filial obedience in Bourguiba's Tunisia—and, by implication, the crisis of affiliation as a result of the clampdown of Bourguiba's authoritarian regime on all forms of political association and dissidence.[16]

14. Walter Benjamin, *Origin of the German Trauerspiel*, trans. Howard Eiland (Cambridge, MA: Harvard University Press, 2019), 195.

15. Mieke Bal, "The Story of W," in *A Mieke Bal Reader* (Chicago: University of Chicago Press, 2006), 41.

16. Aziz Krichen, *Le syndrome Bourguiba* (Tunis: Cérès Productions, 1992), 32. For more on this, see Nouri Gana, "Sons of a Beach: The Politics of Bastardy in the Cinema of Nouri Bouzid," *Cultural Politics* 13, no. 2 (July 2017): 177–93.

The allegorical continuum between the castrating force of paternal-patriarchal authority and authoritarian state sovereignty cannot be overstressed. This explains partly the reason why for Bouzid the renegotiation of filial relations may very well help lift the ban on political affiliations and pave the way for the democratization of political life, whereas the continued patriarchal complicity between the head of the family and the head of the state will only prolong the crisis of postcolonial nationhood not only in Tunisia but also in the entire Arab world, where there is no lack of kings or presidents for life. In fact, the twin crisis of filiation and affiliation becomes even more evident if we place Bouzid's film in the larger context of the Arab world. Accordingly, the slaughtered red rooster represents a transnational allegory of the Arab predicament in the aftermath of the June 1967 Arab-Israeli War. In the very same way the childhood rape that Hachemi and Farfat lived through came to cast a long shadow on their future life, marking them out of the society of men, the legacy of the 1967 defeat dealt a lasting blow to the ideology of Arab nationalism (and to Nasser as a regional father figure), and mortgaged the future of generations of young Arab men and women who would find themselves as grownups belonging to a broken and defeated Arab nation, incapable of addressing, let alone redressing, the transnational and transgenerational stigma of living with the shame of defeat.

In his quasi-manifesto for Arab cinema post-1967, entitled "New Realism in Arab Cinema: The Defeat-Conscious Cinema," which was initially published in Arabic in 1988, Bouzid postulates that the June 1967 defeat "brought into question all belief systems and ideologies," thus leaving "the Arab intellectual, including the Arab filmmaker, endeavoring for his creative work to emerge against this backdrop of failure and disintegration."[17] The post-1967 Arab filmmaker has to confront several urgent questions: Is it possible to produce creative work in the wake of defeat? If so, what would be the aesthetic and political characteristics of such creative work, and how would it be able to tackle the overwhelming sense of national and transnational disintegration, disenchantment and shame percolating across generations and exempting no Arab nation? In fine, how does an artistic articulation of defeat become an inaugural affirmative gesture? Answering these questions, Bouzid lays out the contours of what may be called an affirmative aesthetics of defeat, whose central aim is to bring about a measured recognition of defeat and a heightened sense of the urgency of altering the sociopolitical conditions that led to defeat in the first place.

17. Nouri Bouzid, "New Realism in Arab Cinema: The Defeat-Conscious Cinema," trans. Shereen el Ezabi, *Alif: Journal of Comparative Poetics* 15 (1995): 242.

In terms of his own practice as a filmmaker, Bouzid calls for a programmatic move from the melodramatic realism of state-controlled pre-Naksa Arab cinema, with its "narcotizing doses" of heroic resilience and happy endings, to a new realism, where a happy ending is no longer guaranteed, and a not so happy ending is no longer "blasphemous."[18] Bouzid claims that his generation of filmmakers "declared war on the old emotions. Hitherto the idea had been to make people weep at fate with all the simple, melodramatic tricks. We were fed up with that cinema and wanted to go the other way."[19] Drawing on the pioneering work of Youssef Chahine, Tawfiq Salih, and Shadi Abdel Salam—and, by implication, on the 1968 *Cinema Manifesto* authored by the New Cinema Collective in Egypt as well as on Italy's neorealist cinema, France's Nouvelle Vague, and Latin America's Third Cinema—Bouzid illustrates what he means by "new realism" through a series of astute commentaries on an eclectic group of Arab films, and concludes his article-cum-manifesto by outlining new realism's general characteristics.[20] Unlike melodramatic realism, which "adhered to old formulas" such as the struggle between good and evil and the construction of flat characters (either good or bad), new realism deals with the more complex reality of the culture of defeat from the specific perspective of the *auteur* filmmaker and makes use of largely nonprofessional actors to construct round characters capable of "harboring both good and evil, and living, as a result, in a state of constant inner strife."[21]

"I am," Bouzid intimates, "one of a group of Tunisian filmmakers all from the same generation, who, without getting together without coming to any prior agreement, went in almost the same direction and almost all worked in a similar way. What they have in common is that they decided to make films that were like themselves."[22] While he continually refined its idiom, Bouzid's theory of new realism can be said to revolve around two axes: a characteristic shift toward *auteur* filmmaking, in which the filmmaker stamps his films with his own personality and style, and an abiding preoccupation with defeat as the driving force and organizing principle of dramatic action, dismantling in the process the myth of "the honorable Arab hero," which was in so much demand by the nascent postcolonial state.[23] Bouzid's revolutionary ideas went against

---

18. Ibid., 243–45.
19. Nouri Bouzid, "On Inspiration," in Bakari and Cham, *African Experiences of Cinema*, 49.
20. See Qussai Samak, "The Politics of Egyptian Cinema," *MERIP Reports* 56 (April 1977): 14.
21. Bouzid, "New Realism in Arab Cinema," 246.
22. Bouzid, "On Inspiration," 48.
23. Bouzid, "New Realism in Arab Cinema," 249.

the current of dominant nationalist cinemas across the Arab world, but perhaps most notably in Algeria, where state-funded *cinéma mujahid*/militant cinema, with its epic accounts of the Algerian people's liberation struggles, dominated the public scene at least in the first decade of independence from Mohamed Lakhdar-Hamina's 1966 *Le vent des Aurès/The Winds of Aures* to his 1975 much-acclaimed *Chroniques des années de braise/Chronicles of the Years of Fire*. It was not until Merzak Allouache's 1976 debut feature film, *Omar Gatalto*, that a scrupulous, almost cynical, and resolutely unheroic portrait of everyday Algerian social reality emerges, focusing on the protagonist's crisis of manhood and sociocultural disaffection.

In his 1994 lecture in Villepreux, France, entitled "On Inspiration," Bouzid revisits his new realist theory by mapping the pivotal components of his own cinematic discourse; he comes up with six recurrent sources of inspiration, or what he calls "constants" (i.e., signature leitmotifs), based on all eight scripts he wrote by that time, including the scripts of Moufida Tlatli's *Silences of the Palace* (1994) and Férid Boughedir's *Halfaouine: Boy of the Terraces* (1990), two defining feature films of modern Tunisian cinema. The distinctive elements that constantly preoccupied Bouzid in his scripts range from memory, defeat, and filiation to nudity, pain, and the veil. Clearly these constants are variations on the overarching theme of defeat, or more precisely on the image of the body in pain, which is a common denominator shared by all of his films as well as by a whole host of films across the Arab world that influenced Bouzid's cinematic project, including films by Youssef Chahine, Tawfiq Salih, Shadi Abdel Salam, Mohammad Malas, and Merzak Allouache.

It may not be too far-fetched to suggest that the cultural imaginary from which Bouzid theorizes his own cinematic neorealist approach (and from within which other Arab artists, creative writers, journalists, and intellectuals of various guilds and stripes constitute their own artistic projects) has in the wake of the Naksa become overwhelmingly melancholic. This is not so much about standing by the ruins (*al-bukā' 'alā-l-aṭlāl*), a known motif in the Arabic *qaṣīda*, as it is about a heightened sensitivity to the ruins of history and the ever-receding political horizon of the possible after the collapse of the project of a united Arab nation. A "tragic sensibility" (to use the words of David Scott) has cast a long shadow on the cognitive powers of the imagination to such an extent that Saadallah Wannous could quip, following Sadat's visit to Israel on November 19, 1977, in an article of the same title, "I am the funeral and the funeral-goer, the mourner and the mourned" (*anā al-janāza wal-mushayi'ūn*).[24] History, with its past, present, and future, is reduced here in

---

24. Saadallah Wannous, "Anā al-Janāza wal-mushayyi'ūn" (I Am the Funeral and the Funeral-Goer), *Al-A'māl al-Kāmila* (Damascus: Al-Ahālī, 1996), 3:439.

Wannous's tautological aphorism to a funerary eternity, in which the mourners are simultaneously the mourned. Sadat's visit to Israel would culminate in what would become the 1978–79 Camp David Accords between Egypt and Israel. Wannous was quite justified to add: "The rhythm of the funeral procession is Time-History" (*iqā' mawkib al-janāza huwa al-zamān-al-tārīkh*).[25] When history becomes time, it verges on the unconscious and becomes therefore impossible to historicize. It becomes in the words of Stephen Daedalus of James Joyce's *Ulysses*, "a nightmare from which I'm trying to awake."[26]

Joyce's nightmare is here Wannous's funeral, not least because to be the mourner and the mourned at once, marching in your own funeral, can only be a nightmarish scenario. Obviously, Wannous's allegory of the long funeral procession does not only gesture toward the limitations of the possible or the doable from within the settler colonial and neoliberal dispensation (in which the heterogeneity of history is transformed into the homogeneity of an endless funeral procession), but also stakes a claim to Arab pain and suffering and implies that when colonialism becomes time what it destroys indeed is the ability of those at its receiving end to historicize their own pain and their own suffering. The inability of Arabs to mourn is from this perspective precisely the inability to historicize and quantify grievances, which is why the melancholy disposition of Arab contemporaneity is not a choice that can be, or has been, exercised by Arabs themselves, but is rather the condition of choice, notwithstanding its critical insights and empowering or militant valences. In this sense, Wannous's statement is a melancholy act par excellence given its simultaneously tragic fidelity and enduring claim to an experience of Arab pain and suffering that has been lost or thrust into oblivion and has therefore to be rescued from the anonymity of empty time and inscribed in the history of the present.

Wannous himself, who has contemplated suicide several times, is no stranger to melancholy acts, since his one-act play *Soirée for the 5th of June* (1968) is a melancholy allegorization, reenactment, and indictment of the defeat of 1967, the defeat called by Tarabishi a kind of "trauma without relief" (*al-radda gheir al-qābila li-taṣrīf*).[27] Wannous's play transforms the stage into a battlefield in order to scrupulously scrutinize the root causes of the defeat. The dizzying repetition throughout the play of the expression *"wujūh bilā malāmiḥ"* ("faces without features")—as if the entire complexion from chin to brow were nothing but an expanse of skin—bespeaks a sort of defacement, a crisis of

---

25. Ibid.
26. James Joyce, *Ulysses*, ed. Declan Kiberd (London: Penguin, 1992), 42.
27. George Tarabishi, *Al-Muthaqqafūn al-'Arab wa al-Turāth* (Arab Intellectuals and Tradition) (London: Riad El-Rayyes Books Ltd, 1991), 76.

subjectivity, not unlike the crisis that Bouzid and other Arab filmmakers sought to represent and repair.[28] The raid on the individual in Arab society amounts for Wannous to a form of collective suicide, which is in the end what the Naksa has come to signify, since no war can be won with half-men—faceless, nameless, and spineless. The allegory of defeat becomes a segue way to recovery and renewal, which would not obtain without the liberation of the individual. Almost half a century after Wannous's play, Chokri Mabkhout (Shūkrī Mabkhūt) comes to the same conclusion in his novel *Eṭṭaliyānī (The Italian)*.[29]

The two protagonists of Mabkhout's novel, 'Abd al-Nāṣir and Zīnah, begin their career as two revolutionary and Marxist activists on the campuses of Tunisian universities and end up co-opted by the very system they set out to defeat. The nameless frame narrator, who announces himself as 'Abd al-Nāṣir's neighbor and friend, delves into the psychic and historical archives of 'Abd al-Nāṣir and Zīnah in order to contextualize their manifest behavior, their contradictions, ambivalences, and eventual regressions into self-defensive and offensive stages of childhood narcissism. Meanwhile, the world that unfolds throughout the novel is full of corruption, cronyism, and treachery—it is a world of rape, pedophilia, prostitution, and incest. It is a world founded on patriarchal, matriarchal, and filiarchal power relations but marked emphatically by paternal authority and filicidal fantasies. The confessional progression of the narrative makes it clear in the end that Mabkhout's Oedipus and Antigone (or 'Abd al-Nāṣir and Zīnah) have experienced childhood rape and trauma, like Bouzid's Hachemi and Farfat, and have reached adulthood psychically scarred. There is a sense in which they reckon with their tragedy, defeat, and resignation, and this is partly why they have given up on their leftist dreams of transforming society. Like Wannous's, Mabkhout's point is that to ask of these damaged individuals to liberate society is perhaps to ask too much. They will have to liberate themselves first.

The same applies to Bouzid's defeated characters—they prove unable to liberate themselves, let alone liberate their own societies from the shackles of dictatorship and imperial encroachments. For Bouzid, though, the liberation of the individual must first be rehearsed imaginatively and creatively on the page, in the theater and on stage. This partly explains the reason why in *Man of Ashes* Bouzid's camera confers the dignity of recognition on Hachemi's and

28. Saadallah Wannous, *An Evening Entertainment for the Fifth of June* (in Arabic), in *Complete Works* (Beirut: Dār al-Adāb, 2003), 1:123–229.

29. Chokri Mabkhout, *Eṭṭaliyānī* (Tunis: Dār et-Tanwīr, 2014). See also Shukri Makhout, *The Italian*, trans. Karen McNeil and Miled Faiza (New York: Europa, 2021).

Farfat's childhood rape and plays de facto the role that the community failed to play. It is as if the camera dignifies as it portrays the body in pain, supplementing the aesthetics of defeat with an ethics of defeat—that is, an ethics of responsibility for the defeated. Cinema becomes a hospitable public space for grief and reparation capable of preventing the transformation of vulnerability into toxic vengeance. The representation of private and invisible experiences of pain and suffering humanizes broken and defeated individuals, and, in so doing, extends the concept of the human to all those invisible others at the receiving end of familial, socio-communal, and governmental levers of power. Bouzid's aesthetics of defeat cannot therefore be dissociated from an ethics and a politics of defeat. All the more so given that the tragedy of Hachemi and Farfat is not only that they have been raped but also that they have been raped in a society that is almost predisposed to meet their tragedy with either indifference or shaming.

Bouzid's preoccupation with defeat is not an end in itself; on the contrary, his ultimate goal is the liberation of the body from the memory of pain and the individual from the tyrannical continuum of familial, socio-communal, or governmental and institutional powers. Bouzid wagers on the signifying powers of the powerless individual in order to evoke human exposure and vulnerability, demystify power continuums and produce a rigorous critique of different ideologies, namely of Marxism and Islamism, the two competing and polarizing ideologies that dominated the postcolonial public sphere and that wielded immense influence on the impressionable minds of Tunisian youth. Yet, does this mean that Bouzid's cinema is free from ideology? After all, is liberation from ideology possible without ideology? No. "Style must be understood," Teshome Gabriel observes, "as ideologically determined."[30]

Bouzid's interest in the representation of marginal and defeated subjectivities and sexualities in *Man of Ashes* (1986), *Golden Horseshoes* (1989), *Bezness* (1992), and *Clay Dolls* (2002) may be subsumed under a leftist ideology of social critique while his recent preoccupation with religious fundamentalism in *Making Of* (2006) and *Hidden Beauties* (2012) may be subsumed under a largely secular ideology. Bouzid maintains, however, that making a good film is more about art than it is about ideology: "Making a good film is not a question of telling a story, but of bringing an audience into a cinematic discourse that's new, aesthetic, cinematic, stylistic and dramatic in its totality, and, in the second place, ideological. But never in the first place. If ideology comes first, it's

---

30. Teshome H. Gabriel, *Third Cinema in the Third World: The Aesthetics of Liberation* (Ann Arbor, MI: UMI Research Press, 1982), p. 54.

not cinema."[31] Ideology matters then but only to the extent that it does not compromise the artistic integrity of a given film. In other words, ideology must flow from within the artistic correlatives of a given cinematic vision with dexterity and craft; there is no room for artificial superimposition or projection.[32]

In addition to its openly secular referential points and persuasions, which at times do not seem amenable to self-reflexive critique, perhaps one of the major questions that Bouzid's cinema, or more precisely his new realist aesthetics of defeat, leaves us with is the extent to which it is possible or even legitimate to ask of the broken and defeated characters that teem his films to change reality or transform society (in accordance with the progressive politics of Bouzid's overall cinematic discourse). The reverberations of the rhetoric of failure and defeat in Bouzid's filmography is indissociable from the counterintuitive strategies and visions of enablement that he derives from the overlapping crises of filiation and affiliation in postcolonial Tunisia. While the theme of defeat is central to the entirety of Bouzid's filmography—especially in the case of *Man of Ashes*—*Golden Horseshoes* and *Making Of* are the two films that best dramatize the continuities between the crisis of filiation and the crisis of affiliation and deal head-on with left-wing (socialism) and right-wing (religious fundamentalism) ideologies.

Golden Horseshoes zeroes in on the sociopolitical consequences of the crisis of filiation introduced in *Man of Ashes* by exploring the related crisis of affiliation: the profound loss of any discernible project of psychoaffective investiture, intellectual commitment, or decolonial resistance, especially in the wake of the spectacular dissolution of international socialism and the ensuing triumphalism of global capitalism and financial imperialism.[33] The funereal whiff of defeat that pervades the film is, though, reconfigured into a patient process of reckoning with defeat as an indispensable stage of anagnorisis and autocritique. In fact, Bouzid has gone so far in this direction that he has become one of the rare defendants of what he calls "the right to failure,"[34] the right to

---

31. Bouzid, "On Inspiration," p. 49.

32. Bouzid told me in a personal interview (Tunis, summer 2012) that the problem with Nadia El Fani's controversial documentary *Neither Allah, Nor Master* (aka *Laicism God Willing*, 2011) is that it foregrounds ideology (i.e., laicism) over art. While Bouzid endorses laicism, he finds El Fani's film counterproductive in that it has done an aesthetic disservice to a very serious issue, which has to be treated with acute care and sensitivity.

33. Chapter 3 is devoted to the discussion of left-wing melancholy and the crisis of the Nasserite intellectual in postcolonial Egypt.

34. Bouzid made this statement during a television program titled *Bayt al-Khayāl* (The House of the Imagination) that aired on May 19, 2015; see https://www.youtube.com/watch?v=nJW38GzSxQg.

publicly admit and confront the serial collapses of such progressive sociopolitical projects as Arab nationalism, experimental socialism, and secular modernity. The trials and failures of all these quasi-progressive projects of investiture over the last half-century since 1967 had been shadowed, superseded even, by the resurgence of religious fundamentalism, which is the focal point of *Making Of*, a film about a talented yet failed young dancer and rapper who falls into the hands of a fundamentalist sleeper cell and is thenceforth indoctrinated into carrying out a suicide operation (that is, martyrdom).[35]

Here the "right to failure" becomes a bit risky. In our runaway global capitalist economy, disenfranchised and defeated individuals may become easy prey in the hands of demagogues who would capitalize on their vulnerability and transform it into a vindictive weapon (note here, in passing, that the protagonist of *Making Of* blows himself up at the end of the film inside a container with the word "capital" painted in capital letters on its front side). Bouzid is not unaware of this possibility, since his concept of defeat is capacious enough to include not just the military or political dimensions of defeat, but also the "feeling of helplessness [when] faced with something we're dragged into, something we haven't chosen," including of course being dragged into suicidal terrorist activity.[36] His insistence on the "right to failure," though, is precisely an attempt to secularize and dignify failure and defeat and place them on the continuum of human fragility so as to appropriate them away from fatalistic rhetoric and, above all, from such reactionary and melancholite ideologies as religious fundamentalism. What is worse than failure in the end is to blame it on fate and to succumb to it, without inquiring about who/what is responsible for it, or about one's share of responsibility. In other words, what is worse than the unpreparedness for failure is its denial, disavowal, or displacement into a psychotheological discourse of fatalistic inevitability or divine destiny (note here that the notion of *mektūb*, which indicates that which is written on the forehead, is oftentimes conjured up to defuse and deny human responsibility).

No wonder then that Bouzid's entire cinematic aesthetics of defeat wagers on the significant differentials between the perils of defeat (*hazīma*) and the pitfalls of defeatism (*inhizāmiyya*). While the broad aim of his cinema is to liberate his protagonists and his Tunisian as well as Arab audience from the legacy of the former, his more immediate aim is to make sure that the psychoaffective trauma of defeat does not devolve into a psychopathological cult of defeatism. As Jeffrey Ruoff rightly suggests, "While Bouzid's cinema is conscious

---

35. Chapter 6 is devoted to the discussion of Islamism through the lenses of psychoanalysis and deconstruction.
36. Bouzid, "On Inspiration," 52.

of defeat, it is not defeatist."[37] Determining the responsibility for defeat must not therefore override our responsibility for the defeated. Cinema becomes a powerful tool here insofar as it enables the filmmaker to immunize his audience against the pitfalls of defeatism by walking them visually and vicariously through the fictional experience of defeat that the characters in his films grapple with. Hence, Bouzid's first cinematic act is to wrest away the experience of failure from the realm of divine destiny (the hackneyed notion of *qaḍā' wa qadar*) and place it in the realm of subjectivity and human responsibility. To *fail badly* is to displace and transcend but to *fail well* is to historicize and comprehend. "History," after all, "progresses by failure rather than by success," as Benjamin never tired of insisting.[38] Little wonder then that Sonallah Ibrahim's early fiction maps and remaps everyday failures to appropriate all attention away from the grand narrative of the Naksa in the service of the mundane and quotidian micronarratives of the individual.

Affectlessness between Symptom and Critique

The Naksa has momentarily liberated the individual Arab subject from the illusion of indestructability of Arab military regimes. In his diagnostic canonical film, *Al-'Usfūr/The Sparrow* (1972), Youssef Chahine gestures toward the collapse of the wall of fear through a fleeting scene that occurs toward the end of the film, right after Nasser's televised resignation speech. Johnny (Mahmoud El-Meliguy) releases his sparrow from its cage as masses of people storm the streets, led by Bahiyya (Mohsena Tewfik), the allegorical embodiment of Egypt, who was running and screaming out loud: "*Lā! Ḥanḥārib!* No! We shall Fight!" Chahine's film visualizes the full range of feelings and affects spawned by the defeat from disbelief, denial, and disavowal to shame, resignation, and anger through mourning and melancholia, along with anxiety over future uncertainty as well as nostalgia for lost sovereignty and eclipsed Nasserite glory. Defeated, Nasser is no longer feared.

Rarely has the defeat though been met with more indifference and affectless withdrawal than in the work of Sonallah Ibrahim, namely his novel *67*. The shame of defeat has generally resulted less in the abandonment of the pan-Arabist project than in a melancholy identification with Nasser, the architect of Arab nationalism. In most literary and cinematic engagements

---

37. Jeffrey Ruoff, "The Gulf War, the Iraq War, and Nouri Bouzid's Cinema of Defeat: *It's Scheherazade We're Killing* (1993) and *Making of*," *South Central Review* 28, no. 1 (2001): 31.

38. Cited in Frederic Jameson, *Postmodernism, or, The Cultural Logic of Late Capitalism* (Durham, NC: Duke University Press, 1991), 209.

with the Naksa, self-flagellating shame and diminution of national self-regard are dramatized, only to be simultaneously called off or thwarted by variable rhetorical forms of displacement, disavowal, or defiance. This is not the case, however, with the protagonist of Ibrahim's 67 whose detachment from national politics and devotion to everyday libidinal pursuits bring about an unlikely confluence between cynicism and criticism. There is a slight but crucial difference between the foreclosure of affect and the search for affective closure. Nasser's very reference to the defeat in his resignation speech as a Naksa (a setback) is itself a form of foreclosure of affect, a presidential valediction forbidding mourning! Bahiyya's sprint and scream, however, betray a search for affective closure. In the case of Ibrahim's nameless protagonist, the foreclosure of affect is transmuted into affectless cynicism and sexual deviancy. It assumes somatic and physiological manifestations and vicissitudes.

Ibrahim affected an unconcern for the 1967 war, but its disastrous outcome must have touched him to the quick. The affectual indifference of the protagonist of 67 is a refracted or twisted indictment of Nasserism. Because of its overall clampdown on political dissidents, namely its purge of the communists between 1959 and 1964, Nasserism may have practically made its own demise ungrievable, except that it was not always the case even for a radical leftist and feminist like Arwa Salih. In her searing memoir, *Al-Mubtasirūn* or *The Stillborn*, Salih recalls how the defeat of the Nasserite regime still threw her new generation of leftists in an intense experience of affective turmoil and disarray: "we too [the generation of the 1970s] were overcome by the bitter irony of history. The same regime whose victories against imperialism had knocked them [the generation of the 1960s and 1950s] off their feet for years ravaged us with its defeat in June 1967."[39] The fact that even the third wave communists, Nasser's harshest critics, were aggrieved rather than relieved by Nasser's defeat goes to suggest that Nasserism cultivated unmatched affective mass appeal of the sort that makes it perhaps, as Sara Salem argues, "the first and last hegemonic project in modern Egypt."[40] Sorrow and sadness, though, would only serve to exonerate the regime of the kind of criminal travesties and atrocities that are vividly documented in Mahfouz's 1974 *The Karnak Café*, and especially in the 1975 film based on it, titled *Al-Karnak* and directed by Ali Badrakhan. The novel and, even more shockingly, the film present us with graphic scenes of sexual abuse, torture, harassment, and rape of the detained young students for their alleged left-leaning or communist persuasions. The

---

39. Arwa Salih, *The Stillborn*, trans. Samah Selim (New York: Seagull, 2018), 26.
40. Sara Salem, *Anticolonial Afterlives in Egypt: The Politics of Hegemony* (New York: Cambridge University Press, 2020), 27.

rape of one of the central characters by the name of Zaynab Diyab bespeaks both the rape of Egypt and the Muslim community in its entirety: The very name Zaynab recalls Zaynab bint Jahsh (590–641), the wife of Prophet Mohammed and the mother of all believers, as well as the name of the heroine of the first Arabic novel, Mohammed Husayn Haykal's 1913 *Zaynab*, in which Zaynab is the name of the beautiful and pure peasant who represents the ideal national imago of Egypt.[41]

According to P. J. Vatikiotis, "Nasser maintained complete personal control over the various security services, which competed with one another in displays of loyalty to him; to this end, they invented conspiracies from which they could claim to be protecting him. As a side effect of this competition, thousands (perhaps tens of thousands) of Egyptians were imprisoned during crackdowns on political opposition, and torture was commonplace."[42] Mahfouz's *The Karnak Café*, written in 1971 but not published until 1974, maps through its omniscient viewpoint, episodic narration, and character development the psychoaffective legacy of this dark episode in Nasser's Egypt as the main protagonists slide from committed intellectual optimism to acute despair, disenchantment, and resentment. As Zaynab tells the frame narrator, "We seem to have turned into a nation of deviants. All the costs in terms of life—the defeat and anxiety—they managed to demolish our sense of values."[43] Unlike Mahfouz's *The Karnak Café* and other writings that appeared in the wake of the 1967 defeat, Ibrahim's *67* is unique in its apathy and icy disengagement from the colossal event that bears its title. It however manages to paint a graphic depiction of how Egypt "seem[s] to have turned into a nation of deviants," leaving it for readers to adjudicate whether deviancy is the symptom or the malady or both. Although not published until recently, in 2017, Ibrahim wrote the original draft half-a-century before. In fact, it is arguably his first novel, preceded only by "Tilka al-Ra'iha" (That Smell), the long short story that Ibrahim published in 1966, the same year in which several masterpieces of Arabic literature saw the light of day, including Tayeb Salih's *Season of Migration to the North* and Ghassan Kanafani's *All That Is Left to You*, as well as Abdelkarim Ghallab's *We Have Buried the Past* and Naguib Mahfouz's *Adrift on the Nile*.

Ibrahim's novel comes in a dozen chapters, each of which covers a month of the year 1967. The first mention of the possibility of the "war" does not occur

---

41. See Benjamin Geer, "Prophets and Priests of the Nation: Naguib Mahfouz's *Karnak Café* and the 1967 Crisis in Egypt," *International Journal of Middle East Studies* 41 (2009): 661.

42. In ibid., 658.

43. Naguib Mahfouz, *The Karnak Café*, trans. Roger Allen (New York: Anchor Books, 2007), 75.

until chapter 5 (May). After chapter 6 (June), in which the narrator hears media reports of the war, and then sees the mass demonstrations following Nasser's resignation speech, there is no further mention of it, apart from media reports here and there about intermittent attacks and counterattacks in the Sinai Desert, as well as other glimpses of information about the then much-anticipated Israeli withdrawal from the lands it had illegally captured during the war. Overall, the novel hardly tackles the catastrophic 1967 defeat even though its title proposes to do so. Unlike Saadallah Wannous's *Soirée for the 5th of June*, a play whose title names the start date of the June war and whose content dramatizes the root causes of the defeat, Ibrahim's novel does not even bother to elicit from the protagonist the slightest emotional response to the war.

The disillusionment with Nasserism was a déjà vu experience for Ibrahim's generation when the 1967 war occurred. To write about it is to foreground it yet again; not to write about it is to consign oneself to live with the illusion of its insignificance, which may be seen as a reverse version of false consciousness. The way out of this double bind is to do both at the same time: this may explain why the 1967 war is invoked in the title of the novel yet is almost entirely absented from the preoccupations of the narrative. The narrative concentrates rather on the lived experience of a leftist—in fact, the entire generation of sixties leftists—over whom Nasser had sufficiently triumphed (i.e., he co-opted some of them, disappeared others, tortured and imprisoned most in the years between 1959 and 1964). Through a style of indecorous disobedience, remorseless minimalism and pitiless exposure, Ibrahim's novel proffers us a symptomatic representation of the everyday life of a former leftist, now journalist, experiencing the defeat of the very regime which defeated him and the socialist dreams of his generation. "It takes a special genius," Arwa Salih points out in a laudatory comment on Ibrahim's *Najmat Aghustus* (*August Star*), "for the artist to create a conflict in a novel whose events take place in Nasser's era *in which everything is well and everyone is castrated* (ḥaythu kull shay ʿalā mā yurām wa ḥaythu al-jamīʿ makhṣiyyūn)."[44] The conflict in 67 is created by the disconnect between the protagonist and the central politico-military catastrophe around which the narrative revolves.

For a Marxist, there may be a rationale operative in such a disconnect with historical reality: if it cannot possibly liberate, alienation can potentially repudiate. In this sense, the alienation that pervades the novel is neither an outright aberration nor a straightforward affirmation, only a sustained repudiation of Nasserite mystifications. The first chapter sets the tone for the rest of the

---

44. Arwa Salih, *Saraṭān al-Rūḥ* (*Cancer of the Soul*) (Cairo: Dar al-Nahar, 1998), 76.

novel. The main event here is the New Year's Eve party held in the apartment of the protagonist's brother in Heliopolis. In his characteristically flat prose, and his cryptic and telegraphic style of writing that includes rough cinematic cuts, the chapter makes reference to missed and missing beloved comrades, especially Insaf's husband, who, it is implied, was a political dissident and was, we are further told, tortured, killed, and buried in an anonymous plot of land, without even the dignity of a grave and a stone marker that bears his name. We also learn that many more political dissidents (possibly Islamists but mostly communists, at least by implication, given Ibrahim's own imprisonment from 1959 to 1964) have been arrested and disappeared while others have given up reading and writing, except one fellow journalist and comrade, Sadiq, who still writes op-eds. The party ends with the protagonist's brother vomiting and his wife cleaning up after him; the chapter itself ends with a nightmarish dream in which the protagonist sees himself in a prison cell, trying to repair and shut its broken door, out of fear of being chased down by someone he does not know. Before he wakes up screaming, the protagonist sees the image of his (presumably dead) father dancing at the door, gradually taking on the shape of Satan.

The first chapter introduces the reader to almost all the novel's themes and characters. Nearly all the characters come to the party burdened by their pasts, weary of persecution, hoping for a new future, only to find themselves interpellated by the symptoms of injustice from which they suffered. The symptoms sound a melancholic clamor for the dignity of recognition in the present, or so Ibrahim seems to imply through his narrative obsession with the physiological expressions of his characters. We get a good glimpse of the libidinal passions of the protagonist, who likes rubbing his body against the bodies of plump women, especially the body of his brother's wife, with whom he is having an affair. Not without a measure of bad faith, the secret affair acts like a consolation for the protagonist, who tells her, "If I'd known you before you married my brother, I would have married you myself."[45]

Marriage may be a sacred union, but, as it becomes amply clear throughout the novel, Ibrahim's protagonist is only given to profanity. Not unlike the protagonist of *That Smell*, who was unable to sleep with a prostitute, the protagonist of *67* was likewise unable to sleep with Afef, the veiled young girl whom he met at the party and who offered herself to him on their first date, even inviting him to take her virginity. But, and not for lack of trying, the nameless protagonist was unable to perform. The same protagonist—a journalist and a dissident political writer who locks his notebook in a drawer and puts

---

45. Sonallah Ibrahim, *67* (Cairo: Dār al-Thaqāfa al-Gedīda, 2017), 19.

the key in his pocket—never tires of chasing fleshy women in crowded buses so that he can rub his body against theirs. He even manages at one point to have sex with his brother's wife six times, according to her count.[46] Yet the protagonist's vaunted virility is undercut by the premature ejaculations that seem to characterize his sexual encounters with his brother's wife and, at one point, with a Russian tourist.[47]

The protagonist exchanges declarations of love with his brother's wife but no sooner is love declared than it dissolves or slides into sex and reemerges, in a Lacanian fashion, as an unfulfilled demand.[48] Hence, the chiastic oscillation of the protagonist between the pain of wanting love and the boredom of having sex. Sexual insatiability and excessive virility, along with the shameless public displays of predatory sexual behavior, are all signs of a masculinity in crisis. They signal, as Arwa Salih notes, "the lack of something important," a gaping spiritual vacuum that cannot be filled by sex (as Mahfouz shows in his philosophical novel *The Beggar*, to which I will return in chapter 3).[49] They are physiological and phenomenological manifestations of a besieged (and besieging) masculinity and of a castrating state apparatus. The first chapter of 67 amply indicates that there is something rotten in the Arab Republic of Egypt. Talk of corruption, cronyism, and governmental crackdown on political dissent fills the air. The protagonist's comrades are at the receiving end of the crackdown, the effects of which are mainly physiological; for instance, when Ramzi speaks about his perpetual ejaculatory dysfunctions, he also mentions that Sadiq masturbates nonstop. Later we learn that Sadiq has sex with his wife once a year.

The novel brings into intimate collision the vagaries of authoritarian oppression and its psychosomatic consequences not only on its opponents (Ibrahim's generation) but also on society writ large. Note, for instance, that sexual harassment has transformed in the novel from an aberration into a social relation, a form of intelligibility, that calls for and encodes complicity between men in any public means of transportation so as to preclude competition and contention among them. Treachery, infidelity, and a loose relationship to moral values have become the new norm. In fact, the protagonist (who, it bears

46. Ibid., 41.
47. Ibid., 66–67.
48. For Lacan, "desire is neither the appetite for satisfaction nor the demand for love, but the difference that results from the subtraction of the first from the second, the very phenomenon of their splitting (*Spaltung*), see Jacques Lacan, "The Signification of the Phallus," in *Écrits*, trans. Bruce Fink (New York: Norton, 2006), 580.
49. Arwa Salih, *Saraṭān*, 70.

reminding, is having an affair with his brother's wife) tells his brother after they watch Bernhard Wicki's *The Visit* (1964): "we live among relatives, friends, and loved ones who, unbeknownst to us, could sell us out easily."[50]

The Visit tells the story of Karla (Ingrid Bergman), who returns to the village from which she had been chased out in disgrace by Serge (Anthony Quinn) years earlier and offers a vast sum of money to the villagers provided that they execute him. When they agree to do so, Karla, in a surprise course reversal, stops the execution, opting to punish Serge by letting him live among those who betrayed him. *The Visit* offers an apt allegorical insight into the tangled familial, social, and political relations as well as an indictment of the moral impoverishment of all strata of society. The protagonist may be obligated to the detached neutrality that Ibrahim chose for him, but the enlightened levity with which he informs his brother of his opinion shows the extent to which society has normalized (with) betrayal. It equally demonstrates, albeit tragically, the extent to which the protagonist has himself compulsively repeated, rather than overcome, the stings of betrayal he suffered. It is as if the victim of betrayal must need commit an act of betrayal in order to overcome the trauma of having been betrayed.[51] Clearly, the filial and affiliative betrayals that permeate the novel exist in an allegorical continuum with the prevailing politics of the Nasserite regime—namely, its betrayal of the aspirations of generations of Egyptians for freedom of expression and assembly as well as for socialist democratization and national liberation.

Unaligned with Nasserism but committed to national liberation, Ibrahim's novel suggests that the defeat was devastating yet liberating. As in the cinema of Nouri Bouzid, the allegory of defeat dramatizes here as well the prospect of liberation of the individual from the sociopolitical hegemony of Nasserism and its dialectics of coercion and consent.[52] In Mahfouz's *The Karnak Café*,

---

50. Ibid., 42.

51. It may be worth noting here that Bernhard Wicki's 1964 film, *The Visit*, is an adaptation of Friedrich Dürrenmatt's 1956 play *Der Besuch der alten Dame*, or *The Visit of the Old Lady*. Wicki's Karla replaces Dürrenmatt's Claire, who returns to the village to avenge her banishment by the man who fathered her illegitimate child. In her riposte to the Teacher, who urges her to give up thoughts of revenge and cultivate human kindness, she contends: "The world made a whore of me, now I'll make a whorehouse of the world." See Friedrich Dürrenmatt, *The Visit: A Tragicomedy*, in *Selected Writings: Volume 1, Plays*, trans. Joel Agee, ed. Brian Evenson, Kenneth J. Northcott, and Theodore Ziolkowski (Chicago: University of Chicago Press 2006), 108. I thank Shaden Tageldin for drawing my attention to this play.

52. Sara Salem argues that hegemony under Nasserist rule "signals the presence of notable levels of consent that can legitimize and justify the coercion that co-exists alongside it," *Anticolonial Afterlives in Egypt*, 18.

Zaynab Diyab avows to the frame narrator that she "had the defeat to thank" for allowing her to see Isma'īl, her comrade in arms, after a long interval.[53] It bears recalling the aforementioned scene from Chahine's *The Sparrow* in which Johnny frees his caged bird at the very same time that Nasser announces his resignation from office in his famous televised address to the Egyptian public. In *67*, Nasser's brinksmanship tactics before the beginning of the war are proleptically invoked through a Walt Disney documentary about the (mythical) ritual of collective suicide that lemmings undertake annually.[54] The eventual defeat itself is conjured up metaphorically through an attack by fleas the protagonist suffers at night, and the patches of inflammatory redness and swelling they inflict on his skin. In an interview with BBC Arabic, Ibrahim was asked how he had experienced the 1967 war. He replied that he had an eruption of red spots all over his body, and he concluded that, because he was unable to do anything, his body reacted.[55]

The beginning of the June 1967 war does not seem to make the slightest impression on the protagonist, and he goes on with his daily routine in the coldest and most mechanical manner imaginable, emptying the event of its historical significance, expressing disaffection through affected affectlessness. His comrade Sadiq, who continues to write op-eds and fails to get them published in Egypt, was so jubilant about the outbreak of the war that he promised to write his next op-ed from Tel Aviv. Such hysteria is the material of Ibrahim's scrupulous and satirical scrutiny of wartime propaganda and the production of popular fantasy. At one point, he even relates the story of a fellow journalist named Ali who uses newspapers in the restroom because they clean more effectively than toilet paper. Obviously, the anecdote takes a sidelong jab at state media, especially in light of the role it played in misleading the Egyptian public about the war. After the defeat and Nasser's resignation speech, the protagonist thinks that the communists will be held responsible. He packs his bag and prepares to escape, but then he realizes he has nowhere to go and that they would find him, anyway, wherever he goes.

The protagonist routinely has nightmares about being persecuted and plays dead, opossum-like, in order to evade certain death. Haunted and hunted, he finds refuge in his work at the newspaper and in his routine acts of sexual harassment on public transport. Doubtless the nameless protagonist of *67* is an extension of the protagonist of *That Smell* as well as of the author himself, albeit not entirely. Note, for instance, that upon his release from prison, the

---

53. Mahfouz, *The Karnak Café*, 78.
54. Ibrahim, *67*, 60.
55. BBC News Arabic, https://www.youtube.com/watch?v=Dt-LYa2r8TY, August 11, 2017.

protagonist of *That Smell* makes the following observation: "It was the moment I'd been dreaming of for years and I searched myself for some feeling that was out of the ordinary, some joy or delight or excitement, but found nothing."[56] This inability to feel anything signals the crisis of the leftist subject as both symptom and critique of Nasserism. The unbearable historical weight of 1967 is deflated, displaced, and dispersed into a sustained cultivation of bad taste. The leftist subject is a shell of its former self, emptied of all feelings, and reduced to stupefied inaction. Frederic Jameson's famous thesis about the demise of affect and the disintegration of postmodern subjectivity into fragmentary states of fugacious intensities, devoid of substantive feelings, finds in Ibrahim's protagonist a nigh-perfect embodiment: "the liberation, in contemporary society, from the older *anomie* of the centered subject may also mean not merely a liberation from anxiety but a liberation from every other kind of feeling as well, since there is no longer a self present to be feeling."[57] Yet, while Jameson ties the waning of affect to the crisis of leftist politics, Ibrahim may be seizing on these surface intensities as cynical commentaries on the frivolity of politics.

Ibrahim would not be quick to dismiss the affective flatness of his protagonist. The untrammeled sexual desire of the protagonist is a melancholite or reactionary displacement of political impotence into narcissistic sovereignty. What is disquieting, even disheartening, is that the rebellious practices of Ibrahim's protagonist end up implicating him in reproducing rather than challenging social norms. Sex plays a normative not a transformative, much less progressive, role in the novel. Understandably, Ibrahim may be taking to task the Nasserist regime for outlawing prostitution by showing that the new law resulted less in the embrace of virtue than in the epidemic spread of sexual abuse and harassment. Yet, even for the Sonallah Ibrahim ultras, the novel may be indefensible for creating and unleashing a monstrous sexual predator, especially from the perspective of today's practices of political correctness in which the literary representation of sexual harassment may not always be either the consensual or acceptable means of its denunciation. While appearing as mere deflections of the catastrophic consequences of the 1967 defeat, the libidinal deviancies of the protagonist reflect a more profound crisis of political investiture in transformative social projects, a crisis that has variably befallen the Egyptian left ever since the severe repression of communists of 1959. I will return to a more detailed discussion of this episode in chapter 3; suffice it to

---

56. Sonallah Ibrahim, *That Smell and Notes from Prison*, trans. Robyn Creswell (New York: New Directions, 2013), 19.

57. Jameson, *Postmodernism*, 15.

mention here that the political disengagement and apathy of Ibrahim's protagonist is, as Anouar Abdel-Malek observes, "a new phenomenon. It did not exist before 1959. And it came to an end on June 9–10, 1967."[58]

Ibrahim debunks the grand narrative of revolutionary socialism/Nasserism without naming it. Such foundational narratives no longer carry the same meaning that had hitherto allowed Egyptians and Arabs to thrive toward a better future. Ibrahim does not bother though to offer radical alternatives. He simply soaks the narrative in kitsch, making the protagonist discharge in acts (of sexual assault) what ought to have been disposed of in the work of affect. It is as if the protagonist had to sink so low in order to hammer home, at least allegorically, the filthiness of late Nasserism. The first chapter of 67 is bloated with the victims of Nasserism, and with those who disappeared without leaving a trace as well as with those who were left behind, living with a verdict forbidding mourning. It foregrounds the private, monotonous day-to-day narrative of an individual and a writer to whom the nationalist cause is superfluous to the serious affair he is having with his sister-in-law and to the predatory and daily escapades to which he devotes much of his thinking and which he describes in great detail every time despite their nigh identicalness. Affectlessness in Ibrahim's 67 reenacts a prohibition to grieve for a regime that legitimized itself at the outset by the prohibition to mourn those in whose deaths it is implicated. Whether prescribed or proscribed, mourning becomes here the battleground on which wars for individual and national sovereignty are waged. The question of affect is almost always a question of politics, and, more precisely, of political commitment. The indictment of Nasserism in 67 is indissociable from the melancholy incitement to dissidence that seeps through the entire narrative.

Iltizām under Duress

The uneventful routine in which the protagonist 67 is caught bears witness to the political disarray and stagnation of Egyptian society. The richness, diversity, and sheer vastness of the post-Naksa cultural output should not blind us to the contours of the doable nor to the limits of the possible (that is, to the facts on the ground following the Arab defeat and Israeli superpower dominance), which in one way or another have exerted and continue to exert visible and invisible pressures on the creative imagination. It is not for nothing in this respect that the Syrian intellectual historian Qustantin Zurayq has

---

58. Anouar Abdel-Malek, *The Army Regime, The Left, and Social Change under Nasser*, trans. Charles Lam Markmann (New York: Random House, 1968), xxii.

constantly emphasized the necessity of transforming powerlessness into power and political Arab disempowerment and lassitude into resources for sociocultural empowerment. The rise of the *iltizām* or commitment literary movement in the 1950s across the Arab world highlights the extent to which Arab writers and intellectuals were enchanted by the overnight valorization of literature and culture. For literature to be tasked with *iltizām* amounted to a call to arms in which the pen would play the role of the gun and the word the role of the sword. Fanon had no qualms about calling for a "literature of combat," nor about inciting the native intelligentsia to live up to their historical vocation— the crystallization of national consciousness: "It is a literature of combat, because it molds the national consciousness, giving it form and contours and flinging open before it new and boundless horizons; it is a literature of combat because it assumes responsibility, and because it is the will to liberty expressed in terms of time and space."[59]

Following Jean-Paul Sartre's writings in his journal *Les Temps Modernes* on *littérature engagée* (committed literature), later collected in *Qu'est-ce que c'est la littérature* (1948), Suhail Idriss founded the literary monthly *Al-Ādāb* in 1953, which made *iltizām* a rallying cry for new literary and nonfictional writings. While his first editorial focused primarily on the need for literature to commit itself effectively to society and national liberation (in his words, "to spring forth from society and flow back into it"), he ended his mini-manifesto by casting the net rather widely, stressing that, in its pursuit of social justice and national liberation, the ultimate goal of committed literature is the liberation of humanity from slavery, and from material and intellectual enslavement.[60] Idriss's call for *iltizām*, however, resulted in heated debates regarding the role of the literary in decolonial and neocolonial times, and its tacitly compromised relationship to Arab nationalism, the dominant decolonial ideology in the 1950s and 1960s. Even though Arabic literature has always been more or less engaged with the urgencies of its moments of production, as M. M. Badawi and Verena Klemm argue, the theory of *iltizām* in the decolonial era has come to further radicalize, reinvigorate, and burden literary representation with an intertwined task: the indictment of colonialism and the incitement to rebellion against it.

The fear that *iltizām* was ideologically motivated, that it would end up replicating rather than eradicating censorship and repression, cast a long shadow

---

59. Frantz Fanon, *The Wretched of the Earth*, trans. Constance Farrington (New York: Grove Press, 1963), 240.

60. Suhail Idriss, "Risālat al-Adab" (The Message of al-Adab), *Al-Adab* 1, no. 1 (1953): 1–2.

on the movement, especially from within a Cold War context of competing interests in which the soft power influence of literary magazines was a weapon mobilized by the CIA in the fight against communism (through the foundation of the Paris-based Congress for Cultural Freedom in 1950).[61] Many established Arab intellectuals (including Taha Hussein, ʿAbbas Mahmud al-ʿAqqad, Tawfik al-Hakim, and Mahmoud al-Messadi) mistook committed literature for commissioned and tendentious literary propaganda, and insisted on the autonomy of the aesthetic, all the while stressing the immanence and embeddedness of *iltizām* in literary and cultural creativity. Arab Marxists were weary of the apolitical and solipsistic individualism of some strains of European existentialism, but a few of them stooped uncritically to the juggernaut conformism of some forms of radical Marxism. Others like Najib Mahfouz, Yusuf Idriss, Yahya Haqqi, and Abdel Rahman al-Sharqawi have tacitly embraced the call for *iltizām* and went on to produce social realist fiction.

To my mind the central goal of *iltizām* was and continues to be more of an incitement to make literature matter socially and nationally every day rather than to force writers to follow a stringent roadmap in their imaginative labor. As Verena Klemm rightly argues, "one of the most important achievements of the men of letters of this period of new departures was to have created a relation between literature and the social and political reality around them."[62] It was the fear that *iltizām* might grow into a means of coercion (*'ilzām*) and a sacred duty like obligatory patriotism, party allegiance or military service that ended up, however, arousing incredulity and distrust among the older generation of littérateurs like ʿAbbas Mahmud al-ʿAqqad and Taha Hussein who, it bears mentioning, coined the word *iltizām* as a translation of Sartre's *engagement*,[63] as well as the notion of *al-adab al-multazim* for *littérature engagée*, after having initially flirted with such notions as *al-adab al-muttaṣil*

---

61. For a more recent overview of the CCF's funding of literary magazines, see Zeina Maasri, *Cosmopolitan Radicalism: The Visual Politics of Beirut's Global Sixties* (London: Cambridge University Press, 2020). The earliest article on CCF is by Elizabeth M. Holt, "'Bread or Freedom': The Congress for Cultural Freedom, the CIA, and the Arabic Literary Journal *Hiwār* (1962–67)," *Journal of Arabic Literature* 44 (2013): 83–102. See also Elliott Colla, "Badr Shākir al-Sayyāb, Cold War Poet," *Middle Eastern Literatures* 18, no. 3 (2015): 247–63.

62. M. M. Badawi, "Commitment in Contemporary Arabic Literature," in *Arabic Literature and the West* (London: Ithaca Press, 1985), 1–25, and Verena Klemm, "Different Notions of Commitment (Iltizām) and Committed Literature (al-Adab al-Multazim) in the Literary Circles of the Mashriq," *Arabic and Middle Eastern Literatures* 3, no. 1 (2000), 51–62.

63. See Taha Hussein, "Mulāḥẓāt," *Al-Kātib al-Maṣrī* 6, no. 21 (1947): 9–21, and "Fil-Adab Al-Firansī: Jean-Paul Sartre wal-Sīnemā," *Al-Kātib al-Maṣrī* 7, no. 26 (1947): 179–202.

(connected literature) and *al-adab al-mutaḍāmin* (solidarity literature) as opposed to *al-adab al-muʿtazil* (withdrawn or resigned literature).[64] *Iltizām*, however, proved to be a generative rather than a coercive rallying cry: the fact that it "remained," as Qussay Al-Attabi rightly argues, "an ambiguous concept," "not sufficiently explained," goes to suggest that it was hardly meant to be prescriptive.[65] Ironically, the veritable anxieties over *iltizām*'s potential vicissitudes in the decolonial period of high nationalism gave way in the wake of the Naksa to a profound sense of disenchantment over *iltizām*'s attenuated political mobilizing edge.

Saadallah Wannous recounts how in the aftermath of every performance of his aforementioned post-1967 play *Soirée*, he was not so much haunted by the oppressive-prescriptive dangers of *iltizām* as by the treacherous failure of *iltizām* to segue into concrete action: "I felt a renewed sense of bitterness (مذاق المرارة) the evening of every performance. After the play ended, people would applaud and then leave the theater as they always had after any other performance. They would whisper, laugh, or express amazement. But then what? Nothing. Nothing at all. The audience did not erupt in demonstration."[66] For Wannous, *Soirée*'s aesthetic embodiment of *iltizām* matters only to the extent that it produces the underlying promise of *iltizām*—a concrete move to political action, a fully fledged demonstration. *Iltizām* is an aesthetic ideal that goes beyond abstract intellection and requires the commingling of theory and praxis. Wannous may have had in mind Barthes' argument in *Writing Degree Zero* (*Le degré zéro de l'écriture*) that writing is meant "to unite in a single stroke the reality of the acts and the ideality of the ends."[67] *Iltizām* produces melancholy when it does not live up to the promise it makes. Wannous laments the political insignificance of *Soirée*'s performance, but he perseveres in search of "the word as action" (الكلمة-الفعل).[68] To give up the project of *iltizām* because it has not lived up to its promise would amount to capitulating to the hegemony of Israeli settler colonialism in the Golan Heights, a Syrian territory over which Donald Trump recognized Israeli sovereignty, and in which Israel intends to build a new settlement named in his honor,

---

64. See Taha Hussein, "Al-Adab bayna al-Ittiṣāl wal-Infiṣāl," *Al-Kātib al-Maṣrī* 3, no. 11 (1946),): 373–388.

65. Qussay Al-Attabi, "The Polemics of Iltizām: *Al-Ādāb*'s Early Arguments for Commitment," *Journal of Arabic Literature* 52 (2021): 124–146.

66. Saadallah Wannous, *Sentence to Hope: A Saadallah Wannous Reader*, trans. Robert Meyers and Nada Saab (New Haven, CT: Yale University Press, 2019), 393.

67. Roland Barthes, *Writing Degree Zero*, trans. Annette Lavers and Colin Smith (New York: Hill & Wang, 1968), 20.

68. Ibid., 394.

Trump Heights. Meanwhile, the stark fact that Israel has illegally occupied the Golan since 1967 after it had expelled about 100,000 Syrians out of it does not seem to raise eyebrows anymore in light of the new facts on the ground. From this perspective, the question becomes: Would (giving up) *iltizām* bring back the Golan? There is obviously less of a chance the Golan returns to Syria without *iltizām* than with it. To ask of literature or theater or theory here to liberate the Golan may be to ask too much. Yet, that is precisely the point of *iltizām*: to demand the impossible—that is, to stick to (and be stuck with) such a possibility even while well aware of the limits of the possible. For, "when the necessary and the possible no longer converge, the impossible remains, despite everything, necessary."[69]

Unlike pathologizing melancholization, *melancholicization*, it bears reiterating, is an affirmative gesture insofar as it sustains the commitment to *iltizām* as a cultural project of decolonial critique that is simultaneously challenging and eminently empowering. Recall, as I discussed previously, that Porot melancholized Algerian hetero-destructive tendencies, reducing them to an unenlightened or pseudo-European affect, while Fanon melancholicized them, enlisting them in the collective effort of decolonial struggle. Recall as well that Tarabishi melancholized Arab contemporaneity in the wake of the Naksa but forgot to melancholicize it. The same can be said about Marxist historian Samir Kassir's devastating diagnosis: "The Arab malaise has had such a debilitating effect that Arab history has been entirely hollowed out. What remains is a state of permanent powerlessness that renders any chance of revival unthinkable."[70] Notwithstanding their good intentions, Tarabishi and Kassir failed to inquire about the empowering potentialities of the melancholy disposition they were wont to associate with a generalized geopolitical lethargy, impotence, trauma, and other variably regressive and pathological forms of longing for lost ideals.

Melancholicizing over losses, failures, and defeats need not necessarily induce a regression to despair or depression; on the contrary, for one thing it is always better than repression; for another, melancholicizing over defeat may indeed offer a rare and genuine occasion for introspection and contemplation— really, for repurposing and finding a direction, an orientation, and a horizon for individual or collective action. Indeed, post-Naksa artistic and literary works have grappled with defeat and failure in order to seize and apprehend their root causes (as in the case of filmmaker Youssef Chahine, poet Nizar Quabbani,

---

69. Daniel Bensaïd, *Le pari mélancolique: Métamorphoses de la politique, politique des métamorphoses* (Paris: Fayard, 1997), 255.

70. Samir Kassir, trans. Will Hobson, *Being Arab* (New York: Verso, 2006), 4.

novelists Tayseer al-Sboul and Halim Barakat, and intellectual Sadik al-Azm, in addition to the aforementioned writers and artists), but their artistic output has not always been read or viewed, let alone appreciated, in light of the melancholic sensibility that is subtly woven into its fabric. One will have to read not only symptomatically but also melancholically and scrupulously in order to reckon with the claim—which is etymologically a cry or clamor—for freedom from injustice, for ethical redress and just reparation. In this sense, even seemingly playful innovations in form and language are expressions of melancholic commitment to the decolonial project nationally and transnationally. The commitment or *iltizām* that came after the realist phase and followed the advent of neorealism in cinema and modernism in poetry is in many ways a commitment to and through form; it is not form for form's sake but form for the sake of expressing afresh the same message—freedom from injustice—that has yet to go through and resonate with the powers that be (be they local dictators, occupiers, or colonizers). For Wannous, whose *Soirée*, was an experimental Brechtian play *par excellence*, form is indissociable from content. "The rising tempo, for instance, is motion as effective action. It is both form and content."[71]

The same holds true for Mahmoud Darwish whose tireless work on language and idiom is the exemplar of melancholic commitment. Take, for instance, his famous farewell to martyrs "*tuṣbiḥūna 'alā waṭan*" which literally means "May you wake up to a homeland," and which is clearly a deliberate distortion of the idiomatic nature of the everyday expression *tuṣbiḥūna 'alā khair*, whose equivalent in English would be "good night."[72] Darwish here diverts the direction of the everyday expression without leaving it; that is, he infuses it with both human concerns and political grievances. Not only does *tuṣbiḥūna 'alā waṭan* revitalize the hackneyed expression *tuṣbiḥūna 'alā khair*, but it also brings into bold relief the disconnect between wishing people good night and wishing them a homeland. In no small measure, the intimate overlap or collision here between the residual form of the idiom *tuṣbiḥūna 'alā khair* and its novel configuration *tuṣbiḥūna 'alā waṭan* becomes an allegorical dramatization of the embattled project of Palestinian nationhood, and, above all, a call for a decolonial future. By grafting the loss of Palestine to the everyday expression, Darwish melancholicizes the structure of the everyday idiom, making it simultaneously host the promise of a justice to come and reopen the wound of lived injustice every time it is uttered. "Just as the

71. Wannous, *Sentence to Hope*, 393.
72. Mahmoud Darwish, *Ward Aqall (Fewer Roses)* (Beirut: Almu'assassa Al-'Arabiyya Lildirāsāt wa Al-nashr, 1987).

loss of Palestine will never have been left behind, language in Darwish," Jeffrey Sacks rightly argues, "retains a melancholic relation to loss."[73] Furthermore, this idiomatic neologism *tuṣbiḥūna ʻalā waṭan* not only holds and keeps open the promise of Palestinian nationhood, but it also makes it into the *very condition* for the continued pertinence of the standard expression for wishing people good night, *tuṣbiḥūna ʻalā khair*. The performative élan of the new idiom, a catachresis of sorts, is such that it sets a retroactive imperative claim to historical Palestine upon the conditions of enunciation of the old idiom.

The devastating pungency of Darwish's innovation on the Arabic idiom here is a melancholy act that expresses commitment to the project of Palestinian nationhood and that brings the Arabic language itself up to date with the reality of Israeli occupation. In other words, the idiomatic neologism at work is testament to the extent to which, in the words of Ranjana Khanna, "an inassimilable loss has brought about a manifestation in language."[74] Insofar as this linguistic manifestation coincides with the figure of catachresis, the figure of abuse of language use, it becomes simultaneously "the stamp of the abused" and the badge of melancholic commitment.[75] Aesthetic praxis may never serve as a substitute for political praxis, but, insofar as aesthetic praxis ascribes to artistic form the task of holding on to loss until the promise of a Palestinian homeland is fulfilled, it reinstates the Fanonian nexus between militancy and melancholy. Darwish may be said to have achieved here the kind of language that Wannous had been searching for, a "language in whose syntax both roles, witness (الشاهد) and fighter (المناضل), could be actualized."[76] Darwish's idiomatic neologism suggests that the recovery *from* melancholia as a symptom of the Israeli occupation can only be achieved *through* melancholia as an enduring psychoaffective commitment to the recovery *of* Palestine—the historical homeland of Palestinians. Not only does melancholia here retain, nurture, and sustain a militant commitment to a future homeland, but it also serves as a symptom of and witness to its devastating erasure and expropriation.

Darwish makes the Arabic idiom incorporate and carry the enormity of the Palestinian tragedy, subtly reducing the gap between form and affect, carefully *melancholicizing* the Arabic language in the process, mapping into its

---

73. Jeffrey Sacks, *Iterations of Loss: Mutilation and Aesthetic Form, Al-Shidyaq to Darwish* (New York: Fordham University Press, 2015), 69.

74. Ranjana Khanna, *Dark Continents: Psychoanalysis and Colonialism* (Durham, NC: Duke University Press, 2003), 25.

75. See Nouri Gana, *Signifying Loss: Toward A Poetics of Narrative Mourning* (Lewisburg, PA: Bucknell University Press, 2014), 110.

76. Wannous, *Sentence to Hope*, 391.

syntactic structure the idiomatic plight of Palestinians. Notwithstanding its proverbial poignancy, Darwish's idiomatic reconfiguration of the common Arabic idiom is a product of the coerced imagination, an imagination that is fed by and feeds upon the brutality of the settler colonial state apparatus. This applies to Darwish as much as to other littérateurs and artists, including the notable case of DAM (a Palestinian Arab rap crew from Lyd, inside the 1948 borders of Israel, composed of brothers Tamer and Suhell Nafar and Mahmoud Jreri), which became prominent during Al-Aqsa Intifada (2000–2005) thanks to its explosive 2001 single "Meen Irhābi?" (Who Is the Terrorist?). The song situates historically suicide bombing as the logical offspring of Israeli settler colonial rape and accuses Israel of exclusively and simultaneously playing the roles of the adversary, the witness, the lawyer and the judge, obfuscating injustice and making a hollow mockery of justice. The song is a stark example of a creative imagination saturated by the colossal atrocities of the occupation. In fact, Tamer, one of the crew members, contends that DAM's songs are composed of 30 percent music, 30 percent composition, and 40 percent occupation.[77] "What will you write without the occupation?" asks Darwish rhetorically before he carries on: "What does it mean for a Palestinian to be a poet and what does it mean for a poet to be Palestinian? In the first instance: it is to be the product of history, to exist in language. In the second: to be a victim of history and triumph through language. But both are one and the same and cannot be divided or entwined."[78]

If it is true, in C. L. R. James's rescripting of Marx, that "Great men make history, but only such history as it is possible for them to make," it may as well be true that contemporary Arab writers, especially Palestinians, write only the kind of literature that is possible for them to write, which Frederic Jameson called national allegories.[79] From within this perspective, even the notion of commitment can be seen ostensibly as the byproduct of a coerced imagination, an imagination conscripted by the urgencies of its painful and unlivable geopolitical reality—a reality, in other words, of too much pain and too little hope. From within occupied Palestine, what kind of literature is possible other than committed national allegories? Is *iltizām* still a question, or is it simply a

---

77. See Jacqueline Reem Salloum, dir., *Slingshot Hip-Hop* (Ramallah: Fresh Booza Productions, 2009).

78. Mahmoud Darwish, *In the Presence of Absence*, trans. Sinan Antoon (New York: Archipelago Books, 2011), 126–7.

79. C. L. R. James, *The Black Jacobins: Toussaint L'Ouverture and the San Domingo Revolution* (New York: Vintage Books, 1989), x; Fredric Jameson, "Third-World Literature in the Era of Multinational Capitalism," *Social Text* 15 (1986): 65–88.

matter of doing what comes naturally? It is not for nothing that Kanafani once dismissed the embroiling debates around *iltizām* in the 1950s and 1960s as scholastic; for Kanafani *iltizām* in occupied Palestine is not an "abstract theory" (نظرية مجردة) but an act of resistance, enlisted de facto in the struggle for national liberation. *Iltizām* imbued all aspects of literary and cultural production without being identified as a literary movement. Its oppressive national limitations on the creative imagination may be bargain in the fight against Zionism while the false luxuries (رفاه) of aesthetic autonomy would be as unbearable as unthinkable.⁸⁰

While for Kanafani *iltizām* amounted to doing what comes naturally, for Darwish *iltizām* under occupation is the name of the impossible par excellence:

> Al-'iltizām huwa al-'iḥsās al-ḥurr bi-ṭarīqat al-taʻbīr al-ḥurra 'an mas'ūliyyat al-ḥurr
> [الالتزام هو الإحساس الحرّ بطريقةِ التعبيرِ الحّرةِ عن مسؤوليّةِ الحرّ]
> Commitment is the free feeling to express freely the responsibility of the free.⁸¹

Commitment is a balancing act between freedom and responsibility. And freedom is not freedom from all ties; to the contrary, it is a highly sensitive and sensitized awareness of a given domain of responsibility as a practical limit on (or if you wish signifying practice of) one's freedom. To commit to being free is to commit to being responsible. Isn't Darwish saying or at least implying here that only free people could be said to be responsible, which in turn implies that those who are not (yet) free cannot act responsibly and cannot therefore be held responsible for their acts. They will need to be free first. Here we reach again the same conclusion, the same "subjective impasse," reached by Bouzid, Wannous, and Mabkhout earlier. Yet, there is always a *melancholic swerve* at work: those who are not free, Darwish warns the occupiers, cannot be obliged to act responsibly. *Iltizām* becomes melancholic here because it stakes a claim to the very freedom that the Israeli occupation systematically repudiates. From this perspective, both Darwish's farewell to martyrs and definition of commitment are rhetorically charged melancholic indictments of the Israeli occupation and incitements to rebellion against it. Indeed, Darwish melancholicizes commitment: he exposes its compromised condition of

---

80. Ghassan Kanafani, *Al-Adab al-Filastini al-Muqawim taht-al-Ihtilal, 1948–1968* (Beirut: Institute for Palestine Studies, 1986), 60–61.

81. See Simone Bitton, dir., *Mahmoud Darwish: As the Land Is the Language/Et la terre comme la langue* (Seattle: Arab Film Distribution, 1997).

possibility under settler colonial rule and makes it the object of melancholic recovery. In this sense, freedom becomes paradoxically the end goal and the condition of possibility of commitment. Insofar as he shifts the debate to freedom as the condition of possibility of commitment, Darwish recasts the *iltizām* debate in such a way as to implicate and enlist all (Arab) intellectuals and artists in a collective continuum of struggles against the oppressive alignments of authoritarianism and settler colonialism.

Melancholy Returns

The critique of the occupation is not only addressed to Israel but also to the other Arab and worldwide nations, which for Darwish cannot be considered legitimate nations while another nation remains militarily occupied and its people stateless. The silence of other nations on the question of Palestine, however, has been and is still deafening. This is why the allegorical reach of Ghassan Kanafani's moving novella *Rijāl fī-sh-Shams* (*Men in the Sun*) is quite extraordinary in terms of its subtle melancholic commitment to transformative narrative ethics. Toward the end of the novella, we are presented with the desolation of the Palestinian case and simultaneously with its persistent psychoaffective resonance. Three Palestinian refugees being smuggled from Iraq into Kuwait inside the belly of an empty water tanker suffocate and perish at the border. Just as the refugees lie dying in dreadful agony, the truck driver, a castrated 1948 war veteran, is ridiculously led by the bored and salivating Kuwaiti border guards, in the most farcical of scenarios, into a lewd discussion of his sexual adventures with a belly dancer named Kawkab (literally, Planet)—a name that is very much at odds with the despondency, devastation, and crushing derealization of the refugee experience of which Kanafani's novella is an exemplary performative reenactment. The novella ends with a pseudo-epiphanic moment in which the truck driver, Abul Khaizurān, shouts out loud to the echoing desert, "Why didn't you knock on the sides of the tank? Why didn't you bang the sides of the tank? Why? Why? Why?"[82]

What is poignantly compelling about this novella and its heart-wrenching ending is not the indirectness with which it broaches the question of Palestine and the searing realities of the refugee experience but the very counterintuitive ways and symbolic frames whereby it reconstructs and reinstates the question afresh. It is no exaggeration to suggest that, at least by the sheer force of its allegorical suddenness, *Men in the Sun* performs that very knocking on

---

82. Ghassan Kanafani, *Men in the Sun and Other Palestinian Stories*, trans. Hilary Kilpatrick (Boulder, CO: Lynne Rienner, 1999), 74.

the walls of the metal water tanker that is lacking in the story, and that compelled Egyptian filmmaker, Tawfiq Saleh, to insert it into the diegesis of his 1972 cinematic adaptation of the novella *Al-Makhdūʿūn* (*The Dupes*). What Saleh may not have realized is that the illocutionary force of the novella *transforms* the silence of the suffocating Palestinians into an act of knocking. The issue, though, is less whether Kanafani's protagonists knocked on the walls of the water tanker than whether Abul Khaizurān would have heard their knocking. Does knocking matter at all if there is hardly anyone around to hear it, much less pay attention to it? The crime of Abul Khaizurān (which is by implication the crime of Arab leaders) is to have discreetly yet deliberately abandoned the Palestinians to their own fate. The ending therefore reenacts and accentuates, at least by implication, the resounding silence on the tragedy of Palestinians. *Men in the Sun* is the psychoaffective materialization at the level of language of that scream of despair, agitation, and discontent at the echoing yet indifferent vast desert, located at the center of the slumbering Arab world; it is above all the expression of a bitter yet measured resentment at the entrenchment of the entertainment industry, which has appropriated all attention away from the plight of Palestinians and placed it on belly-dancing spectacles and star belly-dancers like Kawkab, a "Planet" who/which remains, quite ironically, desensitized to its passive-active involvement in the creation, dissemination, and perpetuation of refugee conditions of life.

The post-Holocaust and post-Nakba ethical misgivings about the redemptive and rationalizing impulse operative in every artistic endeavor is weighed against and ultimately overpowered by the smothering and muffled silence of fists and hearts inside the steel water tanker and the reigning void of the echoing desert. Here the requisite suspension of disbelief does not dawn without an affirmation of historical reality, of what happened in the aftermath of the dispossession of Palestine and Palestinians of their rightful home and land. Here the distance between the historical atrocities of 1948 and their patient reenactment and inscription by Kanafani is indeed the measure of the urgent need for a cultural politics of *iltizām* that takes upon itself the task of discerning historical losses melancholically and reckoning with them allegorically. W. J. T. Mitchell's "conviction that a commitment to form is also finally a commitment to emancipation, progressive political practices united with a scrupulous attention to ethical means" finds particular resonance in Kanafani's novella.[83] Kanafani's scrupulous attention to the allegorical ethics of representation matches only the horror of the ending, in which the insolence

---

83. W. J. T. Mitchell, "The Commitment to Form; Or, Still Crazy after All These Years," *PMLA* 118, no. 2 (2003): 324.

of Abul Khaizurān dramatizes less an affront against Palestinianness than a graphic allegorization of the historical predicament of Palestinians as articulated by Edward Said: "finding an 'official' place for yourself in a system that makes no allowances for you."[84]

Never before have the allowances been in shorter supply than in the current historical juncture. And even while Palestinian existence is ceaselessly placed under erasure, the attention of Euro-American policymakers and media outlets is almost always animated by Israel's security and blanket right to immunize itself. The evictions of dozens of Palestinians in the East Jerusalem neighborhood of Sheikh Jarrah, for instance, ought to be seen as the latest installment in a long history of dispossession, displacement and disposal of Palestinians that some historians rightly refer to as an ethnic cleansing.[85] The Israeli occupation of historical Palestine created one of the most disturbing and devasting refugee problems in the decolonial era, with the overnight exodus of thousands of Palestinians in the wake of the Nakba and their transformation into refugees and asylum seekers. The refugee crisis has been exacerbated steadily afterwards: "The original 750,000 displaced persons now exceeds 4.3 million refugees registered with the United Nations, the result of further territorial losses in 1967 and natural growth over sixty years."[86] To add insult to injury, Israel abolished the Palestinian refugees' right of return even while Israel itself is founded on the unconditional right of return of all Jews to their allegedly ancient home in historical Palestine. Israel fears that recognizing the Palestinian refugees' right of return "is bound to raise troubling questions about the moral legitimacy of the Zionist project as a whole."[87] The stakes of the Palestinian refugees' right of return are quite high, even though the promise of return remains elusive.

"Always historicize!"—Jameson's injunction is indisputable in the wake of the Nakba and the creation of the refugee problem—the confinement of Palestinians to the waiting room of history, where the temporary becomes a lifetime, and where the gap between the right of return and the place to return to widens steadily.[88] In the world of *Men in the Sun*, or even at a safe distance from it, historicization is coeval with melancholicization, that is, with the

---

84. Edward W. Said, *After the Last Sky: Palestinian Lives* (New York: Columbia University Press, 1999), 37.

85. See for instance, Ilan Pappe, *The Ethnic Cleansing of Palestine* (Oxford: One World, 2007).

86. Eugene Rogan, *The Arabs—A History* (New York: Basic Books, 2009), 275.

87. Pappe, *The Ethnic Cleansing of Palestine*, 245.

88. Frederic Jameson, *The Political Unconscious: Narrative as a Socially Symbolic Act* (New York: Routledge, 1983), ix.

incumbent task of denouncing settler colonial dispossession and demanding the end of the military occupation. Melancholicization—the enduring return to the origins of Palestinian suffering and allegorization of the primal scene of trauma—is an act of resistance not only against the assimilative resilience and rationalizing logic of Zionism, but also against the "currently dominant humanitarianism that sacralizes the memory of *victims,* and mostly neglects or rejects their commitments" to their right of return to their fast-vanishing homeland.[89] The ending of the novella and the triple repetition of the question— "Why? Why? Why?"—should alert us to Kanafani's careful interruption of the rationalizing and homogenizing impulse that seeks to make sense of historical atrocities. The repetition testifies less to Kanafani's rationalization of "what happened" than to his anxiety that it would be perennially derealized. For what happened in 1948 remains from a geopolitical perspective an embattled field of power relations and manipulations of language, facts, and, above all, truth. Worse still, its lasting legacy has transformed it into a continually unfolding present, an ongoing aftermath without a clear afterness.

Under such settler colonial duress, whose foundational premise is the dehumanization and disposability of Palestinians, there is no transcendental beyond from which the creative imagination can loosen its preoccupation with the embattled situation of the nation. Writing boils down to survival, which is, in turn, indissociable from an indictment of the Israeli occupation, and the incitement of rebellion against it. The vocation of the post-Nakba committed artist (*al-fannān al-multazim*) is, then, to tread the fine and very delicate line between the two incommensurable impulses that structure artistic representation: the redemptive and rationalizing impulse that haunts and torments writing (and the artistic vocation as a whole) and the derealizing impulse that follows from the alternative recourse to silence. In the next chapter, I discuss how various Arab poets have thought about writing in the wake of catastrophe; suffice it for now to point out that Kanafani played silence and writing one against the other by making his novella an inscription of silence, the silence of humanity on the Nakba, and an investment in the transformative possibility of writing. While Kanafani chose writing as a politically urgent task, it is only fair to state that, to his credit, he taxed his imaginative and rhetorical resources to ascertain that he would not accidentally slip into the trap of rationalizing the unthinkable atrocities of the 1948 Nakba, the Catastrophe.

In Kanafani's novella the undertones of fictional veracities are matched by the uncanny lived experiences of refugees who perish in search of a better

---

89. Enzo Traverso, *Left-Wing Melancholy: Marxism, History and Memory* (New York: Columbia University Press, 2016), xv.

elsewhere. Their itineraries, roaming from Palestine to Iraq to Kuwait do not bespeak the pleasures of nomadism and exile but the traumas of displacement. One might argue that because Kanafani was writing *Men in the Sun* in the early 1960s (it was published in 1963), he was actuated by slightly different questions from those that surfaced in the aftermath of 1967 and the rise of an aboveground Palestinian national movement of resistance. Kanafani's writing from *Mā tabaqqā lakum* (*All That's Left to You*, 1966) to *'Ā'id 'ilā Ḥaifā* (*Returning to Haifa*, 1969) through *Umm Saad* (1969) would become variably more politicized and politicizing. Yet, the burden of representing Palestine and the tragedy of everyday Palestinians has become even more taxing imaginatively and artistically in the aftermath of the Naksa. Kanafani was cognizant of this burden of presenting and representing the tragedy of Palestine, which is why he has consistently focused on staging the quotidian lives of those at the receiving end of the Israeli occupation. Representation is a *burden* for Kanafani, not solely because of the possible emotions it is unlikely to arouse in audiences of different sympathies and sensibilities, but also because of the defusing rhetoric with which it is oftentimes displaced or blanketed and surreptitiously perpetuated. It is a burden, not because it is about a biblical and mythical feud for which there can be no solution in the near future, but because the solution is too much in the sun as Hamlet would say and as the title of Kanafani's novella, *Men in the Sun*, forcefully suggests.

The allegorical contiguity between the dispossession and the disposability of Palestinians in the novella attests to Kanafani's melancholic commitment to the imperative urgency of the Palestinian right to national liberation. In *The Dupes*, the aforementioned 1972 film version of *Men in the Sun*, the Egyptian filmmaker Tawfik Saleh makes this allegorical subtext of Kanafani's novella quite explicit. *The Dupes* recreates Kanafani's storyline almost verbatim, except toward the end, where he introduces two significant changes. The first, it bears repeating, is the addition of a sequence in which the three clandestine migrants trapped inside the belly of the water tanker can be heard pounding frantically on the walls. Perhaps for Saleh and others, the fixation on knocking, on making some noise, far surpasses the likelihood of being heard. Even though their cries of despair and desperation hardly reach the offices of the Kuwaiti border guards, the sequence sought to add some modicum of agency to the three Palestinian migrants. All the more so after the establishment of the Palestinian Liberation Organization (PLO) in 1964 and the Popular Front for the Liberation of Palestine (PFLP) in 1967, both of which embodied the national resistance movement and mounted military operations against Israel. By and large, the post-Naksa context of defeat and defeatism might have obliged Tawfik Saleh to seek to boost rather than further crash the morale of Arab and Palestinian audiences. Little wonder, then, that the outrageous scene in Kanafani's novel in which Abul Khaizurān walks back to the dead bodies he disposed of on a garbage heap to take their money and belongings is omitted from the diegesis of the film.

The second addition addresses head-on the existential plight of displacement and statelessness: the film ends with a panning shot of the three corpses atop the trash piles and a postscript that is nonexistent in the novella. The postscript reads as follows: "And my father once said, a man without a homeland will have no grave in the earth, and he forbade me to leave." The added postscript is an interpretation—indeed a *literalization*—of what Kanafani's novella only *indirectly* conjures up. In other words, the film literalizes what Kanafani's novella allegorizes: that "the story of the private individual destiny is always an allegory of the embattled situation of the public third-world culture and society."[90] The film's brief postscript establishes an explicit correlation between, on the one hand, statelessness *and* death in a foreign or no man's land, and, on the other, between having a homeland *and* having access to a final resting place. The allegorical uncanniness of the film's denouement matches only the shock of reckoning with the enormity and perpetuity of the Palestinian plight into the ever more precarious present, in which the longing for the homeland, at least as a final resting place, has receded into profound uncertainty.

"The disorder that Palestinians brought unto themselves by leaving their land in 1948 *would have no meaning*," Fawaz Turki argues, "had they not intended to return."[91] For the Kanafani of *Returning to Haifa*, even while a complete return "will take a war to settle," Palestinians "should never have stopped trying to return."[92] The paradoxical sense of the impossibility yet necessity of return is what continues to inspire the ongoing artistic and psychoaffective investment in its rehearsal. It is not for nothing that Annemarie Jacir, the first female Palestinian filmmaker, returns to the historical dynamics of the aftermath of the Naksa from within the confines of the post-Oslo (1993) and post-Aqsa (2000–2005) Intifada in order to resurrect and reignite the will to return which amounted at the time to doing what comes naturally. In her 2012 feature film *Lammā shuftak* (*When I Saw You*), Annemarie Jacir dramatizes both the will to return and the war it entails. Jacir seeks to recapture a time when

---

90. Jameson, "Third-World Literature," 69.

91. Fawaz Turki, "Meaning in Palestinian History: Text and Context," *Arab Studies Quarterly* 3, no. 4 (1981): 380, italics original.

92. Kanafani, *Returning to Haifa*, 187, 185. The second statement is pronounced by Dov, Said's son and nemesis, who serves in the novel, I would argue, as the voice of self-critique.

the return to Palestine was a matter of individual initiative. She makes use of the pre-political and pre-ideological benchmarks or *points de repère* of a young refugee by the name of Tarek in order to reclaim the lost aura of spontaneity that has historically propelled Palestinians homeward. Indeed, upon finding life in the Harir refugee camp in Jordan unbearable, Tarek embarks on a solitary trek back to Palestine, saddled with nothing but a predilection for the family home. Not least for motivational and inspirational purposes, Jacir recollects and recreates a time when, in the words of Fanon, "spontaneity is king, and initiative is localized."[93]

Born in Bethlehem in 1974, Jacir has grown preoccupied with the issue of return since childhood: "From the earliest days of my life, I crossed the border into Palestine, visiting family and friends, working, making a home for myself. These crossings of the bridge between Jordan and Palestine with my family year after year remain my most humiliating and painful childhood memories. Those experiences shaped forever the person I am today and definitely shape my work as an artist."[94] Jacir's first feature film, *Salt of This Sea* (2008), is about Soraya, an American-born Palestinian woman (played by Palestinian-American poet Suheir Hammad) who goes to Israel to reclaim her family's home and money, both of which were taken during the 1948 Nakba. Soraya's visit to the family house that her grandfather built excited her anger, yet the new occupant, Irit, an Israeli artist, failed to relate to Soraya, much less to reckon with her implication in the confiscation of the family home. The irreceivability of Soraya's intimate Nakba by Irit bespeaks the irreceivability of Palestinian trauma by Israel. David Ben-Gurion once said, "The old will die and the young will soon forget." Jacir's riposte is: "Well, the old are dying and the young are dying too, but nobody is forgetting."[95] The melancholic attachment to the homeland feeds on the credible danger of its disappearance: "Psychodynamically, when a threat confronts human beings, whether as individuals or collectively as a nation, the threat becomes a trigger accelerating the degree of their relatedness to the threatened object."[96]

Ironic as it may seem, what occasions the making of *When I Saw You* is that Jacir, whose cinema is a cinema of return *par excellence*, has been denied entry to Palestine. Settling in Amman, she felt depressed, not just because she

---

93. Fanon, *The Wretched of the Earth*, 131.

94. Estelle Sohier and Clémence Lehec, "Cinema and Palestinian History: Interview with Annemarie Jacir," *Revue du Ciné-club Universitaire* (2015): 45.

95. Annemarie Kattan Jacir, "Refugees and the Right of Return," *Socialism and Democracy* 16, no. 2 (2002): 53.

96. Turki, "Meaning in Palestinian History," 374.

was cut off from her apartment, her partner, as well as her friends and relatives, but also because she could still see Palestine through the Jordan River valley. To manage her depression, she started working on *When I Saw You*, hence the infectious sense of hope that marks the film and that is embodied by Tarek's determination and singleness of purpose.

> *When I Saw You* came after I was denied entry [to Palestine] and I was really depressed. When I made *Salt of This Sea*, which is about the reality of Palestine today—I wasn't depressed when I made it, but it's a depressing reality. And this film was the opposite. I was in deep depression for at least a year and I was trying to figure out a way to do something. I found myself in the position of most Palestinians in the world, who cannot get to Palestine, which is 75 percent of us. I always had the privilege to go back and forth before. So suddenly I was standing there like Tarek, looking at Palestine [from Jordan].[97]

When I Saw You is set in Jordan during the Naksa, which resulted in the exodus of thousands of Palestinians to neighboring countries. The eleven-year-old Tarek (Mahmoud Asfa) and his mother Ghaydaa (Ruba Blal) are among the dislocated families who poured across the border from Palestine into the Harir refugee camp in Jordan. Tarek's father was left behind in the melee of people thronging across the bridge, but Ghaydaa reassured Tarek that if they stay in the camp, he would eventually catch up with them.

The father was nowhere to be found among the truckload of refugees that keep filling the camp daily. Tired of waiting in the miserable conditions of the camp, and longing for his missing father and the fatherland, Tarek decides to walk back home but ends up being taken by Layth (Saleh Bakri) into a *fedayeen* camp, where he was reassured that they all intend to fight their way back to Palestine. Tarek partakes of the brutal training regime and puts his mathematical skills to the service of the commander Abu Akram (Ali Alayan), but soon his mother catches up with him in the camp and asks him to go back with her to the Harir camp. When he categorically refuses to do so, she finds no alternative but to stay with him in the fedayeen camp. Soon, though, Tarek grows weary of the military calculations of the fedayeen, namely the long training period it takes before they are declared ready to go on their mission back home. He therefore took it upon himself to head back home, as he initially

---

97. Maureen Clare Murphy, "Honoring Palestinian history: filmmaker Annemarie Jacir on *When I Saw You*," *The Electronic Intifada*, April 29, 2013, https://electronicintifada.net/blogs/maureen-clare-murphy/honoring-palestinian-history-filmmaker-annemarie-jacir-when-i-saw-you.

planned, alone. The film ends with a freeze-frame of Tarek running toward the border, together with his mother, who catches up with him in his radical yet necessary endeavor. The ending leaves open the possibility of Tarek and his mother making it back home safely, but the actual gist of the film is to resurrect and reactivate the almost mummified hope of return for all the Palestinian refugees and their descendants who grew (up) used to camp life.

Tarek's name is reminiscent of Ṭāriq 'Ibn Ziyād (aka Tarek in English), a Berber Umayyad commander who initiated the Muslim conquest of Spain, then known as Visigothic Hispania, in CE 711–718. He led a large army and crossed the Strait of Gibraltar from the North African coast, consolidating his troops at what is today known as the Rock of Gibraltar. Facing a vastly superior Spanish army, five times the size of his army, Ṭāriq incredulously ordered his men to burn their boats, leaving them with no choice but to either defeat their enemy or die a coward's death. Understandably, Jacir's Tarek and the historical Ṭāriq, conqueror of Spain, may not have much in common, except perhaps the audacity of thinking otherwise, not to mention the perseverance and singleness of purpose that true leadership requires. While their differences outweigh their similarities, namely that Ṭāriq sets out to conquer a new home while Tarek sets out to recover a lost one, what Jacir wants to stress by naming her protagonist Tarek is, I think, the need for fresh and imaginative ideas to deliver Palestinians from their perpetual refugee status. Perhaps the return to Palestine may require an unorthodox strategy like the one devised by the historical Ṭāriq in his conquest of Spain.

Jacir believes that the political process had all along served to undermine rather than facilitate the return of Palestinian refugees to their homes. "Tarek is not politicized," she insists, "he just wants to go back home."[98] In fact, he acts in total oblivion of the revolutionary and military strategies of the fedayeen, their overemphasis on caution to the detriment of action. By telling the story through the eyes of a child, who refuses to accept his fate as a refugee, Jacir reconfigures the Palestinian refugee problem into a question of will and willingness to return rather than a politics of return:

> It's the main issue, the core issue—the return. It's as simple as that. Tarek asks this very logical question: "If you walked [away], why can't you walk back." You can see Palestine from Jordan, you can see cities, recognize towns, everything. It's that stupidly close. The right of return is the central issue and it's not complicated. . . . The media, governments and other interest groups are playing a part in making

98. Ibid.

this issue seem complicated, and that it's so many other things. In reality, the Palestinians are the only refugees who have not been able to return.[99]

All the actors who purport to complicate the Palestinian refugees' right of return have variable interests in its annulment. A prolonged and ineffective peace process has alienated Palestinians from the primacy of acting on the will to return rather than wait endlessly for political negotiations to resume. The negotiations keep resuming and their failure keeps looming, procrastinating, and attenuating in the meanwhile the possibility of return. Yet the desire to return will keep regenerating in spite of, or perhaps because of, its denial; the melancholic attachment to return overrides paradoxically the failure of its concretization. The denial is not only illegal but also untenable in the long run: as long as Palestinians continue to stake melancholic claims to their lost homes, Israeli settlers will continually be haunted and weighed down by the anxiety of usurpation. Even biblical overconfidence will likely displace but not overcome the primal settler anxiety, the specter of illegitimacy.

It is to Jacir's credit that rather than remain a prisoner to her resentment and depression after being banned from Palestine, she turned it into an empowering aesthetic protest against Israel's abolishment of the Palestinian refugees' right of return. Jacir reopens the wound and promise of return without offering an aesthetic form of closure. "The notion of Return," Fawaz Turki argues, remains "an imperative in Palestinian existence, a passionate adventure of spirit and of faith in it."[100] The film ends with the aesthetic dramatization of a *vraisemblable* act of return but leaves it in medias res—an artistic sleight of hand that acknowledges the difficulty of return while holding open its possibility. By no means does the film resolve the emotional turmoil it foments—if anything, *When I Saw You* fosters and cements the melancholic attachment to the Palestinian refugees' right of return. For Palestinians living in refugee camps inside and outside historical Palestine, "It's a constant Nakba. It's happening all the time. It never stopped. It's not something of the past. Houses are still demolished today; people are being ethnically cleansed today. Before moving on from that, this basic thing should be recognized. *People are asking us to move on, to forget the past. But it's not the past—it's now.* That's something that a lot of people forget also or do not realize."[101]

99. Frank Barat, "Why Can't We Walk Back? A Conversation with Palestinian Filmmaker Annemarie Jacir," +972 *Magazine*, December 13, 2013, https://www.972mag.com/why-cant-we-walk-back-a-conversation-with-palestinian-filmmaker-annemarie-jacir/.
100. Turki, "Meaning in Palestinian History," 381.
101. Barat, "Why Can't We Walk Back?"

People are asking us to move on, to forget the past. But it's not the past—it's now. The wound of the Nakba still bleeds through the fabric of Arabic literature and culture wreaking havoc in the conventional historical registers of time, producing and reproducing a spectrum of affective differentials that help sustain the investment in the possibility of ending the military occupation of Palestine. The Nakba is, to paraphrase Benjamin, "a past charged with the time [presence] of the now [*Jetztzeit*]" which will, one day, "[blast] open the continuum of [Zionist] history."[102]

The life of the dispossessed refugee, exile, or migrant worker is a slow affectual and social death, a continual reawakening to the shock of homelessness and to the melancholic commitment to resistance and steadfastness. I have so far painted the broad strokes of my argument about the melancholic turn in Arab literature and culture. The theoretical, literary, and visual examples I have discussed throughout this chapter perform a series of psychoaffective reckonings with the open wound of settler colonialism, the tumultuous embarrassments of military defeat and the *fichue position* of Arab contemporaneity. As such, they are testimonies at once to the precarity of political reality and to the incumbent melancholy tasks of sociocultural and decolonial critique. In the next chapter, I delve more closely into the politics of form, the aesthetic and ethical morass of writing in the aftermath of catastrophe. More specifically, I strive both to discern the psychoaffective dynamics of modern Arabic poetry and to ponder the precarious and elegiac rhetorical modes of its critical intervention in a culture continually strained to its breaking point.

---

102. Benjamin, *Illuminations*, 261.

2
Melancholy Forms
Poetry in the Aftermath of Catastrophe

O my friend,
There's no room for the poem on this earth,
Is there any room for this earth in the poem, after Iraq?
—MAHMOUD DARWISH, "FARAS LI-L-GHARĪB"
(A HORSE FOR THE STRANGER)

To write poetry after Auschwitz is barbaric. And this corrodes even the knowledge of why it has become impossible to write poetry today.
—THEODOR ADORNO, "CULTURAL CRITICISM AND SOCIETY"

I have no wish to soften the saying that to write lyric poetry after Auschwitz is barbaric; it expresses in negative form the impulse which inspires committed literature.
—THEODOR ADORNO, "COMMITMENT"

Perennial suffering has as much right to expression as a tortured man has to scream; hence it may have been wrong to say that after Auschwitz you could no longer write poems.
—THEODOR ADORNO, *NEGATIVE DIALECTICS*

Theodor Adorno's by now infamous dictum that "to write lyric poetry after Auschwitz is barbaric" still weighs heavily on various modern and contemporary representations of war and violence, especially in the Arab world, where the legacy of the Holocaust, entangled with differing or dueling national claims to Israel and historical Palestine, exerts enormous existential pressure.[1] The artistry and lyricism of poetry for Adorno reenact and continue the foreclosure of veritable otherness in favor of the variable cults of selfhood (including self-sacrifice), of which Auschwitz is the product. Wittingly or unwittingly, poetry signals a concern for the subjectivity of the living even when (indeed, precisely when) it addresses itself to the irreducible singularity of the deceased; by purporting to speak in the name of the victims of atrocity, it threatens to defuse and disperse the specificities of their death along the universal continuum between life and death; thus, it not only subtly perpetuates rather than disrupts the rationalizing aims of war and mass slaughter but also, and by the same token, indirectly retards or blocks altogether the very process of apprehending and reckoning with extremity. In short, by offering to represent the unrepresentable and nonsensical nature of military violence and ethnic cleansing, poetry, Adorno cautions us, risks making the unthinkable thinkable.[2] Herein the barbarism that clusters thick

---

1. Theodor W. Adorno, "Commitment," in *Aesthetics and Politics*, ed. Ronald Taylor (New York: Verso, 1980), 189. It will become clear in what follows that even though Adorno revisited and revised his indictment of lyric poetry after Auschwitz, he kept alive the productive tension between aesthetic commitment, which by itself can verge on tendentious propaganda, and aesthetic autonomy, which by itself can boil down to nothing more than the cultivation of art for art's sake—that is, a withdrawal from praxis.

2. Adorno's first mention of "poetry after Auschwitz" occurs rather intrusively in "Cultural Criticism and Society," an essay that was written in 1949 and published in 1951 and that primarily concerned the unmasking of the dialectic of culture and barbarism (of which Auschwitz is the last installment) and, more specifically, the exposure of the complicity of the former with the latter: "The more total society becomes, the greater the reification of the mind and the more paradoxical its effort to escape reification on its own. Even the most extreme consciousness of doom threatens to degenerate into idle chatter. Cultural criticism finds itself faced with the final stage of the dialectic of culture and barbarism. To write poetry after Auschwitz is barbaric. And this corrodes even the knowledge of why it has become impossible to write poetry today. Absolute reification, which presupposed intellectual progress as one of its elements, is now preparing to absorb the mind entirely. Critical intelligence cannot be equal to this challenge as long as it confines itself to self-satisfied contemplation." Adorno, *Prisms*, trans. Samuel Weber and Shierry Weber (Cambridge, MA: MIT Press, 1988), 34. What is important to bear in mind here is that Auschwitz is but one moment, perhaps the most revelatory, in a wide-ranging historical process of "absolute reification" that is about "to absorb the mind entirely." In this sense, Auschwitz is the agent of the impossibility of poetry only insofar as it is the product of this general historical process from which critical intelligence itself is not exempt even though (indeed, in spite of the fact that) it remains the only means of trespass. As an expression of free human intelligence, poetry threatens, should business continue as usual, to give the semblance of freedom from within a context of uncritical unfreedom (i.e., the open-air-prison). For, ideology percolates even "the knowledge of why it has become impossible to write poetry today," and its co-optive ruses cannot therefore be intuited and undone unless we remain constantly on the qui vive.

underneath the act of writing lyric poetry after Auschwitz becomes starkly discernible: while it definitely seeks to fulfill the laudable task of mourning atrocity, poetry seems nonetheless to require atrocity—as its inaugurating principle—in order for it to fulfill *retrospectively* the task of mourning of which it becomes simultaneously the product and the vehicle, if not, indeed, *la flèche et la cible*, the arrow and the target. Obviously, Adorno is not unaware of the equally discomfiting voyeurism of the reverse position—the perplexed resignation to silence—of which the sheer magnitude of his post-Holocaust oeuvre constitutes in and by itself an unequivocal negation.[3] Yet, since the distrust toward poetry might be in excess of our ability to overcome it, it has never ceased to fuel our contemporary disenchantment with representation, casting under the shadow of the culture industry the countervailing ethical powers and politics of the aesthetic in the wake of catastrophe.[4]

While the enduring validity of Adorno's aphoristic indictment of lyric poetry after Auschwitz cannot be overstressed in a world that continues unabashedly to structure itself around the geopolitics of disaster, of resilience, of preemption, of credibility and of deterrence, its distinct configurations in contemporary Arabic poetry fall irresistibly, less under the shadow of the Holocaust than

---

3. Adorno leaves no stone unturned to undermine any uncritical way out of our discomfiting complicity with all cultural formations mediated by Auschwitz: "All post-Auschwitz culture, including its urgent critique, is garbage.... Not even silence gets out of the circle. In silence we simply use the state of the objective truth to rationalize our subjective incapacity, once more degrading truth into a lie." Adorno, *Negative Dialectics* (New York: Continuum, 1973), 367.

4. Julian Barnes once asked, "How do you turn catastrophe into art?" His answer bears witness to what Adorno calls the culture industry, and what Barnes seems to associate with the institutionalization of the atrocity aesthetic and disaster capitalism: "Nowadays the process is automatic. A nuclear plant explodes? We'll have a play on the London stage within a year. A president is assassinated? You can have the book or the film or the filmed book or the booked film. War? Send in the novelists. A series of gruesome murders? Listen for the tramp of the poets. We have to understand it, of course, this catastrophe; to understand it, we have to imagine it, so we need the imaginative arts. But we also need to justify it and forgive it, this catastrophe, however minimally. Why did it happen, this mad act of Nature, this crazed human moment? Well, at least it produced art. Perhaps, in the end, that's what catastrophe is *for*." Barnes, *A History of the World in 10½ Chapters* (Toronto: Random House Canada, 1989), 125, original italics. Barnes's final verdict that catastrophe is clearly the midwife of art makes Adorno's ban on poetry after Auschwitz somewhat justifiable. Nevertheless, both Barnes and Adorno are disenchanted with the ways in which art cannot rise up to the challenge of proffering a measure of aesthetic (I almost said "poetic") justice and a voice to the voiceless victims of catastrophe without ending up commoditizing suffering for the benefit of a runaway consumerist and forgetful culture. While ineluctable, art's failure is perfectible, or so is the fundamental melancholy tonality variably audible throughout modern Arabic poetry.

under the shadow of its proximate historical corollary, the Nakba, or the catastrophe of 1948 (48 نكبة)—that is, the massacre and the dispossession of Palestinians of their lands, homes and other properties as well as the illegal military occupation of historical Palestine by Israel, which continues to this day and is nowadays poised to metamorphose into outright annexation. Like Adorno, many Arab poets have pronounced the impossibility of poetry after every post-Nakba military onslaught on Arab land, from the devastating 1967 Israeli preemptive strike against Egypt, Jordan, and Syria (referred to or sublimated in Arab parlance and imagination as the Naksa, or temporary setback) up to the more recent Operation Iraqi Freedom orchestrated by the so-called Coalition of the Willing against Iraq and beyond. In the Arab world it has become equally barbaric and therefore ethically impossible to write lyric poetry *after* the Nakba; it is as if the lyrical intelligence can no longer redeem (itself from) what happened then, much less aspire thereafter to what can no longer be possible. The Nakba brought to a sudden ending the promise of beginning (i.e., Palestinian national liberation and Arab solidarity), a promise that has nevertheless lived on as an aftereffect and as an ending without end because the moment to realize it was irremissibly missed.[5] After I have grappled with a range of artistic responses to military defeat in the inaugural chapter, and particularly with the ways in which the collective experience of defeat reinvigorated cultural and artistic commitments to freedom from injustice, I focus in this chapter on the ways in which Arab poets have consciously or unconsciously appropriated Adorno's dictum to decry the military atrocities and massacres that have taken place in the Arab world during the decolonization era and beyond. Arab poets have appropriated Adorno's dictum, I argue, less as a death certificate meted out to lyric poetry than as a resolute gesture of inconsolability, less as a license to intellectual gloom or cynicism than as a

---

5. In an important essay on Arabic literature after 1948, Edward W. Said drew attention to the significance and magnitude of the Nakba: "After decades of internal struggle against political chaos and foreign domination, a struggle in which politico-national identity was still at its most precarious initial stage—with religion, demography, modernity, language enmeshed confusingly with each other—Arabs everywhere were forced additionally to confront as their own problem, taking an especially provocative form, one of the greatest and still unsolved problems of Western civilization, the Jewish question. To say that 1948 made an extraordinary cultural and historical demand on the Arab is to be guilty of the crassest understatement." Said, "Arabic Prose and Prose Fiction after 1948," in *Reflections on Exile and Other Essays* (Cambridge, MA: Harvard University Press, 2003), 45–46. Drawing on Constantine Zurayk's provocative book *Ma'nā al-Nakba* (The Meaning of the Disaster), Said goes on to demonstrate that 1948 "on the one hand reveals the deviation from *what has yet to happen* (a unified, collective Arab identity) and on the other reveals the possibility of *what may happen* (Arab extinction as a cultural or national unit)" (47, italics in original).

tacit incitement to poetic insurgency.[6] Above all, Arab poets have implicitly or explicitly conjured up Adorno's celebrated axiom to draw attention to the embattled referential differentials of the geopolitical legacy of Auschwitz in Euro-America, which constituted the limits if not the confines of Adorno's thought from 1949 to 1969, and in the Arab world, where the establishment of Israel, which came on the heels of the unspeakable crimes committed in Auschwitz, went hand in hand with the Palestinian Nakba and therefore amounted for some to nothing more than a form of expiation of European guilt, especially if judged by the unconditional support that Israel has received and continues to receive from Europe and the United States despite its flagrant and repeated violations of international law and the UN Security Council resolutions.[7]

Adorno's ban on lyric poetry after Auschwitz takes on a special significance after the Nakba, which preceded the ban by one year. Lifting the ban would mean not only that lyric poetry must have been transformed but also that it

---

6. Adorno gradually conceded, albeit in a typical admixture of ironic detachment and melancholy disenchantment, that poetry remains necessary: in 1962 he narrows down his 1949 generic indictment of "poetry after Auschwitz" to "*lyric* poetry," arguing that literature "must be such that its mere existence after Auschwitz is not a surrender to cynicism. Its own situation is one of paradox, not merely the problem of how to react to it." For Adorno, the abundance of human suffering ought to make us wonder "whether any art now has a right to exist; whether intellectual regression is not inherent in the concept of committed literature because of the regression of society." Yet, precisely because the "abundance of real suffering tolerates no forgetting," "it is now virtually in art alone that suffering can still find its own voice, consolation, without immediately being betrayed by it" ("Commitment," 188). Almost three years before his death in 1969, Adorno half-admitted art's inalienable right to exist but then immediately complicated it, if not negated it altogether: "Perennial suffering has as much right to expression as a tortured man has to scream; hence it may have been wrong to say that after Auschwitz you could no longer write poems. But it is not wrong to raise the less cultural question whether after Auschwitz you can go on living—especially whether one who escaped by accident, one who by rights should have been killed, may go on living. His mere survival calls for the coldness, the basic principle bourgeois subjectivity, without which there could have been no Auschwitz; this is the drastic guilt of him who was spared" (*Negative Dialectics*, 362–63). Clearly, unless poetry were to desublimate the survivor's guilt, it may not have been wrong to ban it.

7. The disjunctive temporalities of Auschwitz and the Nakba have more to do with their geopolitically polarized and polarizing reception, manipulation, and dissemination than with their historically relational causality or, for that matter, with the dialectic of nationalism and barbarism of which they are de facto the product. Be that as it may, it is ironic that Europe, by supporting the creation of Israel, was indeed, as Gil Anidjar suggests, exporting to the Arab world not only the Jewish question but also the Arab and Muslim question whose history in Christian Europe, particularly during the Holocaust, has been willfully elided. See Nermeen Shaikh, "The Jew, The Arab: An Interview with Gil Anidjar," https://asiasociety.org/jew-arab-interview-gil-anidjar.

must have in the process transformed the conditions that made Auschwitz possible. However, one condition, of which the Nakba is a direct result, is the same old "pathological nationalism" that, according to Adorno, led to Auschwitz.[8] To speak at all of lyric poetry after the Nakba is precisely to wonder whether anything has been learned from Auschwitz.[9] The phrase "lyric poetry

---

8. Adorno, "The Meaning of Working Through the Past," in *Critical Models: Interventions and Catchwords*, trans. Henry W. Pickford (New York: Columbia University Press, 1998), 98. Adorno refers mainly to German nationalism here, but his insights could be applied to all forms of nationalism, including Zionism about which he speaks only indirectly, as when he warns against the internalization and dissemination of the "delusional mania of nationalism": "To the extent that the delusional mania of nationalism openly manifests itself in the reasonable fear of renewed catastrophes so, too, does it promote its own diffusion" (98). Especially revelatory is Adorno's condemnation of the Armenian genocide: "Genocide has its roots in this resurrection of aggressive nationalism that has developed in many countries since the end of the nineteenth century" ("Education after Auschwitz," in *Critical Models*, 192). One might think that the "resurrection of aggressive nationalism" in reference to the "Young Turk Movement" is an implicit criticism of Zionism, yet Adorno did not, to the best of my knowledge, openly condemn or unequivocally criticize Zionism. In 1967, following Israel's preemptive war against Egypt, Jordan, and Syria, he condemned the Arab states for posing "a terrible threat to Israel." Quoted in Andrew Robin, "The Adorno Files," in *Adorno: A Critical Reader*, ed. Nigel Gibson and Andrew Robin (Malden, MA: Wiley-Blackwell, 2002), 189. In *The Psychological Technique of Thomas' Radio Addresses*, Adorno links the anti-Semitism of the American Christian right in the 1930s to Nazism by systematically and comparatively unmasking the devices they both made use of. However, Adorno remains silent about settler Zionism, even though he denounces Thomas for taking issue with Jewish "settlement" (or "resettlement," as Adorno sometimes calls it) of Palestine "without making it clear whether he favors this settlement or resents it": "The weight of the anti-Semitic propaganda within Thomas's speeches is incomparably greater than the actual amount of his frank anti-Semitic statements." *The Psychological Technique of Thomas' Radio Addresses* (Stanford, CA: Stanford University Press, 2000), 120–21. Are we not left to wonder, by the same token, whether the weight of Adorno's silence about Zionism (as well as his later and weightier silence about the colonial occupation of Palestine) is incomparably greater than the actual amount of his frank critique of anti-Semitism and all forms of fascism and nationalism? In general, I find Christopher Wise's provocative remarks about Jacques Derrida on Francis Fukuyama almost applicable to Adorno on Thomas: "While no one can deny that certain forms of evangelical Christianity in the United States, whether they are articulated by sophisticated State Department intellectuals like Fukuyama or Bible Belt Protestants, have served to reinforce historically racist policies aimed at Arab Muslims and Christians in Palestine, it may be worse than misleading to aim exclusively at such targets while remaining silent about actual Zionist policies that have been implemented in Jerusalem/Al-Quds, the West Bank, Gaza, Golan Heights, and so on." "Deconstruction and Zionism: Jacques Derrida's *Specters of Marx*," *Diacritics* 31, no. 1 (2001): 62.

9. I would be remiss not to mention here Adorno's pedagogical imperative: "The premier demand upon all education is that Auschwitz not happen again. . . . Every debate about the ideals of education is trivial and inconsequential compared to this single ideal: never again Auschwitz" ("Education after Auschwitz," 191). This must be understood as an interdiction not

after the Nakba" is a deliberate variation on "lyric poetry after Auschwitz," yet it is also an approximation and a reinstatement of the disaster, and more important by far, a rigorous demand that any discussion of Auschwitz must *confront*, not defuse, the reality of the Nakba, the coercive dispossession and ethnic cleansing of Palestinians and the splintering military occupation of historical Palestine.[10] Above all, the phrase "lyric poetry after the Nakba" enables the literal recognition of evocations of Auschwitz in the Nakba to heighten the intensity, the ironic shock, and the suddenness of an otherwise unexpected scenario (or *l'ironie du sort*) of victim-become-perpetrator. While more of an instance of comparative development than an absolute frame, the reverberations of Adorno's dictum in modern Arabic poetry are ultimately less a matter of verifiable influence than of comparative critical analysis. Arab poets retain the monstrosity that Adorno's master phrase denotes but open it up to the seriality of catastrophes whose disparate monstrosities have yet to penetrate forms of intelligibility and habits of mind alien, if not almost blind, to them.[11] This

---

only of any compulsive tendency to repeat the injustices committed in Auschwitz but also of any conscious manipulation or instrumentalization of the Holocaust to oppress and dispossess others. Indeed, according to Noam Chomsky, Nachem Goldman, who is considered one of the most conservative yet most honest Zionist leaders, deemed it a "sacrilege," if not downright "sick" (as Chomsky himself characterizes it) to use the Holocaust to justify the occupation of Palestine and the dispossession and massacring of Palestinians. See Carlos Otero, ed., *Language and Politics* (Edinburgh: AK Press, 2004), 568. Zionist that he was, Goldman spurned any endeavor that traded on the crimes committed against Jews to warrant the victimization of Palestinians. Yet the visceral denigration and defamation of Goldman (e.g., he was denied a delegation to his burial upon his death in 1982) by other Zionists implies that there is more than a Freudian compulsion to repeat at work here. Gilles Deleuze succinctly and acutely parodizes and challenges Freud's well-known formulation of compulsion-repetition by propounding that "We do not repeat because we repress," but "we repress because we repeat." *Difference and Repetition*, trans. Paul Patton (New York: Columbia University Press, 1995), 105. If we bear Deleuze's dictum in mind, the quelling of Goldman's voice and legacy becomes revelatory of a deliberate inclination to repeat that is engineered by the cognizance that the dispossession of Palestinians *recalls*, more than anything else, the dispossession of European Jews—a dispossession that should have been remembered and mourned, not displaced and reenacted.

10. I borrow the expression "splintering occupation" from Achille Mbembe's masterful analysis of the necropolitics of Israeli occupation, "Necropolitics," *Public Culture* 15 (2003), 28. I will engage with the "necropolitics" of the occupation more fully in chapter 4.

11. During the film *Notre Musique* (Our Music), in an interview with Judith Lerner (pseudonym of Sarah Adler), a journalist from Tel Aviv, Mahmoud Darwish speaks of the precarious positioning of Palestinians in their struggle with Israeli Zionism and propaganda: "Do you know why we, Palestinians, are famous? Because you are our enemies! The interest in the Jewish question is at the origin of the interest in us. So, it is unlucky for us that Israel is our enemy because it has an endless number of supporters around the world. Yet, we are also lucky that

should not be seen as an attempt to chain metonymically or equate *tout court* one extremity with another, but rather as a cautionary reminder that the hierarchical perception of injustices (along with narcissistic and envy-ridden attachments to competing and politicized histories of victimhood) might make their potential recurrence seem palatable—even permissible. After all, nothing could be gained from the mutually insulated monumentalizations of 1948 as a celebration of independence in Israel and as a commemoration of the Nakba in Palestine.

If "poetry after Auschwitz," arguably a periphrasis for the end in Adorno's thought, points allegorically toward a certain irreducible time or temporality to which we are irrecoverably belated, is it necessarily always too early to speak about "poetry after the Nakba"?[12] Might it not be equally too late to speak about it either? I ask these questions because much of the impetus for modern Arabic poetry stems from the chiastic oscillation of the lyric imagination between two psychoaffective temporalities, one contending it is *too early* and the other *too late* to understand what happened in 1948. The latent historical discontinuity evoked by Adorno's ban on poetry after Auschwitz is opened up to include the literality of the sequential adverbial of time, "after," so much so that "poetry *after* the Nakba" emerges along a continuum between the otherwise disjunctive temporalities of Auschwitz and the Nakba. This gliding chiasmus is carried over all the way to the heightened contemporaneity of "poetry after Iraq," underscoring the recursiveness of endings and the recessiveness of the end. In this sense, the poem becomes a contrived space for the dramatization of the psychopoetics of unresolved mourning—*unresolved* because the object whose loss demands mourning (be it Palestine, Iraq, or Arabness *tout court*) is neither completely lost nor fully abandoned. Since the lasting repetition of monstrosities has resulted in a ghastly seriality of contiguous and heterogeneous endings that have not quite coincided with the end, the lyrical intelligence finds itself stranded in an unbearable present, bereft of the very end it professes and hastens to announce again and again, as if each time were

---

Israel is our enemy because the Jews are at the center of the attention of the world. Thus we suffered defeat at your hands and reached fame . . . we suffered defeat at your hands and reached fame. . . . Yes, you are our Ministry of Propaganda because the world has more interest in you than in us and I have no illusions whatsoever about this." See Jean-Luc Godard, *Notre Musique*, Fox Lorber, 2005); see also http://www.youtube.com/watch?v=eTYkPorXxnA. I thank my students in "The Legacy of Mahmoud Darwish" seminar (Spring 2009), particularly Shad Naved, for drawing my attention to this segment.

12. I am referring here to the conclusion of Michael Rothberg's insightful discussion of Adorno's dictum: "If we always come *after* the event in Adorno's thought (both historically and epistemologically), we are also always *too early* to grasp it." *Traumatic Realism: The Demands of Holocaust Representation* (Minneapolis: University of Minnesota Press, 2000), 55, original italics.

indeed the first time. Hence the chiasmus of the too early and the too late suspends the end along a continuum between an *immanent* sense of ending inherent in the lyric and another that pertains to a more mundane apocalyptic imagination for which the end is almost always *imminent*.[13] A *continuum* of chiastic, unreconciled and unsublated relations between Auschwitz and the Nakba, the too early and too late and the immanent and imminent emerges. Each of these chiastic relations is harnessed by Arab poets for empowering psychoaffective and creative purposes.

In what follows, I draw on an eclectic but substantial number of poems composed by such canonical contemporary figures as Nizār Qabbānī (نزار قبّاني), Adonis (أدونيس), and Mahmoud Darwish (محمود درويش) in order to demonstrate how Arab poets strategically and by now even routinely conjure up the muse of impossibility of poetry (in the wake of every act of violence committed against Arab nations since the Nakba) in order to produce poetry. While my focus in this chapter will be on poetry after the Naksa, the importance of the Nakba, as I have suggested earlier, to any rigorous understanding of Arab contemporaneity cannot be overstressed. Indeed, as Edward Said rightly argues: "no Arab could say that in 1948 he was in any serious way detached or apart from the events in Palestine. He might reasonably say that he was shielded from Palestine; but he could not say—because his language and his religion, cultural tradition implicated him in every turn—that he was any less a loser, an Arab, as a result of what happened in Palestine."[14]

Structured by and awakened to its profound impossibility, contemporary Arabic poetry is shot through by the disquiet between two dueling (albeit productive) impulses: one reckoning with defeat and with the violence that poetry shares with the very violence that calls it into existence, and the other revolting against such violence in a carefully nuanced and crafted way, making sure that poetry does not inadvertently fall in the trap of expunging, denying or reproducing the atrocious demarcations of warfare and violence it seeks to contest. Because and in spite of the assaults of historical violence on lyric poetry—confronting it, as it were, with its insignificance amidst the thud and clatter of tanks, of machine-gun fire, of blasts of bombs, of collapsing stonework, and of showering gravel—Arab poets have strenuously exerted themselves by treading the delicate line between the imperative to render violent events in elegiac verse and the fear of defusing their historically aberrant ruptures, integrating them in the process into the intrinsically rationalizing continuum between the horror of reality and the all-too-neat economy of poetic form.

---

13. I am indebted to Frank Kermode for this important distinction, *The Sense of Ending* (New York: Oxford University Press, 2000), 6.

14. Said, "Arabic Prose," 46.

Perhaps the major achievement of contemporary Arabic poetry can be found specifically in the ambivalence of its tenor—really, its dramatization of the discordant experience of the indispensability and impossibility of poetry. The melancholic attachment to poetry becomes, besides its thematic resonances, an organizing principle of poetic creativity. Because its veritable possibility has been stymied by historical violence, Arabic poetry today, I shall argue, is largely post-elegiac and intensely metapoetic in a very specific way: it is an accentuated yet attenuated form of poetry that simultaneously bears the burden of representation but never ceases in the process to undermine any form of consolation or resolution of mourning; it is a poetry that emerges from the full consciousness of its impossibility or, worse, its futility and discomfiting complicity with Arab suffering.

Perhaps Nizār Qabbānī—Syria's and the Arab world's most popular and controversial poet, who died in London in 1988—is the pioneer par excellence of this post-elegiac trend in modern Arabic poetry. Soon after the Naksa, for instance, Qabbānī proclaimed in a scathing poem against the fallacies of Arab nationalism, titled "Hawāmish ʿalā daftar al-naksa" (Marginal Notes on the Book of Defeat; هوامش على دفتر النكسة) that "poems have become like salt in our mouths" (*māliḥatun fī faminā al-kaṣāʾid*; مالحة في فمنا القصائد) and that we have become ashamed of the very thought of writing poetry because the feelings of humiliation and the enormity of our defeat are either in excess or not worthy of poetry altogether.[15] Paradoxically, poetry might serve to rationalize and overcome the lurking sense of failure, yet the insisting indignity of defeat is likely to disenfranchise the poet.

The 1967 Naksa revolutionized the poetry of Qabbānī who until then wrote mostly erotic and ghazal love poems and earned the wide acclaim, or disdain, of being the Arab world's pioneering "women's poet" (*shāʿir al-marʾa*; شاعر المرأة). After the Naksa, Qabbānī admitted that he was no longer capable of writing love poetry. Romantic poetry has exhausted its form and vocation, and the poet, according to Qabbānī, must need give up the pen and take up "the knife" (*al-sikkīn*) to retain a measure of significance and relevance in the aftermath of 1967:

يا وطني الحزين حوّلتني بلحظة
من شاعر يكتب شعر الحبّ والحنين
لشاعر يكتب بالسّكين

---

15. Nizār Qabbānī, "Hawāmish ʿalā daftar al-naksa" (Marginal Notes on the Book of Defeat), in *Qaṣāʾid Nizār Qabbānī* (Poems of Nizār Qabbānī), ed. Nawāl Al-Khālidī (Amman: Dār Osāma li-l-nashr wa-ettawzīʿ, 2005), 199.

Oh, my sad Homeland
You have transformed me in a single moment
From a poet writing of love and yearning
To a poet writing with a knife.¹⁶

While these lines fall within the realm of what has been generally conceptualized since the 1950s as the literature of commitment (*Adab al-Iltizām*; أدب الإلتزام) trend in Arabic literature and culture, as discussed in the previous chapter, "Hawāmish" must be understood first and foremost as an epitaph to an imagined poetic career that has become suddenly impossible after the disastrous setback of 1967—and, ironically, only a year following Qabbānī's decision in 1966 to resign from his other long career as a diplomat and Syrian ambassador (to China, Britain, and Spain) to devote himself more fully to writing love poetry. Not only did "Hawāmish," then, mark a formal and thematic shift in Qabbānī's writings from romantic love poetry to elegiac and political poetry about the malaises of the Arab world, but it has also instilled in his work a new sensitivity with which he has ever since been intensely preoccupied—namely, the very possibility of writing in the wake of catastrophe. Nowhere else is this sensitivity more strikingly operative than in his famous post-elegiac eulogy for his second wife, Balqīs al-Rāwī (بلقيس الرّاوي), who was suddenly killed in 1981 in a bomb attack by pro-Iranian guerrillas on the Iraqi embassy in Beirut, where she was working for the cultural section of the Iraqi Ministry.¹⁷

Qabbānī entitled his elegy *Qaṣīdat Balqīs* (قصيدة بلقيس), or *The Poem of Balqīs*, implying not only that the poem is Balqīs's but also that poetry and Balqīs are indissociable. The death of Balqīs, who inspired much of his poetry, was also for Qabbānī the death of poetry itself. At the very beginning of the poem, Qabbānī screams out—"*qaṣīdatī ughtīlat*" (my poem was assassinated; قصيدتي أغتيلت).¹⁸ The same scream reverberates throughout the moving couplets of the elegy but in a more trenchant manner toward the very end of

---

16. Qabbānī, "Hawāmish," 199.
17. Balqīs was an Iraqi schoolteacher whom Qabbānī initially met at a poetry recital in Baghdad in 1962 and was immediately struck with her beauty, but he could not persuade her family to allow him to marry her until the intervention of the Iraqi authorities on behalf of Qabbānī in 1969, in the aftermath of another Baghdad poetry recital. Qabbānī's reputed *ghazal* or love poetry, singing the praises of more than one woman, and rumored reputation as a womanizer, had not worked in his favor with the family of Balqis.
18. Qabbānī, *Qaṣīdat Balqīs* (The Poem of Balqīs) (Beirut: Manshourāt Nizār Qabbānī, 1982), 1.

the poem where he addresses himself to Balqīs in a mixture of resolve and resignation:

نامي بحفظِ اللهِ..أيّتها الجميلة
فالشِعرُ بعدكِ مستحيل..

> Sleep My Beauty, May God protect you . . .
> For, poetry after you is impossible . . . [19]

Qabbānī's poignant proclamation that "poetry after [Balqīs] is impossible" (*al-shi'ru ba'daki mustaḥīl*) is in itself impossible in that it is announced in the very medium (poetry) it declares to be no longer possible. Qabbānī's poetic verdict on poetry is implicated in an indissoluble contradiction: while contending that poetry is impossible, not only does it participate in the production of poetry, but, above all, it lives through or survives the very impossibility of poetry in order to *announce* it. It is as if the logic of poetry following the death of Balqīs would not unfold without folding back or receding into a reflection about its impossible unfolding in the first place. Qabbānī's poetry had become largely an anachronistic aftereffect of its declared impossibility, an impossibility that had to be repeatedly announced, as if each time were the first. Yet this impossibility is ultimately intelligible only as a gesture of inconsolability. Qabbānī's poetic persona deploys the gesture of impossibility of poetry to interrupt the process of emotional closure set in motion by the consolatory workings of elegy; in so doing, it opens itself up to the alternative possibility of impossible mourning. The gesture of impossibility of poetry functions thus as a figure of reading the decentering of the subjectivity of Qabbānī's poetic persona in tandem with (and as a result of) the unassimilability of the deceased Balqīs to the recuperative curve of the elegiac impulse.

The poetry of Qabbānī—and, as I shall demonstrate, that of Mahmoud Darwish and Adonis (Ali Ahmad Sa'īd), two of the other most innovative and celebrated contemporary Arab poets—withholds the barbarisms of subjectivity, of presence, of meaning and of mourning, all of which poetry is said to fulfill in the sense and scope of Adorno's intransigent verdict. For instance, in the aforementioned poem about the death of Balqīs, the poetic persona of Qabbānī stresses that what is being inscribed is not an elegy:

بلقيس..
ليست هذه مرثيّة

> Balqīs . . .
> This is not an elegy.[20]

19. Ibid., 77.
20. Ibid., 19.

MELANCHOLY FORMS

"This is not an elegy" (*laysat hadhihe marthiya*) is a negative declarative statement whose metapoetic and illocutionary force aims not only at undoing the very act of writing in which the poetic persona is caught but, above all, at disturbing the tenets of the *marthiya* or classical Arabic elegy, namely, its redemptory premises. That is, elegy here is no longer a sublimatory channeling of personal loss onto the body of the poem; it is no longer an ego-consolatory writing exercise, in which the subjectivity of the poet presumably finds substitute solace in the poem; rather, it is a melancholic act of dissidence from normative practices of elegiac mourning—really, a refusal to mourn altogether. In short, the poem not only refuses to presume the triumph of mourning before having it but also, and more radically, drives a wedge between the two topics, mourning and elegy, whose relation to each other it is so difficult not to presume.

The poem is not an elegy because it figures forth the urge for psychoaffective closure only insofar as this urge occasions a subtle reckoning with the impossibility of elegy and the inconsolability of the poetic persona. *Qaṣīdat Balqīs* dramatizes the anxieties of writing: it unfolds in a dialectically negative manner, simultaneously claiming and disclaiming the act of writing. The ethical demand for writing after the death of Balqīs—a demand that aims at inscribing her life for posterity and therefore salvaging her actual death from the final death of forgetting—is foiled against the equally compelling ethical concern for the singularity of the deceased Balqīs whose radical alterity might be compromised by the irresistible slide of elegy toward emotional closure, in which case the poem might amount to nothing less than a second tomb. This eventuality, which seems to structure elegiac poetry, renders the poem for Qabbānī synonymous to a terminal stab in the heart:

هل يُولد الشّعراء من رحم الشّقاء؟
وهل القصيدة طعنة
في القلب..ليس لها شفاء؟

Are poets born out of the belly of wretchedness?
And is the poem a stab
In the heart . . . that has no cure?[21]

Qabbānī's counterelegiac elegy is marked by a willing sustenance of grief predicated upon a critical wakefulness to the ethical limits and limitations of poetry and to the unbearability of writing "just following the death, upon or on the occasion of the death" of the other, as Jacques Derrida would put it.[22]

---

21. Ibid., 59.
22. Jacques Derrida, *The Work of Mourning*, eds. Pascale-Anne Brault and Michael Naas (Chicago: University of Chicago Press, 2001), 49.

Counterelegy emerges in the *meanwhile of mourning*, in the delicate differentials between the demand for writing and the anxiety generated by writing—in short, in playing off the promise of writing against the impossibility of writing. In stark contrast to the imperative dyad of guarding privacy and fulfilling mourning characteristic of the neoclassical *marthiya*, post-elegiac Arabic poetry has become an *accentuated* reenactment of the *attenuated* conditions of possibility of poetry and of affective closure, cutting through the private and the public, the ethical and the political.

It is as if the serial repetition of the impossibility of poetry in the aftermath of catastrophe has become the organizing principle or functional conceit of the modern *marthiya*, whose elegiac object is ultimately poetry itself, though less in the sense of poetry writing than in the writing of the *promise* of poetry, the poetry-to-come in better times. For, the poetry that is now (being inscribed) cannot measure up to the exigencies of its times:

ماذا يقول الشعرُ، يا بلقيسُ . .
في هذا الزَّمانِ؟
ماذا يقول الشعرُ؟

What does poetry say, O Balqīs . . .
In this time of ours?
What does it say?[23]

Like that of Qabbānī, Darwish's poetry, especially following the 1982 Israeli invasion of Lebanon, later recorded in his 1987 memoir proem, *Dhākira li-l-nisyān* (*Memory for Forgetfulness*; ذاكرة للنسيان), constantly integrates a self-reflexive interrogation concerning the pertinence of writing poetry in a world of everyday violence and war. Yet such an interrogation—oftentimes on the re*present*ational limits and limitations of language—is ultimately what importunes the poet to stage the political urgency of representation and the necessity of an ethics of mimetic responsibility that might empower poetry to survive the atrocities of warfare and the cumulative catastrophes of what Walter Benjamin famously called the angel of history or progress. In Darwish, Adorno's dictum can be seen not only as a true intellectual and ethical conundrum, but also as a prelude to multiple beginnings, to poetry about the impossibility of poetry, and, more important by far, to a tireless critique of the axes of global imperialism as well as to an incessant dwelling in the world of possibility, in the very same manner that Emily Dickinson defines poetry.

In a poem titled "Faras li-l-gharīb" (A Horse for the Stranger; فرس للغريب), Darwish wrote perhaps for the very first time directly about Iraq following

---

23. Qabbānī, *Qaṣīdat*, 72.

Operation Desert Storm, in which the American- and British-led forces—equipped with new information technology, wireless communication, computers and robotics (in short, all the fruits of RMA, or Revolution in Military Affairs)—deployed massive aerial bombardments and a very high amount of explosives to destroy systematically Iraq's military and civil infrastructure, leaving tens of thousands of Iraqis dead. While written in the context of Operation Desert Storm, "Faras" was included at the very end of the 1992 dīwān, a poetic corpus or book of poetry, 'Ahada 'ashara kawkaban (Eleven Planets; أحد عشر كوكبًا). Together with the 1990 'Arā mā 'urīd (I See What I Want; أرى ما أريد), the 1986 Ward Aqall (Fewer Roses; ورد أقلّ) and Hiya 'ughniya, hiya 'ughniya (It Is a Song, It Is a Song; هي أغنية، هي أغنية) of the same year, 'Ahada 'ashara kawkaban consolidates a paradigmatic shift in Darwish's poetry from the romance of revolt that marked his early (i.e., post-Nakba and post-Naksa) writings to the post-1982 phase, in which the Sabra and Shatila massacre and the ensuing expulsion of Palestinians from Lebanon compelled Darwish into a profound contemplation of war, ethnic cleansing, exile and the conditions of possibility or impossibility of poetry, not only in the Arab world but also in a worldwide historical context of ancient and constellating or recursive barbarisms that extend beyond Auschwitz or the dissolution of historical Palestine and annex, among other key events, the collapse of Moorish Granada in 1942, the expulsion of the Marranos and later the Moriscos from Spain in 1609 as well as the gradual extermination of the native Indians that went hand in hand with the massive conquest of the Americas.

Darwish's post-1982 poetry surpasses in terms of its poetic sophistication and scope his post-1967 poetry of apprenticeship, which several critics regarded as "more slogan-like than poetic,"[24] attributing its mass popularity largely to its foundational appeal to the injured Arab psyche, a psyche ripped apart by the Naksa and left in search of an assertive and reassuring voice that would reckon with rather than demythologize its grievances, and bring rather than withhold the dignity of recognition to its collective experiences of suffering and dispossession. Born in 1942 in Birweh, a district of 'Akka (Acre) in upper Galilee, Darwish first came to prominence when the Beirut-based modernist poetry magazine, Shi'r (Poetry; شعر), published four of his poems in its summer issue of 1967. He was immediately hailed as the leading figure of Palestinian nationalist poetry of resistance, an overnight rise to fame that cast positive light on his 1960s poetry, ranging from the 1964 'Awarāq al-Zaytūn (Leaves of Olive; أوراق الزيتون) up to the 1969 Al-'aṣāfīru tamūtu fi-l-Jalīl (The Birds

---

24. Munir Akash, "Introduction," in Mahmoud Darwish, *The Adam of Two Edens*, ed. Munir Akash and Daniel Moore (New York: Syracuse University Press, 2000), 20.

Die in Galilee; العصافير تموت في الجليل). Darwish's reputation as Palestine's national poet par excellence was sustained in the 1970s by the publication of, among others, the 1975 *Tilka ṣūratuhā wa hādhā intiḥār al-'āshiq* (This Is Her Image and This Is the Lover's Suicide; تلك صورتها وهذا انتحار العاشق).

His poem "Biṭāqit hawiya" (Identity Card; بطاقة هوّية) became a rallying cry of rebellion and a protest song which resulted in putting him under house arrest in 1967. Addressing an Israeli IDF soldier, Darwish's poetic persona orders the soldier in a defiant voice, "sajjil / 'anā 'arabī" (Write down / I am an Arab; سجّل!/أنا عربي).[25] At the end of the poem, Darwish's poetic persona issues a warning to the IDF soldier that very much reads like a threat or menace:

سجّل . . . برأس الصّفحة الأولى
أنا لا أكرهُ النّاسَ
ولا أسطو على أحد
ولكنّي . . . إذا ماجعتُ
آكلُ لحم مغتصبي
حذارِ . . . حذارِ . . . من جوعي
ومن غضبي!!

Write down . . . at the top of the first page:
I do not hate people
Nor do I encroach on anyone
But . . . if I become hungry
I shall eat the flesh of my raper
Beware . . . beware . . . of my hunger
And of my anger!![26]

"Ḥadhāri . . . ḥadhāri . . . min jū'ī wa min ghaḍabī!!"—the threatening tone of the warning cannot be overstressed. Written in the mid-1960s, "Biṭāqit hawiya" registers Darwish's belated melancholic bitterness at the loss of his home at the age of six, on the heels of the creation of the State of Israel and the Arab-Israeli War of 1948 which resulted in the total erasure of his native village, Birweh, as he discovered firsthand during his allegedly illegal return to Birweh in 1949, a year after he left it to Lebanon as a refugee among hundreds of thousands of Palestinian refugees whose return to their rightful homes has ever since been eternally revoked.[27] Thenceforth Darwish will have to

---

25. Mahmoud Darwish, "Biṭāqit hawiya" (Identity Card), in *Al-Dīwān 1* (Beirut: Riad El-Rayyes Books, 2005), 80.

26. Darwish, "Biṭāqit," 83–84.

27. Anecdotally, Darwish is said not to want to have children of his own because for him one single newborn equals one more refugee. Recently, the Kurdish Syrian novelist and poet,

live as a refugee in his own country; during the 1960s, while working as a journalist in Haifa and acting as a member of the Israeli Communist party, Rakah, he was imprisoned on several occasions for not having a permit to leave Haifa. In the early 1970s, he left Haifa for Moscow and from there went to Cairo where he worked for the daily newspaper *Al-Ahram*. In 1973, he joined the Palestine Liberation Organization (PLO) and was officially banned from reentering Israel until 26 years later. In the late 1970s, he went on to live in Beirut where he became director of the PLO research center before establishing *Al-Karmel* in 1981.

By the time the Lebanese Civil War was raging around him in Beirut, Darwish reached the peak of his reputation: his poetry books sold more than one million copies in the Arab world alone, and a number of his poems were put to song by the Lebanese singer Marcel Khalife, himself an Arab icon of the committed artist (*al-fannān al-multazim*). In the wake of the siege of Beirut by the Israeli army in 1982 and the ensuing massacre of Palestinians in the refugee camps of Sabra and Shatila by Israel's Phalangist proxies, Darwish became an official exile, wandering from and between Syria, Cyprus, Cairo, Tunis, and Paris. It was during his life as an itinerant exile that Darwish produced his most profound verses and rejected most of his early poetry, which his readers dubbed as the poetry of resistance, in an extension of Ghassān Kanafānī's critical qualification of Palestinian literature under Israeli occupation as a literature of resistance in his pioneering study *Al-'Adab al-falastīnī al-muqāwim taḥta al-iḥtilāl: 1948–1968* (Palestinian Literature of Resistance under Occupation: 1948–1968). In his exilic life after 1982, Darwish became particularly cognizant of the confines of labels and sought to release himself from being seen as a Palestinian poet of resistance or as a poet with a cause rather than a poet tout court. With the onset of the first Intifada of 1987, the Gulf War of 1990, and the Madrid peace process of 1991, Darwish's poetry tended toward the worldly, the mythological, the historical, and the human writ large, as well as the oblique and the metapoetic. No longer is the poetry of "Write down/I am an Arab" possible amidst the onslaught on Palestine, Lebanon, and Iraq. No longer is the poetry of resistance possible at a time when the PLO has started to speak the language of its oppressor and practically

---

Salim Barakāt, a longtime friend and editor of *Al-Karmel*, a literary magazine of which Darwish was the founder and editor in chief, divulged a secret that Darwish confided in him, and alleged that Darwish had a daughter out of wedlock with a married woman. Barakat's declaration took the Arab public cybersphere by storm, further testifying to the indestructible mythological stature of Darwish as poet-prophet. See Barakāt, "Mahomoud Darwish wa 'Anā," *Al-Quds Al-Arabī* (6 June 2020), www.alquds.co.uk/محمود-درويش-وأنا/.

compromised the memory of its martyrs in the theatrics and choral chants of a peace process aimed at bringing the Palestinians to unconditional surrender.

Poetry had to reinvent itself in order to survive the ominous demise of the Palestinians' sense of survival at the hands of what would become the Oslo Accords of 1993. In short, poetry had to take stock of the question of survival, which is in turn the question of ending, finality, and dissolution altogether of the resistance and the Palestinian pursuit of national liberation. This is precisely the question Darwish poses rhetorically in one of the most celebrated poems of his 1986 *Ward 'Aqall*, "Taḍīqu binā al-'arḍ" (The Earth Is Closing on Us; تضيق بنا الأرض):

تضيق بنا الأرض. تحشرنا في الممرّ الأخير، فنخلعُ أعضاءنا كي نمرّ . . .
إلى أين نذهبُ بعد الحدود الأخيرة؟ أين تطير العصافيرُ بعد السّماء الأخيرةِ

The earth is closing on us, thrusting us into the last passage
And we pull off our limbs to pass through . . .
Where do we go after the last border?
Where do birds fly after the last sky?[28]

Edward Said uses the last couplet as an epigraph for—and part of the last line as the title of—his poignant photoessay chronicle of Palestinian lives, in collaboration with Jean Mohr, *After the Last Sky*. Said speaks of Palestinians post-1982 as "having had the experience of limits," but remain "enveloped by a nagging disquiet at how much yet needs to be done," on their part, in order for them to articulate a sense of an achievable future and reach a settlement with Israel.[29] He asks, "Can we 'put on' knowledge adequate to the power that entered and dislocated our lives so unalterably in this century? Can we see what we are, have we really *seen* what we have seen?"[30] The rhetorical structure of both Darwish's lines and Said's reflections combine to evoke the uncertainly principle that characterizes Palestinian lives, their present, their past and their future. Said's questions imply that the most devastating aspect of undergoing an "experience of limits" is the resulting inability to fathom and articulate what has been experienced. It is as if what is worse than surviving the experience of limits is the loss of the sense of survival itself: the ability to remember and *to see* what has been experienced preparatory to elaborating narrative departures. For Darwish, the experience of limits—of reaching the last sky, and of having

---

28. Darwish, "Taḍīqu binā al-arḍ" (The Earth Is Closing on Us), in *Al-Dīwān* 3 (Beirut: Riad El-Rayyes Books, 2005), 115.
29. Edward W. Said, *After the Last Sky* (New York: Columbia University Press, 1999), 159, 165.
30. Said, *After the Last Sky*, 159, italics in original.

nowhere else to go—translates into a series of questions he asks to poetry, questions on whether or not poetry can survive the saturation of the horizon of the possible.

For Darwish poetry cannot, or rather must not, survive the demise of its object. Yet for its object to survive its own demise, it becomes necessary for poetry to die and let live. Poetry, in other words, has always to invoke its impossibility, crisis and collapse in order to reclaim and reinscribe the object of memory whose forgetting is required for it to fulfill itself. The reclaiming of the object of poetry must emerge on the pyre of poetry and not thanks to poetry's triumphant survival of its vanishing object. This logic, from which Darwish's post-1982 poetry emerges, is very laconically that of "bright confusion," to borrow Frank Kermode's felicitous expression.[31] Darwish's 1992 dīwān, 'Aḥada 'ashara kawkaban, in many ways the crowning achievement of his post-1982 poetic experiments in form and style, comes at a time when the United States had emerged as the world's only superpower after the collapse of the Soviet-dominated regimes in Eastern Europe in 1989 and the Soviet Union itself in 1991, all of which were hailed by Francis Fukuyama in *The End of History and the Last Man* as the triumph of liberal democracy. The massive display of military power during Operation Desert Storm (1990–1991) against Iraq came as both a proclamation and an implementation of the New World Order led by the unbending hegemony of the United States. At the same time that the United States was eager to flex its muscles in Iraq and prove to the world its uncontestable global dominance, orientalists like Bernard Lewis and Samuel P. Huntington claimed that the conflicts of the future would occur along the cultural fault lines separating civilizations and feature in particular a duel between the Judeo-Christian heritage and the so-called Islamic fundamentalism. No wonder, then, that "Faras li-l-gharīb," Darwish's response to what will become America's serial wars on Iraq, is included as a conclusion to 'Aḥada 'ashara kawkaban, a dīwān whose historical and mythical breadth and depth punctures the logic of the civilization paradigm advanced by Lewis and Huntington and conceives of the future of conflict from within the history of asymmetric power struggles—really, from within the near and yet far barbaric seriality of atrocities that extend from the Reconquista and Inquisition that marked late medieval Europe and the post-Andalusian age up to the irreversible dissolution of historical Palestine and the occupation of Iraq at the hands of the Zionist colonial and the American imperial powers.

"Faras li-l-gharīb" is placed at the end of the 1992 'Aḥada 'ashara kawkaban to act as the last chapter in a dīwān that begins with eleven short poems

---

31. Kermode, *The Sense of an Ending*, 81.

titled "'Aḥada 'ashara kawkaban 'ala 'ākhir al-mashhad al-Andalussī" (Eleven Planets over the Last Andalusian Scene). Darwish clearly wants us to recognize that, at the 1492 quincentennial of the collapse of Granada, Iraq is poised as the last chapter in the historical decline of Arabs, their gradual but steady loss of their rightful homelands culminating in the dispossession of Palestine and the invasion of Iraq. In these eleven short poems whose Quranic invocation of the "Sūrah of *Yūsuf*" connotes betrayal and professes impending doom for the Palestinians in Oslo, Darwish writes:

الكمنجاتُ تبكي على العربِ الخارجينَ من الأندلُسْ . . .
Violins weep for the Arabs leaving Andalusia . . .

أنا آدمُ الجنَّتَيْن، فقدتُهُما مرّتيْنْ . . .
I am the Adam of two Edens, I lost them twice . . .

أنا زفرةُ العَرَبيِّ الأخيرَةْ . . .
I am the last sigh of the Arab . . . [32]

The last Andalusian scene (*ākhir al-mashhad al-Andalussī*) corresponds historically to the scene of "the Moor's last sigh," in which the Nasrid ruler of Granada, Mohammed XI, who was known in the West as Boabdil, was devastated as he de facto surrendered the city to the Catholic monarchs in accordance with the Agreements of Capitulation, signed several months before January 2, 1492, the scene of Boabdil's last sigh of grief and regret. As the anecdote goes, Boabdil was weeping for the inevitable fate of Granada when his mother chastised him, "Do not weep like a woman for what you could not defend like a man." The spot from where Boabdil took his Orphic gaze at the last Muslim stronghold for the previous 250 years, bears to this day, according to Stanley Lane-Poole, the name of *el ultimo sospiro del Moro*, "the last sigh of the Moor."[33] In a proleptic gesture, Darwish appropriates the Moor's last sigh and identifies with Boabdil (*anā zafratu al-Arabī al-akhīra*) to portend the terrible fate of Palestine and Iraq and, above all, his own fate as an Arab and a poet living, as Boabdil did, on borrowed time.

As the last poem of *'Aḥada 'ashara kawkaban*, "Faras li-l-gharīb" is in many ways the epitome of the rhetoric of ending that punctuates the whole *dīwān*. The question that preoccupies the poem and condenses the entirety of the *dīwān* is whether poetry is still possible *after* Iraq, in the exponential curve of aftermaths from al-Andalus onward. The poem is dedicated to a nameless Iraqi poet. It begins with an apostrophic address to the absent Iraqi poet, urging him

---

32. Mahmoud Darwish, "'Aḥada 'ashara kawkaban 'ala 'ākhir al-mashhad al-Andalussī" (Eleven Planets over the Last Andalusian Scene), in *Al-Diwan* 3: 292, 276, 278.

33. Stanley Lane-Poole, *The Moors in Spain* (New York: Putnam, 1911), 267.

to step forward to be elegized, and then slices into a gripping commentary on the implacable recursivity of warfare and violence and on the burden of representation that Darwish's poetic persona sets itself the task to bear following the implied death (or resignation to silence) of the Iraqi poet being addressed:

يا صـاحبي، أين أنتَ؟
تقدّم لأحملَ عنك الكلامَ . . . وأرثيك/
. . . لو كان جسرًا عبرناهُ. لكنّه الدّارُ والهاوية

O my friend, where are you?
Step forward,
So that I bear the burden of your speech,
And elegize you.
If it were a bridge, we would have crossed it already,
but it's a home, it's an abyss.[34]

The fact that Darwish dedicates the poem to an Iraqi poet who is no longer present—and that his poetic persona bears the speech of this absent poet *preparatory* to elegizing him—evokes an anxiety over mourning and, more precisely, over the substitutive and sublative effects of aestheticizing the death of the other. Darwish's poem does not so much restore the subjectivity of the Iraqi poet to the life of the poem, which would result in a tasteless second burial of the deceased poet among the lines of the poem but instantiates a selfless concern for the silence and vulnerability of the addressed poet that might in point fact be of at the very core of any viable ethics of remembering and mourning. Given that this concern for the other takes place following the catastrophic 1991 military assault on Iraq—in which the rhetoric of collaterality and "war without [*American*] casualties" served to conceal the Iraqi death toll—it also constitutes a threshold moment of inquiry about the nature of the implied death of the Iraqi poet, its claim and will to justice from beyond the grave.

Unlike, for instance, Al-Mutanabbī (915–965), the ardent medieval Arab poet whose illustrious elegy for his maternal grandmother constructs death as a natural phenomenon, Darwish's elegy constructs death as a superimposed "home" and "abyss" inflicted on the subaltern, the vulnerable, the one exposed to military violence. In a sense, the poem seems to find no alternative but to reproduce the structural banalization of death in order to expose and resist it. Darwish's lines allow the exposure of the crucial difference between the general

---

34. Mahmoud Darwish, "Faras li-l-gharīb," in *Al-Dīwān* 3 (Beirut: Riad El-Rayyes Books, 2005), 345. See also "A Horse for the Stranger," in *The Adam of Two Edens: Selected Poems by Mahmoud Darwish*, ed. Munir Akash and Daniel Moore (Syracuse: Syracuse University Press, 2000), 105, trans. modified.

"injustice of death" and the "unjust death" to which his writing bears witness.[35] Darwish contends, "Against barbarity, poetry can resist only by confirming its attachment to human fragility like a blade of grass growing on a wall while armies march by."[36] In the face of the derealizing aims of military violence, and the differential allocation of mournability, elegy becomes an insurgent force and an ethical engagement whose ultimate concern is to redeem the dignity and humanity of an otherwise disposable and ungrievable life. Nothing is worse than to be dead and completely forgotten—or, as the Arabic and Quranic idiom of the "Sūrah of Maryam" has it, to be "nasiyan mansiyyā."[37] In this sense, Darwish's poetic persona seeks to reclaim the mournability *right* of the disappeared Iraqi poet precisely by opening the classical lyrical ode (of which Al-Mutanabbī's elegy is a product) to a post-elegiac economy of mourning in which the imperative to mourn incessantly materializes as a vigilant impulse toward psychoaffective irresolution.

No longer normatively bound to a preterit ideal of therapeutic mourning it can no longer deliver, modern Arabic elegy has turned with double zeal to the elaboration of an ethicopolitics of *being in mourning*. According to Max Horkheimer and Adorno, "The respect for something which has no market value and runs contrary to all feelings is experienced most sharply by the person in mourning, in whose case not even the psychological restoration of labor power is possible."[38] Because, according to Roland Barthes, "society codifies mourning in order to assimilate it"[39] and because, according to Horkheimer and Adorno, the "worst possible curse" for a dead person is to be "expunged from the memory of those who live on,"[40] poetry might constitute a rare space for staging and sustaining the experience of unresolved mourning, provided that

---

35. Clifton Spargo makes the important distinction "between the general injustice of death as the end to which any life must come and the particular occasion of the unjust death as a socially determined event," without which victims of war might be consigned to the anonymity of oblivion. *The Ethics of Mourning: Grief and Responsibility in Elegiac Literature* (Baltimore, MD: Johns Hopkins University Press, 2004), 4. This distinction makes possible the critique of the racist apportioning of mournability on the basis of disposability.

36. Quoted in Nathalie Handal, "Mahmoud Darwish: Palestine's Poet of Exile," *The Progressive*, May 1, 2002, https://progressive.org/magazine/mahmoud-darwish-palestine-s-poet-exile-handal/.

37. *The Meaning of the Holy Qurʾan*, trans. ʿAbdullah Yūsuf ʿAlī (Beltsville, MD: Amana Publications, 2006), sūrah19, verse 63.

38. Max Horkheimer and Theodor W. Adorno, "On the Theory of Ghosts," in *The Dialectic of Enlightenment*, trans. John Cumming (New York: Continuum, 1989), 216.

39. Roland Barthes, *The Neutral: Lecture Course at the Collège de France (1977–1978)*, trans. Rosalind E. Krauss and Denis Hollier (New York: Columbia University Press, 2005), 17.

40. Horkheimer and Adorno, "On the Theory of Ghosts," 216.

the poem does not end up substituting the very death of the other whom it sets out to rescue from oblivion. Since the urge to mourn is oftentimes underpinned by the impulse to forget, the poem ought to anchor and express our mourning only to the extent that it renders it hardly possible for us to divest ourselves from the imperative to remember (by displacing it onto the poem as the locus and terminus of mourning as well as the license to forgetting). This is clearly the Herculean task of the modern elegy in general and of Darwish's elegy in particular, for after volunteering to be the custodian of mourning and the bearer of the burden of speech of the Iraqi poet, Darwish's persona finds itself speechless, asking rhetorically, almost in a stunned resignation: "Who will bear the poem's burden for us now?" (*Faman yaḥmilu al-āna 'ib'a al-qaṣīdati 'annā?*).[41]

Given the military buildup that preceded the Gulf War in late 1990, which Darwish calls "Taknūlūjiyā li-qatl al-'Iraq," or the "technology to kill Iraq"— and given the rare multilateralism that in Darwish's words united the East and the West "fī gharīzati qābīl, or "in Cain's instinct"—Darwish is not perhaps unjustified to proclaim that there can be no poetry *after* Iraq:[42]

لم يبقَ في الأرض متّسعٌ للقصيدةِ، يا صاحبي
فهل في القصيدةِ متّسعٌ، بعدُ، للأرضِ بعد العِراقِ؟

O my friend
there's no room for the poem on this earth.
Is there still a room for this earth in the poem, after Iraq?[43]

. . . قبرٌ لباريسَ، لَندنَ، روما، نيويورك، موسكو، وقبر
لبغدادَ، هلْ كان من حقّها أن تُصدّق ماضيها المُرتَقَبْ؟
وقبرٌ لإيتاكةِ الدَّرب والهَدفِ الصَّعبِ، قبرٌ ليافا . . .
وقبرٌ لهوميرَ أيضاً والبُحتُرِيّ، وقبرٌ هو الشِّعْرُ، قبرٌ
من الرِّيحِ . . . يا حَجَرَ الرّوحِ، يا صَمْتَنَا!

A grave for Paris, for London, for Rome, for New York, for Moscow,
and a grave for Baghdad, for did it have the right to take its past for granted?
A grave for Ithaca, the difficult path and the goal,
a grave for Jaffa, for Homer and for Al-Buhturi,
A grave—that is poetry!
A grave of wind . . .
O stone of the soul, O our silence![44]

41. Darwish, "Faras," 349.
42. Ibid., 346, 348.
43. Ibid., 346; "Horse," 106.
44. Darwish, "Faras," 348, "Horse," 109, trans. modified.

These lines subtly express Darwish's uncertainty principle about the political import and ethical implications of poetry. By naming a grave, poetry confirms a graveyard, almost in the same way that "Thinking of the key" in T. S. Eliot's "The Waste Land" "confirms a prison."[45] Nothing can be inscribed on "qabr min-ar-rīh" (a grave of wind) "fī mahabbi-l-'Iraq"—"in the passage wind of Iraq."[46] It is a Sisyphean task that reduces the poet to silence and fails still to stir "ḥajara-l-rūḥi" (the stone of the soul) or end the torment of wordlessness. It bears repeating, moreover, that the real danger of poetry—and of any narrative of war—is its potential imposition of a mantel of coherency over, for instance, the war on Iraq, which might, in turn, result in unwittingly rationalizing and seamlessly integrating it into the annalistic narrative of the champions of history. Poetry is a "grave" in this sense partly because it buries the reality of the war on Iraq—its incongruity with art, its irreducibility to form—in the service of the testimonial obbligato to make the violent event speak, and speak coherently to be witnessable, understandable, and cognizable. Darwish is mindful of the potentially discomfiting complicity of the poet with Arab suffering if the poet were to give in to the rationalizing impulse of poetry and its rhetoric, which may in fact amount to nothing less than a "kind of participation in torture" (*darbun min ḍurūb al-mushāraka fi-t-ta'dhīb*).[47] Poetry can then be said to reenact the violence it seeks to bear witness to and to dig the grave it seeks to protest against precisely because of the violent nature of representation itself, its desire for form, coherency, and credulity. Yet poetry seems to emerge *after* Iraq in a form of contrapuntal irresolution: in the dialectical interplay between the reducibility to silence and the irreducibility to form. While not fully unscathed by the enormity and sheer technological insanity of war, poetry wrests the power of the word from the jaws of futility.

Darwish's apocalyptic tone and vision of vanishing intellectual figures (Homer and Al-Buhturi) and collapsing world capitals (Paris, London, New York, etc.) is framed in an intertextual chiasmus between Eliot's "The Waste Land" and Adonis's "Qabr min 'ajl New York" (A Grave for New York). While Darwish's and Adonis's poems share with Eliot's the outrage against the derealizing thrust of war, they differ quite ostensibly from Eliot in terms of the geopolitical scope and implications of their contestation. Basically, Darwish's outcry is against the West and the United States in particular—what

---

45. T. S. Eliot, "The Waste Land," in *The Complete Poems and Plays 1909–1950* (New York: Harcourt, 1971), 49.

46. Darwish, "Faras," 351.

47. Mahmoud Darwish, *Fī Ḥaḍrat al-ghiyāb* (In the Presence of Absence) (Beirut: Riad El-Rayyes, 2006), 82.

he variably calls "at-Tattār al-judud"/"The New Tatars," "Rūmā"/"Rome," "Qayṣar"/"Caesar," or "Sudūm al-jadīda"/"The New Sodom"[48]—for transfiguring the Arab world into a theater of war, resurrecting and embodying a historical chain of invaders and usurpers. Adonis's poem shares with Darwish's the protest against US imperialism but frames it rather in a transnational context of Third World solidarities with African Americans, American Indians, and many other ethnicities in a manner reminiscent of the planetary reach of the opening concise poems of Darwish's 'Ahada 'ashara kawkaban. However, in the history of modern Arabic poetry, the maturity of Adonis's poem predates that of Darwish's late poetry. "Qabr min 'ajl New York" was published in 1972 in an enlarged edition of Waqt bayna al-ramād wa-l-ward (A Time between Ashes and Roses) whose original publication in 1970 included only two long poems: "Muqaddima li-Tārikh Mulūk-in li-Ṭawā'if" (Introduction to the History of the Petty Kings) and "Hadhā Huwa 'Ismī" (This Is My Name). While these earlier poems constitute Adonis's severe response to the 1967 Naksa, enlisting it as it were in the miserable history of the petty rulers of al-Andalus in Moorish Spain, "Qabr min 'ajl New York" adds a more universal dimension to the first two, as it was written upon Adonis's visit to the United States. Born in 1930 in Syria and brought in the Shi'i tradition of Islamic practices, Adonis, as his pen name indicates, was ceaselessly in search of transformative regeneration in Arab culture, politics, traditions, and thought. Small wonder he was met with formidable opposition at the outset of his poetic and political career and activism and was arbitrarily imprisoned for his radical views in 1955 before he moved to Beirut in 1956 and became a Lebanese national. Frequently shortlisted for the Nobel Prize, Adonis has pursued a literary and critical career that is difficult to categorize: he was an avant-garde poet; a mordant critic of Arabic literature, Arab culture, and politics; and cofounder and coeditor (with Yousef al-Khal) of such modernist journals as Shi'r (Poetry), which published Darwish in 1967, and of the equally influential journal, Mawāqif (Positions), which he founded in 1968.

Consistently preoccupied with the question of modernity and tradition, Adonis's poetic and critical body of work is marked by an unstinting search for the new, the revolutionary, the dissonant and dissenting, which borders quite seamlessly in his case on the mystic and prophetic as well as the anarchistic and apocalyptic. With the 1961 publication of his *Aghanī Mihyār al-Dimashqī* (The Songs of Mihyar the Damascene), in which he deploys the figure of Mihyar as a poetic persona through which he elaborates a new

---

48. Darwish, "Faras," 345, 346, 347, 350.

vision of the world, Adonis ushered Arabic poetry into a new age, not simply of free verse, but also of writing writ large, understood as capaciously inclusive of poetry and prose, irrespective of genre. While his post-1967 poetry indulges in abstraction, symbolism, and surrealism, all of which filtered through an idiosyncratic language that categorically refuses to descend to the level of everyday speech, his more recent poetry is tempered in terms of its language and style; not only is it more accessible but also collapses everyday intelligibility and intellectual elitism in the known style of Arabic poetics of *al-sahl al-mumtani'* or the deceptively simple. However, throughout his works, he remains loyal to his inaugural poetic and critical desire to change the brutal modes of intelligibility that dominate the world scene and that impoverish the Arab world at a crucial historical juncture, when it is caught between dueling currents of modernity, an ancient and almost forgotten current of modernity coexisting in an explosive tension with an encroaching imperial modernity. Palestine, Lebanon, and Iraq remain geopolitical nodal points in his more recent writings, as he attempts to champion the human impulse of transformation and creativity in the face of the graveyard whistling that accompanies war and violence. For Adonis, poetry is never more to be desired than at a time when the truth of humanity, the humanity of the Arab, is crowded out of existence by the cannons of violence.

In "Taḥiya 'ilā Baghdād" (Salute to Baghdad), a poem he wrote soon after the 2003 war in Iraq, Adonis intimates that poetry is at the site of its final demise, that "the killer has eaten the bread of song," and that nothing but raw rebellion can reinstate a glimpse of hope:

يا لهذه البلاد التي نَنْتَمي إليها:
اسمُها الصمّت
وليس فيها غيرُ الآلام
وهاهي مليئةٌ بالقبور ـ جامدةٌ ومتحرّكة . . .

O what a country ours is:
Silence is its name,
And it contains only pain;
There it is, filled with graves,
Some still, some moving . . .

إلى أين نمضي؟
الطّريقُ نفسه لم يعد يصدّق خطواتِنا . . .

Where do we go?
The road itself no longer believes our steps . . .

أكَلَ القاتلُ خُبزَ الأغنيْة،
لا تَسَلْ، يا أيّها الشّاعِرُ، لن يُوقظَ هذي الأرض
غيرُ المَعصِية.

The killer has eaten the bread of song
O poet, never mind asking, for
Nothing will awaken this earth
Except rebelliousness.⁴⁹

Like Darwish, Adonis is on the qui vive about all the ways in which war and violence challenge the very *raison d'être* of poetry. This is not surprising given that war and violence coincide, historically speaking, with imperial expansionism, materialist cruelty and the "lowering of aesthetic standards," as Sigmund Freud argues in his famous exchange with Albert Einstein on how to deliver mankind from the menace of war.⁵⁰ The war on Iraq, like every act of military violence, is waged against poetry and the arts in general (perhaps even more so in a literal sense, given that Iraq's cultural patrimony, for instance, was either looted or callously bombarded). War challenges the poem to try to keep its form and still accommodate realistically the suddenness and rupture of violence. In short, the challenge of war is the challenge for poetry to exist outside the logic that underpins war. Adorno even suggests that "works of art which by their existence take the side of the victims of rationality that subjugates nature, are even in their protest constitutively implicated in the process of rationalization." For Adorno, "the organizing, unifying principle of each and every work of art is borrowed from that very rationality whose claim to totality it seeks to defy."⁵¹ "The killer has eaten the bread of song" (*akala-l-qātilu khubza-l-'ughniya*), reiterates Adonis, testifying thus to the pitiful failure of poetry not only to take stock of the unreality of war but also to alter that unreality of which it is a product and to which its failure bears witness.

In a style of deceptive literality and ironic distancing, Darwish actually inscribes the damages incurred by poetry in his 2002 dīwān of post-al-Aqṣā Intifada of 2000, *Ḥālit Ḥiṣār* (State of Siege), as follows:

خسَائِرُنا: من شهيدَيْن حتى ثمانيةٍ
كُلَّ يوم،
وعشرةُ جرْحَى
وعشرونَ بيتاً
وخمسونَ زيتونةً،
بالإضافة للخَلَل البنيويّ الذي
سيُصيبُ القصيدةَ والمسرحيةَ واللوحة الناقصةُ

---

49. Adonis, "Taḥīya 'ilā Baghdād," http://www.arabiancreativity.com/salute.htm; "Salute to Baghdad," trans. Sinan Antoon, *Al-Ahram Weekly* 634 (17–23 April 2003), http://weekly.ahram.org.eg/2003/634/bsc13.htm.

50. Sigmund Freud, "Why War?" in *Civilization, Society and Religion*, trans. James Strachey, ed. Albert Dickson (London: Penguin Books, 1991), 362.

51. Adorno, "Commitment," 191–92.

> Our losses: Between two and eight martyrs every day
> Ten wounded
> Twenty homes
> And fifty olive trees . . .
> In addition to the structural defect that
> Will afflict the poem, the play, and the incomplete painting.[52]

Clearly, war is a raid on poetry, which has, if it were to survive the onslaught, to incorporate the devastating and eviscerating effects of war within its form. While the critical incredulity toward poetry seems to be self-defeating at times, it is best understood in terms of its empowering presentational wherewithal. I would argue that such an attitude of "objective cynicism" toward poetry becomes crucial to signifying the "unmeaning" of violence itself, and, in the process, to reinstating (in a series of metapoetic interpellations) the discontinuity of war that might otherwise be diluted by the poem's desire for form. Poetry becomes, pace Eliot, a raid on the articulate.[53] For Darwish (as much as for Adonis), then, to call poetry a "grave of wind" that, in W. H. Auden's words, "makes nothing happen" is—far from being an inclination to debunk poetry—a way of slicing into the disastrous repercussions of war and, more programmatically, a kind of a counterredemptory gesture of negative dialectics toward both the poem and the catastrophe it seeks to represent.[54] For the poem to approximate and expose the carnage of the battlefield, it must be "nāqiṣa" or "incomplete," containing "khaṭa' kabīr" or a "grave mistake" in its structural rib.[55] In *After the Last Sky*, Said stages and articulates an argument similar to the one operative in Darwish's and Adonis's poetry and prose: "Since the main features of our present existence are dispossession, dispersion, and yet a kind of power incommensurate with our stateless exile, I believe that essentially unconventional, hybrid, and fragmentary forms of expression should be used to represent us."[56] In Adonis's poem, there is an overwhelming sense of fatigue, dissipation of energy, and saturation of the horizon of the doable. The poetic persona asks, "'ilā 'ayna namḍī?" (where do we go?), for "ḥattā-l-ṭarīq

---

52. *Ḥālit Ḥiṣār* (Beirut: Riad El-Rayyes, 2002, 38, *State of Siege* in *The Butterfly's Burden: Poems by Mahmoud Darwish*, trans. Fady Joudah (Port Townsend, WA: Copper Canyon Press, 2007), 136–37.

53. Eliot, "The Waste Land," 128.

54. W. H. Auden, "In Memory of W. B. Yeats," in *Selected Poetry of W. H. Auden* (New York: Random House, 1969), 53.

55. Darwish, *Fī Ḥaḍrat*, 84; Darwish, *Ka-zahr al-Lawz aw ab'ad* (Like Almond Flowers or Further) (Beirut: Riad El-Rayyes, 2005), 69.

56. Said, *After the Last Sky*, 6.

lam yaʿud yuṣaddiqu khaṭawātinā" (the road itself no longer believes our steps), and the temperament becomes reminiscent of Eliot's J. Alfred Prufrock's dizzying repetition, "I have known them all already, known them all."[57] However, this poem, which mocks the overlordly preemptive strike or preventive war (ḥarb wiqāʾiya) against Iraq and the embarrassing complicity of the Arab world, calls for revolt and political and religious disobedience (al-maʿṣiyah), in a manner reminiscent of the 1960s committed poetry of, among others, Muẓaffar Al-Nawwāb, Khalil Ḥawi, Qabbānī as well as Adonis's own poetry (such as Fāris Al-Kalimāt Al-Gharība, or The Knight of Strange Words).

Darwish, for all his complaints in his writings about the power and legitimacy of poetry at a time of imperial warfare and diurnal occupation, also asserts that poetry, regardless of its end results, does not need a podium, any more than bread needs to announce itself to the hungry. Adorno had "no wish to soften the saying that to write lyric poetry after Auschwitz is barbaric" because it expressed "in negative form the impulse which inspires committed literature."[58] To express the empowering potential of poetry in a negative register—in a simulacrum of impotence and inarticulacy—has become a mark of Darwish's own reverse raid on the articulate. Rhetorical questions such as "Is poetry still necessary?" or "Is poetry still possible?" are scattered here and there in his writings.[59] In the 1987 Dhākira li-l-nisyān (Memory for Forgetfulness), his somewhat belated passionate outcry against the Israeli invasion of Lebanon and the siege of Beirut in 1982, which resulted in the suicide of Khalil Hawi and the Sabra and Shatila massacre, Darwish wonders again about the pertinence of writing poetry while a city and a people are under siege: "Who can sleep, with these packs of fighter jets above? I'm curious to know how a poet can write, how he can find the words for this language" (lughatun li-hadhihi al-lughah).[60] In the 2005 dīwān titled Ka-zahr al-Lawz aw abʿad, his poetic persona reframes the question about the burden of representation, which figures as discussed earlier in "Faras li-l-gharīb," as follows: "how do I bear for you and for myself the burden of the poem?" (Kaifa aḥmilu ʿibʾa al-qaṣīdati ʿanka wa ʿannī?).[61] One would go on citing examples of this theme,

---

57. T. S. Eliot, "Love Song of J. Alfred Prufrock," in The Complete Poems and Plays 1909–1950 (New York: Harcourt, 1971), 5.

58. Adorno, "Commitment," 188.

59. Mahmoud Darwish, Ḥayrat al-ʿāʾid (The Hesitant Homecomer) (Beirut: Riad El-Rayyes, 2007), 130.

60. Mahmoud Darwish, Dhākira lil-nisyān, (Beirut: Riad El-Rayyes, 2007), 58.

61. Mahmoud Darwish, Ka-zahr al-Lawz aw abʿad (Like Almond Flowers or Further) (Beirut: Riad El-Rayyes, 2005), 121.

or variations on it, which are oftentimes situated in a dialectic of ambiguity, not to say negativity, coexisting with and within the very act of writing poetry—really, the act of writing poetry on the pyre of poetry, as if poetry were indeed necessary and impossible at the same time.

In *Dhākira li-l-nisyān*, for instance, Darwish returns again and again to the question of the "whenness" of poetry, only to contend—not without equivocation, of course—that poetry cannot possibly unfold in parallel to the unfolding of a violent event, and that it is impossible to write or bear witness to a massacre while it is taking place. To write poetry *during* Sabra and Shatila is barbaric. Writing occurs *after* the event and in retrospect, but it is by no means less barbaric. In between, the poet writes, as it were, his silence (*aktubu ṣamtī*). When asked by an American journalist during the 1982 Israeli siege of Beirut—"What are you writing in this war, poet?"—Darwish responds retrospectively in 1987 in the following staged dialogue between Darwish's poetic persona and the journalist:

— أكتب صمتي.
— هل تعني أن الكلام للمدافع؟
— نعم. صوتها أعلى من أي صوت.
— ماذا تفعل إذن؟
— أدعو إلى الصّمود.
— وهل ستنتصرون في هذه الحرب؟
— لا. المهم أن نبقى. بقاؤنا انتصار.
— وماذا بعد ذلك؟
— سيبدأ زمن جديد.
— ومتى تعود إلى كتابة الشعر؟
— حين تسكت المدافع قليلا. حين أفجر صمتي المليء بجميع هذه الأصوات. حين أجد لغتي الملائمة.
— أليس لك من دور؟
— لا. لا دور لي في الشعر الآن. دوري خارج القصيدة. دوري أن أكون هنا، مع المواطنين، ومع المقاتلين.

—I'm writing my silence.
—Do you mean that now the guns should speak?
—Yes. Their sound is louder than my voice.
—What are you doing then?
—I am calling for steadfastness.
—And will you win this war?
—No. The important thing is to hold on. Holding on is a victory in itself.
—And what after that?
—A new age will start.

—And will you go back to writing poetry?
—When the guns quiet down a little. When I explode my silence, which is full of all these voices. When I find the appropriate language.
—Is there no role for you then?
—No. No role for me in poetry now. My role is outside the poem. My role is to be here, with the citizens and fighters.[62]

On the one hand, writing poetry seems to be impossible during war; on the other, poetry seems neither necessary nor guaranteed when the war is over, since it hinges on whether or not the poet finds "the appropriate language" (*al-lughah al-mulā'imah*). It might seem that Darwish's persona perceives of poetry as subordinate to silence and fighting, but a deeper look reveals that the figures of silence, fighting or being with the citizens and fighters are deployed to conjure up the incubational moment of poetry (in Darwish's by now familiar indirectness). Darwish's poetic persona is already at work on its silence, exploding it in the *promise* of writing while looking for the appropriate language, the language whereby to reframe the familiar question—the possibility of writing poetry in the aftermath of catastrophe: after the siege of Beirut, after the war on Iraq, after the occupation of Palestine, after the siege of Ramallah or the serial raids on Gaza. In a precious aside in a *Ḥālit Ḥiṣār*, he writes:

[إلى الشَّعر:] حاصِرْ حِصارَكَ

[To poetry:] Besiege your siege.[63]

This clear imperative is addressed to a captive poetry (in a poem written during the siege of Ramallah in 2002 which Darwish experienced firsthand); it proffers us not only with a way of weighing on the psyche of the surrounding oppressors (which is alluded to throughout the poem), but also a way for poetry to preclude the poeticidal demarcations of war and violence. Already in *Dhākira li-l-nisyān*, Darwish invented the proverbial formula with which to address the question of siege, the siege of Beirut: "besiege your siege . . . no escape" (*ḥāṣir ḥiṣāraka . . . lā mafarru*).[64] In "Faras li-l-gharīb" he lays the axiomatic ground for addressing the question of exile, urging the Iraqi poet to "open up an exile for his exile" (*Iftaḥ li-manfāka manfā*).[65] It is perhaps the first time that Darwish uses this counter-intuitive formula to ask of poetry to lay siege to its siege. Yet, in the same poem, he also addresses the reader, warning

---

62. Darwish, *Dhākira*, 65–66, *Memory*, 24.
63. Darwish, *Ḥālit*, 57, *State*, 149.
64. Darwish, *Dhākira*, 61.
65. Darwish, "Faras," 346.

him or her not to trust poetry, before he concludes: "Writing is a small puppy biting the void/writing wounds without drawing blood" (*al-kitābatu jarwun saghīr yaʿaḍu al-ʿadam / al-kitābatu tajraḥu min dūni damm*).⁶⁶

As the opening of Ḥālit Ḥiṣār suggests, writing poetry—while symptomatic of "dāʾ al-amal,"⁶⁷ or the poison of hope—"nurtures hope":

هنا، عند مُنحَدراتِ التلالِ، أمام الغروبِ
وفُوَّهةِ الوقتِ،
قُرْبَ بساتينَ مقطوعةِ الظلِّ،
نفعَلُ ما يفعلُ السُجناءُ،
ومايفعلُ العاطلون عَن العَمَلِ:
نُرَبّي الأَمَلْ.

Here, by the downslope of the hills, facing the sunset
and time's muzzle,
near gardens with severed shadows,
we do what the prisoners do,
and what the unemployed do:
we nurture hope.⁶⁸

In "Atadhakkaru al-Sayyāb" (I Recall al-Sayyāb), his more recent poem about the more recent invasion of Iraq, Darwish addresses yet another Iraqi poet, Al-Sayyāb, one of the pioneers of free verse in Arabic poetry; unlike the earlier address to the nameless Iraqi poet, his address to Al-Sayyāb centers on a sequence of remembrances that Darwish's persona reactivates and inscribes. Literally, Darwish's persona bears the burden of Al-Sayyāb's speech and honors it by citing it. Citation is perhaps the most refined form of hospitality and elegy by which Darwish's persona is unsettled and haunted while hunting for an answer for the meaning of poetry after Iraq; Al-Sayyāb's scream, "Iraq, Iraq. Nothing but Iraq," searing in its sadness and honesty, has a performative élan that extends into the present of writing:

أتذكّرُ السّيّابَ، يصرخُ في الخليج سُدَىً:
"عراقٌ، عراقٌ، ليس سوى العراقْ . . . "

I remember Al-Sayyab screaming into the Gulf in vain:
"Iraq, Iraq. Nothing but Iraq . . ."

أتذكّرُ السّيّابَ. إنّ الشعرَ تجربةٌ ومنفى
توأمان. ونحن لم نحلُمْ بأكثر من
حياةٍ كالحياةِ، وأن نموت على طريقتنا

---

66. Darwish, *Ḥālit*, 83, *State*, 167.
67. Darwish, *Ḥālit*, 81, *State*, 167.
68. Darwish, *Ḥālit*, 9, *State*, 120–21.

> I remember Al-Sayyab . . . poetry is experience and exile
> Twins . . . and we didn't dream of more than a life
> as life and to die in our own way[69]

By coming to the succor of the otherwise forgotten scream of Al-Sayyāb, Darwish's poem is indeed, if figuratively, reclaiming and calling for the rescue of Iraq. After all, "The poet cannot free himself from his historical condition [*sharṭahu a-t-tārīkhī*]. But poetry," Darwish contends, "proffers us with a margin of freedom and a figurative compensation for our inability to change reality."[70]

Perhaps poetry after Auschwitz—perhaps poetry after al-Nakba, after al-Naksa, after Iraq, after every massacre and after every genocide—is no more than a melancholy rehearsal or compensatory act of what could have been done or undone. But we cannot but be struck by the tenacity with which poetry dramatizes its attenuation, as if that were its new vocation at a time of cumulative horrors and recursive war aftermaths, as if its attenuation cannot but be accentuated. This might very well be poetry's way of laying siege to its siege, of opening an exile to its exile from the world of nonviolence, but it might as well be poetry's way of envisioning modalities of breaking through the siege of imperial warfare and disaster capitalism.[71] Whether in Qābbanī's, Adonis's, or Darwish's poetry, Adorno's verdict on lyric poetry is appropriated and infused into an untiringly accentuated yet profoundly attenuated search for significance amidst the absurdities of war brutalities. The metapoetic economy that structures most of modern Arabic poetry—cutting across poetic form and meaning, the private and the public, the ethical and the political, the historical and the mythical—largely invalidates even while it consciously accommodates the impossibility of writing lyric poetry in the aftermath of catastrophe. No longer beholden to the aesthetics of redemption that govern the classical and neoclassical marthiya, post-elegiac Arabic poetry figures forth its revolt against normative practices of mourning as a shock of incompleteness, as a mode of total self-relinquishment, and as a conceit of impossibility and afunctionality that dramatizes the sustained duel between form and reality. Ultimately, it is in this fringe or margin of militancy that poetry holds open a transcultural and transnational space for psychosocial and geopolitical transformation in a

---

69. Mahmoud Darwish, "Atadhakkaru al-Sayyāb," *Lā taʿtadhir ʿamma faʿalta* (Beirut: Riad El-Rayyes, 2007), 121, "I Recall al-Sayyāb," *Don't Apologize for What You've Done*, in *Butterfly's Burden*, 281, trans. modified.

70. Darwish, *Ḥayrat*, 149.

71. I have borrowed this felicitous term from Naomi Klein, *The Shock Doctrine: The Rise of Disaster Capitalism* (New York: Metropolitan Books, 2007).

world that continues to be persistently structured around colonial and imperial violence.

While the political and the military convulsions of the Arab world in the aftermath of the Nakba, and especially in the aftermath of the Naksa, confronted Arab poets with the unbearable lightness of their creative endeavors in the face of the overwhelming seriality of defeats at the hands of Israeli settler colonial aggression and American imperial campaigns, the rapid collapse of the Berlin Wall in 1989 and demise of the Soviet Union in 1991 shocked socialists around the world and Arab leftists, in particular, because they were caught since the 1967 Naksa between the Scylla of religious fundamentalism and the Charybdis of state authoritarianism. The dissolution of the USSR as the loadstar of revolutionary socialism since the Bolshevik Revolution of 1917 fomented an immeasurable amount of grief that transformed in part into what several commentators dubbed, following Benjamin, as a form of left-wing melancholy. In the following chapter, I examine the crisis of the Arab left with particular focus on the Egyptian left. I do so by way of a critical analysis of Naguib Mahfouz's compelling 1965 novel, *Al-Shahḥadh (The Beggar)*. I argue that the Arab and Egyptian left more specifically had long before the collapse of the Berlin Wall experienced the rise and consolidation of Nasserism in the decolonization era as an affront to its socialist agenda. The crisis of the leftist intellectual in the mid-1960s that is at the center of Mahfouz's novel becomes therefore of particular relevance to an inquiry into the melancholy disposition that inaugurated and sustained the socialist project during and after the national struggle for liberation.

3
Enduring Left Melancholy
Recasting the Crisis of the Nasserite Intellectual

> Il est forcément mélancolique, ce pari, puisque les dés roulent toujours à contretemps, toujours trop tard, toujours trop tôt, lorsque le nécessaire et le possible ne s'accordent plus ou pas encore.
> — DANIEL BENSAÏD, *LE PARI MÉLANCOLIQUE*

> What lies beyond involves a Leap of Faith, faith in lost Causes, Causes that, from within the space of skeptical wisdom, cannot but appear as crazy.
> — SLAVOJ ŽIŽEK, *IN DEFENSE OF LOST CAUSES*

Mahfouz's *Al-Shahhadh* (الشحّاذ; *The Beggar*) is a wondrous testament to the crisis of the Arab left in general and the Egyptian left in particular. Published in 1965, at the height of the socialist experiment in Nasserite Egypt, this novel tells the story of Omar Al-Hamzawi, a successful lawyer and upper-bourgeois intellectual who succumbs to a devastating psychoaffective crisis when he learns about the approaching release from prison of his old comrade-in-arms, Othman Khalil. Together with Omar and Mustapha Al-Miniyawi, Othman was involved in an underground cell that in the mid-1930s carried out militant operations against the British colonial establishment. In one of these operations, Othman was chosen by lot to throw a bomb at a British target, in the course of which action he was shot in the leg, caught, tortured, and sentenced to more than twenty years behind bars. Unencumbered by their militant past— especially because Othman, despite being tortured, never discloses their names—Omar and Mustapha went on to enjoy successful careers, the former as a lawyer and the latter as a journalist. Now, with Othman's imminent release, Omar is consumed by a sense of debt, guilt, and regret as well as by an incessant and involuntary recall of a revolutionary past he can neither mourn nor ignore.

The narrative follows the unfolding of Omar's psychic disarray, which soon becomes an existential crisis, and an indefatigable search for the mystical experience that would fulfill what he calls the "long-sought ecstasy."[1] In this chapter, I explore how this novel uses the theme of journey to stage the spiritual bankruptcy and political insignificance of the Nasserite intellectual. I argue that *The Beggar*, while it encodes Mahfouz's ongoing quarrel with the military regime, presents Nasserism as both symptom and precipitating cause of the failure of the Egyptian left to apprehend the character of post-1952 Egypt and to elaborate viable alternatives. The crisis that Omar undergoes is, in turn, as much a symptom of as a response to the collapse (and later in the novel, the persistence and indispensability) of leftist worldmaking imaginaries. Broadly speaking, the Arab left is a constellation of communist, Marxist, and even Islamist-leaning movements, parties and groups that initially adhered to a decolonial and nationalist agenda and advocated in the wake of independence a transformational socialist vision. These groups were to different degrees weakened by, among others, the lack of an overarching and unified socialist movement across the Arab world. The Egyptian left in particular was practically marginalized by the emergence of Nasser in the mid-1950s as a popular leader who gradually acquired socialist and revolutionary credentials.

The question that preoccupies Mahfouz in *The Beggar* and in a number of other novels, such *al-Liṣṣ wal-kilāb* (1961; اللص والكلاب; *The Thief and the Dogs*), is apparently a simple one: how has the Egyptian or Arab left dealt, if at all, with its (unfolding) crisis? Of course, such a question is pertinent not only to the Arab left but would also become increasingly relevant to left-wing politics on a global stage, particularly following the dramatic collapse of the Soviet dominated regimes in Eastern Europe in 1989 and the Soviet Union itself in 1991—events which led to the consolidation of the capitalist system and to the emergence of the United States as the only global superpower. Examining the reactions of the left-wing intelligentsia in West Germany to "the unstoppable exit of 'empirical socialism' from the world state," the German

---

1. Naguib Mahfouz, *The Beggar, The Thief and the Dogs, Autumn Quail* (New York: Anchor, 2000), 52.

sociologist Helmut Dubiel suggests that such reactions generally "conform to a pattern that invites psychoanalytic interpretation":

> On the one hand, the postmodern reaction, reflecting a presently erupting trend that sacrifices leftist identity altogether—admittedly the maintenance of which had been a matter of excessive exertion for some time. But in the process, it is not only dead weight that is being thrown overboard, but also the very passenger basket itself. Thus the affair might continue to have the appearance of flight. On the other hand we find those who have been beset by a fear of flying. Instead of pitilessly taking stock of a self-destructing reality, their first concern is preserving their identity. They too are throwing off dead weight. But what characterizes them is the deliberate conscientiousness with which they are doing it. Scrupulously, they make a list of those political and intellectual stocks in the tradition that they want to know are secure against the downdraft caused by the tailspin of empirical socialism.[2]

Drawing on Freud's well-known essay "Mourning and Melancholia" (1915), Dubiel characterizes the first leftist trend as "manic," that is regressive, and the second as "melancholic," that is, melancholite—the former viscerally detaching itself from its leftist identity while the latter narcissistically adhering to it even in the face (or perhaps because) of its virtual implausibility.[3] Dubiel is right in positing that these two psychoaffective dispositions exemplify the failure of the work of mourning (*Trauerarbeit*) on the part of the left-wing intelligentsia. As defined by Freud, the work of mourning entails a rather "piecemeal" and "painful" psychic process at the end of which the mourner would have successfully withdrawn all (libidinal) attachments from the lost object and simultaneously reinvested them in a new object.[4] Dubiel champions the fulfillment of the task of mourning and urges leftists everywhere to work through their manic or melancholite socialist affiliations. For him, as much as for Claus Offe before him, socialism has become an "operationally empty" concept and cannot therefore pave the way to a "post-capitalist state of affairs."[5]

---

2. Helmut Dubiel, "Beyond Mourning and Melancholy on the Left," *Praxis International* 10, nos. 3–4 (1990–91): 241.

3. Ibid., 242.

4. Sigmund Freud, "Mourning and Melancholia," in *On Metapsychology: The Theory of Psychoanalysis*, trans. James Strachey, ed. Angela Richards (London: Penguin Books, 1991), 253.

5. Dubiel, "Beyond Mourning and Melancholy on the Left," 244.

Dubiel's reading of the psychic apparatuses of left-wing intelligentsia through the lenses of mania and melancholia is reminiscent of Walter Benjamin's 1931 scathing critique of Erich Kästner, a left-wing poet from the Weimar Republic. Benjamin traces in Kästner's poetry "a transposition of revolutionary reflexes into objects of distraction, of amusement, which can be supplied for consumption."[6] This "metamorphosis of political struggle from a compulsory decision into an object of pleasure" corresponds, for Benjamin, to a state of "tortured stupidity"—"the latest of two millennia of metamorphoses of melancholy."[7] Unlike Dubiel's generic characterization, left-wing melancholy for Benjamin is specifically a *vicissitude* of melancholia: it represents neither melancholia's full scope (including its productive and empowering potentials) nor its bleak and lethal aspects (such as mania and suicide). Wendy Brown rightly conjectures: "Benjamin treated melancholia itself as something of a creative well-spring. But 'Left melancholia' is Benjamin's unambivalent epithet for the revolutionary hack who is, finally, more attached to a particular political analysis or ideal—even to the failure of that ideal—than to seizing possibilities for radical change in the present."[8] In *The Origin of German Tragic Drama*, Benjamin indeed argues, "Melancholy betrays the world for the sake of knowledge. But in its tenacious self-absorption it embraces dead objects in its contemplation, in order to redeem them."[9] For Benjamin, Hamlet is the exemplar of melancholia's contemplative and redemptive forces precisely because the work of melancholia confronts Hamlet with his own melancholia, which simultaneously awakens in him "the clear light of self-awareness" and inspires his ultimate course of action.[10] Left-wing melancholy, by contrast, enacts a state of political exhaustion in which the involuntary disposition to remember the revolutionary past is unaccompanied by any "corresponding political action" in the present.[11]

I read Mahfouz's *The Beggar* not merely as a proleptic reflection of these global debates about the condition of left-wing politics but also as a creative intervention and reconfiguration, from an Arab and Egyptian perspective, of the stakes involved in these debates. For one thing, socialism in the Arab world

---

6. Walter Benjamin, "Left-Wing Melancholy," in *Selected Writings: Volume 2: 1927–1934* (Cambridge, MA: Belknap Press, 1999), 424.

7. Ibid., 425–26.

8. Wendy Brown, "Resisting Left Melancholia," in *Loss: The Politics of Mourning*, ed. David L. Eng and David Kazanjian (Berkeley: University of California Press, 2003), 458.

9. Walter Benjamin, *The Origin of German Tragic Drama*, trans. John Osborne (New York: Verso, 1998), 157.

10. Ibid., 158.

11. Benjamin, "Left-Wing Melancholy," 425.

has existed in miniaturized and variably experimental forms and constituted more of a promise of a future to come rather than a lived empirical reality. For another, the left-wing Arab intelligentsia has not been offered the luxury of embarking on the project of mourning its revolutionary past at a time when the Arab world has been and continues to be the scene of colonial and imperial campaigns and simultaneously of decolonial insurrection and revolt. While mourning here would amount more or less to the surrender of freedom, sovereignty, and national identity, melancholia stakes a claim to what is unjustly lost in order to redeem it and protest against those who engineered it, be they colonial and imperial powers or oppressive local regimes. Melancholia in the neocolonial and settler colonial contexts of the Arab world is therefore not the preferred choice (over mourning) that can be or has been exercised by Arab leftists but is indeed the very condition of choice itself. The logistical and geopolitical conditions necessary for mourning to become a realistic possibility have yet to materialize; melancholia is in part the only objective alternative left to Arabs and in part an incubational haven for future psychopolitical engagements whose incumbent mandate would be first to transform the indignity of defeat into the fuel of militancy and second to bring about the just, proper, and appropriate conditions of an eventual reconciliatory mourning—all the more so given that melancholia is indeed the apt response to what Freud calls "a loss of a more ideal kind."[12] In the case of Omar in *The Beggar*, the lost object is socialist utopia, which is not a concrete object whose demise can be objectively verified; rather, it is a *promise* whose fulfillment might be frustrated or deferred but whose *force* may live on undiminished. Dubiel's socialism may have become "operationally empty," but its promise of a "post-capitalist state of affairs" remains alive. I do not mean to suggest that this promise is fulfillable in a near or foreseeable future, but I argue that Mahfouz's novel holds open the possibility of its fulfillment. Really, what else could this promise signify nowadays other than the precarious materialization of possibility? And what can literature do other than host and rehearse this possibility, fan out the imagination, and propel the drive toward it?

Given the ideal nature of the promise of socialist utopia, the promise's object transforms at the very moment of its apprehension into an ambient source of melancholia. As Peter Schwenger observes, there is something melancholy about the act of perception itself: "through perception, [an object] is simultaneously apprehended and lost." "This perception, always falling short of full possession," Schwenger further argues, "gives rise to a melancholy that is felt

---

12. Freud, "Mourning and Melancholia," 253.

by the subject and is ultimately *for* the subject."[13] Although this melancholy informs the mode of existence of all physical objects, it is even more pertinent to nonphysical objects, objects such as socialist utopia whose mode of existence is in excess of the melancholy that structures the mode of existence of physical objects. In contradistinction to the melancholy that structures physical objects and holds captive the subject of perception in the process, the melancholy that structures an ideal object is always already a given: the subject is at the outset cognizant of the lack of the ideal object in the world of reality but is wedded to such a cognizance only to the extent that it grounds and enables the pursuit of this ideal object. Melancholia is thus the initiatory and driving force of any socialist project that aspires to a postcapitalist state of affairs. This is to my mind the argument that Mahfouz's *The Beggar* permits us to reach and contemplate. The manic and melancholite reactions of the West German left-wing intelligentsia about which Dubiel speaks are secondary to the melancholia that inaugurates and sustains the founding of the socialist revolutionary project. This melancholia is obviously not the actual foundation of the socialist revolutionary project but is rather coextensive with its foundation and development since it anchors and sustains the psychoaffective investments necessary for its fulfilment. Similarly, Benjamin's left-wing melancholy is but a detour or deviation from the vital role of melancholia in the formation and consolidation of leftist politics. Not infrequently, failing to acknowledge this foundational melancholia, which has for long fueled and cemented the commitment to revolutionary praxis, Arab leftist intellectuals experience the nonfulfillment of the socialist promise, like Mahfouz's protagonist, as a loss of a concrete object, a loss that necessitates the adoption of reactionary or prophylactic strategies of damage control—the kind of manic or melancholite recourses that Dubiel disdains.

The singular venture of Mahfouz's *The Beggar* lies in its attempt to deconstruct and reconfigure these reactionary, manic, and melancholite strategies in light of the foundational and empowering premises of melancholia in relation to the object of socialist promise. Mahfouz's painstaking dramatization of Omar's crisis and reactionary melancholia becomes an occasion to confront Omar with the foundational melancholia that made possible his former socialist commitment in the first place. Insofar as it is a promise whose materialization is projected into the future, the object of socialist struggle can neither be said to be fully obtainable nor completely losable, yet the leftist intellectual experiences it as a concrete object that is always under the threat of being

---

13. Peter Schwenger, *The Tears of Things: Melancholy and Physical Objects* (Minneapolis: University of Minnesota Press, 2006), 2, original italics.

lost even while it can never be said to have been fully possessed. A melancholy dialectic emerges: the relation between the leftist intellectual and the object of socialist promise generates the melancholia of which it is a product. The actual breakup of such a relation, for one reason or another, engenders what might be called reactionary melancholia—really, a second-degree melancholia whose shadow more often than not falls on foundational melancholia and threatens to empty it out of its empowering potency. The epiphany that Omar experiences at the end of the novel—and that reawakens him to reality—constitutes precisely what would have already been the condition of his old socialist struggle: foundational melancholia. This epiphany permits the remetamorphosis or reconversion of reactionary melancholia into foundational melancholia. While Omar's late awakening to foundational melancholia proves liberating, as I argue toward the end of this chapter, his earlier entanglement with reactionary melancholia has proved impoverishing *yet* necessary for his ultimate transformative reckoning.

Rather than simply *resisting* left melancholia, as Wendy Brown seems to suggest in her essay of the same title, Mahfouz's novel calls for the necessity of *enduring* it so that its reactionary direction can be redirected into the service of the foundational melancholia from which the left derives its persisting political potential. What else could be more melancholically empowering for leftist intellectuals at this point in history than to reclaim and reactivate their originary melancholia? There may be no better wager than the wager on the originary wager—all the more so, as the epigraph by Daniel Bensaïd suggests, when the necessary (postcapitalist socialist utopia) is no longer possible at the current historical juncture (global neoliberal dystopia). We ought nonetheless, as Theodor Adorno had so melancholically once urged us, to "patiently trace the ambiguity of melancholy in ever new configurations. Truth is inseparable from the illusory belief that from the figures of the unreal one day, in spite of all, real deliverance will come."[14] From this perspective, it becomes clear that only through a continually unsatisfied melancholic reattachment to and re-enactment of the moment of incubation of the socialist project, could we possibly flesh out the promise of a postcapitalist world order. It is a demand for the impossible, "a Leap of faith, faith in lost Causes," as Žižek maintains.

In this chapter, I trace the genealogy of left melancholia in post-1952 Nasserite Egypt, then examine its configuration in *The Beggar*. Left melancholia functions in Mahfouz's novel as a psychodynamic of disavowal and fetishism—*disavowal* of an insistent revolutionary past that can neither be overcome nor

---

14. Theodor W. Adorno, *Minima Moralia: Reflections from Damaged Life*, trans. E. F. N. Jephcott (London: Verso, 2005), 121–122.

disregarded and *fetishism* of whatever object that might help cushion or deflect its full impact. I read Omar's detour into Sufism—his indefatigable search for ecstasy, whether through whimsical sex or through abstinence from pleasure and devotion to inward contemplation of the heart, the spiritual organ by means of which divine essence is revealed—as an apotheosis of the psychodynamics of disavowal and fetishism. Sufism here can be seen as a form of escapism similar to opium in *Tharthara fawq al-Nīl* (1966; ثرثرة فوق النيل; *Adrift on the Nile*), but Mahfouz is less critical of Sufism than of a condition of enlightened complicity toward which we might all—not just (Arab) leftist intellectuals—be moving. In this pseudo-enlightened condition, we voluntarily abdicate our political choices and responsibilities in the name of soul-searching, nomadism, or any other such alibi that serve to defuse our consciousness of and commitment to our human, historical, and sociopolitical vocation.

Mahfouz cautions us that, along with Omar, we are all becoming beggars, preoccupied with our own particular needs and pursuits, leaving the incumbent task of actuating real change in the sociopolitical sphere to crony politicians and corporate capitalists. "I wonder, with the state so intent on applying its progressive ideals, isn't it better for us to be concerned with our own private affairs?" Mustapha asks Omar rhetorically.[15] Far from being a "novel of compliance" with the Nasserite regime, as Halim Barakat hastily concludes, *The Beggar*, I contend, relays and contests the post-1952 conditions of which compliance is a product. It is not its advocate.[16] What is more, by gradually and steadily deconstructing the affective economies and figures of compliance—such as reactionary melancholia, Sufism, disavowal, and fetishism—Mahfouz's novel fleshes out the promise of transforming Omar's escapism, complicity, and compliance into critical and political defiance.

Genealogies of Left Melancholy

The Arab left refers less to a homogenous or pan-Arab entity than to a broad spectrum of sociopolitical movements, alliances, and factions whose common roots lie in the ideological prism of empirical socialism and the ethos of social equality as much as in the nationalist struggles against European colonialism and settler Zionism. Most of these movements sprang into existence between the two world wars and appealed to intellectuals, workers, and students as well as to anticolonial and nationalist militants and activists. The mass

---

15. Mahfouz, *The Beggar*, 85.
16. Halim Barakat, *The Arab World: Society, Culture, and State* (Berkeley: University of California Press, 1993), 218.

attraction of leftist thought stemmed from its resonance with anticolonial and national liberation struggles in the Arab world, but the actual agendas of the movements have shifted foci over the years even while they preserved a number of constants which have recently coalesced around the resistance to the neoliberal takeover of the economies of the majority of Arab states as well as the resistance to the rise of the religious right and political Islam. Leftists have variously promoted social welfare, pressed for the redistribution of wealth, and called for communist seizures of the means of production as well as for the concretization of the vision of a classless society. Additionally, they generally professed secular and progressive approaches to personal status law and gender issues, freedom of expression and assembly, and so on.

The pressing priority on the agendas of the early leftist movements that took shape between the two world wars was arguably the anticolonial struggle for national liberation.[17] As the well-known Egyptian socialist Salama Moussa used to say, "Independence is our first goal and socialism is our second."[18] The extent to which the Arab nationalist struggles for independence have been informed by Marxist, socialist, and leftist latencies may not have been sufficiently discernible for the generation of Salama Moussa. Indeed, it may very well be the case, as Joel Beinin and Zachary Lockman have argued, that, because of the inextricable relation between Egyptian capitalism and British colonialism from 1882 to 1956, most leftist agitations and labor "demands for greater autonomy and respect in the workplace were seen as part of the nationalist struggle."[19] The nationalist struggle in Egypt, as elsewhere in the Arab world, can be said to have appropriated attention away from the leftist and socialist struggles with which it so closely converged and merged.

The economic demands for higher wages and better working conditions as well as for social justice writ large became more pronounced in the post-World War II period and particularly after the 1952 revolutionary coup by the "free officers." Not surprisingly, the majority of the Egyptian left condoned the ouster of the monarchy and contributed productively to the Revolutionary Command Council's immediate policy measures, especially the land reform

---

17. The more or less standard chronology of the Egyptian left among historians, researchers, and former militants is as follows: *al-ḥaraka al-'ūla*, or the first movement (from the mid-1920s, and the establishment of the first party, to the early 1930s); *al-ḥaraka al-thāniya*, or the second movement (from the 1940s to the mid-1960s); and *al-ḥaraka al-thālitha*, or the third movement (from mid-1960s to the present).

18. See Hasan Yusuf, *Al-Mufakkir Al-Ishtiraki fi fikr Naguib Mahfouz* [The socialist thinker in Naguib Mahfouz's thought] (Cairo: Dar Al-'Alim Al-Thalith, 2005), 14.

19. Joel Beinin and Zachary Lockman, *Workers on the Nile: Nationalism, Communism, Islam, and the Egyptian Working Class, 1882–1954* (London: IB Tauris & Co., 1988), 450.

program inaugurated in September 1952. This otherwise sanguine collaborative prospect proved no more than a temporary appeasement, for the seeds of an eventual face-off with the ruling Revolutionary Command Council (RCC) were sown as early as August 12, 1952, during a labor strike at the Misr Fine Spinning and Weaving Company at Kafr al-Dawwar, about nineteen miles south of Alexandria. Leftists, communists, and trade unionists were outraged by RCC's deployment of the army to violently suppress the August 13 demonstration by the textile workers, killing four demonstrators, injuring dozens, and arresting hundreds, some of whom were varyingly sentenced to hard labor while the two alleged leaders, Mustafa Khamis and Muhammad al-Baqari, were sentenced to death by an ad hoc military tribunal and hanged on the premises of the textile factory on September 7 in order to deter further labor mobilizations and agitations.[20]

By the end of 1952, the military regime started a clampdown on leftist media and went on to abolish all political parties by January 1953, which resulted in a litany of arrests, detentions, trials as well as demonstrations. HADETU, or the Democratic Movement for National Liberation (DMNL), the main branch of the Egyptian left, lost no time in denouncing the new military regime as "fascistic," despite its overall support of the RCC before (and well beyond) the Kafr al-Dawwar events.[21] Egyptian politics gradually leaned afterward toward the right, partly because the right wing was never completely neutralized and partly because the RCC "began to take measures to isolate the communists in its own ranks and remove them from all positions of power," a tendency that culminated in a brutal crackdown on leftist and communist movements between 1959 and 1964.[22] Ironically, though, it was during this large-scale crackdown and torture of leftists and communists that Nasser would start to veer leftward (as if it were necessary to persecute the leftists in order to emulate, dissimulate and assimilate them at once).

---

20. See Selma Botman, *The Rise of Egyptian Communism, 1939–1970* (Syracuse, NY: Syracuse University Press, 1988), 123–139.

21. James Jankowski, *Nasser's Egypt, Arab Nationalism, and the United Arab Republic* (Boulder, CO: Lynne Rienner, 2001), 21. Yet, notwithstanding their criticism of the ruling RCC, "when the communists began to reassess their attitude toward the regime in 1955, the impetus lay primarily in the government's anti-imperialist foreign policy. Therefore, the economic struggle of the working class and other social questions became largely subordinated to the task of uniting with the regime against the imperialist enemy," see Joel Beinin, *Was the Red Flag Flying There?: Marxist Politics and the Arab-Israeli Conflict in Egypt and Israel, 1948–1965* (Berkeley: University of California Press, 1990), 91.

22. Beinin and Lockman, *Workers on the Nile*, 426.

Nasser's popularity became overwhelming in the aftermath of the 1955 Bandung Conference and the 1956 Suez War, both of which brought him worldwide acclaim and conferred on him a leadership role of the Third World and the nonaligned movement, along with Tito and Nehru. Nasser's embodiment of a revolutionary leader of Arab nationalism was cemented by the union with Syria in 1958 and the formation of the United Arab Republic (UAR). The formation of the UAR caused panic among Syrian communists and further divided the Egyptian left and cast doubt over its revolutionary credentials. The tendency to collapse the differences between socialism and communism by the detractors of the Egyptian left undermined the credibility of its noncommunist adherents and practitioners. What further isolated and diminished the legitimacy of the Egyptian left was the oppositional vitality and mass appeal of the anticommunist Muslim Brotherhood, which was not banned until January 1954. Ironically, though, even the Brothers' targeting of Nasser for assassination—and Nasser's impromptu assertion that "if Gamal Abdel Nasser shall die, each of you shall be Gamal Abdel Nasser"—only added to Nasser's revolutionary legitimacy and self-esteem.[23] Leftists and Islamists alike were weakened and marginalized by the emergence of Nasser as a populist leader and prime architect of the 1952 revolutionary coup, as illustrated by his slim book-cum-manifesto *The Philosophy of the Revolution* (*falsafat al-thawrah*; فلسفة الثورة), published in September 1954; allegedly, the book was put together by Nasser's confidant and vocal supporter, the prominent journalist Mohammed Hassanein Heikal.

Leftist movements' sectarianism and fragmentation stem partly from their centralized leadership and partly from their intellectual dependency on Soviet-style socialism and international Marxism, which resulted in plural and at times conflictual interpretations, Cold War conspiratorial visions, and divisive organizational stratagems. In an interview with Hala Halim, Egyptian leftist intellectual Ibrahim Fathi recalls his move to Cairo and recounts how shocked he was by the disunity of the capital's communist milieu: "I had thought there was only one and the same communism in the whole world, but in Cairo I was shocked to find that there are many different organisations, that each one accuses the others of treason."[24] Repeated attempts to urge rival communist movements to move beyond factional contentions and ad hoc coalitions and create an opposition bloc to the threat of long-term military rule finally came to fruition in January 1958 with the formation of the Communist Party of Egypt (الحزب الشيوعي المصري). The consensus among communists, however, was not

---

23. Jankowski, *Nasser's Egypt*, 25.
24. Hala Halim, "Ibrahim Fathi: Curbstone Critic," *Ahram Weekly*, 5–11 (September 2002).

so much to oppose as to support the decolonial endeavors of the post-Suez Nasserite regime and even "to subordinate the struggle for democracy and socialism to the formation of a 'popular front' against imperialism."[25] Be that as it may, the unification of communists proved short-lived: the party ended up reproducing the perennial doctrinal disputes that dogged communists since times past; it split by the end of 1958 over deep disagreements caused by the Iraqi revolution of July 1958. In the meanwhile, the formation of the UAR appeased Nasser's distrust of the communists who largely aligned with his vision of pan-Arabism as an antidote to imperialism, especially in the wake of the Eisenhower Doctrine of January 1957, which sanctioned America's interventionist policy in the region as the guardian of Western interests after the tripartite Suez fiasco.[26] Ironically, while the Eisenhower Doctrine viewed Nasser as a communist agent, Nasser was worried and wearied by the threat of a communist takeover in the Hashemite Kingdom, since the Iraqi communists are the ardent allies of the leader of the new revolution, Abd al-Karim Qassim, an outspoken opponent of Nasser's expansionist pan-Arabism.

With the exception of the DMNL, the majority of Egyptian communists threw their support behind Qassim and their Iraqi comrades, which incensed Nasser and reignited his obsessive distrust of the communists. Nasser was so entangled in the inter-Arab strategic and precarious game of Cold War military and political power jockeying that he perceived all forms of internal dissent, or even critical and conditional support, as forms of disloyalty; on day one of 1959, he embarked on a merciless campaign of repression of communists whose endgame is the elimination of Egyptian Marxism altogether. Hundreds of communists were subjected to arrest, imprisonment, and torture, including Shuhdi Attia al-Shafie, a visionary activist and organic intellectual, who died under torture on June 15, 1960, in the notorious Abu Zaabal prison, a concertation camp in the Egyptian desert known as *maqbarat al-ḥayāt*, or the cemetery of the living. Shuhdi is widely remembered and lauded by his communist comrades in their fictional and nonfictional works as a symbol of what Anouar Abdel-Malek calls the "mutilation" of Egyptian Marxism.[27] Nasser did

---

25. Brecht De Smet, *A Dialectical Pedagogy of Revolt: Gramsci, Vygotsky, and the Egyptian Revolution* (Leiden: Brill, 2015), 167. See also Gennaro Gervasio, *al-Ḥaraka al-mārkisiyya fī miṣr (1967–1981)*, trans. Basma Muḥammad 'Abd al-Raḥmān and Carmine Cartolano (Cairo: al-Markaz al-qawmī li-l-tarjama, 2010), 23.

26. For more on the interventionist-imperial scope of the Eisenhower Doctrine, see chapter 5 and 6 of Saïd K. Aburish, *Nasser: The Last Arab* (New York: St. Martin's Press/Thomas Dunne Books, 2004).

27. The great Egyptian Marxist sociologist Anouar Abdel-Malek devotes his major work on Nasserite Egypt to "the fraternal memory of Shohdi Attia el-Shafei, who brought honor to our

not release the communists from concentration camps and prisons until Nikita Khrushchev's widely acclaimed and much celebrated two-week visit to Egypt in May 1964 for the official inauguration of the construction of the Aswan High Dam.

As Abdel-Malek recounts, "never before had the people of Egypt hailed a foreign visitor with so much fervor and enthusiasm. Here was a visitor in whom the Egyptian people saw the standard bearer of socialism, the representative of the state that had halted the aggressor at Suez and done everything to ensure the success of the Aswan High Dam."[28] Indeed, the building of the Aswan High Dam with Soviet funding and technical design goes a long way to explaining Nasser's drift into the Soviet communist orbit. There is also the collapse of the UAR after a military uprising in Damascus by aggrieved Syrian army units on September 28, 1961, which reclaimed Syrian autonomy. Syrian secession affected Nasser so deeply that he made a radical political reorientation toward Arab socialism—"an ambitious if quixotic reform agenda fusing Arab nationalism and Soviet-inspired socialism."[29] Nasser paid little attention to the quasi-colonial manner in which he ruled over Syrians but "came to the conclusion that Egypt and Syria had failed to achieve the degree of social reform necessary for such an ambitious Arab unity scheme to work."[30] The radical reform agenda Nasser embarked on revolved around the Soviet model of state-led economy; it resumed and accelerated the nationalization of private enterprise begun in the aftermath of the 1956 Suez Crisis.

While the Cold War geostrategic rationale for the leftward and pan-Arabist drift of post-Suez Nasserite Egypt cannot be overstated, the regime co-opted and institutionalized the oppositional valences of the Egyptian left and labor movement, especially since Nasser had already encouraged the creation of an Arab Socialist Union and a Ministry of Labor. Nasser carefully maintained his margin for maneuver in internal and international affairs even at the height of the socialist experiment. "By adopting a policy of [positive] neutralism he manipulated both American and Soviet interests, utilizing their conflict to his own advantage."[31] Unlike empirical socialism in China or Cuba, Nasserite socialism was, like its cognates across the Arab world, more of a tactical Cold

---

generation and who was my friend." Abdel-Malek, *The Army Regime, The Left, and Social Change under Nasser*, trans. Charles Lam Markmann (New York: Random House, 1968), 133.

28. Ibid., 349.
29. Eugene Rogan, *The Arabs: A History* (New York: Basic Books, 2011), 321.
30. Ibid.
31. Rami Ginat, *Egypt's Incomplete Revolution: Lutfi Al-Khuli and Nasser's Socialism in the 1960s* (London: Frank Cass, 1997), 195.

War ploy in response to Euro-American and Zionist encroachments rather than a deliberative strategy for democratizing and modernizing the postcolonial state. The May 1962 National Charter, which sought to weld together Islam, Arab socialism, and socialism into a coherent triptych, gave rise to the only official political party in Egypt, the Arab Socialist Union. Not only was the evolution into socialism supposed to occur without socialists but also without class conflict and without social dialectic.[32] Much to the left's chagrin, Nasser's doctrine of Arab socialism boiled down to state ownership and management of the means of production, which resulted in the largescale nationalization of key sectors of the industry, finance, and commerce. The aforementioned nationalization of the British and French companies in Egypt, which led to the Suez War of 1956, set a precedent for many later seizures and sequestrations of private property by the Nasserite regime.

Curiously enough, Nasser's socialist turn gained momentum well before Khrushchev's visit and at a time when communists were behind bars. His dislike of organized Marxism did not seem to contradict his endorsement of nationalist socialism, which he perceived as a pragmatic and étatist means "to combat conditions which would lead to communism."[33] While many communists looked favorably at Nasser's socialist turn and retained the promise of a productive and organic fusion between nationalists and leftists, their "enforced alienation from the actual political situation" reduced their posture "to theorizing about reality, but not changing it."[34] Given that they neither enlisted mass support nor developed a Pan-Arab party—and given that Islamist groups in Egypt and throughout the Arab world professed anticommunism while most pan-Arabist movements and Arab regimes felt threatened and delegitimized by the encroachments of international Marxism and Leninism alike—Egyptian leftists (namely, the two main communist parties, DMNL and ECP) were left with little margin for maneuver, and eventually succumbed to the "practical pressures from the regime to dissolve," which they did in 1965 in the hope "that socialism was possible in Egypt through Nasser."[35]

By the time Mahfouz wrote *The Beggar* in the mid-1960s, he was fully aware of the mood of despondency that had swept the Egyptian left, which faced the choice of either hitching its wagon to Nasserism (understood as a mishmash of anticolonialism, pan-Arabism, and noncommunist socialism) or going underground and facing persecution. The disenchantment with Nasserism was

---

32. Abdel-Malek, *The Army Regime*, 378–79.
33. Ibid., 197
34. Botman, *The Rise of Egyptian Communism*, 144–45.
35. Ibid., 145.

a déjà-vu experience for Mahfouz since 1959, when he resumed writing and when Nasser began literally hunting down the members of an entire generation of leftists. "The severe repression of 1959," Anouar Abdel-Malek contends, "affected not only Marxists but progressive groupings in general. The attempt to destroy this body of thought and action was to bring about a general crisis in all fields of intellectual and political life."[36] As in Sonallah Ibrahim's *67*, which I discussed in chapter 1, the betrayal of promises and democratic ideals on the part of the Nasserite regime has de facto transposed into a mode of social intelligibility in society at large. Likewise, leftist normalization or accommodation with the regime or the upper bourgeoisie is a form of betrayal. But while Ibrahim banalizes betrayal to shock and awaken the reader, Mahfouz adopts a more cautious approach which views betrayal as the exception and not the norm.

Mahfouz's *The Thief and the Dogs* stages the theme of betrayal of leftist and revolutionary thought on the part of some members of the Egyptian intelligentsia. Said Mahran, a thief with something of Robin Hood in him, is betrayed not only by his wife and friend but also by Rauf Ilwan, his leftist mentor and comrade. From a scribbler in an obscure magazine, *Al-Nadhir*—and from a socialist who once reassured Said "that what is taken by theft should be retrieved by theft"[37]—Rauf had climbed the social ladder overnight and become an upper bourgeois and careerist columnist working for a mainstream newspaper, *Al-Zahra*. Not only had he become the beneficiary of a system he once philosophized against, but he had also become its agent, one of the "dogs" that force Said to surrender for his vindictive misfires, which are reminiscent of Hamlet's killing Polonius instead of Claudius. Mahfouz majestically straddles the conventional divide here between family or social betrayal and leftist or political betrayal. He emphasizes, however, the enormity of leftist betrayal—"a betrayal so vile," in the words of Said, "that if the whole Muqattam hill toppled over and buried it, I still would not be satisfied."[38]

While Omar Al-Hamzawi in *The Beggar* shares more or less the past leftist activism and late bourgeois status of Rauf Ilwan, he is not as oblivious as Rauf to the fact that the bourgeois status is a betrayal. Moreover, if Rauf typifies opportunistic compliance with the new regime—much as Mustapha al-Minyawi does in *The Beggar*—Omar remains the new regime's tragic conscript. He is a deserter, a renegade, and an escapist of sorts, but only in the sense that he is diurnally interpellated by a leftist past that he can neither put

36. Abdel-Malek, *The Army Regime*, xxii.
37. Mahfouz, *The Beggar*, 232.
38. Ibid., 181.

to rest nor completely disregard. Unlike Said Mahran, whose revolutionary struggle in the name of the poor and powerless morphs into a futile pursuit of personal vendetta, Omar languishes in a liminal state of melancholy self-impoverishment, oscillating between, on the one hand, disavowals of his past leftist engagement, and, on the other, recessive entanglements in the resurrectionary and insurrectionary returns of this very past's unexorcised phantoms. While Said's hopeless struggle matches only the promise of freedom and social egalitarianism that inaugurated it, Omar's melancholy ambivalence symptomizes the demise of this very promise. Insofar as he experiences the nonfulfillment of the promise of socialist utopia as an object loss, Omar wallows under the shadow of reactionary melancholia, oscillating between manic detachment from and narcissistic attachment to his revolutionary past.

In both *The Thief and the Dogs* and *The Beggar*, Mahfouz dramatizes the persistent demand for socialist revolution even while stressing how localized and splintered it has become, being, as it were, contingent upon isolated cases of individual suffering (as in the case of Said Mahran and Othman Khalil) rather than organized around a movement against systematic injustice and inequality. The revolutionary elite (Rauf Ilwan, Mustapha al-Minyawi, and Omar Al-Hamzawi), whose task is to educate and mobilize the masses toward revolutionary action, have gone back on their commitments. Little wonder that Othman Khalil asks Omar during their first encounter after Othman's release from prison, "Be frank with me, my dear friend. Are you a true believer as you once were?" Aware of his betrayal but trying to preserve a patina of respectability, Omar responds thusly: "I was until the Revolution broke out, then I felt reassured, began losing interest in politics, and turned in another direction."[39] Notwithstanding its seductive appeal, the bulk of this argument falters under Othman's probing gaze. Having sacrificed twenty years behind bars for the sake of socialist utopia, Othman holds fast to his principles, pointing out to Omar and Mustapha that it is still absolutely necessary (ḍarūra ḥatmiya)—indeed, never more to be desired than at a time when the Nasserite regime has become a defaced simulacrum of the ancien régime.[40] Filled with recrimination and resentment, Othman rages against Omar and Mustapha, scrupulously scrutinizing their many lamentable travesties: "If you hadn't trusted into hiding, you wouldn't have lost the field."[41] "Just because you have changed doesn't

---

39. Ibid., 115.
40. Ibid., 120.
41. Ibid., 115.

mean truth has changed."[42] "How pathetic. . . . I can't believe how degenerate you've both become."[43]

Buoyed by an undiminished utopian vision, particularized and kept intact by his long experience of "classless" life among prisoners, Othman's impulsive reaction to Omar's and Mustapha's accommodation with the regime and abdication of their responsibilities as custodians of revolutionary struggle may very well symbolize leftist critique par excellence.[44] Yet, given its anachronism, it reflects or symptomizes rather what Brown calls a "reproachful moralizing sensibility."[45] The cruelty of Othman's critique may stem not only from the hopelessness of his moralizing exhortation to revolutionary action in the face of the deterrent powers of the Nasserite regime, but from its latent operation as "a strange substitute for action."[46] Othman's fidelity to his principles is far from hypocritical, but his complaint reveals the profound disempowerment of the leftist position. Disavowing such disempowerment and claiming the moral high ground may end up foreclosing rather than keeping open the possibilities for transformative action or radical change in the sociopolitical sphere.

The danger of Othman's moralizing enterprise is that it tends to slip into the self-impoverishing rhetoric of leftist impotence it seeks to repudiate. Its incitement to action might be read paradoxically as a sign of the broken promise of socialist revolution. While it limns an otherwise galvanizing leftist moral and political vision, it remains incapable of enlisting the support of either Omar or Mustapha, notwithstanding their past leftist activism. Clinging to the habits of mind of a prerevolutionary leftist position, for which no compelling alternatives have been forged, Othman experiences his commitment more as an entitlement to rather than a demand for revolution, mistaking the *promise* for the *object of the promise*. Meanwhile, he apprehends neither the character of Nasserite Egypt, particularly its preemptive assimilation of socialist rhetoric into its revolutionary apparatus, nor the pervasive crisis of the Arab left of which he is a product and to which his resentment bears witness. In this sense, Othman is no less melancholic than Omar, but while Othman narcissistically disavows the demise of the old leftist position, Omar manically denies his very attachment to it. In other words, if Othman's undifferentiated identification with his old leftist position is inextricably bound up with the imperative to preserve his leftist identity, Omar's proscribed identification with that position

---

42. Ibid., 120.
43. Ibid., 121.
44. Ibid., 118.
45. Wendy Brown, *Politics out of History* (Princeton, NJ: Princeton University Press, 2001), 21.
46. Mahfouz, *The Beggar*, 40.

figures forth the identity crisis and the psychoaffective disarray and disorientation of the Egyptian left.

Manifestations of Left Melancholy

The Beggar begins with a poignantly compelling scene of Omar sitting in a doctor's waiting room, contemplating a painting of a child riding a wooden horse:

> White clouds floated in the blue expanse overlooking a vast green land where cows grazed serenely. . . . In the foreground a child, mounted on a wooden horse, gazed toward the horizon, a mysterious semi-smile in his eyes . . . he liked the searching child, the tranquil cows. . . . There the child looks at the horizon, and how tightly it grips the earth, closes in upon the earth from any angle you observe it. What an infinite prison. Why the wooden horse, why the cows so full of tranquility?[47]

Appropriating a technique most commonly used in film, *The Beggar* starts in medias res and then unfolds chronologically. Antedating the beginning of the novel is the scene in which Omar encounters a client who most memorably rebukes him for worrying that the government might confiscate the client's land. Omar asks the client: "Suppose you win the case today and possess the land only to have it confiscated tomorrow by the government?" The client responds in a way that would mark Omar's life indelibly: "All that matters is that we win the case. Don't we live our lives knowing full well that it is going to be taken away by God?"[48] Retrospectively, Omar believes that these words precipitated his disease, which in turn prompted him to see his old friend and doctor, Hamid Sabry. The beginning of the novel coincides with his visit to the doctor's office where, while awaiting his turn, he reflects on the painting of the child riding a wooden horse. As in *The Thief and the Dogs*, where he originally put it to full use, Mahfouz draws extensively here on the stream of consciousness technique which was most notoriously brought to perfection by James Joyce in *Ulysses*, a novel that Mahfouz castigated as "terrible."[49] Although Mahfouz dismisses Joyce and the excessive psychologism that permeates his novel, rendering it nothing more than "licensed chaos" (الفوضى المباحة), he includes what he calls a "Joycean moment" in the life of

---

47. Ibid., 6–7.
48. Ibid., 40–41; trans. modified [ألسنا نعيش حياتنا ونحن نعلم أنّ الله سيأخذها].
49. Mahfouz, *Ataḥaddathu Ilaykum*, 94.

his protagonist at certain narrative junctures.[50] What we witness in the aforementioned opening scene is just such a Joycean moment in which the reader is given access to the interior thoughts and desires of Omar while he reflects on the painting.

The opening scene offers us a very important segue into Omar's unfolding psychoaffective crisis following his chance encounter with the litigant and the alleged onset of his disease. Omar's nonchalant gaze at the painting quickly spills over into a consuming concern—really, a hobbyhorse of sorts which he couldn't fully relinquish. The word *hobbyhorse*, as the Merriam-Webster online dictionary has it, may denote "a stick having an imitation horse's head at one end that a child pretends to ride" or may convey the more contemporary sense of "a topic to which one constantly reverts." Interestingly enough, the two meanings overlap here: the insouciant child riding his hobbyhorse adds but more grist to the mill of Omar's metaphysical obsession with death which was set running in full throttle following his chance encounter with the client. Before Omar leaves the doctor's office, he examines the painting one more time, as if he were expecting a change in the child's posture. Alas, "the child was still riding his wooden horse, gazing at the horizon.... The horizon still closed in upon the earth."[51] Back at home, his thoughts drift again to the painting, delivering a final judgment, no less perplexing and gloomy than the earlier ones: "The child imagines he's riding a real horse. 'He was exasperated, he is exasperated, be exasperated, so he is exasperated, she is exasperated, and the plural is they are exasperated.'"[52] Clearly, the hobbyhorse cannot be forgotten; it will keep intruding at different phases and under different guises in Omar's unfolding crisis. Mahfouz uses the interior monologue to draw attention to what he calls "moments of ill-health" or morbidity (لحظات مرضيّة) in the life of his protagonist.[53] Throughout *The Beggar*, this device acts as an economic stylistic register of Omar's psychoaffective convulsions.

I shall return to Omar's obsession with his client's words, his subsequent existential crisis and search for the secret of life and long-sought-after ecstasy, but suffice it to mention here that Omar is gripped by what Freud calls "a revolt ... against mourning."[54] At first "he [likes] the searching child, the tranquil cows," but he cannot help but color the scene with a lyrical sensibility,

---

50. Ibid., 105, 95.
51. Mahfouz, *The Beggar*, 15.
52. Ibid., 19. [ضجر يضجر أضجر فهو ضجر وهي ضجرة والجميع ضجرون وضجرات].
53. Mahfouz, *Atahaddathu Ilaykum*, 106.
54. Freud, "On Transience," in *Art and Literature*, trans. James Strachey (London: Penguin Books, 1990), 288.

worthy of the poet still throbbing inside him. Now he perceives only the "infinite prison" that engulfs the child and the earth, in a way reminiscent of Hamlet's similar verdict on Denmark and the world.[55] Omar's perception of the painting is traversed by his foreknowledge of the transience of the romantic world of oblivious joy it evokes, a world irrecoverably lost to him. But on many occasions, he expresses his fascination with this quasi-Nietzschean world of productive forgetting,[56] or of "bestial oblivion" as Hamlet would put it,[57] which the grazing cows and the child riding his wooden horse incarnate. For instance, when in Alexandria, Omar writes the following to his friend Mustapha: "Buthayna is happy—how I wish I could read her mind—but the happiest of us all is certainly Jamila, who as yet understands nothing.... I met a mad man.... I wish I could have read his mind, too."[58] If Omar longs for this world of blissful ignorance or exquisite madness, then what must have troubled him about the painting is that it actually bears witness to such longing whose object loss he can neither recover nor recover from. Hence, his perception of the painting becomes nothing but the outward projection of the "infinite prison" within—a heap of broken promises and dead dreams, belatedly conjugated and dispersed into the grammar of exasperation (*dajar*).

The world that the painting conjures up could be catalogued under the same rubric as Omar's past promissory world of love and romance, socialist utopia, committed art, leftist engagement, and organized struggle. In the same letter to Mustapha, he writes:

> By chance I overheard a conversation between two lovers in the dark ... God, what a long time has passed without love! All that is left are *mummified memories* [!؟ذكريات محنّطة]. How I would like to sneak into the heart of a lover. As you know, Zeinab has been my only love; but that was more than twenty years ago.... However, the memory of insanity is not like insanity itself—the feverish thoughts, volcanic heart, and sleepless nights. Agony lifted me to poetic ecstasies. Tears streamed from my eyes and I approached heaven. But these are no more than *mummified memories*.... Honestly, I've lost interest in everything. Let them take the three apartment buildings and the revenues. I won't claim that the principles which once nearly landed

---

55. Mahfouz, *The Beggar*, 68.

56. Friedrich Nietzsche, *Unfashionable Observations*, trans. Richard Gray (Stanford, CA: Stanford University Press, 1995), 89.

57. William Shakespeare, *Hamlet*, ed. Susanne L. Wofford (Boston: Bedford Books, 1994) 115; 4.4.40.

58. Mahfouz, *The Beggar*, 23–24.

us in jail along with Othman make it easy to accept, for those days of strife are themselves no more than *mummified memories*.⁵⁹

Along with the painting in the opening scene, this letter has a powerful proleptic force, conveying Omar's unfolding affective ambivalence toward the past and anticipating his future detour into Sufism. His mental condition may invite psychoanalytic interpretation, but it defies any analytic pattern, running the spectrum of affects from mourning and manic detachment to nostalgia, melancholite, and melancholic attachments. No sooner do we get the sense that Omar is nostalgic for the past (about which he speaks with warm and pastoral imaginativeness) than he declares that the past is no more than a cluster of "mummified memories," no more than an accumulated dead weight whose burden he has cast off. This magic release from the past is undercut by his intense repetition or overfiguration of the expression "mummified memories" (*dhikrayat muḥannaṭa*), which suggests that the release is incomplete. Far from exemplifying his complete detachment from the past, Omar's letter to Mustapha is suggestive of an unfolding affective response to this very detachment. This response unravels Omar's ungrieved and ungrievable alienation from the ideal objects of his mummified memories—objects that embed not only his love for Zeinab and his dreams of socialist utopia but also his passion for writing poetry and his commitment to socialist struggle. While these same objects can be said to have precipitated the formation of his new identity as a lawyer in post-1952 Egypt, they have become quite inaccessible to him beyond their haunting insistence on his psyche and their simultaneous withdrawal into the fractured horizon of loss and longing. How does Omar then sustain a sense of belonging in the wake of this ache of longing?

Omar's longing is at two removes from the foundational melancholia that must have inaugurated and sustained his youthful pursuit of socialist utopia, a pursuit that nearly landed him and Mustapha in jail along with Othman. First, Omar does not reckon with the persistence or *endurance* of this originary melancholia in his longing for the cluster of ecstatic effects the "mummified objects" used to generate. Benjamin asks, "What . . . does the 'intellectual elite' discover as it begins to take stock of its feelings? Those feelings themselves? They have long since been remaindered."⁶⁰ Omar has not yet taken stock of the "feelings" (i.e., foundational melancholia) that went hand in hand with his former commitment to socialist struggle, a struggle whose object (i.e., socialist utopia) was lacking from the outset, and has thereafter

---

59. Mahfouz, *The Beggar*, 25–26, trans. modified, italics mine
60. Benjamin, "Left-Wing Melancholy," 424–25.

continually fallen short of full possession. The socialist project is clearly inaugurated by a melancholic longing for the possible materialization of a postcapitalist state of affairs that has proved necessary yet elusive, neither fully possessed nor completely lost. In a book of the same title, Daniel Bensaïd calls this melancholic longing for what is necessary yet impossible, *le pari mélancolique*, the melancholic wager. "This wager cannot but be melancholy—given that the dice always rolls out in an untimely manner, either too late, or too early—when the necessary and the possible no longer or not yet converge."[61] Second, Omar experiences his alienation from the objects whose effects he cherishes as an alibi to construct them as lost. Omar's longing does not follow the normal process of mourning, whereby libidinal investments are withdrawn from lost objects and lavished onto fresh ones. Nor does it follow Freud's conceptualization of melancholia, whereby lost objects are recuperated through an economy of identification mounted by the ego of the bereaved subject. Given the *incomplete* loss of the objects whose effects he seeks, Omar constructs them *as lost*. Yet constructing these objects as lost does not result in mourning since in order for mourning to occur and be accomplished the loss has to be complete (which is neither the case with, for instance, Zeinab who is still around nor with socialist utopia, which, while apparently lost, continues to exist by other means, namely as a force of social justice and of leftist critique and the like and cannot therefore be fully mourned). What transpires instead is a twisted process of manic detachment or reactionary melancholia whereby melancholia mediates Omar's "capacity," in the words of Giorgio Agamben, "to make an unobtainable object appear as if lost."[62] Indeed, socialist utopia, as an object of his former leftist commitment, could not be said to have been obtained in order to be then declared lost; what is more, even the construction of socialist utopia as lost does not warrant its abandonment, since the initial pursuit of the utopia was conditioned and set in motion by the acknowledgment of its very lack; finally, socialist utopia is not prior to the initiatory melancholia of which it is a product and, simultaneously, a driving force.

Whether in his manic detachment from the object of his former leftist commitment or in his narcissistic attachment to the ecstasies it once produced, Omar bathes in reactionary melancholia, which is at two removes from the productive melancholia that must have anchored and enabled his old socialist struggle. Unlike Freud's melancholic subject who simulates the continued

---

61. Daniel Bensaïd, *Le pari mélancolique: Métamorphoses de la politique, politique des métamorphoses* (Paris: Fayard, 1997), 14–15.

62. Giorgio Agamben, *Stanzas: Word and Phantasm in Western Culture*, trans. Ronald L. Martinez (Minneapolis: University of Minnesota Press, 1993), 20.

existence of an irrecoverably lost object, Omar's brand of left melancholia feigns the loss of his unmasterable objects but longs for the effects they used to create. What Omar longs for is not Zeinab, who once defied her family and converted to Islam in order to marry him, but the experience of love she evokes in him; nor is poetry writing, which he considers a thing of the past, the locus of his longing but the upheavals of emotion that the writing experience generates in him; and, above all, he yearns no longer for direct socialist engagement but for the transcendental dreams and impersonal pursuits to which such engagement gives rise. Yet, what would break the hold of longing except the cultivation of the objects that Omar holds at bay against the incessant returns of the leftist past by which he is held at bay?

Sufi Detours

Omar's longing for forgone ecstasies bespeaks a brand of left melancholia that disavows the very objects whose significance it fetishizes. Perhaps nothing more attests to the psychodynamics of disavowal and fetishism than Omar's tireless search for what he initially calls in his letter to Mustapha ثرثرة لا نهائية (*tharthara lā-nihā'iya*; "endless chatter").[63] His search, prompted by his client's words—"Don't we live our lives knowing full well that it is going to be taken away by God?"—soon finds utterance in a rich battery of Sufi metaphors such as نشوة (*nashwa*; ecstasy) or يقين (*yaqīn*; intuitive certitude), or variations on both. Being too unpregnant of his past revolutionary cause, Omar wants to experience the ecstasy of revelation it used to mediate without investing enough stamina in the accomplishment—that is, without subscribing to the tenets of socialist struggle on which Othman insists still. Hence his detour into Sufism: an attempt on Omar's part to experience the ecstasy of divine revelation *directly* and without any corresponding concern for or involvement with sociopolitical reality. Benjamin's terse dismissal of what he calls the "flight into theosophy" is relevant here: "Never have such comfortable arrangements been made in such an uncomfortable situation."[64] *The Beggar* suggests a counterintuitive connection between the crisis of the Arab left and the resurgence of Sufism in post-1952 Egypt.

By no means am I saying that Mahfouz empties Sufism of its spiritual and sociocultural valences, nor of its vital challenge to orthodoxy, or its long political history—including its contribution to the resistance to European colonial conquests. Sufism played an important role in the 1881 Mahdist revolt

---

63. Mahfouz, *The Beggar*, 23; trans. modified.
64. Benjamin, "Left-Wing Melancholy," 425.

against Anglo-Egyptian influence in Sudan. The Sufi emir 'Abd al-Qadir fought the French for years in Algeria until he was defeated in 1847, imprisoned, and eventually exiled in Syria, where he wrote extensively on Sufism. Rather, Mahfouz mainly registers some reservations about the potential slide of the political under the spiritual in Omar's flight into Sufism. It is not for nothing that *The Beggar* ends with a scene that stages Omar's emergence from an ecstatic trance into the frying pan of sociopolitical reality. Before it reaches this denouement, the novel charts the trajectory of his Sufi journey, which has three interrelated phases. First is the *awakening*, which is provoked by Omar's encounter with his client. Second is the *search*, which first compels Omar to pursue the pleasures of the flesh as a potential mediator of ecstasy; when that fails, he resorts to the heart as a mirror of divine omnipotence and to a number of abstemious practices that range from meditative exercises and other innocent methods of autohypnosis to total retirement from society and disengagement of the mind from all worldly concerns and responsibilities. Third is the phase of *arrival*, which coincides, much to Omar's surprise, with his reawakening to the exigencies of sociopolitical reality instead of to the knowledge of the secret of creation and the ecstasy of direct communication and unity with divine life or فناء (*fana'*).

Mahfouz makes use here not of exact Sufi concepts but of a contiguous chain of metonymic signifiers that charts a poetics of Sufism of its own. The first part of Omar's search revolves around the hunt for love as a means to ecstasy; it is conjured up by a sequence of metonymic expressions that portray Omar's longing for "the pleasure of madness" (لذة الجنون), the "strange intoxication," "the long-sought ecstasy" (النشوة المستعصية المنشودة), "the first ecstasy of creation" (نشوة الخلق الأولى), "the raptures of love" (نشوة الحبّ), and, last but not least, the "fire-brand of sex" (لذعة الجنس السحريّة).[65] His extramarital pursuits with other women such as Margaret and Warda do not result in *nashwa*, or ecstasy, given the irreducibility of love to sex, as in Lacan's well-known formulation of desire in terms of a continual split between demand (love) and need for satisfaction (sex). Intensely invested in metonymy, Mahfouz's language here is performative of the fullness and futility of Omar's search—*fullness* because, like the constant slide of desire along the metonymic chain of signifiers, the search can never be fulfilled; *futility* because the void that fuels the search is in excess of the capacity to fulfill it. Omar concludes this first part of his search with a saturnine declaration: "The ecstasy of love fades and the frenzy of sex is too ephemeral to have any effect" (نشوة الحبّ لا تدوم ونشوة الجنس أقصر من أن يكون لها أثر).[66]

65. Mahfouz, *The Beggar*, 24, 50, 52, 56, 61, 63.
66. Ibid., 96.

Hence, erotic pleasure is incapable of mediating *nashwa* and the new love objects are but transient entrapments that lure Omar away from his metaphysical destiny. By repudiating the body's pleasures, Omar repudiates all forms of sociality in search of the pure, unmediated, and eternal *nashwa* that the soul's transcendentalizing impulse is finally deemed capable of generating.

Omar's detour into Sufism intensifies both his longing for ecstasy and alienation from all the objects, old and new, that are deemed no longer capable of producing the rapturous effects associated with the experience of ecstasy. Insofar as it has confronted him with the necessity of deserting all worldly matters to devote himself to the rapt contemplation of the soul, Sufism can be seen to accommodate and aggravate Omar's reactionary melancholia and its psychodynamics of disavowal and fetishism. Sufism is, after all, a license to suffering on the path to divine ecstasy, yet Omar suffers not only because he has not suffered enough (as a Sufi wayfarer would) but also because he can never suffer what Othman must have suffered in prison. Omar bears and wears his illness like a badge of honor: it draws him close to divine ecstasy and gnosis (معرفة, *ma'rifa*) and allows him to make up for his failure to suffer for the same principles for which Othman suffered. Sufism then contains melancholia in the double sense of containing and containment. Little wonder that the second part of Omar's search runs in tandem with his gradual disengagement from society in an attempt to find in solitary life "the ecstasy which gives assurance without proof" (النشوة الّتي تحقّق اليقين بلا حاجة إلى دليل), "to listen to the silence,"[67] "[to be cured from] the call of life" in order "[to see His face]."[68] This part also ends with yet another yearning *cri de cœur*, "When would he see His face? Hadn't he deserted the world for its sake?"[69] Omar's failure to find Sufi ecstasy expresses Mahfouz's unequivocal indictment not of Sufism as such but of the banality with which it is perceived as the "magic key of escape" (مفتاح الهرب السّحري) from the iron grip of history and sociopolitical reality.[70] In fact, Mahfouz insists that he "loves Sufism" provided that it does not become a rejection of life: "Sufism is like a mirage in the desert. It says to you, come and sit, relax and enjoy yourself for a while. I reject any path that rejects life."[71]

The title of the novel acquires a concrete yet tragically ironic dimension as it encapsulates Omar's narcissistic regression into an infantile stage in which

---

67. Ibid., 122, 135.
68. Ibid.; trans. modified.
69. Ibid., 143; trans. modified.
70. Ibid., 41.
71. Charlotte El-Shabrawy, "Naguib Mahfouz: The Art of Fiction," *Paris Review* 123 (1992): 17.

he becomes a mere beggar for ecstasy, as if ecstasy were to be bestowed from a benevolent outside rather than achieved from within. Omar has taken literally Mustapha's cynical statement, "And since there is no revelation in our age, people like you can only go begging."[72] Yet, begging for revelation is a far cry from the old activist struggle in which Omar was one of the agents of a revelation in the making—socialist utopia. Ironically, on the night that he gets a tiny glimpse of divine revelation, his wife is in the delivery room, giving birth to their first boy. Belatedly, Omar laments: "Here she is, able to create, while all his efforts have failed."[73] Although Omar is fixated on creation as a means to ecstasy, he is incognizant of the extent to which the rightful path toward it has been transposed by the Sufi ideal which places the heart at the center of all knowledge. For Othman, whose penchant for secular and leftist critique is perhaps without equal in Mahfouz's oeuvre, "the heart is a pump operating through the arteries and veins. To see it as a means of apprehending the truth is sheer fantasy. . . . You will not attain any truth worth speaking of except through reason, science, and work."[74] When Mustapha tells Othman that Omar is going through a crisis, as if he's "searching for his soul," Othman responds laconically, "Wasn't he who lost it?"[75]

Georges Tarabishi rightly suggests that Omar's search for ecstasy is but a search for "the ecstasy of being free of all ties."[76] Omar's journey into Sufism, though, is as much a break of all ties with the world for the sake of ecstasy as it is indeed a psychoaffective response to the *already broken* ties with the world. Given that the inaccessible objects of his longing—objects he deliberately constructed as lost—return with the force of the repressed to weigh heavily on his psyche, there lie underneath Omar's leap into Sufism the contours of fetishism. The fetishism of ecstasy enables Omar to avoid (as in a-void-dance, or Sufi whirling trance) the unbearable truth of the vitality and viability of transformative sociopolitical action in the present. This unbearable truth insists, after Othman's release from prison, that their old cell be resurrected and their socialist struggle be renewed. It relentlessly asserts in the wake of Zeinab's ability to create a newborn, in the wake of the burgeoning of Bouthayna's poetic talents in parallel to her scientific pursuits, and finally in the wake of the engagement of Othman and Bouthayna whose marriage and offspring may unite

---

72. Mahfouz, *The Beggar*, 76.
73. Ibid., 106.
74. Ibid., 122.
75. Ibid., 121.
76. Georges Tarabishi, *Allah fi rihlat Naguib Mahfouz al-ramziya* (Beirut: Dar al-Tiba'a wa-nashr, 1988), 61.

seamlessly science, poetry, and socialism. Throughout the novel, Omar fetishizes a cluster of events, scenes, and intensities—ranging from his obsession with the painting, his client's words, his illness, the secret of creation and the meaning of life to his search for ecstasy and divine revelation—"to cancel the full impact of reality" and disavow the continued existence of the objects of longing whose loss he manufactured.[77] Joined-up disavowal and fetishism prolong Omar's detour into Sufism. Yet, what would break the hold of Sufism except the melancholic cultivation of the objects whose endurance Omar holds at bay against the ecstatic longings by which he is held at bay?

Enduring Left Melancholy

If Mahfouz begins *The Beggar* with a Joycean moment, he ends it with a sequence of disparate surreal moments in which Othman taxies toward the Sufi experience of ecstasy but never quite reaches takeoff speed. In the penultimate chapter, he is in a state between sleep and waking, close to divine revelation when the world of reality makes an intervention: Bouthayna's reproachful queries, Mustapha's derisive repartees, and Othman's menacing incitements. A free-floating seriality of scenes unfolds in his eyes and ends with a compressed vision of the history of humankind from primitive battles to civilization and modern warfare. In the final sequence, just at the moment when his heart throbs with expectation, on the verge of the ecstasy of revelation, Omar sees not the divine face but the faces of Zeinab, Bouthayna, Samir, Jamila, Othman, Mustapha, and Warda. They exchange heads and assume hybrid shapes. The newborn Samir puts on Othman's head and chases Omar until he falls on the ground, admitting to himself that "ecstasy has become a curse, and paradise a stage of fools" (بدلا من النّشوة حلّت اللّعنة واستحالت الجنّة ملعبا للمهرّجين).[78] The last installment in this sequence portrays Omar communicating with insects, reptiles, and animals in a scene that collapses Sufism and surrealism, as in Adonis's book of the same title.[79] By blending the two, Mahfouz not only intensifies Omar's failure to achieve ecstasy but also reduces Omar's journey to pure phantasmagoria, likening it to the fantasy of a cow giving up the milk business in order to study chemistry.[80] It might not be impossible for the fox to become the guardian of the chicken and for the scorpion to wear a nurse's

---

77. Slavoj Žižek, *Enjoy Your Symptom* (New York: Routledge, 2008), x.
78. Mahfouz, *The Beggar*, 137.
79. Adonis, *Sufism and Surrealism*, trans. Judith Cumberbatch (London: Saqi, 2016).
80. Mahfouz, *The Beggar*, 137.

uniform, but "it is utterly impossible," as Tarabishi concludes, "for Man to absent himself from the world."[81]

While this penultimate chapter may seem to suggest Omar's failure to reach the long-sought ecstasy, its proleptic thrust paints in broad strokes Omar's eventual awakening to reality. The last chapter of *The Beggar* shows how his disavowal of the call of life (نداء الحياة) is *rerouted*—in the very process of its unfolding—into a poetic reckoning with reality and, ultimately, with the call of life itself. While in his Sufi shack, Omar is visited by Othman, who, true to his socialist ideals, got involved in a new underground operation and comes to Omar looking for a place to hide from the police:

> [OTHMAN:] "Listen, Omar, I'm in a bad situation. They are looking for me everywhere. If they catch me I'll die."
> [OMAR:] "So it's you who is running away this time (إذن فأنت . . . الهارب هذه المرّة)"[82]

Omar makes a subtle reference to the primal operation undertaken by Othman, Omar, and Mustapha together in the mid-1930s, in which Othman was chosen by lot to throw a bomb on the "pigs" (a reference to the British colonial powers) who "sucked our blood long enough."[83] This operation, in which Othman was shot in the leg, captured, and incarcerated while Omar and Mustapha escaped unscathed, is, curiously enough, reversed in the last chapter of the novel. It is Othman who is trying to escape and not Omar, even though both of them end up being caught. And it is Omar who bears the brunt of Othman's actions and is shot in the shoulder. Given the overdetermined history between the two comrades, this *reversal* is key to understanding the symptomatic modality of Omar's melancholite disavowals and fetishistic Sufi detours.

Throughout the narrative, Omar has been psychically unhinged by an overwhelming sense of guilt. The closer Othman's release from prison approaches, the deeper Omar sinks into illness, as if illness were a prophylactic tactic that enables him to cope with his inexpiable debt to Othman. When Omar finally meets Othman for the first time after his release from prison, Omar wonders, "He doesn't want to budge. How strange, it's as though you'd never wanted this meeting at all. You share nothing but a dead history, and he arouses in you only feelings of guilt, fear and self-contempt."[84] Apart from melancholy

---

81. Tarabishi, *Allah fi rihlat Naguib Mahfouz*, 62.
82. Mahfouz, *The Beggar*, 139.
83. Ibid., 112.
84. Ibid., 113.

self-impoverishment, this unremitting sense of guilt must have precipitated Omar's "flight into illness," to use Freud's felicitous expression—a flight that makes it possible for Omar "to evade a situation of conflict which is generating tension, and to achieve a reduction of this tension through the formation of symptoms."[85] This explains why time and again, Omar tells his doctor and himself that he is "not ill in the usual sense" or that he is the "invalid without illness" (المريض بلا مرض).[86] His constant harping on illness provokes Othman's rebuke: "It's unfortunate that the ill only think of disease."[87]

An unsettling emotional constellation of guilt, debt, and self-contempt as well as of empathy with and envy of the ethical enormity of Othman's sacrifice prompt Omar's flight into illness and from there into Sufism. It is as if the fetishistic mode of his illness—really, an illness without illness—enables Omar to stake a belated claim to victimhood and to balance the unquantifiable suffering that Othman has incurred and that Omar can only vicariously—and through illness—approximate. If illness sanctions his victimhood, then his loss of what Othman calls "the healthy and sound part" of his self might be a price willingly paid to expiate the debt.[88] Illness affords Omar the reversal of fortunes necessary to compensate for the better life he led while his old comrade-in-arms was in jail. Not surprisingly, Omar constantly belittles his achievement as a renowned lawyer: comparing himself with his doctor in the opening scene of the novel, he reflects, "a distinguished physician is widely known; who hears of the lawyer other than those with legal cases?"[89] Omar's self-berating revels in self-engineered symptoms: illness, victimhood, and Sufi intoxication. Yet the sudden reversal of roles in the final chapter of the novel—and the fact that Omar is literally shot back into life—can be seen to achieve just that, that is, to fulfill what vicarious victimhood could *only* approximate.

The bullet that fractures his collarbone pays, albeit belatedly, Omar's share of the implacable debt or just enough of it to supplement the consolatory vistas already operative not only through his flight into illness and vicarious victimhood but also through his detour into Sufism, which becomes, ironically, the midwife of a concrete reckoning with the world of reality. Hence his poetic epiphany at the end of the novel:

---

85. J. Laplanche and J. B. Pontalis, *The Language of Psycho-analysis*, trans. Donald Nicholson-Smith (New York: Norton, 1973), 164.
86. Mahfouz, *The Beggar*, 38.
87. Ibid., 115.
88. Ibid., 121, trans. modified.
89. Ibid., 7.

He had the feeling that his heart was beating in reality, not in a dream, and that he was returning to the world.

He found himself trying to remember a line of poetry. When has he read it? Who was the poet?

The line reverberated in his consciousness with a strange clarity: "If you really wanted me, why did you desert me?" (إن كنت تريدني حقًا فلم هجرتني!؟)[90]

Melancholy disavowal gives way to poetic acknowledgment! Omar awakens to life, to reality, rather than to divine revelation when he impulsively reclaims a long foreclosed *nashwa*—the ecstasy of poetry. Poetry for him conjures up the world of leftist engagement, socialist struggle, and all the objective coordinates of his past. It comes back at a fitting time, when he is caught in a scene from that world's gripping actuality: he is taken in a police car with Othman after having already become a suspect whose family is in danger and whose office has been searched by the authorities. Omar's line of poetry is a reversal of Jesus's *cri de coeur*, "My God, My God, why hast Thou forsaken Me?"[91] Instead of pointing to a future crucifixion, it stakes a claim to an abandoned life, a claim that has endured the cruelty of reactionary melancholia and Sufi detours. In fact, Omar's very Sufi detour or diversion could be seen as a condition for his later reversion to reality—really, for his "return to the point of entanglement from which [he was] forcefully turned away."[92] In other words, Omar returns to the point of incubational melancholia, the driving force of his past socialist struggle, equipped with cognizance rather than disavowal, with the energy to *create* rather than to *search* for the meaning of existence, and with the impulse to confront the actuality of the past rather than to transcend or evade it in the name of a metaphysical or a spiritual truth that is somewhat irreducible to sociopolitical reality.

The political force of *The Beggar* comes from its unapologetic assertion that the spirit of revolutionary change cannot be reduced to the failures of the Arab left or empirical socialism on a world stage. The novel's painstaking dramatization of the crisis of the Arab left and of the Egyptian left in particular becomes an acknowledgement of the ways in which the past continues to impinge on the

---

90. Ibid., 143.

91. Ps. 22:1 in *The Bible: Authorized King James Version* (New York: Oxford University Press, 2008).

92. Edouard Glissant, *Caribbean Discourse*, trans. J. Michael Dash (Charlottesville: University Press of Virginia, 1992), 26.

present, wreaking havoc in the psychic apparatuses of former fervent socialists such as Omar Al-Hamzawi. It forces a reckoning with the consequences of living in a state of disillusionment and disenchantment with a utopian past that never comes to pass. While it stages the trajectory of the Arab left's melancholia (as in Omar's vertiginous detours through disavowal, fetishism, and Sufism), *The Beggar* wagers on the enabling potentiality of foundational melancholia, its power to ground and reactivate the pursuit of the object of socialist promise. "If you really wanted me, why did you desert me?"—a vague line of poetry, indeed; yet, it conveys a sense of reckoning and reconciliation with what Omar deserted to pursue an elusive ecstasy. Omar has become cognizant of an uncannily familiar love object he has so far abandoned but cannot afford to do so any longer—not after having lived through, witnessed, and survived the drama of its concealment and repression.

Because reactionary melancholia is the symptom rather than the cause of the collapse of the Arab left, it becomes in the process of its unfolding a segue into the originary melancholia that constitutes not only the condition of possibility of the promise of socialist utopia, but also the condition of its renewal and reinstatement as a political and critical force in the sociopolitical sphere.[93] Unencumbered by the therapeutic rhetoric it reproduces, *The Beggar* is not unmindful of the potential slide of the political predicament of the Arab left into a psychoaffective discourse of pathological overtones as long as the former should find interwoven in the latter a concrete itinerary for the contemplation and elaboration of transformative visions and counterintuitive tactics. Omar endures reactionary left melancholia despite its compromised political potential and debilitating thrust toward compliance and indifference. Afflicted with all the tensions of which human beings are capable, reactionary melancholia sustains Omar's endurance and leads to his final reawakening to his and every leftist's originary melancholia.

Seizing left melancholia away from the psychodynamics of disavowal and fetishism, *The Beggar* is an empowering and visionary novel. Not only does it stage left melancholia while enduring it, but it also confronts Omar and the (leftist) reader alike with the foundational melancholia from which the socialist project continues to derive its enormous sociocultural, critical, and political potential—especially at a time when empirical socialism had exited the world stage. Socialist critique is never more to be desired than at the current

---

93. In his discussion of Hamlet, Benjamin speaks about the necessity of confronting melancholia with itself: "Only in princely life such as this is melancholy redeemed, by being confronted with itself. The rest is silence," *The Origin of German Tragic Drama*, 158.

historical juncture of runaway (disaster) capitalism. Yet "it remains for the person whose cause it is to make the final determination, to keep the initiative, retain the prerogative."[94] By subtly underscoring the viability of *enduring* rather than *resisting* left melancholia, Mahfouz's novel has limned one crucial condition of its own possibility, and, I should add, of ours—really, of the indispensability yet fragility of our demand for and endurance in proximity to the object of socialist promise, the promise of a post-capitalist state of affairs.

The lesson of Mahfouz's *The Beggar* is even more urgent today given the surprising decline of the Arab left after its promissory revitalization during the Arab uprisings. Its poor performance in the post-uprising elections beggars the imagination, especially that the popular demands that ignited the mass protests across the Arab world were very much in sync with the long-standing leftist tenets and goals of socialist political struggles. Although Hamdeen Sabahi emerged as a major leftist figure and campaigned vigorously on a nationalist socialist platform in the 2012 Egyptian presidential elections, he did not reach the final round which ended up bringing Mohammed Morsi and the Islamists to power. Sabahi may have voluntarily squandered his political clout when he decided to throw his weight behind Abdel Fattah El-Sisi's 2013 coup d'état. Accommodation with yet another military regime is not an unprecedented happenstance in the post-1952 trajectory of the Egyptian left. On the contrary, it has become a measure of leftist impotence: the compulsion to repeat the same mistakes of earlier generations of leftists.

In her heart-searing memoir about the late 1960s and 1970s student movement and the new and more radical generation of communists, Arwa Salih reflects back on the inhibitory influence of the previous generation of communists on her own generation, implying that the legacy of leftist failures is transgenerationally transmitted: "The communists of the sixties generation took different positions on the Nasser regime and on a host of other questions besides. Not all of these positions were worthy of respect, emerging as they did from a cloistered clique of leftists ravaged by the Defeat of 1967. Instead of leaving us to our own devices—of giving us the space to work out our living reality and to let experience sift out left from right—they nursed us on their poisoned milk."[95] The "poisoned milk" from which Salih's generation imbibed seems to be the same from which Sabahi's generation drank. The point of Mahfouz's *The Beggar* is not somehow to unburden ourselves from the legacy

---

94. Edward Said, "On Lost Causes," in *Reflections on Exile and Other Essays* (Cambridge, MA: Harvard University Press, 2003), 529.

95. Arwa Salih, *The Stillborn: Notes of a Woman from the Student-Movement Generation in Egypt*, trans. Samah Selim (New York: Seagull, 2017), 60–61.

of leftist failures but to endure in the face of and in spite of failure in the realm of the promise, and to search for inspiration in the initiatory moment of melancholicization at the origin of the socialist pursuit.

The realm of the promise remains hospitable, even if it may seem at times no longer within sight, as is the case in the aftermath of the Arab uprisings with refueled authoritarian and neoliberal retrenchments. While the religious right remains the historical foe of the old and new generation of leftists, and one of the nonnegligible reasons for leftist accommodations with authoritarian regimes whether in Egypt or Tunisia, much of the impetus of the melancholy disposition toward melancholy in Arab culture derives from the reduction of oppositional cultural and political forces to irrelevance by the ruthless repression or assimilation of postcolonial authoritarian regimes. The Arab left may seem perennially caught between the Scylla of Arab despotism and the Charybdis of political Islam. Mahfouz's *The Beggar* moves beyond the exigencies of realpolitik—and the rampant melancholite language of crisis, failure, and defeat that has become synonymous with the Arab left—and reminds us that leftism is not solely about fulfilling pragmatic necessities, however urgently important they remain, but also about a substratum of promise and a set of worldmaking imaginaries that cannot be reduced to electoral outcomes, failures, or crises. Through Mahfouz's Omar, we are served a much-needed dose of Sufi spiritualism to move forward and forge in the smithy of our souls the foundational psychopolitical conditions at the origin of the socialist promise of worldmaking, the pursuit of a world in the making.[96] Every failure and every setback becomes from this perspective a station in the Sufi path toward the ecstasy of completion and the elation of creation, a mere postponement of the rendezvous with victory, or, at least, a postponement of complete capitulation.

In the following chapter, I will focus on a related project of worldmaking that took place in Tunisia in the wake of its independence from France. While in this chapter I have focused on the trials of the bottom-up project of socialist utopia, in the next chapter I will shift the focus to the top-down project of secular modernity and explore its psychoaffective imprint on conceptions of gender and masculinity, which are tightly connected to the preoccupations of secular leftists, not least because of their desire to unsettle traditionally Islamic and patriarchal sedimentations. Not unlike Egypt, the duel between

---

96. I have deliberately paraphrased James Joyce's Stephen Dedalus: "I go to encounter for the millionth time the reality of experience and forge in the smithy of my soul the uncreated conscience of my race," James Joyce, *A Portrait of the Artist as a Young Man* (Ware, UK: Wordsworth Editions Limited, 1992), 196.

Arab leftists and Islamists in Tunisia may not end any time soon, but it has almost always pushed leftists to gravitate in the orbit of secular authoritarianism. After they supported an old Bourguibist, Beji Caïd Essebsi, in the Tunisian 2014 presidential elections, Tunisian leftists were completely disunited, co-opted, and reduced to empty shells. Leftist parties managed to send only one representative to the parliament in the 2019 elections. Although there are still several leftist-leaning representatives in the Tunisian parliament, leftist agendas have either been diluted or appropriated by grassroots activists, civic society actors, NGOs, or syndicalists, and labor unions, especially the Tunisian General Labor Union (UGTT).

The neocolonial and later neoliberal politico-economic dispensation has not only imposed debt dependency, aggressive privatization, and renewed structural adjustment programs but also has produced a pattern of governance in which authoritarian regimes maintained themselves in power by, initially, playing the Islamists against the leftists and, after 9/11, by framing the Islamists as a national and global threat. Meanwhile, they harped on their own inimitable role as both protective shields against any possible Islamist takeover at home and credible allies in the American-led global war on terror. The war on terror and the Bush-Blair invasion of Iraq may have retarded the Arab uprisings because Arab dictators "found in the War on Terror and the so-called Islamist (aka terrorist) threat a convenient ruse to recast allegations of human rights violations, along with various abuses of democracy and freedom of speech, as part of the global effort to fight terrorism."[97] The repression of the Islamists may have paid dividends to authoritarian regimes across the Arab world, but the Arab left has benefited neither from the rise of the Islamists as a political nightmare, or force to be reckoned with, nor from their routine repression in Egypt, Syria, Algeria, or Tunisia. Leftist agendas have mostly benefited the enemies of the left, especially those who were in power and who assimilated them, at least in part, into their own visions of transforming postcolonial societies.

The case of postcolonial Tunisia is quite revealing in this regard. The first president of the country, Habib Bourguiba, sought to modernize and revolutionize society in such a way as to bring about gender equality through a slim document titled the Personal Status Code (PSC), passed on August 13, 1956. A self-professed secular nationalist who sought to hitch the wagon of the young nation state to the train of European modernity both socially and economically, Bourguiba sustained a steadfast westward gaze but suffered from an en-

---

97. Nouri Gana, ed., *The Making of the Tunisian Revolution* (Edinburgh: Edinburgh University Press, 2013), 5.

during neopatriarchal hangover. While Tunisian leftists sought to liberate the individual from the clutches of postcolonial dictatorship, Bourguiba chose to liberate Tunisian women and oppress Tunisian men—not to liberate both women and men from the conditioning vagaries of traditional mindsets, but to weaken his male political opponents and coup-proof his regime from any potential challengers, especially from male political dissidents who denounced the centralization of all the powers in his hand. Not only did Bourguiba lay the foundation of what is now known as state feminism but also set in motion a disorienting project of modernity which professed enlightened values, democracy and free expression but practiced oppression and repression. Bourguiba may be seen as the liberator of women, but only insofar as they remained de facto under his patronage. As will become clear in the following chapter, which is devoted to the psychopolitics and subtle melancholy dynamics of gender representation in postcolonial Tunisian film, the contradictions of Bourguiba's project of modernity not only reproduced the colonial pact between modernity and oppression but also enlisted Tunisians as agents in their own cultural belatedness by virtue of melancholizing their traditional habits of mind. Postcolonial Tunisian cinema maps the contours of the dialectic between postcolonial modernity and tradition, dramatizing their moments of entanglement and psychoaffective disengagements, and enlists Tunisian audiences as participants in their own cultural and national liberation.

4
Melancholy Manhood
Modernity and Neopatriarchy in Tunisian Cinema

A civilizational mutation occurs whenever change affects the constituents of the pentahedron (time, *jouissance*, alterity, death and truth) and brings about a new status quo in the connections among men and in their relation to the world. As a result, cultural work (*Kulturarbeit*) is necessary so that the new status quo can be assimilated by the psychic life of the individual and can ensure its unconscious anchorage in the human collectivity.

— FETHI BENSLAMA

I think it is important to drive a wedge in, early and often and if possible conclusively, between the two topics, masculinity and men, whose relation to one another it is so difficult not to presume.

— EVE KOSOFSKY SEDGWICK

In the Arab world, it is the differential wedge between masculinity (*dhukūra*) and manhood (*rujūla*)—otherwise unequivocal in the Arabic language—that is rather difficult to presume. In a culture gradually but steadily alienated from the conceptual subtleties of its linguistic heritage—and profoundly unsettled by the unrelenting and disorienting encroachments of Western cultural hegemony—it is less obviously ironic, but all the more alarming, that the spawning historical and cultural amnesia of Arab contemporaneity has come to converge with the imperative to resist global cultural imperialism. For instance, the irresistible impulse to counter the surreptitious imperialist ideology of Western feminism, has fostered an overall insouciance about the "ever-growing cultural retardation" and "drift into ahistoricity" of modern-day Arabs,[1] which has amounted at times to a sanctioned ignorance about the initially promissory status of women under Islam to which scholars from Qasim Amin (1863–1908) through Tahar Haddad (1899–1935) to Leila Ahmed (b. 1940) have variably drawn attention.[2] In a climate of fear of insidious and alienating Westernization—which intensified in the era of decolonization and high nationalism—the proximity between forgotten moments of cultural modernity in Arab history and Western modernity tends to be overlooked, if not rejected altogether, as a ruse of Western imperialism. Likewise, anything that might retrospectively contain latencies of Arab modernity becomes suspect and objectionable if recycled, repackaged, and indexed as Western.

The imbrication between modernity and coloniality has not only inhibited the emergence of a noncoercive discourse of progressive politics but has also elided the forward vision of many aspects of Arab culture. The persistent disavowal in most Arab neopatriarchal societies of Arabic's avant-gardist differentiation between masculinity and manhood—as well as between sexuality and gender—would seem utterly at odds with the postcolonial wave of Arabization if understood separately from the composite forces that provoke and sustain it, namely (1) a hypersensitiveness to the "woman question" (قضيّة المرأة) and to the universalization of Western feminism, and, more recently, to the rise of the "Gay International," combined and/or alternating with (2) a sanctioned amnesia of the progressive Arab Muslim past, which is sufficiently manifest at the level of the Arabic language alone (insofar as language is an exemplary reflection of culture and civilization). While in French, for instance, there is no distinctive word for *manhood* apart from *masculinité* (which is an offshoot of *masculin*, the French word for sexual, not gender, differentiation), in English the homology between *men* and *manhood* makes linguistically discreditable the reason why, for that matter, it is difficult not to presume the collapsibility of the two, as Eve Sedgwick points out in the epigraph to this chapter. The wholesale appropriation of *masculinity* from the French *masculinité* resulted only in a homonymy between men and masculinity instead of the homology between men and manhood. However, a reconfiguration of the

---

1. Abdallah Laroui, *The Crisis of the Arab Intellectual: Traditionalism or Historicism?*, trans. Diarmid Cammell (Berkeley: University of California Press, 1976), 159.

2. Qasim Amin, *The Liberation of Women and the New Woman: Two Documents in the History of Egyptian Feminism*, trans. Samiha Sidhom Peterson (Cairo: American University in Cairo Press, 2001); Tahar Haddad, *Imra'atuna fi al-Shari'a wa al-Mujtama'* (Our Woman in Islamic Law and Society) (Sousse: Dar al-Ma'arif, 1930); Leila Ahmed, *Women and Gender in Islam: Historical Roots of a Modern Debate* (New Haven, CT: Yale University Press, 1992).

whole problematic in terms of a distinction between masculinity and manhood is more attuned to the logic of the Arabic language, even though masculinity has more currency in English than in Arabic and manhood more currency in Arabic than in English.

In Arabic, *dhukūra* (masculinity; ذكورة) is oceans apart from *rujūla* (manhood; رجولة). Etymologically, *dhukūra* comes from *dhakar* (male; ذكر), which refers also to the male sexual organ. As much as *dhukūra* is thusly an accented sexual category, *rujūla* is a neutered cultural construction whose connotative reach (i.e., gender-defying evocations of human attributes and virtues) is by no means reducible to the sexual binaries of *dhukūra* and *'unūtha* (femininity; أنوثة), with the caveat that these two categories might interchangeably pertain to men and women alike. Without diminishing the etymological polysemy of *rujūla*,[3] it is important to stress its cultural polyvalence and unequivocal difference from as well as excess of both femininity and masculinity, let alone virility or sexual potency (*fuḥūla*). If we take into consideration the special place of language in Arab consciousness—namely, its affiliation with the authority and holiness of the Quran—this linguistic distinction between masculinity (ذكورة) and manhood (رجولة) is, in no small measure, a locus of modernity. And by modernity here, I mean specifically the timeless modernity of insight, vision, and values, which is not easily subsumable under the temporal, processual, and instrumentalist drive of techno-industrial modernity. As the ardent modernist Arab poet Adonis observes: "I find no paradox in declaring that it was recent Western modernity which led me to discover our own, older, modernity outside our 'modern' politico-cultural system established on a Western model."[4]

Apart from the long Ottoman interim and the Crusades that preceded it, from the first to the second fall of Baghdad (at the hands of, respectively, the Mongols in 1258 and the so-called Coalition of the Willing in 2003), no other factor had played a more detrimental role in neutralizing and diminishing the core vitality of Arab modernity than European colonialism and now neoliberal American imperialism. One of the most crippling legacies of the colonial conquest—which first came to the fore in the period of al-Nahda, or Arab

---

3. For a definition of manhood, see *Lisan Al-Arab*, s.v. *rajala* (رجل). For further definitions, see *Qamoos* online.

4. Adonis, *An Introduction to Arab Poetics*, trans. Catherine Cobham (London: Saqi Books,1990), 81. Adonis adds that soon afterward he realized "that modernity was both of time and outside time: of time because it is rooted in the movement of history, in the creativity of humanity, coexisting with man's striving to go beyond the limitations which surround him; and outside time because it is a vision which includes in it all times and cannot only be recorded as a chronological event" (99).

renaissance, from the beginning of the nineteenth to the mid–twentieth century—is that it charted, at least retrospectively, the postcolonial duel between secularism and Islam. French colonial modernity censored and embargoed Islam and the Arabic language because they constituted the mobilizing forces of anticolonial discourse and militant resistance. Islamist resistance to secular colonial modernity emerged and flourished in the colonial period before it had come to cast a long shadow on the postcolonial futures of the Arab world. Under the direct influence of Euro-American imperialism and its Zionist proxy, there precipitated a rift in Arab contemporaneity between, on the one hand, the call to return to the Arab Islamic past (advocated by the Salafists and traditionalists writ large) and, on the other, the call for a secular (intellectual) alternative advocated by the nonconformists and progressives who played a major role in the decolonial movements of their own countries and some assumed the leadership of the nascent postcolonial nation-states.

It is from within these entangled dynamics of colonial modernity and counter–colonial modernity that emerges the longstanding duel between Islamism and secular authoritarianism, a duel that has never ceased to gain center stage in the Arab world, especially in the wake of the 1967 Naksa and, more recently, in the aftermath of the 2010–2011 Arab uprisings. The legacy of colonialism continues to weigh heavily on Arab collectivities, unsettling their cultural tenets, communal ethos, traditional power structures, and forms of governance. The postcolonial nationalist elites strived to modernize and reform their countries, only that they internalized and reproduced the very same colonial systems of rule they had previously resisted. As Wael Hallaq rightly observes, the majority of the newly independent countries "inherited from Europe a readymade nation-state (with its constitutive power structures) for which the existing social formations had not been adequately prepared."[5] Modernization amounted to Westernization without cultural preparation, or cultural work (*Kulturarbeit*), as Benslama calls it after Freud. Tunisia's first postindependence president, Habib Bourguiba (1956–1987), distinguished himself from the rest of Arab presidents and monarchs by his unequivocal embrace of secular modernity and by the brazen legal and social reforms he immediately introduced (particularly with regard to women's rights). Bourguiba's own hegemonic stature as the father figure of the postcolonial nation created a generation of Tunisian men who tried to straddle both modernity and patriarchy but failed at both. As will become clear in what follows, this verdict is reached, with different degrees of severity, by a host of postcolonial

---

5. Wael B. Hallaq, *The Impossible State: Islam, Politics, and Modernity's Moral Predicament* (New York: Columbia University Press, 2013), 2.

filmmakers, whose films best exemplify the sociopolitical and psychoaffective legacies (complexities and complexes) of the arranged marriage between colonial modernity and local culture in Tunisia and beyond.

Postcolonial Tunisia and the Leap into Modernity

The values and attitudes of patriarchal relations internalized in early childhood underlay the "modernized" surface and determined the deep structure of personality and orientation.

HISHAM SHARABI[6]

Our collective consciousness is indeed marked by a double mutilation, alienation vis-à-vis what is foreign, and alienation vis-à-vis what is past, the mimicry of modernity and the mimicry of tradition.

AZIZ KRICHEN[7]

Unlike any other country in the Arab world, Tunisia is the exemplum of an Arab country that wanted to waste no time in rehearsals or gradualisms but was eager to leap briskly into the frying pan of modernity. Tunisia gained its full independence on March 20, 1956, after having been, following the 1881 Treaty of Bardo, a French colony for almost three-quarters of a century. Apart from the day of Independence and the more recent Revolution of Freedom and Dignity (December 17, 2010–January 14, 2011), August 13, 1956, occupies pride of place in the national memory of Tunisians. On that day, the now proverbial *majallat al-aḥwāl al-shakhṣiya,* or Personal Status Code (PSC), was promulgated by Neo-Destur Party leader Habib Bourguiba. Unmatched in the Muslim world except perhaps by the 1924 Turkish Civil Code, the Tunisian Code did not, however, abolish the Sharī'a, or Islamic law, altogether, nor did it proceed to sweepingly mimic, somewhat à la Atatürk, the French model of *laïcité (laiklik)*. Even while it abolished, in a move to unify, centralize and simplify jurisdictions, both Maliki and Hanafi rival jurisdictions as well as the Sharī'a courts, it was still presented as an eclectic and intelligible amalgam of pressing concerns, faithful to the spirit of Sharī'a and ijtihād, or independent reasoning, as well as to the exigencies of modernity and postcolonial statehood.

---

6. Hisham Sharabi, *Neopatriarchy: A Theory of Distorted Change in Arab Society* (New York: Oxford University Press, 1988).

7. Aziz Krichen, *Le syndrome Bourguiba* (Tunis: Cérès Productions, 1992).

Some of the boldest reforms the PSC brought into force pertain to the reconfiguration of social life, opting for the nuclear family, and the emancipation of women, which has come to be synonymous with Tunisia's project of modernity. The cataclysmic reforms entered in this area are predicated on the animating principle of equality between men and women (even though such a laudable principle of gender equality is yet to be extended, according to Tahar Haddad's teachings, to the thorny issue of inheritance laws). These include the debunking of the Maliki principles regarding compulsory marriage by requiring the mutual consent of the spouses prior to marriage; interdicting marriage before spouses reach the age of puberty; urging the wife to contribute to the household expenses if she has the private financial means to do so; prohibiting polygyny; repudiating repudiation (i.e., the thrice-repeated divorce initiated by the husband in the privacy of his home) by decreeing that divorce outside a court of law is without legal effect; and, finally, permitting either spouse to file for divorce at the expense of a juristically justifiable financial indemnity.[8]

It is these last two provisions of the code that represented the most startling innovations and for which the trail had hardly been blazed by any other Arab Muslim country. Not unexpectedly, therefore, they were met with the utmost opposition from the 'ulama' or judges, as well as from the remnants of the 1920 Old Destur Party. Attentive to the clearly political agenda of the opposition, Bourguiba not only tilted the political playing field to his own advantage but also hammered home his vision of modern Tunisia by pointing out to the preexisting socioreligious logic on which these legislations tack and by reiterating that they have been approved by notable and highly esteemed jurists and scholars, including the Sheikh of the Zaytuna Mosque and Muhammed Ju'ayit, Sheikh al-Islam. Moreover, and in a spirit of intellectual self-adulation that would become characteristic of his dismissal of counterarguments, Bourguiba challenged his detractors that the abolition of polygyny is by no means a deviation from the encoded meaning of the Quran, which he treated as an open book and deemed himself (by dint of his training in law and graduation from Sorbonne with a degree in law and political science in 1927) more than juristically qualified to interpret in view of the alleged sociopolitical urgencies of modernity.[9]

---

8. For a concise critical description of the code, see J. N. D. Anderson, "The Tunisian Law of Personal Status," *The International and Comparative Law Quarterly* 7, no. 2 (1958): 262–79.

9. While a number of religious judges resigned in protest of the new reforms, Bourguiba insisted nonetheless that in abolishing polygyny he was very much in line with precepts of the Qur'an: "I respect this religion . . . but through my functions and responsibilities I am quali-

Given the decisiveness of the moment of birth of the postcolonial nation-state, Bourguiba's effort was twofold: to neutralize political opposition and to conciliate a discontented population, abruptly alienated from habitual societal practices hitherto thought beyond human intervention. It is not surprising therefore that Bourguiba sought to weaken the centers of command from which these practices derive their continuing appeal and authority such as the Zaytuna Mosque, the prestigious bastion of Islam in Tunisia, which came to be placed in 1956 under the supervision of the Ministry of Education before it was completely absorbed into the Faculty of Theology at the University of Tunis by 1961. Bourguiba's efforts to secularize the nation morphed unwittingly, however, into an incensed raid on the observance of such foundational pillars of Islam as the holy month of Ramadan. Bourguiba exempted himself from fasting and unilaterally decreed that Tunisians ought to follow suit because Tunisia is engaged in a major jihad or holy war against economic underdevelopment.[10]

It is no exaggeration to suggest that Bourguiba's vision of Tunisian modernity was somewhat beclouded by his brazen undifferentiation between the amorphousness of the political system of the postcolonial nation, which needed

---

fied to interpret religious law." See Derek Hopwood, *Habib Bourguiba of Tunisia: The Tragedy of Longevity* (London: Macmillan, 1992), 140. Bourguiba refers to verse 4:3 in the *Quran*, which can be seen to encourage polygyny only to the extent that the husband has the capacity to treat his wives justly: "marry such women as seem good to you, two and three and four; but if you fear that you will not do justice (between them), then (marry) only one or what your right hands possess." Verse 129 of the same *Surat al-Nisā'*, or *The Surah of Women*, however, reedits the aforementioned caveat and states unequivocally that it is impossible for a husband to be just and equitable to all his wives: "And you will never be capable of being just between your wives no matter how hard you tried" *(wa lan tastatī'ū an ta'dilū bayna al-nisā' wa laou haristum)*. In abolishing polygyny, Bourguiba was clearly influenced by Tahar Haddad, a progressive Zaytuna intellectual who, in one of the pioneering works about the emancipation of women in the Arab Muslim world, laments that "had not the practice of polygyny continued after the revelation of this verse, this would have been the most frank call for its complete abolition." Haddad, *Our Woman in Islamic Law and Society*, 55.

10. "In a 1960 speech Bourguiba asserted that Tunisia's involvement in a *jihad* against underdevelopment absolved its citizens from fasting, just as warriors in a jihad in defense of Islam were exempted. To sanction this as a product of *ijtihad* (as he had justified controversial provisions of the Personal Status Code), Bourguiba demanded a fatwa of endorsement from the mufti of Tunis. When his statement failed to offer unequivocal support, he lost his job." Kenneth Perkins, *A History of Modern Tunisia* (New York: Cambridge, 2004), 141. On one infamous occasion, Bourguiba drank a glass of orange juice on public television to incite his people to quit fasting: "I tell you that administrative and school timetable will not be altered for Ramadan. I am only interpreting the letter of the Koran. If you are not convinced you are free not to follow me," see Hopwood, *Habib Bourguiba of Tunisia*, 140.

to take a particular form in order for it to function properly, if not efficiently, and the overestimated sociocultural malleability of his people who are inherently shaped by Tunisia's placement in the Arab Muslim world. This is not to say that Bourguiba was incognizant of the country's enduring Islamic heritage, which would be inexcusable, but that in his attempt to hitch the wagon of the fledging postcolonial state to the train of modernity, he was reluctant to attend to, if not quick to underestimate, the everyday sociocultural leverage of this heritage. Regardless of whether the new reforms derived their raison d'être from building craftily on arguably deep-seated Islamic values, they were perceived, in part, as masks of a corrosive ideology of neocolonial secular modernity (especially in the sense of French *laïcité* or laicism) that sought to deny Tunisia its sociocultural specificity.[11] Such views gained momentum as Bourguiba accented the linkages between modernity and French language and culture, presenting himself as the exemplar of the new breed of the proposed grafting: "This Arab is Frenchified to the tips of his fingers, a living example of assimilation."[12] Indeed, Bourguiba had already married a French woman, Mathilde Louvain, in 1927, and had consistently refuted accusations of complicity with neocolonialism in an intransigent and complacent manner, resting on his laurels and basking in his glory: "I do not cry neocolonialism or imperialism when difficulties arise in my country. . . . Having struggled most of my life against the colonial régime, having freed my country of its after-effects, I need not take lessons from anyone about colonialism."[13]

Parallel to this project of modernity, which boasts of gender equality and socioeconomic advancement, there emerges a more gendered and male biased narrative of nationhood, which revolves around the pivotal figure of Bourguiba as the architect of modern Tunisia. In a series of conferences presented in the early 1970s at the Institut de Presse et des Sciences de l'Information on the history of the National Movement, Bourguiba constantly reminded his

---

11. Secularism protects religious plurality, whereas *laïcité* protects against it in the public sphere. *Laïcité* is a militant form of secularism that requires that any sign of religious identity be confined to the private sphere. It is a statist ideology contrived mainly to confront and contain Islam in France. In other words, and as Oliver Roy argues, "we must draw a distinction between secularization, whereby society emancipates itself from a sense of the sacred that it does not necessarily deny, and *laïcité*, whereby the state expels religious life beyond a border that the state itself has defined by law." Roy, *Secularism Confronts Islam*, trans. George Holoch (New York: Columbia University Press, 2007), 13.

12. Hopwood, *Habib Bourguiba of Tunisia*, 142.

13. Habib Bourguiba, *Ma vie, mes idées, mon combat* (Tunis: Ministère de l'Information, 1977), 486.

audience, most of whom were students, that the Tunisian nation is his sole creation. The following statement is typical of Bourguiba's modesty: "J'espère que vous connaîtrez mieux l'histoire de notre pays en écoutant celui qui l'a faite" (I hope you get to know better the history of our country by listening to the person who made it).[14] While Bourguiba insists that Tunisia is *notre*, or *our*, country, he reserves the privilege of having forged it to himself. Blending the narrative of the nation with his own image reached its zenith in 1975 when he proclaimed himself, thanks to parliamentary support, president for life. As Derek Hopwood muses: "If Bourguiba had taken to heart lessons from French history his favorite must have been Louis XIV's *l'état c'est moi*. He did not distinguish any longer where he ended and where the state began."[15] By introjecting the nation, blurring the dividing lines between nation and self, and anointing himself the Supreme Combatant (*al-mujāhid al-akbar*), Bourguiba painted a male biased and cultish picture of the nationalist project of modernity despite his enthusiasm for the emancipation of women from patriarchal binds. In fact, his 1960s infamous campaign against the veil can be seen, at least retrospectively, as an attempt to veil male privilege precisely by unveiling women's faces (an act he himself categorically opposed during the anticolonial struggle because he deemed the veil then, much like Frantz Fanon, as the last frontier of sorts against complete assimilation to the hegemony of French culture).[16]

Hardly respectful of the democratic conventions he initiated, arrogant, and prone to opting for heavy-handed methods and cavalier policies, he ruled over an overawed population, fretting at the bondage imposed upon them in what practically constituted in the words of Hisham Sharabi an "etatist patriarchy,"[17] or what Hélé Béji calls "nationalitarisme,"[18] which blends unabashedly the all too neat rhetoric of nationalism, the instrument of resistance under colonial rule, with political oppression, the instrument of cultivating postcolonial nationhood. It is as if Tunisians surrendered their right to challenge the ideology of state nationalism no sooner had they subscribed themselves to it in their collective struggle for independence, hence the sense of *désenchantement national*, or national disenchantment, of which Hélé Béji speaks dispassionately.

14. Ibid., 75.
15. Hopwood, *Habib Bourguiba of Tunisia*, 84.
16. "To the colonialist offensive against the veil, the colonized opposes the cult of the veil." Frantz Fanon, *A Dying Colonialism*, trans. Haakon Chevalier (New York: Grove Press, 1965), 47.
17. Sharabi, *Neopatriarchy*, 65.
18. Hélé Béji, *Désenchantement national: Essai sur la décolonisation* (Paris: François Maspero, 1982), 19.

Bourguiba's cult of personality had gradually insinuated itself into the national imaginary and became synonymous with the very idea of Tunisian nationalism. Rather than a mere psychological prop or a crude expression of self-glorification, which it is in some ways, Bourguiba's personality worship is an extension of the political system he instituted after Tunisia's independence from France in 1956. It magnified his personal will, elevated his ideas to the status of oracular infallibility and bestowed on him limitless powers to justify his tyranny and pursuit of longevity.

Bourguiba's pursuit of presidency for life, and of a deformed ideology of postcolonial nationhood that demands and manipulates the tacit commitment of every Tunisian to the collective imperative of *"tunisianité"* or "Tunisianness," symptomizes the persistence of the patriarchal impulse underneath the modernist project he spearheaded—a project that promised a genuine break with the incongruities and anachronisms of traditional culture in the service of progressive secular modernity. The result is what might fittingly be called, following Hisham Sharabi, "a bastardized form of modernization" which produced a "modernized" patriarchy, "a neopatriarchy," very much in synch with the prevailing neopatriarchal paradigm that gradually set in Arab society during al-Nahda period and tightened its grip in the postcolonial era.[19] Being a combination of colonial paternalism and state bureaucracy, the neopatriarchal system thrived on contradictions such that the more entrenched it is, the more exaggerated its contradictions become, and vice versa. As Sharabi rightly observes: "In this type of polity the gap between appearance and reality took on exaggerated forms. . . . Stark contradictions between verbal and actual behavior produced no problematic tensions for consciousness."[20] Teeming with contradictions, Bourguiba's project of modernity unfolded as a series of desiderata from which he maintained a curious insularity; even though he is the initiator of the modernist rupture with beylical and colonial Tunisia, Bourguiba showed no willingness to subscribe to the political entailments of modernity thought to be his singular mark. On the contrary, he was much in the gravitational pull of neopatriarchy, which seemed to gratify power and longevity, if not eternity, as might be worthy of a presidency for life (رئاسة مدى الحياة).[21]

---

19. Sharabi argues that "modernization within the structure and relations of colonial or imperialist-dominated patriarchy was no more than a bastardized form of modernization: it only produced a 'modernized' patriarchy." *Neopatriarchy*, 64.

20. Ibid., 66.

21. While it is all too common that leaders of newly decolonized nations revert to applying to their own peoples the same colonial practices to which they once submitted at the hands of

Bourguiba's rule over Tunisia (1956–1987) produced a breed of men that might be aptly called Bourguiba's sons. Not being a homogenous group, the contradictions, confusion, and confusedness of Bourguiba's sons is the measure of their filial relation to him as well as of their kinship and belonging together. Under the westward gaze of modern Tunisia, beclouded by the enduringly patriarchal strain of societal and family practices, the acute disorientation of Tunisian men cannot be overstated. Suspended in a state of mutability that is simultaneously cultivated and frustrated, they have been able neither to come to terms with the challenges of modernity, of which gender equality is part and parcel, nor to relinquish fully the protective shelter of traditional patriarchy, in which male supremacy is the grantor of psychosocial stability. Modern Tunisian cinema is abundantly invested in unraveling the ways in which Tunisian men are stranded in the pull of neopatriarchy, even while attempting timidly or defiantly to break out of its molds. Somewhat like Bourguiba, their exemplary modern patriarch, while they can be enlightened about the workings of gender in the patriarchal unconscious—and even about the regulatory or naturalized nature of such collective unconscious—they will nonetheless guard and perpetuate, quite ferociously at times, its tenacious patrilineal precepts. The affective apparatus that produces and sustains such a psychosocial behavior can be confidently called *melancholite* because it professes consciously or unconsciously to straddle two contradictory (yet, eventually, mutually reinforcing) logics at one and the same time—the logic of modernity and the logic of patriarchy, and specifically the logic of gender equality and the logic of male privilege—which might otherwise be mutually exclusive. Were Bourguiba's modernity not parachuted on an already entrenched patriarchal apparatus, inculcated by decades of colonial domination and decolonial struggle, but rather worked out from within (and in excess of) its everyday reenactments, generations of Tunisian men and women might have developed the necessary psychic wherewithal whereby to participate in it in ways that would surely redound to their own and others' benefits.

---

colonial European powers, Bourguiba's case beggars the imagination since (or, perhaps, because) he was precisely an intellectual who graduated from Sorbonne and wrote against colonialism in newspapers such as *La Voix du Tunisien* and *L'Etendard Tunisien* before he launched his own militant newspaper *L'Action tunisienne* in 1932, founded the Neo-Destur party on socialist and communist models in Europe two years after, and began direct decolonial struggle which resulted in his imprisonment and exile before it led to Tunisia's internal independence on June 3, 1954, and full independence on March 20, 1956. For more on Bourguiba's curious legacy, see, among others, Krichen, *Le syndrome Bourguiba*; Béji, *Désenchantement national*; and Michel Camau and Vincent Geisser, *Le syndrome autoritaire: Politique en Tunisie de Bourguiba à Ben Ali* (Paris: Presses de Sciences Politiques, 2003).

Undoing Manhood

> Manliness, it can be seen, is an eminently relational notion, constructed in front of and for other men and against femininity, in a kind of fear of the female, firstly in oneself.
>
> PIERRE BOURDIEU[22]

> Je le répète, il y a un décalage actuellement entre l'émancipation de la femme et celle de l'homme, une distorsion entre la théorie et la pratique, la tradition et la modernité. Les lois existent mais peuvent-elles changer les blocages dans les têtes? Pourtant, j'ai la faiblesse de croire que le cinéma peut à sa façon aider à changer les choses.
>
> It bears repeating, there is a gap currently between the emancipation of women and that of men, a discrepancy between theory and practice, between tradition and modernity. Laws exist but are they capable of removing mental blocks? And yet, I would like to believe that cinema can, in its own way, help change things.
>
> MOUFIDA TLATLI[23]

The National Union of Tunisian Women (الإتحاد القومي النسائي التونسي and now الإتحاد الوطني للمرأة التونسية) was founded as early as 1956, shortly after the promulgation of the PSC. The Union's mission consisted largely in promoting and improving the status of women throughout the country by fostering awareness of the benefits of the PSC and by eliminating gender discrimination and ensuring that the new reforms are implemented. The very foundation of the Union right after the promulgation of the PSC sufficiently signals the anticipated disjunction between legal reform and social practice that Moufida Tlatli evokes. What is worse than the assumption that legal reforms will translate into everyday practices is, as Theodor Adorno had warned us, their all too abstract compatibility with "the most insidious tendencies of society."[24] It is a mistake, as Judith Butler reminds us, "to understand all the ways in which gender is regulated in terms of those empirical legal instances [here, the PSC] because the norms that govern those regulations exceed the very instances in which they are embodied."[25] In other words, the sociocultural forces that regulate

---

22. Pierre Bourdieu, *The Masculine Domination*, trans. Richard Nice (Stanford, CA: Stanford University Press, 2001), 53.
23. Moufida Tlatli, "Une affaire de femmes/Stories of Women," *Ecrans d'Afriques* 8 (1994): 11.
24. Theodor Adorno, *Minima Moralia*, trans. E. F. N. Jephcott (London: Verso, 1984), 102.
25. Judith Butler, *Undoing Gender* (New York: Routledge, 2004), 40.

gender roles override, as it were, the top-down imposition of new rules of engagement. More precisely, and insofar as modern Tunisian society is concerned, it is the intractable workings of neopatriarchal dispositions that routinely frustrate the laws and obligations juristically attendant upon gender roles. While the Union's mission is to contravene the myriad functioning of gender discrimination in everyday societal practices, it remains itself a symptom of the yawning gulf between the new legal reforms and the hegemonic norms of social intelligibility that continue to be largely influenced by neopatriarchal sensibilities.

The real venture of postcolonial Tunisia cinema is that it has given pride of place to the sociopolitical urgencies of closing the rift between abstract legal reforms and quotidian practices, namely by visualizing the cognitive tensions between theory and practice, confronting Tunisian male viewers in particular with the obligation to ponder and resolve the operative disconnect between their belief in gender equality and their embodiment of male privilege. A series of postcolonial films directed by male directors—ranging roughly from Omar Khlifi's *Hurlements* (*Screams*, 1972), Abdellatif Ben Ammar's *Sejnane* (1973) and *Aziza* (1980), Rachid Ferchiou's *Les enfants de l'ennui* (*The Children of Boredom*, 1975), and Sadok Ben Aïcha's *Le mannequin* (*The Mannequin*, 1978) to Khaled Ghorbal's *Fatma* (2001)—have staged the sedimentations of the neopatriarchal mentality and demanded the furtherance of the modernist project of gender equality. Parallel to these films, there emerged a number of more or less feminist films that followed a slightly autobiographical *auteur* thrust and posed bold questions about women's oppression, sexuality, and liberation while deconstructing the neopatriarchal hold on social behavior by forcing into cognizance more ungendered conceptions of manhood. These films stretch from Selma Baccar's documentary *Fatma 75* (1978) to her most recent feature film, *Khochkhach* (*Flower of Oblivion*, 2006), and include, among others, Nejia Ben Mabrouk's *La trace* (*The Trace*, completed 1982); Moufida Tlatli's *Les silences du palais* (*Silences of the Palace*, 1994) and *La saison des hommes* (*The Season of Men*, 2000); Nadia Fares's *Miel et cendres* (*Honey and Ashes*, 1996), and Raja Amari's *Satin Rouge* (*Red Satin*, 2002) and *Les secrets* (*Buried Secrets*, 2009). While these films by female directors relied on the progressive feminist wager to undo normative constructions of manhood, other films by male directors such as Nouri Bouzid's films from *L'homme de cendre* (*Man of Ashes*, 1986) to *Le dernier film* (*Making Of*, 2006); Ferid Boughedir's *Halfaouine: L'enfant des terraces* (*Halfaouine: Boy of the Terraces*, 1990) and *Un été à la Goulette* (*A Summer at La Goulette*, 1995); Jilani Saadi's *Khorma, la bêtise* (*Khorma, Stupidity*, 2002) and *'Urs el-dhīb* (*Tender Is the Wolf*, 2006), as well as Abdellatif Kechiche's *La faute à Voltaire* (*Blame It on Voltaire*, 2000) and *La graine et le mulet* (*The Secret of the Grain*, 2007) delved into the experiences of male characters in order to unravel the neopatriarchal modes of production of manhood and to examine its constraining effects on unconventional sexual practices, homosocial space, and socioeconomic mobility. In what follows, I shall discuss an eclectic number of films from the two latter categories in order to show how female and male directors have, while focusing on seemingly dissimilar issues, collectively constructed, reproduced, and exposed a master narrative of melancholy manhood.

I understand this melancholy narrative of manhood in two significantly distinct ways, one is melancholite, the other melancholic: *melancholite* because it is shot through with fetishistic nostalgias for or narcissistic attachments to neopatriarchal reflexes and gendered constellations of social intelligibility and psychoaffective sovereignty; *melancholic* because it would conversely stake a claim to a set of historical or individual grievances and traumas (such as childhood molestation, rape, incarceration, torture, and other forms of abuse) that would have been thrust into oblivion were it not for melancholia's Janus-faced contemplation and scrutiny of the past—really, melancholia's creative and analytical potential to intuit the injustices that the past, any given past, might have assimilated en route to becoming recognizable as *past*. The retrospective provenance, particularism, and provincialism of melancholia, far from being counterproductive to forging livable futures, might potentially constitute an incubational moment for the emergence of just and perfectible futures, all the more so given melancholia's critical latencies and scrupulous vigilance to projects that seek to defuse or elide the past for the sake of convenience or for whatever sociopolitical exigencies, ideological calculations, and concrete immediacies invested in or attendant upon the inscription and interpretation of history. Insofar as melancholia is evocative of psychoaffective dissidence from regulatory practices of mourning, it offers a vantage point or methodological armory for any revisionary project of close reading, redress, and reparation (provided that the initially disoriented and generalized state of discomfiture it represents comes to be gradually transformed into particular critical and narrative investitures). Melancholia has, in short, the potential to bring the dignity of human recognition to those who may have incurred historical injustices of various kinds but have not yet been able to frame or work through them via homeopathic and publicly adequate measures of empathic witnessing and societal solidarity.

Tlatli's *Silences of the Palace* (صمت القصور) and *The Season of Men* (موسم الرّجال) are not technically and thematically very dissimilar. In both films, Tlatli relies squarely on the convenience of the flashback technique to underline how heavily the past experiences of her female protagonists still weigh on their present lives and to assess the extent to which, if at all, the modernist reforms entered after independence have changed the subordinate conditions of Tunisian women. Tlatli's findings are disconcerting, to say the least. Set in beylical Tunisia (the Hussein dynasty of beys, 1705–1957), which is technically part of the Ottoman Empire but de facto a French protectorate, *Silences* stages an initially promising reversal of fortunes both for Tunisia and for its women insofar as the independence of the country from France would usher in the independence of women from patriarchal bondage, as Lotfi (Sami Bouajila) himself assures Alia (Hend Sabri): "You're as indecisive as our country. One word thrills you, the next scares you. Things are going to change. A new future awaits us. You will be a great singer. Your voice will enchant everyone."[26] Such a reversal, however, hinges squarely on whether or not beylical conceptions of manhood would, following the exponential curve of decolonization, shrink into obsolescence in postcolonial Tunisia. Tlatli does not suggest that the effervescence of national liberation and the legal reforms that followed suit were calibrated with genuine changes in societal practices. Her verdict aligns with Marnia Lazreg's astute observation: "Consciousness of difference between women and men as an instance of social inequality, instead of the expression of biological difference ordained by a divine force, is not the automatic outcome of militancy in a decolonization movement."[27] It

---

26. For more on the intersection or correlation between the independence of Tunisia and the liberation of women, see such feminist readings by, among many others, Suzanne Gauch, *Liberating Shahrazad: Feminism, Postcolonialism, and Islam* (Minneapolis: University of Minnesota Press, 2007; Droit Naaman, "Woman/Nation: A Postcolonial Look at Female Subjectivity," *Quarterly Review of Film and Video* 17, no. 4 (2000): 333–42; Dina Sherzer, "Remembrance of Things Past: *Les silences du palais* by Moufida Tlatli," *South Central Review* 17, no. 3 (2000): 50–59; Catherine Slawy-Sutton, "*Outremer* and *The Silences of the Palace*: Feminist Allegories of Two Countries in Transition," *Pacific Coast Philology* 37 (2002): 85–104; Lindsey Moore, *Arab, Muslim, Woman: Voice and Vision in Postcolonial Literature and Film* (New York: Routledge, 2008); and Roy Armes, *Postcolonial Images: Studies in North African Film* (Bloomington: Indiana University Press, 2005). Gil Hochberg argues, quite suggestively, that *Silences* "invites" to be read as a national allegory yet "constantly undermines" such a reading in order to highlight "the disjunct between the 'national story' and Alia's 'personal story' as a woman" whose "own situation has not improved" in the wake of Tunisia's independence. To further understand such an allegorical disjunct, as Hochberg rightly suggests, it is necessary to examine, as I do here, the all too neat convergence between national allegory and Bourguiba's cult of personhood and the ways in which it has come to imperil for generations to come the incipient postcolonial liberation of men and women alike from the matrix of neopatriarchy, see Hochberg, "National Allegories and the Emergence of Female Voice in Moufida: Tlatli's *Les Silences du palais*," *Third Text* 14, no. 50 (2000): 42–43.

27. Marnia Lazreg, *The Eloquence of Silence: Algerian Women in Question* (New York: Routledge, 1994), 141.

MELANCHOLY MANHOOD 173

is not for nothing that Tlatli deems it indispensable to overcome the disjunctive temporalities, or *décalage* (lag), between the liberation of women and that of men.

While it is undeniably true that the narratives of manhood staged in *Silences* cannot be dissociated from the economic and bourgeois status of which they are a product, it does not necessarily follow that the emergence of more gender tolerant forms of manhood is contingent on the disruption of the economic and political privileges of beylical manhood. Indeed, while the Bey of Tunisia, Sidi Lamine, was deposed following a vote of the constituent assembly, which subsequently made the country a republic and Bourguiba first president, the postcolonial nation did not go farther than the promulgation of the PSC in ridding itself of the sedimentations of beylical manhood. Consider, for instance, the differences between the revolutionary nationalist Lotfi and the fervent antinationalist Sidi el-Bechir (Hichem Rostom), and, to a lesser extent, Sidi Ali (Kamel Fazaa) who remains caught in the trappings of beylical supremacy even though he definitely shows more sensitivity than his brother toward both nationalists and women servants. Discussing the riots and protests which were shaking apart at the seams French colonial power and its beylical acolytes, Sidi el-Bechir traces the origins of such a state of emergency/emergence to the crisis of manhood that had swept the Palace of the Beys. There ensues an intense dialogue between the two brothers, which dramatizes vividly the fallacious veneer of manhood that Tlatli is interested in undoing in her directorial debut:

> SIDI EL-BECHIR: There are no more powerful men left in the palace (*oufet er-rjāl esshāh mil-qsar*)
> SIDI ALI: They are on the other side (*esshāh duhru fil-wājha lukhra*)
> SIDI EL-BECHIR: But they have no class (*el-wahra*); class cannot be seized; it takes generations to nurture
> SIDI ALI: The country's had enough of us (*el-bled feddit mil-wahra wil-kbarāt*); we may end up facing the same sad fate as Farouk of Egypt and you're still dreaming of greatness and bigness (*el-wahra wil-kbarāt*)

This dialogue brings into prominence the clash between two constructions of manhood, one associated with the beys and the other with the revolutionary nationalists. It is the former conception of manhood sustained by class, greatness, and bigness (*el-wahra wil-kbarāt*) that seems to falter under the scrutiny of the nationalist gaze whose brand of manhood relies less on *el-wahra* than on braving storms of bullets from French machine guns. Indeed, when Khalti Hadda feared that the country would be lost were the Bey to leave, one of the servants firmly reassured her that "nothing would be lost, since the men who expose their chests to bullets know what they are doing" (*meydī' shey, er-rjāl ellī m'arḍa zdirha lirṣāṣ ta'rif esh-ta'mil*). These two scenes provide perhaps the most revelatory instances of the trembling of beylical manhood, long associated with *wahra* and socioeconomic privileges as well as with sexual exploitation of female servants. Sidi el-Bechir took umbrage at his brother's remark that the powerful men (*er-rjāl esshāh*) are on the other side of the conflict, regardless of whether they lack class and greatness, the touchstones of beylical manhood. His complaint that there are "no more powerful men left in the palace" is a melancholite disavowal of the agonizing narrative of beylical manhood.

The film's articulate undoing of beylical manhood is far from being an endorsement of revolutionary nationalist manhood, given that the latter seems to have failed to live up to its promises of gender equality, as Lotfi's relation to the adult Alia (Ghalia Lacroix) attests to. In his constant exhortations of Alia to abort time after time, there seems to be a dormant Bey at the heart of Lotfi's initially enchanting promises of new beginnings. As a colonized man, Lotfi's anticolonial struggle for basic human rights does not make him, as Lazreg rightly points out in the context of colonized Algerians, "a perfect human being. For him to understand the meaning of modes of suffering and inequality other than those inflicted upon him by colonial might requires attaining a form of consciousness that is willing to rise above its own victimization and implicate itself in that of others."[28] Far from attaining such self-reflexive and transformative consciousness, Lotfi has in fact internalized and applied to Alia the very protectorate system that France imposed on Tunisia. Upon picking her up from a wedding ceremony where she was singing, Lotfi assures Alia that she shouldn't worry about being harassed by other men because they know she is with him. While Alia was so inspired by his anticolonial nationalist zeal that she summoned up sufficient strength to sing the forbidden national anthem, *Tunis al-khaḍra'* (Green Tunisia)—and while he seems to have continued to offer her the protection she needed after her escape from the palace the very night her mother died in a botched abortion—Lotfi failed to offer her the family she had longed for in a free Tunisia, uninhibited by its oppressive past. It is as if her interruption of Oum Kalthoum's song *Amal ḥayātī* (The Hope of My Life) at the beginning of the film is a reenactment of the successive abortions she has been having and of the ungrievable life she has been living. Lotfi's first words in the film, "You're late," moreover, are suggestive of the hurdle of belatedness with which postcolonial subjectivities are plagued

---

28. Ibid., 140.

at the outset. Alia's later defiance of Lotfi, her decision to keep the child after having agreed to abortion, constitutes not only her next step on the ladder of individuation but also a blow to the intransigence of beylical manhood. Tlatli's melancholic scrutiny and commitment to undoing the melancholite beylical unconscious of manhood in Tunisian society does not stop at presenting her viewers with a more or less "feminist" challenge but proceeds to lay bare women's discomfiting complicity with the preponderance of beylical manhood. Indeed, in 2001, she told *The Guardian* that "Arab women are not oppressed by men; it is women who perpetuate the tradition. The decrees are there, the laws are there, but women did not immediately assimilate the possibilities."[29]

The Season of Men (2000), Tlatli's second feature film, though not as critically acclaimed as her debut feature, is I think a more mature and critically balanced film than the first. Counting as many flashbacks as *Silences*, *Season* chronicles the lives of women in the island of Djerba during the eleven-month absence and one-month presence of their husbands, who own bazaar shops in Tunis, the capital of Tunisia. Unlike *Silence*, which takes us to the inside of the opulent palaces of the Beys, *Season* is more concerned with (lower) middle-class women; it tackles the issue of *nuzūḥ*, internal migration or rural exodus, of the males of Djerba in southern Tunisia to the capital city for work, leaving their wives at the mercy of the despotic *la-ḥma*, or the mother-in-law, Oummi Sallouha (Mouna Noureddine). While not unmindful of the interdependencies of the economic and the social independence of women, Tlatli seeks rather to explore the labyrinthine thread of gender oppression as perpetrated by women against women in the absence of the men of the house. Tlatli sets herself thereby the task of complicating the verticality of oppression (i.e., of men enslaving women) she foregrounded in *Silences*. By staking women against women, Tlatli's film unveils the often overlooked female zeal to enforce the neopatriarchal and male-worshipping system from which women try to break free. In fact, the men in the film, whether the aged Am Ali (Sadok Boutouria) or the two brothers who work in Tunis, seem to have little to no role to play in a system that is nevertheless acted out in their name. While this is by no means

---

29. Tlatli, "Moufida Tlatli Showcases the Inner World of Women's Emancipation," *Magharebia: The News and Views of the Maghreb* (March 3, 2005). Tlatli's sensitivity to the active role women play wittingly or unwittingly in patriarchal and neopatriarchal practices contradicts Ella Shohat's argument that women in *Silences* "become a non-patriarchal family within a patriarchal context." *Taboo Memories, Diasporic Voices* (Durham, NC: Duke University Press, 2006), 303. While definitely not to an equal degree, for Tlatli men and women alike are subjects *of* and *to* patriarchy and cannot therefore be freed separately from its myriad twists and turns.

in contradiction with the logic of normative power, which works by absence, it is nonetheless crucially important to see the confluence of absence and presence of this patriarchal domination in the mother-in-law. *La-ḥma* presides over the house at will and urges her son, Said (Ezzedine Gannoun), to make clear to his rebellious wife, Aicha (Rabia Ben Abdallah), that as long as she is alive no other person's word but hers must be followed (*yilzim tfahhamhā 'illī hney ma dem enī ḥeiyah, mātham kān kilmtī timshī*).

Season dramatizes what Suad Joseph aptly calls "patriarchal connectivity": a form of sociality in which males and females collaboratively internalize, observe, and produce the norms of relationality and intelligibility by which they are governed. These norms are shot through by transgenerational patriarchal psychodynamics, lineaments, and proclivities. As Joseph argues, "connectivity and patriarchy have helped produce selves trained in the psychodynamics of domination, knowing how to control and be controlled."[30] No wonder then that the film's aim is to embarrass the brokered connectivities of patriarchy by figuring forth its underlying contradictions, hypocrisies, and naturalized injustices. Tlatli upsets this patriarchal apparatus by means of a gnawing irony whose performative effect is meant to set in motion a collaborative choking-off or disruption of patriarchal connectivity. *Season* dramatizes the ironies of a male-worshipping society, in which a woman is valorized in the eyes of her husband and other women only by her ability to give birth to male offspring. Regardless of the generally sanctimonious nature of patriarchal logic, for Aicha—who is, as it were, "plagued" by two daughters, Meriem (Ghania Benali) and Emna (Hend Sabri)—the key to earning the respect of the archmatriarchal *la-ḥma* is to give birth to a male child. Moreover, her husband, Said, had hypocritically exploited the situation in his favor, and in order to rid himself of her constant naggings and pleadings to take her to Tunis with him, he made that conditional on her bearing him a son. There follows, of course, the obsessions with, the anxieties over and difficulties of getting pregnant when the husband is absent for eleven-months-a-year from the household. But such a hardly conducive state of affairs does not seem to curb the amazement of

---

30. Suad Joseph, *Intimate Selving in Arab Families* (Syracuse, NY: Syracuse University Press, 1999), 13. Joseph further elaborates: "Patriarchy has operated effectively in part because both men and women were socialized to view themselves relationally. Connectivity has held family together in part because men and women, adults and children internalized the psychological demands of compliance with gendered and aged hierarchies. Intertwined, patriarchy and connectivity have underwritten the crafting of relationally oriented selves, socialized to negotiate gendered and aged hierarchies and *locally* recognized as healthy, mature, and responsible" (13–14, emphasis in original).

Aicha's mother at her inability to get pregnant: "How is it," her mother exclaims, "I want to understand, that you can't get pregnant?" (*ma'ṭānī nifhim kifesh 'āmla besh mā tiḥbilsh?*).

When Aicha finally gives birth to Aziz (Adel Hergal), the joys of *la-ḥma*, the husband, and the rest of the extended family reach an unprecedented pitch. Unfortunately, while the family was finally able to move to Tunis, this joy will prove short-lived. Aziz grows up as an autistic and emotionally troubled child who is subsequently rejected by, among others, his father, the very person who initially wanted to have a son. Indeed, the father wants to institutionalize him, but Aicha categorically opposes the idea, jeopardizing irreparably her marriage to Said who would then move out to a separate apartment. It is ironic that Aicha, the last person to have desired a son, is the only one who devotes her life to his well-being; indeed, in an admixture of resignation and defiance, she moves back with him to the old house in Djerba, which she thought she left forever when Aziz was born. It is as if, she finally realizes that, to borrow György Lukács's words, "the profound hopelessness of the struggle" to undo patriarchal connectivity is as taxing as "the still more profound hopelessness of its abandonment."[31] Her dedication to an autistic child and her opposition to his institutionalization both evoke, I think, the severity of her desire to expose the symptoms and anomalies of male-worshipping patriarchy; since relinquishing the child to a psychiatric institution would from a Foucauldian perspective amount to nothing more than a further acquiescence to the regulatory machinery of patriarchy, holding fast to an autistic child constitutes thus more than a sufficient excuse to embarrass the overestimated health of patriarchal logic, its facade of identification with sanity rather than with the conditions of human vulnerability that belie life and that ought therefore to govern social and family ties. Along the same lines, I find it particularly suggestive that the opening scene of *Season* dramatizes Aziz's refusal to take a bath, which is, symbolically, a refusal to undergo the rituals of cleanliness that patriarchal manhood cultivates and that the women of Djerba themselves undergo in their immaculate preparations for the sexual encounters involved in the one-month season of men back home. It is not for nothing also that *Season* concludes with a final fade-out, a close-up scene of Aziz in front of the loom, trying clumsily to weave a woof of thin red threads, as if acting out the melancholy impasse of patriarchal manhood, weighed down by its stubborn devotion to masculinity, sanity, and regulatory repression. It is as if Aziz, by virtue of reenacting his

---

31. Georg Lukács, *The Theory of the Novel*, trans. Anna Bostock (Cambridge, MA: MIT Press, 1971), 86.

mother's household craft, undoes, what Pierre Bourdieu has called "the fear of the female, firstly in oneself."[32]

By regulatory repression I mean to suggest the ineluctable performative confluence between normative power and its diurnal actualizations by compliant, complicit, or, really, regulated subjectivities. Even while I fully understand that subjects are products of the norms of which they become extensions and active perpetuators, I do not subscribe to the seemingly dizzying and unbreakable circularity of regulatory power. Neither do I subscribe to a revolutionary dialectic of reversibility whereby norms could be supplanted or subverted by others, and so forth, as is undoubtedly the case with Bourguiba's vision of Tunisian modernity. It seems to me that the ineluctability of submitting to regulatory power matches only the insurgent force with which this power is paradoxically reproduced, challenged, and ultimately mutated through localized and stylized exercises of close reading and regenerative critical wakefulness to the workings of power relations in all spheres of life. While unquestionably constant, regulatory power, scanned through a span of time, reveals that it is actually neither immune to mutability nor in excess of immanent transformation in everyday practice. This is perhaps a rather roundabout way of concluding my discussion of *Season*, but it is important to stress that *la-ḥma*'s presidency for life, as it were, over the household is inextricably tied to the transgenerational fact that she in turn had once submitted to the regulatory repression of her own mother-in-law, as Aicha's mother explains to her daughter. *La-ḥma* merely applies to her daughter-in-law the same patriarchal practices to which she once submitted at the hands of her own mother-in-law. It becomes clear, therefore, that the circularity of regulatory power within patriarchal connectivity owes a much more colossal emotional debt to the dialectics of primary vulnerability than to the regulatory functioning of the system avows or allows us to see. Regulatory repression, when actualized in the patriarchal sphere, is, in earnest, a regenerative attempt to surpass a scene of primary vulnerability that can neither be fully remembered nor assimilated, only compulsively acted out in spectacles of invulnerability. This is precisely the *melancholite* side of patriarchal manhood that Nadia Fares's *Honey and Ashes* (1996) delves into, exposes, and critiques. I call it melancholite not so much because of its disavowal or repression of primary vulnerability but because of its elegiac pursuit of the fantasy of invulnerability. Melancholites almost always fail to transform the apprehension of their profound vulnerability

---

32. Bourdieu, *The Masculine Domination*, 53.

into a condition of sociality, in which we become very much implicated in each other's vulnerability.

Fares's way of undoing the melancholite subsistence of patriarchal manhood proceeds, preparatory to anything else, by scandalizing its material effects: scenes of male abusive behavior toward women such as beating, harassment, and rape punctuate the film's action. Fares does not bother, in turn, to offer her viewers with alternative models of uninhibited and meaningful gender relations in what seems to be like a Tunisian battle of the sexes but forces them instead to leave the theater with bitterness and resentment, if not outrage. While I do not want to minimize the potential critical valences of such intense emotions, I nonetheless think that their thought-provoking and transformative force risks being crucially vitiated by the film's failure to furnish its male viewers with ideal or model characters they can possibly identify with—characters such as Sami (Nejib Belkadhi) in Tlatli's *Season*. Yet perhaps Fares should be credited precisely for just doing that—that is, for not attempting to offer us a reassuring model of manhood that might inadvertently result in rationalizing the melancholite violence inflicted by her eclectically chosen male characters on her eclectically chosen female characters.

Fares's *Honey and Ashes* relies on shock effect and scenes of recursive demonstrativeness of aggression against women in order to hammer home the unfaltering resoluteness and sorority of the feminist challenge to patriarchal manhood as well as to underscore the compulsive violence with which it is subsequently met. In a gesture reminiscent of Tlatli's *la-ḥma* character, Fares's film also drives a wedge between masculinity and patriarchal manhood by inserting a matriarchal figure who ends up practically forcing her son Hassan (Slim Larnaout) into an arranged marriage with his cousin instead of the girl he loves, Leila (Nozha Khouadra), and who would subsequently make a sudden and an unexpected swerve into freelance sex work. Briefly, the film depicts how Leila runs away from her father's house and takes up sex work to cover the costs of her studies. Just when Leila earned enough money and decided to quit, Idriss (Jamel Sassi), a fellow student madly in love with her, finds out about her secret job and decides to pay her a visit. Enraged and inconsolable, Idriss perceives her profession as an affront on his ego and tries to rape her; overpowered but unsubmissive, she suddenly grabs a knife and stabs him dead. When in prison, Leila's case draws the attention of Naima (Samia Mzali), a single mother—really, a know-it-all female figure who once fled to Russia to avoid entering into an arranged marriage with a man she does not know. She now works in a hospital where she meets, treats, and offers help and solidarity to Amina (Amel Hedhili) who has taken a beating from her husband, Moha (Naji Najeh).

Although the film is forcefully about the intersecting lives and common struggles of three different women within and against patriarchy, it does not proceed independently of a concomitant construction of a narrative of manhood. Indeed, *Honey and Ashes* dramatizes the matriarchal-patriarchal continuum and brings it under the critical scrutiny of the melancholic female gaze. The severity of this gaze must have impelled Leila and Naima in *Honey and Ashes* and Alia in *Silences* as well as Aicha in *Season* to challenge the hold of beylical manhood; similarly, it must have sustained Fares and Tlatli in their artistic mapping and exposure of the melancholite apparatus of manhood. As a psychoaffective formation, the melancholia of these female characters/filmmakers can be seen as both the symptom of and the impetus to confront the historical injustices of patriarchal manhood—a manhood that has yet to come to terms with the legacy of colonial shame, let alone with the added postcolonial blow to its patriarchal privileges. By reproducing the psychodynamics of extreme male violence and extreme male powerlessness, Fares's laudable intent is to paint a complex picture of Bourguiba's sons suspended in Tunisia's modernist project, unable to reconcile themselves to the exigencies of gender equality and to the hegemony of patriarchal mores. Fares's ambitious tapestry of male characters includes insanely jealous men, *ḥazzāra*, drunken machismos, clandestine prostitution clients, sanctimonious peasants, and so forth. I shall examine only the three major characters: Hassan, Leila's boyfriend; Idriss, Leila's fellow student; and Moha, Amina's husband. While these characters are different, they can be seen as variations on one modern Tunisian man caught in the disorienting incongruities of an arranged marriage between tradition and modernity and between theory and practice. Hassan who is in love with Leila proves gutless in front of his authoritative mother who forces him to marry his cousin. His behavior is typical of a mama's boy (*weld-'ummū*)— which in this context means someone who cannot possibly muster up enough courage to say *no* to the choices his mother makes for him. He is, I think, the aberrant example of weakness that patriarchal manhood, exemplified by his mother, exploits in order to enforce its regulatory rationale.

In the extended prologue to the film (which presents echoes of women's voices discussing male-female relations), one of the women declares that she cannot tolerate a man's weakness (*faiblesse*) while another maintains that weakness in a man can be very touching (la faiblesse chez un homme, ça peut être quelque chose de touchant aussi). In either case, it is important to stress that weakness in a man, which might be taken also as a signal of impotence or lack of manhood, is codetermined by the desires and aspirations of both men *and* women within patriarchy. Otherwise, how can we even begin to understand the coexistence in Tunisian society of the kind of logic that compels Naima to decline an arranged marriage and Hassan to succumb to one? Such a scenario is the measure of the film's sustained attempt to pry apart the sociocultural attributes of manhood (here, the mere courage to say *no*) from the biological differentials between masculinity and femininity. Without undermining or romanticizing the weakness of Hassan and the courage of Naima, I would like to argue that a combination of both casts a melancholy pall on patriarchal manhood—a manhood that feeds on the unacknowledged and disavowed rift between masculinity and men. What further muddies the waters is that for Hassan's mother, the task is to overcome the very modernity that emancipates the likes of Naima from the patriarchal mold. The dialectic between Hassan's mother (matriarchy) and Naima (modernity) yields Leila, Bourguiba's daughter *par excellence,* an admixture of contradictions, a character who depends on men (male clients) to liberate herself from them (Idriss).

Weakness is what patriarchal manhood paradoxically depends on and defends against. One might wonder whether Hassan is a victim of male powerlessness or of matriarchal supremacy, but, really, the latter is only an effect of the former. Consider, for instance, Idriss's visceral attempt to rape Leila when he discovers she is a clandestine prostitute by the name of Theresa. While Idriss is indubitably in love with Leila, he is in love with her only to the extent that she is a function or an extension of his own manhood. Such manhood is founded, as Abdelwahab Bouhdiba propounds, on the "kingdom of mothers," according to which the respect and idealization of the mother-imago is directly transferred onto the woman one loves. "Hence," Bouhdiba rightly concludes, an "excessive idealization of [a] woman [is] inevitably followed by disappointment," since the loved woman would certainly fall short of supplanting the aura of the mother-imago.[33] Enchanted by the mother-imago, Idriss's discovery that the woman he loves is a prostitute cannot be more revolting and

---

33. Abdelwahab Bouhdiba, *Sexuality in Islam,* trans. A. Sheridan (Boston: Routledge & Kegan Paul, 1985), 224. Bouhdiba goes on to argue the following: "Respect of our mothers prevents us from flying with our own wings. We have to see the mother, that is to say the truth, in her complete nakedness, face to face, without blenching, without accepting the slightest veil." Bouhdiba, *Sexuality in Islam,* 227. Indeed, this view seems to echo Assia Djebar's rhetorical queries in *A Sister to Scheherazade (Ombre Sultane)*: "Are men ever really naked? You are never free of fetters, you are bound fast by fears of the tribe, swathed in all the anxieties handed down to you by frustrated mothers, shackled by all your obsessions with some ill-defined elsewhere! . . . Show me one really naked man on this earth, and I will leave you for that man!" see Djebar, *A Sister to Scheherazade* (Portsmouth: Heineman, 1987), 86. Both Bouhdiba and Djebar

embarrassing a betrayal. Conversely, even though he tells his friend that it is sinful (*e-ḥrām*) to sleep with prostitutes, he spitefully tries to rape Leila, all the while threatening to denounce her. Unbeknownst to him, however, Leila had already quit the clandestine job. Idriss's attempt to rape her can therefore be understood as a melancholite attempt to suture the fissuring narcissistic wound of his manhood—a manhood that is demarcated by the dominance of the mother-imago as well as by the otherwise all too human defenselessness against suffering that accompanies falling in love with another person. For the inevitability of grief and suffering regulates erotic expenditure and structures libidinal approaches, encounters, and cathexes such that love is indeed unthinkable outside the parameters of grief and grieving. Idriss's injured ego, however, is blind to the chiastic gliding of vulnerabilities that inaugurates libidinal ties and seeks instead to reaffirm a fantasy of mastery and control over his unimmunized exposure to his love-object, Leila.

By refusing to prostitute herself to him, Leila denies him an immediate vehicle of mastering and making up for the foundational vulnerability of having been in love (with the allegedly wrong mother-imago). In other words, by refusing to participate in what would have amounted to his ego-consolatory process of mourning, Leila can be seen to have exposed and further compounded the vulnerability of Idriss's patriarchal manhood. Leila's refusal to participate in his consolatory mourning process is in fact a refusal to mourn him mourning himself for his inability to come to terms with his vulnerability. If Leila were to participate in his spectacle of mourning and give herself to him, not only would she have thwarted his healing process ("lies don't heal," says Naima), but she would also have become an accomplice in the consolidation of the repertory of lies that sustains patriarchal manhood. When she stabs him to death with a knife, she can therefore confidently claim: "I killed him with the truth, not with a knife" (Quand je l'ai tué, je l'ai fait avec la vérité, pas avec un couteau).

Lies should here be understood in their interactive literal and figurative senses. Every time Moha—who is not only a former professor of his wife, Amina, but also of both Idriss and Leila—beats Amina, he tells his daughter and the doctor in the hospital (who happens to be the know-it-all Naima) that she fell down the stairs. Only lies can close the yawning gap between traditional manhood and the simulacrum of French modernity, that is, between being a wife-beater in the privacy of one's house and a professor of French at the university. Insofar as "the most extreme idealism . . . could co-exist, without con-

---

point toward the necessity of encircling and rechanneling the influx of matriarchal-patriarchal reflexes into uninhibited and ungendered projects of selfhood.

scious contradiction, with everyday social cynical practice" in neopatriarchal societies, Moha is the prototype of Bourguiba's sons.[34] The task of modernity becomes a mask of traditionalism in neopatriarchy. Although he claims to have deemed himself the only person who could make Amina "happy and free," he ironically sees no contradiction between such idealism and his male-worshipping mentality: "If you had really loved me," he tells Amina, "you would have given me a son." Furthermore, even though he once offered Amina one volume of Foucault's *Dits et écrits* and appears aware of Foucault's useful insights into regulatory power, he fails to integrate an element of self-scrutiny and consistency as he navigates the private and public spheres of his life as a husband and a father as well as a professor and public intellectual. Indeed, in the classroom, he seems to maintain a gendered sensibility in his relationship with his students, assigning, for instance, research topics about "love" to female students and others about "money" to male students. In sum, Moha is as frenchified (to use Bourguiba's word) modern Tunisian as he can possibly aspire to be from within the citadels of neopatriarchy and facade of modernity.

There is a very precious moment in *Honey and Ashes* when Moha is crying solitarily in front of his desk, but as soon as Amina comes into the room, he stops, and quickly masks with a stern face, bristling with anger, what could have possibly been a productive homeopathic experience of mourning. *Honey and Ashes* deconstructs the melancholite recourse of Bourguiba's sons to masks of invulnerability in order for them to continue to command the credibility of patriarchal manhood. In this respect, the riddle (*tshanshīna*) that the young Safiyya plays with her mother is very suggestive. Safiyya asks her mother about who she thinks is the "biggest" and "strongest" of all; when her mother, Amina, interrupts her half-way through, "I know—God" (*e'raftū—Rabbī*), Safiyya corrects her: "No, it isn't God, it's Papa!" It is this kind of knowledge instilled in the minds of young girls at an early age that ultimately contributes to the perpetuation and intensification of a distinctive linkage between masculinity and male supremacy in society at large. Tlatli's and Fares's films expose the unacknowledged or disavowed chasm between masculinity and manhood and caution against the melancholite dispositions generated by Bourguiba's gendered project of modernity. By conferring on their female protagonists the attributes of *rujūla* or manhood (such as courage, defiance, solidarity, and perseverance), their aim is not only to subvert gender biases but also to undo the schizophrenic premises of the patriarchal collective unconscious and to embarrass its unjust hold on the forms of sociality and intelligibility that regulate relations between Tunisian men and women.

---

34. Sharabi, *Neopatriarchy*, 66.

Manhood Undone

> Generally, the image people have in their heads is one which has to be favorable; they can't imagine anyone presenting an unfavorable image of themselves to them. So I almost rape them with my images so that they shan't be raped elsewhere.
>
> NOURI BOUZID[35]

> No later undoing will undo the first undoing.
>
> JAMES JOYCE[36]

While Tlatli and Fares undo the "genderational"[37] impress of patriarchal manhood by bringing it into collision with economized female and feminist challenges, Férid Boughedir and Nouri Bouzid provide a rationale for comprehending the "undoing effects" of manhood, whether by constructing its passage rites (Boughedir) or by discerning the heterosexist biases on which it is predicated and the residual grievances of which it is a product (Bouzid). In *Halfaouine: Boy of the Terraces*, Boughedir maps the different stages that the twelve-year-old protagonist, Noura (Selim Boughedir), goes through in the process of being socially instituted, constituted, and accepted as a member of the fellowship of men. The film can be seen as a visual assemblage or inventory of signals that attest to the rituals of virilization (and, simultaneously, defeminization) that mark a child's crossing of the threshold of the male world. These signals start with circumcision (which Noura reexperiences vicariously during his brother's circumcision ceremony) and range thereafter from Noura's growing sexual curiosity and subsequent banishment from the women's ḥammām (i.e., public bath) after having been caught by the manageress gazing at a local beauty, trying to steal her underwear, to his first sexual encounter with an orphan-girl servant and his eventual rebellion against his father, Si Azzouz (Mustapha Adouani), which signifies his triumphant resolution of the oedipal struggle/complex. The making of Noura's manhood throughout the film runs parallel to the unmaking of his father's authority, as if to underscore, and rightly so, the transgenerational transmission of the patriarchal order and conversely

---

35. Nouri Bouzid, "On Inspiration," in *African Experiences of Cinema*, ed. I. Bakari and M. Cham (London: British Film Institute, 1996), 56.

36. James Joyce, *Ulysses*, ed. Declan Kiberd (New York: Penguin Books, 1992), 251.

37. This neologism is used by Anthony R. Berkley to refer to the overlap between gender and generation in Maya society, but I use it here to stress the transgenerational transmission of gender discrimination in patriarchy. See Berkley, "Respecting Maya Language Revitalization," *Linguistics and Education* 12, no. 3 (2001): 345–66.

the vulnerability of patriarchy, its susceptibility to change, if not transformation altogether. While Boughedir's film details the rituals, challenges, frustrations, and pleasures of Noura's initiation process to manhood—and of the seamless compatibility, if not collapsibility, of masculinity, manhood, and heterosexual practices—Bouzid's Man of Ashes draws out and enacts manhood as the scene or site of infantile traumata, and of acute anxiety, despair, and inconsolability. If Boughedir's film documents the various social incitements to "manning up," and the becoming man of Noura following his discovery of the female body, Bouzid's directorial debut, my focus henceforth, accents the process of "becoming undone" in the very roadmap to becoming man.[38]

Man of Ashes chronicles the crisis of manhood that Hachemi (Imad Maalal) experiences at a time when the ceremonial preparations for his arranged marriage are well underway, that is, at a time when the social expectations of virility become the ultimate litmus test of manhood. The crisis is provoked by the circulating graffiti rumor about the alleged lack of manhood of Farfat (Khaled Ksouri), his childhood friend. The many graffiti on street walls, which announce that Farfat is not a man (*Farfat mush rājil*) have brought back with them a seriality of traumatic flashbacks or *screen scenes* of childhood rape. The viewer gradually realizes that when they were young carpentry apprentices, Hachemi and Farfat were both molested by their mentor, Ameur (Mustafa Adouani), and they both grew up indelibly marked and precariously bound up by this closet trauma even though it functions as a mere open secret in the public sphere. While both of them suffered their mentor's sexual assaults, it is Farfat alone who seems to bear the heavy burden of its public disclosure since Hachemi sustains quite an intact public reputation, hardly tarnished by his intense homosocial relationship with Farfat. Director Nouri Bouzid insists, however, that Farfat is but Hachemi's "double, the other side of the coin," he who would have no qualms to say to society: "Get stuffed, I will do what I like."[39] As the figure of the double, Farfat personifies the "internal" drama within Hachemi's psyche, lifts up a flap of the veil on the heterosexist unconscious of society—really, positions and implicates the viewer as a witness to or accomplice in the stressful and frustrating conditions of patriarchal manhood. Little wonder, then, that it is via Farfat that the film strains in the lumpy bits of child molestation, homophobia, and erotic vengeance—verities that would certainly prove hard to swallow for the majority of the beneficiaries of patriarchal manhood. Indeed, by the end of the film, Hachemi releases Farfat from his tight hold—as if letting loose a long pent-up instinct or a repressed desire

---

38. Judith Butler, *Undoing Gender* (New York: Routledge, 2004), 1.
39. Bouzid, "On Inspiration," 50.

for vengeance—so that he confronts the pederast Ameur and stabs him in the groin.

Throughout the film, the protagonist and his double struggle with the psychosocially daunting task of being (validated as) *men*—that is, of being, paradoxically, members of a rigid community they can neither fully join nor leave behind even though Farfat's fantasy of departure from Sfax to Tunis animates his rebelliousness against his biological father and ultimately against his father figure or, as it were, mentor-cum-molester, Ameur. This is a community in which the melancholite anxieties of male supremacy (of which the gendered construction of manhood is a product) are augmented by the devirilizing heterosexist fears of emasculation, effeminacy, and homosexuality. Manhood in this community is, it bears repeating Bourdieu, "an eminently *relational* notion, constructed in front of and for other men and against femininity [and, I would add, queerness], in a kind of *fear* of the female [and the queer], firstly in oneself."[40] Like other docile members of their community, Hachemi and Farfat are already undone by the constitutive heterosexist norms of intelligibility of patriarchal manhood; however, at the level of personal history, they are more profoundly undone by the sexual assaults of their mentor-cum-molester—assaults that, while evidentially incriminating, must remain unspeakable, not least because they carry the taint of homosexuality, or of what is commonly referred to in Tunisian pejorative parlance as *wabna* (i.e., *coitus a tergo* between men). Being victims of pederasty, Hachemi and Farfat grew up to be victims of homophobia in a community hypocritically bent on shaming its victims and glorifying its rapists, molesters, or active homosexuals (*ṭaffāra*). Consider, for instance, "Ameur's standing in the community as a respected family man who, naturally, will be invited to the wedding" at the very same time that Farfat is banished from his father's house, vilified and denigrated by Azaiez (Mohamed Dhrif) as less than a man.[41]

The tragedy of child molestation, far from being ethically and therapeutically reckoned with, is disavowed, displaced, and thus aggravated by the scapegoating and blackmailing effects of homosexual shaming rituals, in which "aggressors" (here Ameur) are associated with male power while the "aggressed" (here Farfat in particular) are cast aside as effeminate weaklings. It is as if patriarchal manhood cannot appreciate the pain, let alone denounce the crime, of child molestation unless as a defamatory scandal of homosexuality! Worse, the Manichean logic of patriarchal manhood would stop at nothing to

---

40. Bourdieu, *The Masculine Domination*, 53, original italics.

41. Martin Stollery, "Masculinities, Generations, and Cultural Transformation in Contemporary Tunisian Cinema," *Screen* 42, no. 1 (2001): 53.

stigmatize and shame Farfat and Hachemi as aberrant models of manhood. Such cruelty is surely symptomatic of the agonizing vulnerability that drives melancholites into prophylactic and deceptive bonds of "real men" and melancholics into careful reexaminations of the all too familiar cognitive modalities that inhibit melancholites from extending human solidarity and empathy to the victims of the cisgender habitus. Few things are worse than suffering from the long shadows of a childhood trauma in a culture marked by the lack, or the foreclosure altogether, of the adequate conventions that would otherwise acknowledge such a trauma and initiate the reparative work of mourning necessary for its treatment. Ironically, while the trauma of child molestation is disavowed, its resultant effects (i.e., the public invalidation of Farfat's manhood, for instance) are recognized, sought after, and disseminated as hot entertainment items. The distance between the tragedy/injustice of child molestation and the scandal/stigma of homosexuality is the real measure of the melancholite disposition of the patriarchal apparatus of manhood, its sadistic, Manichean and *heteroimmunitary* pursuit of the fantasy of invulnerability.[42]

As I mentioned earlier, I reserve the term *melancholite* to describe the visceral and somewhat neurotic defensiveness with which the beneficiaries of patriarchal manhood guard ferociously against the encroachments of the feminist challenges of gender equality as well as the growing challenges of new sexualities, new masculinities, and transgendered identities, not least because of the discursive incitements of what Joseph Massad calls the "Gay International" whose universalizing pretentions and homogenizing politics of gay identity/rights/pride are, according to Massad, not only destroying formerly tolerated same-sex practices in the Arab world but also endangering the lives of LGBT subjectivities and exposing them to police identification and harassment, detention, imprisonment, torture, and forced exile, as was the case with the Egyptian LGBT activist Sara Hegazy.[43] In its melancholite form,

---

42. By *heteroimmunitary*, I refer to the frantic reinvestments in the heteronormative patriarchal orders of manhood in the wake of global LGBT challenges to conventional forms and norms of sexuality, sexual practices, and gender identities. *Heteroimmunization* is what melancholites do to preserve the spurious familiarity that binds them to their patriarchal habitus.

43. Joseph Massad, "Re-Orienting Desire: The Gay International and the Arab World," *Public Culture* 14, no. 2 (2002): 361–85. Massad's article predates Sara Hegazy, the Egyptian LGBT activist who was imprisoned and tortured in Abdel Fattah el-Sisi's Egypt after she was photographed flying a rainbow flag at a *Mashrou' Leila* concert in 2017 in Cairo. She suffered from intense PTSD and ended up taking her own life in exile in Canada. Perhaps the issue with the Gay International is less whether its soft power influence has been detrimental for pre-identitarian homosexual practices in the Arab world—it has—than whether such closeted

manhood is a fragile repository of psychoaffective and sociocultural dispositions, fears and anxieties, a saturated cushion of vulnerabilities, whose guardians and beneficiaries color it with fantasies of androcentric supremacy in order to confer on it the power and privilege to command credibility and gain legitimacy, that is, patriarchal perpetuity. I distinguish this largely unfounded—and quite pathologically disposed—melancholite form of manhood from the more retrospective and introspective melancholic form of manhood which is often grounded in an unequivocal event of historical injustice, or as is the case with Hachemi and Farfat in a traumatic experience of rape that can neither be forgotten nor openly confronted in the public sphere without further reactionary complications (i.e., stigmatization) from melancholites at large. In addition to being a posttraumatic formation, the melancholic form of manhood in *Man of Ashes* becomes a necessary tool to denaturalize and deconstruct the deceptive familiarity that binds melancholites to phallocentric modes of behavior embedded in the sexist ideology of patriarchy.

Farfat's own public disclosure that he is "not a man" is symptomatic of his melancholic insurgency—his "insistent communicativeness which finds satisfaction in self-exposure," unashamed self-flagellations, and ego-impoverishments.[44] Being a highly explosive force of emotional flux and fluidity, it is quite hard to determine whether melancholia is all suffering or perverse pleasure—and, in turn, whether Farfat is masochistically emptying his ego or luxuriating in his symptom via his self-engineered and wall-graffitied claim that he is not a man.[45] Farfat's melancholic diminution of self-regard cannot be understood

---

practices themselves can be sustained in the long run. All the more so given the rise of homonationalism in parallel to the Gay International, namely Israel's campaign to brand itself as a gay haven in contrast to the surrounding Arab world, and, worse still, Israel's attempt to harness these pinkwashing methods to appropriate all attention away from its settler colonial apartheid practices. That being said, there is a related issue that has hardly so far caught the attention of gender studies specialists writing on the Arab world—the question of *homosociality*.

Unquestionably, the Gay International has, I would argue, strained homosocial relations and, because of homosexual panic, eroded the spontaneous intimacy of greeting, feeling, and touching that, in a not so distant past, used to mediate relations between men, especially in the case of friendship. This is of course most obviously true about Hachemi and Farfat whose homosocial entanglements could easily be mistaken for unspoken or unspeakable homosexual desire. It still might be so, but the film does not provide any solid evidence in that direction, which leaves us with the homosocial bond as the overarching one.

44. Freud, "Mourning and Melancholia," in *On Metapsychology: The Theory of Psychoanalysis*, ed. Angela Richards (London: Penguin, 1991), 255.

45. Lang and Ben Moussa exaggerate quite a bit Farfat's turn against society and against its constrictive strictures of manhood all the while overlooking Farfat's struggle to reintegrate

separately from the nonexistence of any conventional strategy that would help him process and overcome his trauma of childhood rape. Along with the coercive violence of heterosexist manhood, the lack and/or foreclosure of a socially honored framework of mourning renders the injuries of trauma ungrievable, and explains therefore the "circuitous route by which the psyche accuses itself of its own worthlessness."[46] Yet, is not this self-inflicted violence, as Butler rhetorically asks, "a refracted indictment of the social forms that have made certain kinds of losses ungrievable?"[47] While this might surely be the case, I would like to further suggest that Farfat's public self-denunciation or disclosure that he is "not a man" is, in fact, a tactical move from a solitary suffering of the effects of childhood trauma to a deliberate implication of his entourage in such a process of suffering and public shaming; since the beginning of the end of solitary suffering occurs when it is witnessed and reckoned with by community members, Farfat is, in so publicly denouncing himself, attempting to engineer or solicit witnesses, regardless of whether or not they prove credibly empathic enough to bring him what Peter Shabad calls the "dignity of recognition."[48] Clearly, Farfat's melancholia is expressive of a hybrid strategy of *resisting* patriarchal manhood while *enduring* it.

By implicating the community to which he belongs (or rather from which he is ostracized and banished) in his public melancholic turn, Farfat is implicating us all in his suffering, not because we have experienced what he experienced firsthand, but because we cannot deny what his experience entails for us symbolically (especially for those of us who happen to be Arabs) living in the aftermath of 1967. Bouzid himself avers that he wanted to address "what makes up our present situation of crisis, the bankruptcy of our society. Thus, my first film [*Man of Ashes*] addresses childhood, not exactly mine but rather my generation's, how we were 'broken' from the beginning, how we suffered

---

himself into the community by, among others, wreaking vengeance on his molester. After all, "Farfat" literally means to flap one's wings against the earth as the slaughtered red cockerel in the beginning of the film does before gasping the last breath. If anything, Farfat's relation to the community remains shrouded in ambivalence, attraction and repulsion, insurrection and revolt. See Robert Lang and Maher Ben Moussa, "Choosing to Be 'Not a Man': Masculine Anxiety in Nouri Bouzid's *Rih Essed/Man of Ashes*," in *Masculinity: Bodies, Movies, Culture*, ed. Peter Lehman (New York: Routledge, 2001), 81–94.

46. Butler, *The Psychic Life of Power: Theories in Subjection* (Stanford, CA: Stanford University Press, 1997), 184.

47. Ibid., 185.

48. Peter Shabad, "The Most Intimate of Creations: Symptoms as Memorials to One's Lonely Suffering," in. *Symbolic Loss: The Ambiguity of Mourning and Memory at Century's End*, ed. Peter Homans (Charlottesville: University Press of Virginia, 2000), 210.

from adult violence."⁴⁹ While Bouzid might be referring here to the inaugurating, constitutive and inscriptional violence that accompanies our introduction to a sociality that prefigures our existence, his remarks take on a specific historical and political dimension in the context of *Man of Ashes*, besides the allegorical dimension which I delved into in chapter 1. Without diminishing the importance of the political allegory of French colonial and neocolonial rape or of Israel's ongoing occupation of Arab lands following the 1967 war (both of which are at the origin of the persisting malaise of postcolonial nationhood and the counterrevolutionary turn of the Arab uprisings), Bouzid's film is concerned with the immediate material and psychoaffective effects of these wider transnational Arab historical and societal crises as they become manifest—in a rather condensed and indirect form—at the inscriptional level of individual history. Moreover, while the correlative trajectories or allegorical correspondences between the neopatriarchal dispensation of Bourguiba's postcolonial Tunisia and the dramas of manhood of Hachemi and Farfat cannot be overstated, it is crucial to economize, and not to overemplot, the allegorical mode of reading, since it threatens to defuse the specificities of the historical case studies at hand onto the grand narratives of colonialism, postcolonialism, globalization, and so on.

Bourguiba's personification of the neopatriarchal cult of personhood informs, as I have shown, the melancholite proclivity of men portrayed in modern Tunisian film. Bourguiba's autocratic rule is, in turn, informed by the history of French colonialism as well as by the trials of Arab nationalism against Zionist settler colonialism and predatory Western imperialism. Both Bourguiba and sons are belated to a historical condition that contributed to their deformation and continues to exert immense psychic pressure on their present and future. The importance of Bouzid's *Man of Ashes* is the severity of its critique of the allegorical continuum between patriarchal manhood and Bourguiba's brand of Tunisian modernity and nationhood. Both Hachemi and Farfat renounce any possible identification with their biological fathers and their mentor-cum-molester who nevertheless boasts of having initiated them. For Hachemi, the only remaining model of manhood is Monsieur Lévy, the old Tunisian Jew, who dies just when Hachemi opens up to him and starts telling him about his secret trauma. The fact that by the very end of the film Hachemi seeks out but is not granted permanent refuge in the clandestine brothel run by Sejra is expressive of the ways in which the play of identifications in this scene is mobilized to recast widely the nets of paternity, fatherhood,

---

49. In Viola Shafik, *Arab Cinema: History and Cultural Identity* (Cairo: American University in Cairo Press, 1998), 194.

motherhood, and, really, manhood insofar as it is now irreducible to the empty but injurious rhetoric of men and masculinity. Manhood is persistently wrested away from normative patriarchal sedimentations throughout the film. In this respect, the opening scene of a slaughtered red cockerel, flapping its feathers and gasping its last breath is indeed a performative trope of the melancholic predicament of manhood. The cockerel, a symbol of virility and masculinity, conjures up less the fear of castration than the imperative to pry virility and masculinity apart from manhood. From the outset, the film deploys what might have been a castrating historical situation of colonial rape or child molestation to prod the viewer to rethink manhood beyond the fallacies of virility and masculinity.

There is something politically redemptory in Bouzid's preoccupation with staging "broken" individuals in a decadent society—a society unable to take stock of its glaring moral bankruptcy, never mind its sociopolitical failures. Small wonder that one of Bouzid's preeminent keywords is "defeat," or, more precisely, the inexhaustible drama that follows from the disavowal of defeat in a world traversed by a "pair of contradictions—greatness and impotence."[50] For Bouzid, the incumbent task of the filmmaker is to force the recognition of defeat on the viewer who might have formerly lived in the fantasy of a balmy elsewhere, unencumbered by the fleeting thought of an imminent downfall. The cinematic image must deal a rude awakening to the viewer, rape him out of his world of fantasy "so that he shan't be raped elsewhere."[51] Bouzid's preoccupation with defeated individuals whose manhood has already been undone must be confidently understood as an attempt to explore the critical, transformative, and empowering emotional valences of aestheticizing failure, hammering home melancholic men, and *melancholicizing* the spectators in the process—awakening them to the historical injustices of which they are the product and in which they are implicated. As Rey Chow observes in a not so dissimilar a context, "the powerless provides a means of aesthetic transaction through which a certain emotional stability arises from *observing* the powerless as a spectacle."[52] Through the chiasmus of proximity and distance, of identification and disidentification with the powerless, the viewer becomes cognizant of the imperiling structures of manhood in which he is involved, of the melancholic and melancholite anxieties attendant upon such structures, and of the necessity of reconfiguring manhood as a locus and force of cultural

---

50. Bouzid, "On Inspiration," 54.
51. Ibid., 56.
52. Rey Chow, *Primitive Passions: Visuality, Sexuality, Ethnography, and Contemporary Chinese Cinema* (New York: Columbia University Press, 1995), 135, italics in original.

malleability, unbundled from gender and sexual practices—and, above all, at a safe remove from the heteroimmunitary exit strategies of melancholites at large.

Bouzid's *Man of Ashes* becomes in this respect a veritable artistic vehicle that permits us to undertake the indispensable work of puncturing the fantasy of melancholite invulnerability, all the while implicating ourselves in the experiences of powerlessness that mark the melancholic condition of manhood and subjectivity. Bouzid has been preoccupied with powerless and defeated individuals throughout his cinematic career; it is as much an obsession as a mission whereby he seeks to incite empathy, project, and rehearse a sense of communal and collective solidarity among Arab audiences. It is not a fetishization of defeat, much less of defeatism, but an indefatigable effort to contribute a cultural politics of empowerment to the larger political context in which the crisis of Arab subjectivity and manhood has been artistically inscribed through chronicles of individual histories of political impotence, castration, or suicide protest, as is most notably the case in Palestine during the Second Intifada (2000–2005). As long as the Arab world continues to be unfree from Euro-American and Zionist domination, even more so after the Arab uprisings, the everyday fetishization of virility and masculinity can only breed melancholites, not foster a collective consciousness of the melancholic predicament of manhood in the current historical juncture of Arab contemporaneity. Without such collective consciousness, at a remove from the melancholite reflexes of quotidian patriarchy, not even the potentially redemptory valences of melancholia can be productively redirected into the critique of the joined-up forces of settler colonialism and global neoliberal imperialism.

In the following chapter, devoted entirely to the psychoaffective politics of resistance in Hany Abu-Assad's 2005 film *al-jannah-tul-'ān* (*Paradise Now*), I will move from the context of Tunisia, in which the imposition of modernity in an authoritative and authoritarian presidential style resulted in a spectrum of psychoaffective resistances, to the context of occupied Palestine, in which the imposition of a military occupation, settler colonial style, has resulted in the emergence of twisted forms of complicity and resistance that range from coerced collaboration to martyrdom and suicide operations. Melancholy forms in the interface between the hopelessness of resistance to the mighty occupation (a hopelessness that is best captured by the resort to acts of martyrdom or suicide protests) and the alternative hopelessness of giving up the struggle altogether. There emerges a cruel psychoaffective struggle between the necessity of not giving up the resistance and the impossibility of forging a meaningful, let alone productive, strategy of resistance to the iron cage or tight grip of the Israeli military occupation. The resigned attachment to the impossibility of resistance in this particular historical disjuncture makes nothing happen, except perhaps a complete Israeli annexation of what is left of historical Palestine. It is the melancholy attachment to resistance in the face of its impossibility that deserves our critical attention, not least because it attests to the steadfastness of the human will in the face of the macabre apparatus of the occupation. What is worse than the impossibility of armed resistance, however, is for it to take forms that have been made possible wittingly or unwittingly by the splintering occupation. After all—and as Said, the protagonist of Abu-Assad's *Paradise Now*, rightly points out—"it is the occupation that decides 'the space of Man' (*masāḥit el-'insān*) and 'the space of struggle' (*masāḥit el-niḍāl*)." Ironically, the occupied are always decried and denounced for whatever means (left to them by the occupation) they may decide to make use of in their own resistance to the occupation.

It is worth recalling another part of the same memorable scene, with which I started chapter 1, from Gillo Pontecorvo's 1966 classic *The Battle of Algiers*. This is the part in which Larbi Ben M'Hidi, the historical FLN leader who was captured by mistake and brought to a press conference, was asked by a journalist—"Mr. Ben M'Hidi, isn't it cowardly to use your women's baskets to carry bombs, which have taken so many innocent lives?" Ben M'Hidi's reply debunks with cutting irony the brazen assumptions of the question: "*évidement, avec des avions ça aurait été plus commode pour nous*" (obviously, planes would have made things more comfortable for us). Ben M'Hidi ends his statement with an even more scathing irony: "Give us your bombers, sir, and you can have our baskets." *The Battle of Algiers*, which enjoyed a second life after 9/11, allows for something that is terribly missing in the political discourses against terrorism—contextualization and historicization. Condemnation alone forecloses interpretation, narrative, and critique. The rhetoric of terrorism has become, especially during Al-Aqsa Intifada, part of the ideology of the occupation: it aims to confine Palestinians to a choice between two alternative states of nonexistence. First, there is the state of nonexistence that is defined by the nonresistance to an occupying and dispossessing settler colonial power. It is precisely the dehumanizing and degrading state of allowing others to have total sovereignty over you, that is, allowing them most importantly the privilege of determining your life and your death. These are of course extreme forms of sovereignty, the privilege of sovereign power, a power that determines who must die and who must live. Second, there is the state of nonexistence that follows almost automatically upon any kind of resistance to the occupation. It is precisely the scandal of being called a terrorist. To be called a terrorist is by definition to become nonexistent, to disappear from the face of the earth, and to become a disposable subject, a subject that can, if captured beforehand, be detained, tortured, and ultimately destroyed. It is clear then that whether in the context of the Algerian armed resistance or in the context of Palestinian resistance to the occupation, there hides behind the dizzying rhetoric of terrorism the pernicious ideology of reducing to silence any form of armed or unarmed resistance. As I will show in the next chapter, Abu-Assad's *Paradise Now* dramatizes the stakes of resistance, or what is left of it, in the aftermath of Al-Aqsa Intifada. The film treads a fine line between the commitment to militancy and the incumbent critique of the pitfalls of martyrdom operations, namely their desensitized commodification in Palestinian society at large. All of these critical, theoretical, economic, and sociopolitical dynamics are variably broached at the inscriptional level of the individual histories of the two protagonists, Khaled and Said.

5
Melancholy Ends
Palestinian Film and Narrative Martyrdom

A photograph has two dimensions, so does a television screen; neither can be walked through.

—JEAN GENET

We Palestinians are a human phenomenon facing a gigantic colonizer, and we refuse to give up . . . We are facing a project of ethnic cleansing. Our only weapons are persistence, knowledge, culture and art.

—HANY ABU-ASSAD

There are a great number of war films with pretensions of denouncing war which at the same time are great spectacles of war; and in the end the spectacle is what you enjoy about them. So to speak clearly: art is essentially a disinterested activity, but if we're in a phase when we have to express interests, then let's do it openly and not continue to camouflage it. And therefore, if art is substantially a disinterested activity [*actividad desinteresada*] and we're obliged to do it in an interested way, it becomes an imperfect art.

—JULIO GARCÍA ESPINOSA

In a triumphantly planetary age, comfortably abandoned to the hypnotizing lures of reality shows and the implacable whims of entertainment industries, the aestheticization and consumption of atrocity, horror, violence, and so on, it is indubitably a daunting task to seek to produce by way of critique an appraisal of film that might move us beyond its inaugurating spectacular appeal. If film is nowadays unthinkable outside the conscripts of an economy of the spectacle—or without the mediatory interposition of the screen that cannot "be walked through," as Genet pinpoints in the epigraph—it becomes incumbent upon us to discern, following Espinosa's critical insight in the above epigraph, the artistic imperfections which would make film irreducible to a spectacle, pandering, as it were, to audiences' unwitting lust for melodramas, intrigues, kinesthetic thrills, and technically sophisticated stunts, dazzles, or visual gags.[1]

Surely film cannot evacuate its spectacular entertainment principle or be redeemed *from* it, but it can, or so I hope to contend, be redeemed *through* it—by continually raising the threshold beyond which it ceases to be a readily consumable good, and, in particular, by committing to the exigencies of historical veracity with the sense and force, patient and persistent, of responsible mimetic urgency. Without diminishing the crucial importance of always approaching film critically—and interrogating its unavoidable complicity with the historical moment of global capital of which it is a product—my priority in this chapter is to extend the thematic discussion of film in the previous chapter and attend more closely to the critical valences of cinematic form, its optical fecundity and potential for fostering critical consciousness and precipitating political dissidence. I intend to do so partly by exploring the paradox of the spectacle in Hany Abu-Assad's *Paradise Now* (*al-jannah-tul-ān*): the ways in which film can surpass itself in the process of becoming itself—becomes otherwise than spectacle in the very route to becoming spectacle.

The paradox of the spectacle is an offshoot of our residual ambivalence toward the persistently solidifying visual cultural dispensation in which we are caught, and which has installed in us two contradictory and dueling sociopolitical malaises: an impulsive cynicism toward the visual (whether because of its mimetic unreliability or insidious conditioning forces) combined or alternating with a reluctant cognizance of its ineluctability, or, worse still, its indispensability in a world-wide society that Guy Debord had characterized as the "society of the spectacle."[2] It is necessary therefore to pinpoint and affirm

---

1. Julio García Espinosa, "Meditations on Imperfect Cinema ... Fifteen Years Later," Trans. Michael Chanan, in *New Latin American Cinema: Theory, Practices and Transcontinental Articulations*, ed. Michael T. Martin (Detroit, MI: Wayne State University Press, 1997), 84.

2. It is worth noting that, for Debord, "the spectacle is not a collection of images; rather, it is a social relationship between people that is mediated by images," *The Society of the Spectacle*,

the many ways in which film might mobilize the visually enchanting aura of the spectacle in order to envision and elaborate new corridors to a historical reality that might, ironically, be no longer recognizable if it were to be "walked through" firsthand, that is, without the sheltering, balmy and even desensitizing mediation of the screen. In fact, whenever/wherever the reality of catastrophe and violence is "walked through," it does not necessarily mean that it has become witnessable (least of all from a psychoanalytic point of view), comprehensible or graspable as such (since its effects are usually *perceived* as *surreal* rather than real).[3] Reality itself might no longer be sustainable if it can no longer be discernible through the visual, virtual, or fictional writ large.

Since many of us nowadays "experience" reality virtually and visually, it is oftentimes argued by critics as diverse as Jean-François Lyotard, Frederic Jameson, Martin Jay, Alain Badiou, and Jean Baudrillard, among others, that we are inhabited by a nostalgia or passion for lived experiences, for a naked return to the desublimated real (through, for instance, extreme sports, reality shows, and so on, which both embody and displace this insatiable *passion du réel*). Such configurations of the passion for the unmediated real, however, pale into insignificance if compared to the brisk surfacing of the "desert of the real" at the heart of American soil, as Slavoj Žižek puts it following the cataclysmic attacks on the World Trade Center in New York and the Pentagon in Virginia on September 11, 2001.[4] The arguments about the return to/of the real are but fodder, in my view, for a scholastic debate at best and a dangerous one at worst—"scholastic" because we indisputably, not to say hopelessly, live under the ineluctable modalities of the virtual and the visual, and "dangerous" because such arguments about the return to/of the real stealthily imply that, without having experienced the same, we cannot have access to the mediated experiences of others, regardless of where they come from, how near or far, or what they went through, how tragic, cruel, or, to put it bluntly, unfortunate.

---

trans. Donald Nicholson-Smith (New York: Zone Books, 1995), 12. In other words, the spectacle is a function of social intelligibility and cannot therefore be rethought separately from the unwritten norms that govern social relations at large. What I will be calling the "collapse of the spectacle" is a threshold moment in the process of disarticulating the existing sociocultural norms of intelligibility in order to bring under critical scrutiny their assumptions and (oftentimes, devastating political) implications.

3. Jean Genet, "Four Hours in Shatila," *Journal of Palestine Studies* 12. 3 (1983), 4.

4. Slavoj Žižek, *Welcome to the Desert of the Real: Five Essays on September 11 and Related Dates* (New York: Verso, 2002).

In no small measure, to applaud the return to/of the real is to tacitly consent to the nonexistence of the Other prior to the burst of the real on the Western front. Indeed, what remains after the so-called return to/of the real, after every return, is the foreclosure of the real that structures this very return. It is this foreclosure of the real therefore that should be interrogated, not its assumingly terrorizing (also in Kantian terms) returns, which deflect all attention away from the constitutive foreclosure of the real at the heart of global imperialism. Obsessive consumptions of and nostalgias for the fake-real in reality shows are in this sense but symptoms of this systematic and ambient foreclosure on a massive scale.

With the many atrocities materializing in front of our eyes since the turn of twenty-first century—in, among other places, Gaza, Lebanon, Iraq, Libya, Syria, Yemen, and Egypt—it is dubious, not to say utterly naïve and disingenuous, to maintain that the smacks of the desert of the real we experienced at home did indeed bring closer to us (let alone bringing us closer to) the deserts of the real and banal tragedies of everyday Palestinians, Iraqis, and Syrians, to name a few of the peoples whose sufferings have become so permitted that they can neither be numbered nor mourned, neither prevented nor halted, let alone acknowledged. Has our experience of the desert of the real at home helped us reckon with the deserts of others? No. On the contrary, it has fueled, in a frenzy of compulsive repetition and retribution, the obscene and self-righteous desire to raise the threshold of the desert beyond any foreseeable "empathic unsettlement," to borrow Dominick LaCapra's felicitous expression.[5]

Hany Abu-Assad's 2005 *Paradise Now* reopens the corridors of distant empathizing and shakes awake the intoxicated slumbering of our sobering imaginative impulses. It treads the fine line between objectively interpreting and critically interrogating martyrdom operations, ensuring that these complementary and simultaneous hermeneutic tasks do not slither accidentally into the hegemonic and hegemonizing discourse of the "war on terror," whose binary logic forecloses reflection altogether. The film makes use of a minimalist and stylized version of the thriller genre (minus tension music, sound, and special effects) and camera malfunction as well as the humorous register to undo the spectacle of martyrdom and articulate a more nuanced and challenging narrative of Palestinian nationhood—a narrative that has so far been both impermissible and/or readily discreditable by the colossal system of Israeli occupation. In chapter 2, I reflected on the possibility of poetry, particularly the poetry of

---

5. Dominick LaCapra, "Trauma, Absence, Loss," *Critical Inquiry* 25 (1999): 699.

resistance that emerges in a seriality of aftermaths—after the Nakba, after the Naksa and after Iraq. I explored the melancholic commitments to resistance at the level of poetic form, the attenuation and tenacity of form in expressing and sustaining resistance to the Israeli occupation. In this chapter, I move the discussion from poetic to cinematic form and inquire about the ends of resistance to the omnipotent system of the Israeli military occupation in Palestine, which strategically transforms any form of opposition to its atrocities into a productive force.[6] The questions that foment the melancholy anguish throughout *Paradise Now* are as follows: Is resistance to the Israeli occupation still possible? If yes, how? If not, is an end to the occupation still possible without resistance? The framing argument of my discussion is as follows: as melancholy acts, martyrdom operations testify to two impossibilities, the impossibility of resistance and the impossibility of liberation without resistance. As Emad Burnat's *Five Broken Cameras* (2012) harrowingly attests, any form of resistance to the inhumane system of Israeli occupation is suicidal: nonviolence, steadfastness or *sumūd*, and mobility are intimidating and incriminating daily acts in the eyes of the occupier. Whoever engages in those acts in the open-air prison of the Palestinian Territories is therefore committing what Huey Newton would call "revolutionary suicide."[7] Melancholy is the symptom, the testimony, and the driving force behind the psychopolitical commitment to freedom from injustice. As Jacques Derrida once argued, "when he testifies the martyr does not tell a story, he offers himself. He testifies to his faith by offering himself or offering his life or his body."[8] Derrida is probably unpacking here the double meaning of martyrdom in Arabic (*shahāda*), which is both the act of self-sacrifice and the act of bearing witness (to one's faith). As a film, *Paradise Now* is precisely the reverse: it seeks to tell the story of the one whose story did not get through.

---

6. "Zionism is successful because it is a global project with no head and a lot of hands. It sets out a modern framework or even template for Jewish tribalism by incorporating all elements into a dynamic power, and transforms its opposition into a productive power." See Gilad Atzmon, *The Wandering Who? A Study of Jewish Identity Politics* (Washington, DC: Zero Books, 2011), 76.

7. See Huey P. Newton, *Revolutionary Suicide* (New York: Harcourt Brace Jovanovich, 1973).

8. Jacques Derrida, Demeure (1998), in Maurice Blanchot, *The Instant of My Death*, and Jacques Derrida, *Demeure: Fiction and Testimony*, trans. Elizabeth Rottenberg (Stanford, CA: Stanford University Press, 2000), 38.

Tarrying with Terror

> The very indiscriminateness of terrorism, actual and described, its tautological and circular character, is anti-narrative.
>
> EDWARD SAID[9]

> There seems to be nothing in the world that sustains the [Palestinian] story and keeps it there; in other words; unless you're telling it, it is going to drop and disappear.
>
> EDWARD SAID[10]

> If thought is to do more than merely confirm dominant regulations, it must appear more universal and authoritative than when it simply justifies something that already holds.
>
> MAX HORKHEIMER AND THEODOR ADORNO[11]

Few things are worse than the contestation or negation that one might experience or confront of one's own identity—national, racial, ethnic, cultural, religious, sexual, or otherwise. A contested identity is essentially an identity forced not only to despise itself, but also, and whenever possible, to reduce itself to (the status of) nonexistence, or of disposability—really, to liquidate or annihilate itself *tout court*. A contested identity is, above all, an identity that is usurped from the otherwise inalienable right to re-present, assert and liberate itself—that is, in many ways, to narrativize itself.[12] You would agree that today there is nothing more contested than the "identity" of "terrorists": constantly constructed in Western media as an uncanny breed of embittered global vampires, thirsty for blood and vengeance, envious of freedom and democracy, rejectionists of progress and Western civilization—in short, practitioners of terrorism, oftentimes

---

9. Edward Said, "Permission to Narrate," *Journal of Palestine Studies* 13, no. 3 (1984): 36.

10. Edward Said Interviewed by Salman Rushdie, https://www.youtube.com/watch?v=vAmLNc_4VtE.

11. Max Horkheimer and Theodor W. Adorno, "Contradictions," in *The Dialectic of Enlightenment*, trans. John Cumming (New York: Continuum, 1989), 237.

12. I use "to narrativize" rather than "to narrate" in order to stress the challenges confronting contested identities. A contested identity *narrativizes* itself insofar as its narrative is isomorphic with an accented counternarrative because its narrative is preceded and provoked by its contestation. It is an elaborate defense and vindication, an account of both grievances and aspirations. See also Hayden White, "The Value of Narrativity in the Representation of Reality," *Critical Inquiry* 7, no. 1 (1980): 6–7.

suicidal (airborne) attacks, bombings or any other acts of violence deemed illegal because, inter alia, aimed at noncombatant civilians.

Categorical in style and apocalyptic in tone, terrorism brooks, as Said's epigraph demonstrates, no narrative—no space for communicative dialogue, vindication, or rebuttal. Terrorism is inconclusive in content and form; it breaks off, it interrupts, and it terminates. While the broad aim may be to draw media attention to a gross injustice, the immediate consequence is affective and emotional: installing fear and disseminating terror. Terrorists are—and insofar as they are identifiable before (or after) the act—hardly permitted to narrativize themselves out of their otherwise largely disposable condition, and mainly *because* of it. In the context of the post-9/11 "war on terror," the prohibition on "narrative terrorism" had exerted such pressure on critical thinking that it could not be dispensed with even when prefaced by the forthright condemnation of terrorism: any supplementary undertaking, be it interpretive or psychoanalytic, risks bringing upon itself the reproach of condoning terrorism. As such, responsible discussions or representations of terrorism have been destined to muddle through a conceptual terrain marked by what might be called an *implicatory fallacy*—a stubborn imposition of a mantle of continuity and inseparability between interpreting and condoning terrorism. This implicatory fallacy serves to delegitimize and silence (counternarrative) resistance to imperial hegemony and sanction instead étatist terrorism by imperial and settler colonial powers such as the United States, Israel, and their allies, which include Arab monarchies and dictatorships.

The war on terror is in equal measure a war on hermeneutics, on understanding, on counternarrative writ large; it approves only of one streetcar named condemnation. Yet, while the condemnations of terrorism are a déjà-vu, there seems to be no foreseeable end to terrorism in the Middle East, South Asia, and elsewhere in the world. What is less obviously ironic, but all the more telling, is that terrorists themselves have no qualms about condemning terrorism. The war on terror has clearly been a war of clattering and dueling rhetorics sustained on the pyre of self-reflexivity—in short, what was disturbingly hijacked all along, in the enthusiasms and fanaticisms of the long war on terror, is the very impulse and power of self-reflection and critical dissidence. It is against this background that we must situate the singular venture of *Paradise Now*, its counterintuitive and counternarrative freshness, challenging lucidity, and compellingly detached seriousness.

By converting the "antinarrative" nature of terrorism into a condition of narrativity, *Paradise Now* achieves, in no small measure, the impossible. In most Euro-American films, as well as Arab-Egyptian films that engaged with terrorism, not infrequently the requisitory condemnation of terrorism precedes the narrative and conditions it, foreclosing thus the more challenging venues of reflection that terrorism might hurl before our eyes; *Paradise Now*, however, accomplishes the exact reverse.[13] Only at the end of the film, when we have rounded out all the competing factors that regulate and precipitate the terrorist act, are we prodded to ponder its intricately complex economy.

Plotwise, the film is set in the occupied West Bank city of Nablus and follows the last two days of the lives of Said (Kais Nashef) and Khaled (Ali Suliman)—two humble auto mechanics and childhood friends—as they prepare to undertake voluntary martyrdom missions (*'amaliyyāt 'istishhādiyya*) for which they had signed up; the missions were not, however, assigned to them by Al-Kataeb of Liberation and Resistance until approximately two years later, which coincides with the beginning of the film. In terms of its dogged pursuit of a hermeneutics of martyrdom as a form of protest, and of its various originating and teleological forces, the film can be situated in league with other variously provocative films of this sort that range from Gillo Pontecorvo's *The Battle of Algiers* (1966) and Nouri Bouzid's *Ākir Film/Making Of* (2006) to Ziad Doueiri's *The Attack* (2012) and Nabil Ayouch's *Horses of God* (2013). However, as a film about the complex conjunction between the phenomenon of martyrdom missions and the persistence of the Palestinian question more than half a century after Al-Nakba (1948), it is quite unprecedented, and mainly because this phenomenon is a fairly recent response to the intransigence of the occupation after the Oslo Accords (1993). While drowned in accolades, including a Golden Globe and an Oscar nomination, the film was petitioned and lobbied against at the Oscars, and the ceremony at which it was named the Best European Film was picketed by demonstrators.

By virtue of its polarizing and brokered subject matter, the film was somewhat destined to court controversy, to earn the contempt of some and the appreciation of others, and, in the process, to run the risk of undermining its many artistic merits. Ironically, however, the controversial nature of the film is but an effect of its inaugural artistic impulse: the elaboration of a narrativizable and visualizable account of voluntary martyrdom. The narrativization of martyrdom missions, the "antinarrative" *par excellence*, is inhabited by two rival impulses that seek to reveal to understanding what passes beyond understanding while sustaining intact its unthinkability. Herein lies the film's

---

13. For a concise overview of Hollywood's orientalist depiction of terrorism, see, for instance, Carl Boggs and Tom Pollard, "Hollywood and the Spectacle of Terrorism," *New Political Science* 28, no. 3 (2006): 335–351. For a more detailed account, see Jack Shaheen, *Guilty: Hollywood's Verdict on Arabs after 9/11* (Northampton, MA: Olive Branch, 2008).

daunting venture, and, really, of any likewise artistic endeavor worthy of its name: to focalize the unthinkable and to accentuate the sense of the unrepresentable or inarticulable. For, and as I discussed in chapter 1, any artistic endeavor after the Holocaust (not just lyric poetry) that engages with catastrophe would, following Adorno, ineluctably verge on barbarism: its rationalizing impulse (without which it is neither conceivable nor consequential) would stealthily and against the grain "make an unthinkable fate appear to have had some meaning."[14] Inversely, it is no less "barbaric" to remain silent about this "unthinkable fate," to thrust it into oblivion, and kill it, as it were, for the second time.

Several decades passed after the Holocaust, yet the aporetic polarities of representing the unrepresentable have never ceased to gain center stage in the circuits of aesthetic, cultural, and critical debates. Ironically, the numerous reviews of the film show little to no reckoning with the film's fundamental theoretical and aesthetic burden: the narrativization of the so-called suicide bombing. Not that the reviewers focus solely on the polarizing *effects* of this narrativization; indisputably, that is *precisely* the case. Pro-Palestinian and pro-Israeli reviewers alike have managed to agree that the problematic nature of the film revolves around the mutually exclusive "humanization" and "dehumanization" of both Palestinians and Israelis, as if either were inherently more or less than human. The dehumanization/humanization argument risks deflecting attention away from the illegitimacy of the occupation to the illegitimacy of the resistance. Besides, who but the settler colonial apparatus has the sovereign power and the military clout to generate, distribute and redistribute as well as withhold the human?

By inciting and enticing those it oppresses to engage in its discursive construction of who would qualify as human and who would be relegated to the status of the less than human, the settler colonial state tightens its grip on Palestinians, and delegitimizes their own conception of the human, martyrdom, and terrorism.[15] As'ad AbuKhalil is not unaware of how the discourse of dehumanization is manipulated by Israel to repress Palestinian resistance, yet he focuses his review on what he perceives as the humanization of the occupiers and the IDF soldiers. AbuKhalil writes passionately and irascibly about the "commercial" palatability of the film to "Western audiences and sensibilities,"

---

14. Theodor W. Adorno, "Commitment," in *Aesthetics and Politics*, ed. Ronald Taylor (New York: Verso, 1980), 189.

15. I am thinking along with Samera Esmeir's excellent study on law and the politics of the human in colonial Egypt. See Samera Esmeir, *Juridical Humanity: A Colonial History* (Stanford, CA: Stanford University Press, 2012), 6.

to Sally Fields's "seal of approval," and, above all, to the eagerness of Arab audiences "for any semblance of positive portrayal" after they have suffered for quite a long time from "racist and negative" stereotyping. He then questions the film's positive portrayal by way of a rhetorical question: "if Arabs/Muslims have been portrayed as one-fourth of human beings, should we celebrate when they are portrayed as one-half of human beings? Is that reason to cheer? Or should we aim higher, simple [sic] to portrayal of them as full human beings?" Hammering home his argument on the dehumanization of Palestinians in the film, AbuKhalil concludes: "I dare say that Israeli civilians in the movie are more civilian than Palestinian civilians in the movie. Even Israeli soldiers were portrayed quite humanely."[16]

It is hard not to appreciate the counterintuitive insights of AbuKhalil, one of the wittiest political commentators on the Mashreq, but his comments here raise serious questions about the relationship between the film's reception in the West and its aesthetic value: he suggests that if an Arab film (about Palestine) succeeds in the West, it follows that it must have been "driven by and designed around" the sensibilities and horizon of expectations of Western audiences. Surely, a Westerner's appreciation of an Arab film or any work of art might constitute critical grounds for suspicion, but suspicion must be economized lest it should become a rule of aesthetic judgement, in which case we may all slide into what Rey Chow calls a self-defeating mode or mood of "ethnic *ressentiment*,"[17] which would reproduce the very problems of validity and bias associated with the Westward gaze. This is perhaps another facet of the implicatory fallacy I mentioned earlier and that has plagued several Arab artists (including Nobel Laureate Naguib Mahfouz) in that it projects an objective correlative between the reception of a work of art in the West and the politics of its author or his ulterior motives. While the politics of reception of Arab literature and culture in the West should never be neglected, it should

---

16. As'ad AbuKhalil, "Paradise Now? Paradise Never. Not With. . . . Sally Field," available at http://angryarab.blogspot.com/2006/04/paradis-now-paradise-never.html. Generally, AbuKhalil's critique seems to me to stem from a broader perspective in which the humanization of Palestinians happens oftentimes hand-in-hand with their dehumanization. For instance, when Israeli companies showcase their Detection System Products (SDS), they boast that "the products were road-tested on Palestinians," in which case it becomes clear that when Palestinians are not dehumanized as terrorists, they are rehumanized only to be redehumanized as "guinea pigs," see Naomi Klein, "Israel thrives, Gaza suffers," http://www.straight.com/article-96202/israel-thrives-gaza-suffers.

17. Rey Chow, *The Protestant Ethnic and the Spirit of Capitalism* (New York: Columbia University Press, 2002), 189.

not be allowed to override our critical engagement with such works. Otherwise, the grounds of suspicion could expand ad infinitum, voraciously enlisting any Arab's artistic achievement in the West within the orbit of the West's expectations and the artist's own personal motives. Aside from his negative reception of the West's reception of the film—which is quite telling about the level of our involvement in, rather than volunteering for, the West's cultural hegemony—AbuKhalil's commentaries swiftly morph into a Manichean certitude about the film's humanization of Israeli soldiers and dehumanization of Palestinian civilians, overlooking thus the more crucial and problematic issues of narrativization and visualization without which the question of dehumanization or humanization cannot be broached critically.

The Jerusalem Post's editorial review of the film, "Humanizing Terror," follows the same logic as AbuKhalil's, only to reach the opposite results. Rather than humanize Israeli soldiers and civilians, the film, the editorial contends, humanizes Palestinian terrorists, "making the worst monsters look human."[18]

18. See *The Jerusalem Post*, "Humanizing Terrorism," January 17, 2006, https://www.jpost.com/opinion/editorials/humanizing-terrorism. Another review by Irit Linor also accuses the film of humanizing terrorism. After having slammed the film as an "exciting, quality Nazi film," Linor goes on to argue, with self-contented sarcasm, that the film "sells us a humanity whose outer characteristics we find palatable: young heroes, sweet families—like us—not religious fanatics, but marginally traditional, t-shirt wearing secular folk. You know, just like us." These comments, and many similar ones in numerous biased reviews of the film blindly decontextualize and dehistoricize terrorism, presenting it as more of a moral aberration than an offshoot of colonial struggle against occupation, as if it were neither reminiscent of FLN (National Liberation Front) decolonization maneuvers against the French in the 1950s, nor of the Zionist recourse to terror in the 1940s, especially the Stern Gang, which drove a truckful of explosives into a British police station in Haifa in January 1947 and massacred Palestinians before the 1948 war broke out. Rather than accept the film's invitation to address the root causes of terrorism, bigoted reviewers symptomatically choose to defuse history, abstracting the degrading human conditions of the occupation into, in the words of Linor, no more than a "ritual cleansing bath for every Palestinian moral blight." Really, however, Occupation is not a "cleansing bath" for Palestinian violence and, should that be the case, God knows how many would prefer to stay unbathed. See Irit Linor, "Anti-Semitism Now," available at http://www.ynetnews.com/articles/0,7340,L-3212503,00.html. Finally, Roger Ebert offers no exception to the dizzying number of reviewers who attack the film on the grounds of humanizing suicide bombers: "*Paradise Now*, like another 2005 film, *The War Within*, and the 1999 Indian film *The Terrorist*, humanizes suicide bombers. But in my mind, at least, that creates not sympathy, but pity; what a waste, to spend your life and all your future on behalf of those who send you but do not go themselves." See "Paradise Now: Questions from Here to Eternity," https://www.rogerebert.com/reviews/paradise-now-2005. Ebert exaggerates the religiosity of the protagonists and misses on the humorous register with which the idea of paradise as a reward is broached and debunked.

It is no exaggeration to suggest that there is something quite disturbing about the alleged concern over the humanization of the so-called suicide bombers. First, I would say it would be utterly misguided if film director Abu-Assad *intended* to humanize Khaled and Said. For what is less obviously ironic, but all the more insidious, is that—were it indeed compelled by the urge to prove the humanity of the two childhood friends—the film would more likely converge with, rather than depart from, the logic of the Israeli oppressors who infinitely urge their Palestinian victims to prove their humanity. The victims acquiesce, but to no avail—terrorists must remain terrorists despite piling evidence to the contrary.[19] Besides, and similarly to my approach throughout this chapter, Abu-Assad does not defend what he tries to understand.

Second, one should ask what is really at stake, if that is the case, in such a monstrous feat as that of the film's humanization of the so-called suicide bombers. Does it mean that the film somewhat condones suicide bombing? Or is it because the film does something else altogether—something, I think, that is likely to fall afoul of the sensibilities of audiences who are wholly committed to the denial of their illicit complicity in the ongoing occupation of Palestine and the dispossession of Palestinians? What is at stake is not the horror of a film that, if this is indeed the case, humanizes suicide bombers; rather, it is the bankruptcy of the deeper rationale that sustains that horror, namely the differential allocation of humanity. While the exclusive nature of the "human" might just be the flipside of its inclusive horizon, the way the "human" is structured has to be carefully discriminated from the way it is appropriated to structure our experience of history, the conferral and withdrawal of meaning—only then can we be able to ask ourselves boldly whether our human and humane task is to search for and host the human wherever it might seem least expected or to foster a differential system of assigning it to some and denying

---

19. Given the pliancy of international law, the seemingly incurable structural weaknesses of the United Nations and the very crude fact that, as Jean de La Fontaine put it, "the strong are always best at proving they're right," it is unfortunate that oppressed peoples end up internalizing and enacting the logic of their oppressors. The task at hand is to envision and elaborate novel logics, more indirectly suggestive than purely evidential, which is what *Paradise Now* seeks to accomplish. See Jean de La Fontaine, "The Wolf and the Lamb," in Jacques Derrida, *Rogues: Two Essays on Reason* (Stanford, CA: Stanford University Press, 2005), x. The United Nations has persistently failed to condemn Israeli abuses of human rights in the West Bank and Gaza and Israel has persistently been able to deny any responsibility for its atrocities. For a cogent analysis on how governments respond to human rights abuses, see Stanley Cohen, "Government Responses to Human Rights Reports: Claims, Denials, and Counterclaims," *Human Rights Quarterly* 18, no. 3 (1996): 517–43.

it to others. What is at stake is the fear that the film might disarticulate the exclusive assignation of humanity, extending it to those who are not its beneficiaries, even while they remain its tragic subscribers.

Clearly, then, the concern over the humanization of the so-called suicide bombers betrays, wittingly or unwittingly, an ideologically motivated interest in their dehumanization. Few things are worse than the will to dehumanization to which Palestinians are subjugated in theory and in practice. The core issue is, though, less the danger posed by the humanization of suicide bombers than the claim to *narrative* legitimacy of which such humanization is an effect. Narrative suicide bombing is terrifying because it inscribes the suicidal act within a *historical continuum* of a people's struggle for self-determination. Khaled and Said do not see themselves as suicide bombers but as militants tasked with a martyrdom mission. Insofar as it voraciously appropriates all concern away from the fundamental question of the Israeli occupation, subtly displacing the Palestinian right to statehood, the controversy over the humanization of suicide bombers is disingenuous at best.

In general, it is undeniably true that the narrative visualization of suicide martyrdom might eventually expunge the horror of the act; however, such a flagrant shortcoming of narrative pales into insignificance if compared to the reverse course—resignation and silence—which would not only desensitize us to the historical and material realities of the Palestinian resistance movements, but also somewhat align us, embarrassingly so, with the occupation. Worse still, to resign to silence would further opportune the occupation of the definitional pliancy of the concept of terrorism to stretch its application to any form of resistance to its obstinate settler (postcolonial colonial) annexational desires and designs. Indeed, the strategic goal of the occupation is not only to identify metonymically suicide protest with terrorism but also to establish an allegorical correspondence between terrorism and Palestinian resistance. Such strategic syllogism discredits the resistance and, not inconsequently, disposes of it in the widening gyre of terrorism, licensing thus its historical derealization, or, as it were, "storycide." Above all, this strategy authorizes the ultimate ruse: the displacement of terrorism from the realm of history and everyday politics to that of abstract structural deficiencies (namely, the congenital disposition of Arabs and Muslims toward violence and terror).[20]

---

20. In *Terrorism: How the West Can Win*, Benjamin Netanyahu claims that, "The root cause of terrorism lies not in grievances but in a disposition toward unbridled violence," in Edward Said and Christopher Hitchens, *Blaming the Victims: Spurious Scholarship and the Palestinian Question* (New York: Verso, 1988), 154.

Narrative suicide resistance à la *Paradise Now* nuances the untoward condemnation of suicide bombing on licensed premises, all the while calling for dialogue and contemplation, or, at least, for a condemnation that passes through understanding—one that does not override or eclipse the historical facts and material realities at the origin of suicide resistance. One can safely posit that the narrative structure of the film unfolds in the pressing logic of a double-bind: a critique of suicide resistance (as a sociopolitical movement toward liberation from Israeli occupation) punctuated by intimate forays into the grassroots conditions that lead some to think that self-sacrifice (*shahāda*) is the only plausible alternative left that will, in time, bring about positive change on the ground and restore dignity. After all, violence in all its forms, and inasmuch as it structures any (settler) colonial project, is by no means a choice that native resistance movements can *exercise* but, rather, one of the principal conditions of choice. For instance, by settling for the assigned martyrdom mission in Tel Aviv, Said is not oblivious to the fact that he is thus acting in line with, not in excess of, the regulating power of the Israeli occupation: "It's not we who decide," he tells Suha (Lubna Azabal)—"it is the occupation that decides 'the space of Man' (*masāḥit el-'insān*) and 'the space of struggle' (*masāḥit el-niḍāl*)."[21]

By virtue of its superior military capabilities and sovereignty over all aspects of Palestinian lives, the occupation, according to Said, not only generates the very forms of resistance it subsequently crashes, but also converts, in calculated measures, resistance into an extension of its rule. By unhinging resistance's *substance* (struggle for freedom, national liberation) from its *form* (martyrdom, suicide bombing), the occupation achieves the strategic goal of discrediting the legitimacy of resistance. When unhinged from its substance, the form, by virtue of its pliancy, is further instrumentalized in the service of the "intrinsically propagandistic" discourse of terrorism to warrant any atrocious acts,[22] which will be then cloaked under such newspeak euphemisms or "syndromes" (Noam Chomsky's characterization) as "retaliation," "self-defense," or "disproportionate response," leaving it thusly up to the more powerful side to calibrate the allowable measure of disproportionality.

---

21. *Paradise Now* (Al-Jannah-tul-'Ān), dir. Hany Abu-Assad (Burbank, CA: Warner Home Video, 2006).

22. Alain Badiou, *Infinite Thought: Truth and the Return to Philosophy* (London: Continuum, 2005), 109. Joseph A. Massad rightly argues that "what the discourse on terror seeks is the erasure of power relations as the central problematic of violence." *The Persistence of the Palestinian Question: Essays on Zionism and the Palestinians* (London: Routledge, 2006), 8.

The Matereality of Struggle

> Suicidal resistance is a message inscribed in the body when no other means will get through.
>
> GAYATRI SPIVAK[23]

> And so many autoimmunitary movements. Which produce, invent, and feed the very monstrosity they claim to overcome.
>
> JACQUES DERRIDA[24]

The threat and promise of *Paradise Now* lie in its effortful scrutiny of the metonymic bundling together of suicide martyrdom and terrorism and of, specifically, the unchecked expropriation of the precarious substance of the former under the immensely nihilistic and propagandistic form of the latter. Shot on location (in Nablus, Nazareth, and Tel Aviv, and only at an arm's length away from daily firefights and missile attacks by the Israeli occupying army and the various Palestinian armed factions), the film brings the current mind-numbing—albeit mobilizing—credulity of the "grand narrative" of terrorism into intimate collision with the micronarratives of Palestinian youths, their diurnal psychosocial, economic, and political small-scale struggles for identity, for dignity, and for a life worthy of its name. While resolutely taking upon itself the incumbent task of elaborating a narrative of suicide resistance, *Paradise Now* is nonetheless marked by a tenacious reluctance to impose a veneer of coherency and wholeness over its narrative design. The distance between suicide resistance and the promise of Palestinian liberation is the measure of the film's insistent demand for and recessive withholding of narrative form or closure. Being the latest offspring of what Nouri Bouzid had conceptualized as the "new realism in Arab cinema/the defeat-conscious cinema," the film invests in staging contradictions and acute existential dilemmas and, in the process, investigates a "defeated" consciousness's infinite vulnerability to hope—its "malady of hope" (*dā' al-'amal*), as Mahmoud Darwish is wont to say.[25]

In the opening sequence, the film juxtaposes the historical juncture of occupied West Bank city of Nablus and the public/private spheres of the three

---

23. Gayatri Spivak, "Terror: A Speech after 9–11," *Boundary 2* 31, no. 2 (2004): 11.

24. Jacques Derrida, "Autoimmunity: Real and Symbolic Suicides—A Dialogue with Jacques Derrida," in *Philosophy in a Time of Terror: Dialogues with Jürgen Habermas and Jacques Derrida*, ed. Giovanna Borradori (Chicago: University of Chicago Press, 2003), 99.

25. Nouri Bouzid, "New Realism in Arab Cinema: The Defeat-Conscious Cinema," *Alif: Journal of Comparative Poetics* 15 (1995): 81; Mahmoud Darwish, *Halit ḥiṣār* (Beirut: Riad El-Rayyes Books, 2002), 81.

leading characters. While presented briskly, these fleeting segments are crucial to an understanding of the broad context, dense and multilayered, within which the action leading up to the martyrdom mission in Tel Aviv develops. Take, for instance, the very first segment which introduces us to Suha (Lubna Azabal) being searched at an Israeli checkpoint: her apprehensive and mute exchange of gazes with the Israeli soldier, compressing in a fleeting moment a long history of distrust and condescension, immediately sets the tone for the enveloping sense of captivity, daily humiliation, outrage, exhaustion, and hopelessness—all of which will later be articulated by Said and Khaled as they come to ponder their suicide mission.

Equally important is the following segment, featuring Said and then Khaled in front of the auto garage where they work, arguing with the client, a car owner, who complains that the bumper of his car is crooked. Although Said and Khaled try to reason with him, demonstrating with a water level that it is not crooked and that he might simply be mistaking the sloped surface of the ground for the apparent crookedness of the bumper, the client insists on reporting the matter to Abu Salim, their boss; meanwhile, he obdurately substantiates the crookedness of the bumper by way of analogy with the "crookedness" of Said's father (*māyil zay 'abūk*: "it's crooked like your father")—a direct reference to Said's father's collaborative past with Israel and to the treacherous heritage Said has to put up with on a daily basis.

In no small measure, this well-contained scene is a telescoped parable (or an extended simile) of the Israeli-Palestinian "conflict," and of the unequal power relations that subtend and precondition it, even while they remain horrendously mystified and disfigured under the guise of equitable, peace-talk negotiations. The scene brings to the fore all the ingredients/elements of salubrious communication in view of a friendly settlement of the matter at hand, but to no avail. While Said insists on the deceitfulness of appearances, urging the client to verify again the "straightness" of the bumper, which is judiciously confirmed by the water level test, the client holds fast to the infallibility of his eyesight and to the veracity of his observation. The staggering discrepancy between the factual and tested result (that the bumper is indeed straight) and the tenacity with which the client sticks to his erroneous judgment proved so taxing on Khaled's composure (or, otherwise, "oppressive tolerance"—Herbert Marcuse) that he grabbed a mallet and hammered the right side of the bumper to the ground, acting out what would retrospectively constitute a rare staging of visceral violence in the entire film.[26]

---

26. Herbert Marcuse, "Repressive Tolerance," in *A Critique of Pure Tolerance*, by R. P. Wolff, B. Moore Jr., and H. Marcuse (Boston: Beacon Press, 1965), 81–117.

Shot slightly from above the eye level, perhaps with a fittingly "crooked" posture of the camera, the scene is shadowed by the ambient voice of Lebanese diva, Nancy Ajram, pleading helplessly to be heard out—Di hāga motʻeba!/Ekmennī tayyiba/Mustaḥmilāk wa baʻālī ktīr (Oh, how tiring this thing is becoming!/How kinder can I be?/You know I've been putting up with you for a long time). While Nancy Ajram's words evoke Said's pleading with the client to resolve the problem with calm, the overflowing Arab coffee onto the portable stove (towering at the left side of the screen, a close-up shot from below the eye level) craftily prefaces Khaled's combustible temper and ultimate explosion. But the difference in temperament between Said and Khaled is not as clear cut as it might seem, since there emerges a subtle allusion that Khaled might not be other than a foil to Said, or, simply, his alter-ego. Such a hypothesis can nuance further an already nuanced ending in which the initially hesitant Said transforms into the formerly determined Khaled.

The client's sheer negligence of the evidence of the facts matches only the deep determination with which he insists he is "right" about them. When the whole matter is reported to Abu Salim, the client takes up the position of the *wronged*, even though he has been and remains evidentially wrong throughout the concourse of tests and observations that led up to the confrontation and Khaled's ultimate reaction, for which he was subsequently fired by Abu Salim. This scene subtly condenses the entire trajectory of the peace process between the Palestinians and the Israelis and unmasks the inequality of power relations on which the rhetoric of peace settlements is predicated and by which, in turn, "victimhood" is *always already* determined.[27] Thus, while it might seem prima facie quite irrelevant to a film about two potential suicide martyrs, this sequence poignantly captures the historical logic of violence, its genesis in concrete grievances, and in the everyday travails to sustain dignity in the face of an adversarial power whose victimhood precedes and automatically covers up for its brutality—all the more so since Abu-Assad is prudent enough not to suffuse his narrative and character driven film with a documentary-style demonstrativeness of the devastating effects of the Israeli matrix of control over the West Bank and Gaza.

---

27. Debunking the abuse of the anti-Semitic charge and the sickening slandering of any constructive criticism of Israel, or of its ethnic cleansing of Palestinians, Judith Butler is severely critical of the ways in which the Jewish tragic heritage has constantly been peddled about to warrant current Israeli aggressions: "It seems . . . that historically we are now in the position in which Jews cannot be understood always and only as presumptive victims." *Precarious Life: The Powers of Mourning and Violence* (New York: Verso, 2004), 103.

Note, for instance, that in the same year the film was shot, Israel committed with the overt support of the United States massive violations of basic human rights in the West Bank and Gaza, including the imposition of severe restrictions on the movements of Palestinians such as curfews, checkpoints, and roadblocks; the expansion of illegal settlements and the network of "bypass" roads for exclusively "Israeli" settlers; and the building of a huge, unlawful (according to the International Court of the Hague) wall (not "fence") nearly 375 miles long, annexing, caging, and isolating Palestinian cities and suburbs, shredding the very humble idea of a road-map Palestinian state, barring the access of Palestinians to their richest agricultural land and water, to healthcare facilities, places of work and schools, and to numerous workaday activities.[28] Worst of all is the frantic bulldozing of Palestinian homes and infrastructure, a long established form of collective punishment that aims to turn Palestinians into homeless refugees. A UN Humanitarian Fact Sheet indicates that, "Between September 2000 and through September 2004, more than 24,000 living in the Gaza Strip have been made homeless by Israeli house demolitions. In the first nine months of 2004, the Israeli Defense Forces (IDF) demolished on average 120 residential buildings each month—or four each day."[29]

The demolition of Palestinian homes goes hand in hand with the uprooting of thousands of olive and fruit trees, the confiscation of Palestinians' fertile lands, water resources and livelihoods, resulting in a dire humanitarian situation: unemployment, homelessness, poverty, and acute health crises. All of this has spurred and intensified Al-Aqsa Intifada and, in turn, Israel's heavy-handed military offensives. From the beginning of the Intifada in 2000 through the 2002 massive IDF military operation in the Jenin refugee camp and up until 2004, when *Paradise Now* was being shot, the Palestinian death toll reached about 3,196 civilians, including 618 children. In the year 2004 alone, the Israeli army killed 834 Palestinians (of which 667 were civilians, among them 167 children, 13 women, and 19 older than sixty years) and injured 1,884 people.[30]

In a manner somewhat reminiscent of Genet in Shatila, Abu-Assad "walked through" the West Bank and filmed amidst the looming danger of gunfire, landmines and, worst of all, missile attacks by the Israeli army. Suspicious that

---

28. See Amnesty International Briefing Paper to the CERD, "Israel/Occupied Territories: Briefing to the Committee on the Elimination of Racial Discrimination (CERD)," https://www.amnesty.org/download/Documents/76000/mde150022006en.pdf.

29. United Nations, "Humanitarian Information Fact Sheet (January 2005)," https://www.un.org/unispal/document-category/report/page/96/.

30. See Amnesty International Briefing Paper to the CERD, available at https://www.commondreams.org/organization/amnesty-international?page=50.

the film would likely misrepresent suicide martyrs, a Palestinian armed faction asked the crew to stop filming while another kidnapped the location manager (later released following an appeal to Yasir Arafat). The worst, however, was yet to come: as Abu-Assad recalls, "on the 20th day of shooting [the film] an Israeli rocket struck close by. . . . Six German technicians left the set. I can't blame them. Life is more important than film. So we all left and shot instead in Nazareth."[31]

While attentive to these "facts on the ground" as he "walked through" them firsthand, Abu-Assad relies nonetheless on the suggestiveness of the opening sequence to evoke the material and historical realities of his Nabulsi protagonists' everyday lives in the occupied West Bank and tacitly "refuses the mimetic burden of documentary (associated with the Palestinian experience)."[32] The economy and circumspection with which he recreates the historical circumstances of the action (limiting the portrait to checkpoints, one explosion in the horizon, and demolished houses) should ideally put us on the qui vive as to the subtlety with which Abu-Assad broaches the subject of suicide martyrdom operations. It seems that what is important for him is not whether the atrocities of the occupation are sufficiently portrayed but whether there can be a way of sufficiently portraying them if the viewer, like the client in the opening sequence, is instinctively or deliberately blind to them. As I suggested earlier, the client is only formally engaged in dialogic exchange, and not so much for the sake of formality as for the sake of maintaining he is right and, in the process, disempowering Said and Khaled. This is, I think, emblematic of the way in which Israel, according to Jeff Halper, has never been genuinely interested in negotiating with the Palestinians: "The truth is that Israel has nothing to negotiate. 'Greater' Jerusalem is ours, the settlement blocs are ours, the borders are ours, the water is ours, even the sky is ours. What's left to negotiate?"[33]

Rather than opt for a dramatic and spectacular rendition of the grinding system of occupation, Abu-Assad finesses what would be an easily visualizable spectacle into an allegorical reenactment of the ways in which violence à la Khaled is precipitated on the pyre of a communicative system preconditioned by disparate power relations. What does Khaled achieve, one might ask, by

---

31. Hany Abu-Assad, "Shooting *Paradise Now* amid Israeli Rockets," https://en.qantara.de/content/interview-with-hany-abu-assad-shooting-paradise-now-amid-israeli-rockets.

32. I draw on Kamran Rastegar's reflections on a similar tendency in Elia Suleiman's filmmaking technique. See Kamran Rastegar, *Surviving Images: Cinema, War, and Cultural Memory the Middle East* (New York: Oxford University Press, 2015), 7.

33. Jeff Halper, "Countdown to Apartheid," *The Israeli Committee Against House Demolition*, https://icahd.org/2019/05/24/countdown-to-apartheid/.

hammering the left side of the bumper to the ground? Does he do it out of sheer wastefulness, an unbridled compulsion toward violence? Since, if anything, his action *confirms* that the bumper is crooked (huh, *wella mazbūt—māyil* / "Now, you're right—it's crooked"), why did he resort to it? A patient answer to these interlaced questions will benefit from a close reading of the unlikely conjunction I would like to make between the logic of violence in the opening sequence and the logic of suicide martyrdom in the entirety of the film.

To understand Khaled's melancholy act—that is, to read it closely—one has to open up to its contradictory impulses and, really, to its performative unpredictability: the attempt to embarrass the logic of the client by embracing it. What looks awry about this act of violence is, however, that its somewhat Fanonian and creative potential to critique the logic of the client *converges* with the ineluctability of affirming that same logic. Given this ultimate convergence, the act enunciates the limit of possibility and, above all, the fantasy of omnipotence that is coextensive with the exhaustion of all hope. Having lost all hope, exhaustion stages itself as a wish that overrides hope.[34]

Independent of fulfillment, wish survives as a testimonial to hope, a residual vindication of a life that has lost all hope. It is in this sense that Khaled's melancholy act furnishes us with the logic of suicide martyrdom in miniature. Apart from the fact that violence is obviously a currency of social interactions under occupation—and among Palestinians themselves (as is, for instance, cleverly elaborated in Elia Suleiman's 2002 feature film *Divine Intervention*)—it is important to bear in mind the ways in which an act of violence testifies simultaneously to the system of occupation and to the movement of resistance. When armed resistance exhausts itself—when it is denied the economy of resistance and the means to channel the surplus anger and energy excited by the occupation, when it is forced to turn in the void or face its own extinction—it partakes of the exterminating logic of brutality to which it is subjected, and stages its own demise/existence by recourse to the remainder (i.e., the material body).[35] Hence, Spivak's pronouncement that suicide resistance "is a message inscribed in the body when no other means will get through."[36]

---

34. "The wish," according to Hans-Jost Frey, "is independent of the possibility of fulfillment; it is a pure crossing of borders, a hopeless breakout [*Ausbruch*], a setting out [*Aufbruch*] into the impossible," *Interruptions* (Albany: State University of New York Press, 1996), 81.

35. According to Jacques Derrida, "Brutality is not only an unrefined violence, it is a bad violence, impoverishing, repetitive, mechanical, that does not open the future, does not leave room for the other." *A Taste for the Secret* (Cambridge: Polity Press, 2001), 92.

36. Spivak, "Terror." Note that the very Arabic word for "suicide resistance" in this context is *shahāda*, which means not only *martyrdom* but also *testimony* and therefore implies a strong

Suicide resistance proceeds logically from the ethnocidal and politicidal practices of the occupation. If suicide bombing is an aberration, there must be, one suspects, conditions aberrant enough to precipitate it.[37] "And when a people has no choice but how it will die; when a people has received from its oppressors only the gift of despair, what does it have to lose?"[38] Said stresses this fact in his farewell speech: *"Lam yabqa lanā gheiru ajsādinā"* (We have nothing left to fight back with except our bodies). Suicidal resistance is not historically incongruous to the logic that furnished the rationale for the many massacres that Zionists had committed en route to founding the Israeli state and establishing it as a regional super power.[39] Furthermore, and as is widely known, the suicidal phenomenon in the Israeli-Palestinian conflict is reminiscent of the biblical story of Samson who, when humiliated by the Philistines, knocks down the pillars of their house, proclaiming, "Let me die with the Philistines," and kills himself along with his enemies.[40] According to Michel Warschawski, this parable of Samson recurs regularly today in Israeli politics under what is known as "the Samson option," suggesting that "Israel's course is unquestionably suicidal" in that, now that it presumably has a nuclear arsenal, neatly named "the Samson Option," it "is ready to destroy itself together with those who aim to destroy it."[41]

---

sense of enduring occupation while bearing witness to and contesting its devastating practices. To a large degree, then, suicidal operations are testimonials, desublimated and demetaphorized representations as well as lethal contestations of the everyday realities of Palestinians under occupation.

37. Interrogating what he calls the sanctioning of the "condemnation imperative" in public and academic discourses about (contextualized understandings of) suicide bombing, Ghassan Hage maintains that he is "certainly more comfortable with absolutely condemning the living conditions that make people into suicide bombers than with absolutely condemning suicide bombers as such," "'Comes a Time We Are All Enthusiasm': Understanding Palestinian Suicide Bombers in Times of Exighophobia," *Public Culture* 15, no. 1 (2003): 67.

38. Jean-Paul Sartre, "Introduction," in Albert Memmi, *The Colonizer and the Colonized*, trans. Howard Greenfeld (Boston: Beacon Press, 1991), xxix.

39. See, for instance, Samera Esmeir's compelling discussion of the massacre of the natives of the Tantoura village by Zionist forces, "1948: Law, History, Memory," *Social Text* 21, no. 2 (2003): 25–48.

40. "And Samson took hold of the two middle pillars upon which the house stood, and on which it was borne up, of the one with his right hand, and of the other with his left" (Judges 16:29 KJV); "and Samson said, Let me die with the Philistines. And he bowed himself with all his might; and the house fell upon the lords, and upon all the people that were therein. So the dead which he slew at his death were more than they which he slew in his life" (16:30).

41. Michel Warschawski, *Toward an Open Tomb: The Crisis of Israeli Society* (New York: Monthly Review Press, 2004), 99. For an analysis of the Samson story, see also Talal Asad, *On Suicide Bombing* (New York: Columbia University Press, 2007), 74–76.

The very idea that a few countries, including Israel, have a nuclear arsenal capable of permanently damaging, if not terminating, life on earth should alert us sufficiently enough to the suicidal foundation of the modern state in the nuclear age—that is, to the consensual fantasy of the modern state with its annihilation. In fact, the sovereignty of the nation-state today is indissociable from the state's instituting and nihilistic aura, its nuclear "new-clarity," invincibility and deterrence capabilities. Now, to be accepted in the club of nations with a suicidal foundation, it might as well help if you are already a member or, at least, a neutralized outsider; otherwise, you're a rogue (*voyou* or *suʻlūk*) state. It seems that what is really worrisome about the logic of suicide bombing is that it enacts and duplicates the very suicidal foundation of the modern state, bringing about into the theater of the real its disavowed thanatophilic fantasy. More than ever, it is not radical difference but veritable proximity that is repelling—a proximity that has not so far led (as one might expect of recognizing oneself in another) to the renunciation of identity politics in the service of solidarity. The war on terror campaign and the construction of suicide bomber-monster can surely be seen as ruses modern nuclear states make use of to evade—as they hold fast and tight to—their suicidal foundation.

The phenomenon of suicide resistance signals first and foremost the extent to which the brutality of the occupation is performed and inscribed (i.e., exposed and resisted) in and through the formation of the suicidal other, the would-be martyr. That suicide resistance carries, as Spivak contends, a counterinscriptive message on the body is not a foregone conclusion; the message is intelligible only to the extent it is in excess of—not indispensable to—the war on terror. That remains to be determined, but the ways in which the taboo on (unofficial/group) terrorism has furnished the rationale for the acceptability of (official) state terrorism should provide some pointers. The world's acceptability of the war on terror is the measure of intelligibility (or nonintelligibility) of the counterinscriptive message of the militant martyr, the *shahīd*. Israel wastes no time to retaliate with choking security measures to whatever Palestinians do to resist its colossal settler apparatus, which thrusts Palestinians into a damned if you do, damned if you don't catch-22. Clearly, and as Darwish had best verbalized this melancholic anguish, or Hamletian impasse:

> The earth is closing on us,
> Pushing us through the last passage,
> And we tear off our limbs to pass through . . .
> Where should we go after the last frontiers?
> Where do birds fly after the last sky? . . .

We will die here, here in the last passage. Here and here our blood
Will plant its olive tree.[42]

These lines re-create with gripping poignancy life under Israeli occupation. A splintering occupation in which the right of passage hinges on a slow process of mutilation and dismemberment—a geobiological dismemberment of human body and the body land of Palestine. The settlements and the checkpoints, not to mention the contempt that accompanies them, make the occupation such a vision of the end before the end that to survive it is perhaps synonymous to being martyred without the commemorative accolades of martyrdom. The ineluctable implication of this constant mutilation of the Palestinian body is to appropriate the attention of Palestinians away from what they lost to what remains to be lost. Once melancholicization (the persistent psychic investiture in what is lost) is reduced to an anticipation of loss rather than to an attachment to loss, it becomes easier for the occupation to naturalize loss and turn it into a matter of facts on the ground. When loss is preceded by its anticipation, it becomes less of a loss, only a foretold fact. This insidious and numbing strategy is in full display in the recent West Bank Annexation plan.

Melancholicization (not to be confused with melancholization, which often means pathologization) ought to remain about attachments to what is lost; it ought not slide into an expectation of what more can be lost, lest it should reduce loss to a structural fact of object-relations, or lack thereof (as in structuralist approaches to melancholy from Lacan to Žižek through Agamben). Any form of resistance to the occupation understands innately this settler colonial dispossessive psychopolitical tactic of appropriating attention away from what is lost to what remains. Not infrequently, what intensifies the urge toward martyrdom operations is the refusal to countenance the integrity of the struggle against occupation, namely, its claims to what is lost beyond recognition and to the right of return to the refugee population. Israel's strategic manipulation of the war on terror to diabolize a long tradition of unarmed Palestinian resistance movements (especially, during the 1987 intifada) has made it almost impossible to engage in any form of legitimate resistance and simultaneously keep at bay the scandalmongering terrorist identifications so gratuitously bandied about nowadays even in academic circles. It seems that the unfocused and tendentious foisting of the heinous label "terrorist" or

---

42. Mahmoud Darwish, "The Earth is Closing on Us," in Adonis, M. Darwish and S. al-Qasim, *Victims of a Map: A Bilingual Anthology of Arabic Poetry*, trans. Abdullah al-Udhari, (London: Saqi, 1984), 13.

"apologist," or even anti-Semite, on all forms of opposition to Zionism and to the war on terror has spawned a fearful confluence (or, "an overlap without equivalence," to use Derrida's felicitous expression) between the *erasure* of the everyday materealities of struggle in the West Bank and Gaza and the *erosion* of terrorism's concrete sociopolitical devastation, producing, all along, the necessary insensitivity and surety for the perpetuation of settler colonial terror in the theater of cruelty. By delving into the intimate lives of everyday Palestinians, *Paradise Now* compels the viewer to ponder and problematize the question, are Said and Khaled terrorists?

The Collapse of the Spectacle

> We are lacking an art of multiple senses, multiple ways, of the equivocal and even of veiled senses, veiled ways, of suspended sense or of ab-sense. An art, or rather . . . a sense (of direction)?
>
> JEAN-LUC NANCY[43]

> It is not the office of art to spotlight alternatives, but to resist by its form alone the course of the world, which permanently puts a pistol to men's heads.
>
> THEODOR ADORNO[44]

> What I did with Paradise Now is take a formulaic film language—a genre, the thriller, a very artificial language—and remove the artificiality to tell a story as close to reality as possible.
>
> HANY ABU-ASSAD[45]

The force of *Paradise Now* resides in its acute awareness of its audiences' multiple and diverse horizons of expectations as well as in its incumbent attempt to nuance and, whenever possible, transform those expectations, which would have already been established or spoiled by trailers and reviews. The trailer of Warner Independent Pictures, for instance, intimates (with a suspense-sugared voice) that the film is a thriller of the utmost quality: it will take you to "a land forsaken by hope" and to "a culture searching for its place" in order

---

43. Jean-Luc Nancy, "Consecration and Massacre," *Postcolonial Studies* 6, no. 1 (2003): 47–50.

44. Adorno, "Commitment," 180.

45. Hany Abu-Assad, "Dear ()," http://angryarab.blogspot.com/2006/05/hani-abu-assads-reply-to-my-review-of.html

to show you how "two lifelong friends struggle with an impossible choice."[46] Warner Independent Pictures capitalizes on the exotic whiff and provenance of the film in order to foster mass-market consumption rather than artistic perception. The form and content of the trailer as a schematic and vicarious experience of the film speaks volumes about the ways in which the logic of reification and commodification overrides the film's encoded intent. Gravely still, this somewhat "spoiling trailer narrative" undercuts—precisely by projecting a sense of a suspense thriller in thrall of the exotic—the artistic freshness of the film and relays it back to the very same thriller genre that Abu-Assad painstakingly seeks to surpass.[47]

What I am suggesting here is that the ways in which artistic productions are marketed and codified very much trivializes beforehand the serious subject matter they broach, snipping in the bud their potential for resistance (Adorno) and for producing multiple and equivocal senses (Nancy). The mobilizing force of mass marketing bears significant continuities with the mobilizing force of the war on terror in that it foregrounds consumption and forecloses reflection. This detrimentally compounds the already difficult attempt of *Paradise Now* to demystify the prediscursive currency of terrorism, and, as it were, prematurely suspends its artistic suspension of the spectacle of terror. Perhaps the fact that the film has been co-opted by a Warner Bros. distributor (i.e., Warner Independent Pictures) is indicative of the relatively easy convertibility of resistance art into mainstream culture; perhaps this bespeaks, in turn, the acute fragility and precariousness of cultural politics in the age of terror; clearly, however, a critical scrutiny of the film's "multiple senses" and "veiled ways" of resistance is never more to be desired than at times when, from excess of commodity fetishism and mass-consumerism, the entertainment industry has never ceased delocalizing and leveling out complex historical experiences into mainstream culture.

Paradise Now invests in its own cinematic medium to resist paradoxically the desire for form, for reel narrative terror, and to paint a vividly complex yet

---

46. Warner Independent Pictures, available at https://www.youtube.com/watch?v=C9xmEBs_FoM.

47. Nadia Yaqub situates *Paradise now* in the context of two other film genres—the wedding and the road movie—and concludes that Abu-Assad's film is rather an anti-wedding and an anti-road film. Yaqub largely approaches *Paradise Now* as a pessimistic commentary on the political failure of the Second Intifada, but she ends her essay by taking note of the artistic productivity in film and literature that proliferated in the aftermath of the Intifada. See Nadia Yaqub, "Paradise Now: Narrating a Failed Politics," in *Film in the Middle East and North Africa: Creative Dissidence*, ed. Josef Gugler (Austin: University of Texas Press, 2011), 219–27.

realistic picture of Palestinian lives under occupation. The film might be accused of a certain mimetic irresponsibility, of reproducing terrorist stereotypes about Palestinians, a suspicion that might be at the core of its worldwide acclaim, acceptability, and circularity in the West; but insofar as the stereotype is not utterly unrealistic, it is, at least at a deeper and more worthwhile level of reflection, a realistic representation—and, I must add, *denunciation*—of the publicly held *image* of Palestinians. The collapse of the public image is precisely what the film dramatizes, all along inviting the unavoidable question: Are these two young men to be branded as terrorists?

As I pointed out earlier, the film invests in staging contradictions in order to disidentify with and discredit the credulity of homogenizing terrorist identifications, urging the viewer to reckon with the unruly micronarratives of everyday struggles against the Israeli occupation, the decentralized but intricately intertwined and overlapping forces that propel the cumulative and explosive thrust of that struggle. It makes sense then to rely on mostly round rather than flat, one-dimensional characters. Additionally, the significance of the names of the leading characters is not incompatible with the latencies of meaning, "of the equivocal and even of veiled senses" (Nancy) that the film makes use of to illuminate the everyday, which is relentlessly brought under erasure, cast into amnesia so as to stress the presentist but lasting exception: the frantic war on terror. "Said," which means "happy," is basically dissonant with the sense of shame, boredom, and disenchantment with life he experiences and conveys. "Khaled," which means "eternal" or "immortal," is also at odds with the character of Khaled who, while lured by the posthumous heroic commemoration that voluntary martyrdom promises, fails in the end to go ahead with the mission, the guarantor of immortalization. "Suha" invokes the dim star Alcor ("the pious woman") in the constellation of Ursa Minor while its root verb in Arabic (*saha*, "to lapse") evokes inattentiveness, absent-mindedness, and, in a stronger sense, obliviousness. This is quite unfortunate for a character whose generally one-dimensional role in the film consists of representing the exile's perspective, the embodiment of reason, intellect, and critical distance.[48] In the case of Said and Khaled it is the character that un-

---

48. Suha might be seen as the spokesperson of Palestinian intellectuals such as Hanan Ashrawi who issued a statement calling for the cessation of suicide bombing operations: "We call upon the parties behind military operations targeting civilians in Israel to reconsider their policies and stop driving our young men to carry out these operations. Suicide bombings deepen the hatred and widen the gap between the Palestinian and the Israeli people. Also, they destroy the possibilities of peaceful co-existence between them in two neighboring states," "Palestinian Intellectuals' Urgent Appeal to Stop Suicide Bombings," *The Middle East and Islamic World Reader*, ed. Marvin Gettleman and Stuart Schaar (New York: Grove Press, 2003), 231.

dermines the name, while in the case of Suha it is the name that undermines the character.

There are other contradictions and differences between the characters that I will not go into, but one in particular bears mentioning: unlike Said, who is plagued by his father's collaborative history with the Israelis, Suha derives her social stature and patina of respectability from the fact that she is *bint* abu-Azzam, the daughter of a renowned Palestinian martyr. Yet her intellectual detachment from the Nabulsi ways of resistance is seriously at odds with the cult of martyrdom from which she has earned and continues to earn her social aura. Said is initially presented as equally detached, enjoying the companionship of his friend Khaled and a *nargila* (hubble-bubble) smoke on a hill that overlooks Nablus, imparting thus a sense of noninvolvement, oftentimes idiomized in Arabic as *al-julūs 'alā al-rabwa afḍal*—literally, "better to be sitting on the hill" (rather than get bogged down the frustrating morass of politics). But the viewer later learns that Said had indeed requested and committed himself to a martyrdom operation (*'amaliyya 'istishhādiyya*) and that, given the compromised legacy of his father, he had been carefully monitored and tested (along with his lifelong friend Khaled) by Jamal (Amer Hlehel), for no less than two years.

Without exaggerating or diminishing the psychic components that underlie Said's transformation into a voluntary martyr, it is important to stress the extent to which they bear the impress of his father's embarrassing legacy. Here *Paradise Now* proceeds in a way no less obviously accusatory of the Israeli occupation for generating and recruiting collaborators than subtly critical of the hypocritical socioeconomic norms whereby the tragic execution of a collaborator (*'amīl*) is denied the dignity of public grief, on the one hand, and, on the other, is reified and commodified into a sought-after item in a lucrative video rental business. For Said and his family, however, few things are worse than a legacy of intimate grief forever barred from the public rituals of mourning deemed necessary for its uninhibited assimilation. Such a legacy of inarticulate grief, withdrawn from but hardly spared the shaming tirades of the public eye, is likely to set in motion, at least form a psychoanalytic perspective, a psychoaffective response of disparate incubational intensities—ranging from narcissistic and manic to melancholic rages—of suicidal proportions.[49] Given

---

49. "Insofar as the grief remains unspeakable, the rage over the loss can redouble by virtue of remaining unavowed. And if that rage is publically proscribed, the melancholic effects of such a proscription can achieve suicidal proportions." Judith Butler, *The Psychic Life of Power*, (Stanford, CA: Stanford University Press, 1997), 148. Similarly, Eric Santner contends that "mourning without solidarity is the beginning of madness," *Stranded Objects: Mourning, Memory, and Film in Postwar Germany* (Ithaca, NY: Cornell University Press, 1990), 29.

that the continuity between melancholy and suicide is a well-developed thesis of Freudian psychoanalysis, it is safe to posit that Said's strain toward suicide boils down to an *accented* or *late* melancholy, a post-Aqsa Intifada psychoaffective product of life under the mutilating system of Israeli occupation—a twilight zone in which the dividing lines between life and death start gradually to blur.[50] Yet, the auto- and simultaneously hetero-destructive nature of this melancholy suggests that we are at the site/sight less of compulsive and vicissitudinal behavior than of compulsory and political resistance.[51] The compulsive in psychoanalysis becomes the compulsory under Israeli occupation. In the settler colonial context, psychoanalysis runs less of a risk to privatize the political because the private must have always been penetrated by the political.

I will say more about the private and the political in what follows. Suffice it for now to say that I do not mean to calibrate completely Said's melancholy effervescence with his ultimate self-sacrificial act even though it is a melancholy act *par excellence*. Rather I mean to suggest that there is no master narrative of suicide resistance, and that melancholy is an incisive psychoaffective precipitator or supplement of a piece with a course of action that is determined at the outset by *status occupation*, its stifling socioeconomic hegemony, military siege, and political regulation of every aspect of Palestinian everydayness. Yet I would be remiss not to insist, conversely, that an end to the occupation and the betterment of socioeconomic conditions of lives would not simultaneously result in the dissipation of melancholy or any other psychic and traumatic symptoms originating in and testamentary to the trauma of the occupation; melancholy weighs on the system of occupation of which it is a product, but their relationship is far from being mutually exclusive: it would insuperably lurk and fester in the incubational disjuncture between the hypothetical demise of occupation and its *Zeitlos*, or timeless, psychic demarcations. By and large, the psychological interest of the film, far from domesticating and undermining the political, imparts a more complex and stronger sense of the

---

50. On the continuities between melancholia and suicide, see, for instance, Sigmund Freud, "The Ego and the Id," in *On Metapsychology: The Theory of Psychoanalysis* (London: Penguin, 1991), 341–401; Peter Shabad, "The Most Intimate of Creations: Symptoms as Memorials to One's Lonely Suffering," in *Symbolic Loss: The Ambiguity of Mourning and Memory at Century's End*, ed. Peter Homans (Charlottesville: University of Virginia Press, 2000), 197–212.

51. As I previously mentioned, Fanon overturns Freud's conception of pathological and auto-destructive melancholy in the service of a hetero-destructive conception of melancholy, embodied by, for instance, the Algerian *mujāhid*, or freedom fighter: "The illness of the moral consciousness, which is always accompanied by auto-accusation and auto-destructive tendencies, took on in the case of Algerians hetero-destructive forms. The melancholic Algerian does not commit suicide. He kills." Frantz Fanon, *The Wretched of the Earth*, trans. Constance Farrington (New York: Grove Press, 1963), 299.

degree to which the familial and private are shot through with the political status quo. But while the *matereality* of everyday lives is structured by status occupation, in many ways it exceeds and gnaws at the very system to which it is submitted.

If the occupation is a "necropolitical" system that assumes and exercises exclusive sovereignty not only over life ("bio-politics") but also over death ("necro-power"), it is not inconceivable for any logic of resistance to proceed by reclaiming sovereignty over life and, if not, over death.[52] In its unchecked compulsion to "autoimmunize" itself against Palestinian resistance by suppressing it (under a litany of guises ranging from security and democracy to sovereignty), the occupation intensifies its illusion of invulnerability to the threat of resistance from/against which it seeks to protect itself.[53] Meanwhile, it creates the objective conditions for the emergence of Palestinian resistance, which can be deconstructed as a symptom or counterproduct of the occupation's obliviousness to (or inability to contain) its "autoimmunitary aggression."[54]

This deconstructive analysis might be a crude and apologetic summation of the structural fragility/aggressivity of sovereignty. It is, however, important to stress that the autoimmunitary fervor of the Israeli occupation is heightened by its disavowed historical injustices toward the Palestinians—really, its cynical exploitation of their extreme vulnerability (to violence) to dispossess them (by violence) of their geopolitical identity. Rarely has there been an autoimmunitary and necropolitical system more compulsive-repetitive and contradictory than the Israeli occupation in Palestine: it regularly wheels out the proverbial vulnerability of the Jews throughout (modern) history to displace and disperse any concern for the actual vulnerability of the Palestinians. As Edward Said mentions during the Q&A part of his talk on "The Myth of the Clash of Civilizations," "You cannot continue to victimize someone else just because you yourself were a victim once. There has to be a limit."[55] The

---

52. Achille Mbembe contends that "the most accomplished form of necropower is the contemporary colonial occupation of Palestine" in that it not only exercises tight control over bodies but also creates death- or necro-scapes, disposable subjects and massacres, subjugating vast populations (as in the West Bank and Gaza) to a "vertical" and "splintering occupation." Mbembe, "Necropolitics," *Public Culture* 15, no. 1 (2003): 27–29. Suicide resistance in this context becomes threatening precisely because it wrests away from the Israeli occupation its exclusive sovereignty over life and death—really, because it brings about a form of *unauthorized death*. See also Talal Asad, *On Suicide Bombing* (New York: Columbia University Press, 2007), 67.

53. Derrida, *Rogues*, 123.

54. Jacques Derrida, "Autoimmunity: Real and Symbolic Suicides—a Dialogue with Jacques Derrida," in Borradori, *Philosophy in a Time of Terror*, 95.

55. Edward W. Said, "The Myth of the Clash of Civilizations," *Media Education Foundation*, https://www.youtube.com/watch?v=aPS-pONiEG8.

counter-autoimmunitary (desperate and despairing) measures undertaken by some Palestinians cannot be understood, as Said is well aware of, in stark contrast to the logic of victim-cum-perpetrator that the occupation brought to perfection. The logic of resistance seeks to override its perennial vulnerability and "living dead" status by appropriating and countering the autoimmunitary sovereignty to which it is forcibly conscripted. In this manner, the occupation precipitates the resistance, and its necropolitical practices precipitate what I will call the *fantasies of necromnipotence* that structure martyr operations.

Paradise Now focuses squarely the expropriation of the corporeal, on the bodily unfolding of this logic of rescue and liberation of a captive sovereignty; indeed, the film *deliteralizes* the auto- and hetero-destructive processes through which the body expropriates its matereality in the name of appropriating its own sovereignty. For the body to have an absolute dignity and value, it must be worth more than its material reality, more than its *matereality*. In other words, the value of the body is in excess of its own *matereality*; it is a measure of its *potent*ial spectrality, or of its "invisible and spectral survival."[56] No wonder, then, the film throws into bold relief the *immunopoetic* practices through which the body is gradually inoculated against and catapulted out of its own matereality.

The elaborate preparations leading up to the martyrdom mission are carried out in quasi-mechanical, matter-of-fact and circumambient apprehension; they include, in particular, videotaped martyr farewells (mission exalting speeches and "valedictions forbidding mourning" for families), shaving and bodily washing (a rite of passage that suggests they are "dead corpses" or "living dead"—but in an *agentive replication* rather than in the passive sense of bare living under occupation), and dressing up in tailored suits, making them look like Israeli settlers (the cover story being that they are heading up to a wedding in Tel Aviv). In addition, photos of the protagonists are put on posters (later to be displayed in the town center, as a showcase of martyrdom), and their torsos are strapped with explosives before they are offered a "Last Supper," intimating thus their progress toward their voluntary crucifixion for the sins of the Israeli occupation.

Although inflected by the redemptory lore of religion, Said's desire (and to a lesser extent Khaled's) to work through his father's crime and his daily shame or character-assassination by the public gaze—and commit or commit to, as it were, "suicifixion"—is prodded less by the ostensibly redemptory cult of martyrdom than by the *fantasy of necromnipotence*, which institutes and sustains martyrdom's seductive appeal (by means of a vast husk of paradisiacal and com-

---

56. Jacques Derrida, "Faith and Knowledge," in *Acts of Religion* (New York: Routledge, 2002), 87.

memorative heroic lures). *Paradise Now* explores the psychic life of resistance at the nexus of the religious, the national, and the personal. Void of scenes of carnage or thriller suspense tarnish (no sound music and no special effects), the film stages the "ab-sense" (Nancy) and collapse of the spectacle of terror, pointing instead toward an unlikely conjunction I would like to make here between close reading and the body strapped in explosives.

This whole ceremonial procession gravitates toward the agentive duplication or "cloning" of the body from its *passive* "living dead" state *under* status occupation to an *active* and *actantial* "living dead" motor force *against* the occupation—resulting, in the process, in an assault on figurative language.[57] No longer is one capable of recognizing the signifying metaphoricity of the "living dead"—it is demetaphorized in the service of its agentive replication. If the literality of the "living dead" trope is isomorphic with its metaphoric intelligibility, then it is now deliteralized and demetaphorized, as it were, for the sake of a literality that is in excess of representation (specifically because it is a deliberate activation of the literality of figurative language). It is also in this sense that the body wrapped in explosives is the "antinarrative" *par excellence*, the threshold moment of generative collapses: the collapse of narrative, the collapse of figurative language as well as the collapse of the spectacle of terrorism. Yet, this is, compellingly enough, what *Paradise Now* seeks to achieve: narrating the unnarrativizable through the punctilious staging of the transition from the tropology to the immunology of the "living dead" body. This involves (1) the evacuation of the "living dead" body from its tropological signature and (2) its transformation, by way of immunizing techniques, into a living specter, a *corpsofactual entity*.

The image of Said's torso strapped with explosives presents us with a rare confluence between the ostensible physical vulnerability (for instance, when Said sits in a washroom and wipes the sweat from under his bomb strap) and the spectral immunity/invulnerability of the suicide martyr's body (as Said feels in the same washroom that the bomb had become part of him—his destiny—and resolves to go on with his mission). The film tries to walk the fragile line between these two poles of extremity, prodding viewers to contemplate their veritable proximity: how the *radical* vulnerability of Palestinians (who have lost everything, and, as Darwish would put it, tore off their limbs in the passage) to

---

57. W. J. T. Mitchell, "The Unspeakable and the Unimaginable: Word and Image in a Time of Terror," *ELH* 72, no. 2 (2005): 292. Mitchell uses the concept of "cloning" to highlight the terror of cloning as such and the ways in which terror as a violent sociopolitical movement infinitely produces and reproduces itself. I am using "cloning" here to stress the autoimmune movement through which the "living-in-dying" body under the Israeli occupation becomes a corpse incarnate, a function of its spectrality, a master of its destiny, and not just a bare matter of its own matereality.

the violence of the occupation can give rise to the kind of *deliberate in*vulnerability to violence that the suicide martyr (who has nothing more to lose) appropriates. By its economized play on the spectacle—by building toward but ultimately withholding the spectacle of terror—the film might be seen to give the viewers what they want with one hand and take it back with the other. In other words, rather than stage the suicidal act as a climactic spectacle, the film arouses in its viewers the desire for the spectacle of terror, the desire to enjoy what is morally reprehensible, and simultaneously disallows the spectacle from materializing. This is clearly a subtle artistic detail through which Abu-Assad attempts to inscribe the contemplative faculty in place of the spectacle of terror, and, in turn, set in motion an imaginative and empathizing process through which viewers can determine for themselves the degree to which they might be unwittingly involved as subjects in historical circumstances that might not initially qualify even as objects of remote concern for them.[58]

Paradise Now stages the collapse of the spectacle of violence and terror by encoding the very collapse of the visual medium in which it is anchored. This is perhaps one of the most innovative artistic contributions of the film: elaborating and visualizing a narrative of suicide martyrdom that is simultaneously sustained by an acute critical wakefulness to the economy of the spectacle, and the ways in which such a hegemonic economy of spectatorship regulates global literacy and social intelligibility from the West Coast to the West Bank. Perhaps it is in this sense then that the collapse of the spectacle at the end of the film and even prior to that (following the camera malfunction during the filming of Khaled's farewell speech) testifies to Abu-Assad's search for what might be called a post-spectacle filmic expression: while acknowledging the indispensability of the spectacle to its visual medium (as well as the fact that historical matereality itself is nothing more than an effect of the spectrality of that medium), this novel art demonstrates nonetheless a willingness to scrutinize the limits/inadequacies of its medium to stress the irreducibility/excess of matereal history. The film evidences this creative and critical sobriety by thoughtfully incorporating the camera failure scene like a reel "dead corpse" in the film's entire narrative/visual texture, imparting thus a strong sense of its message precisely by exposing the collapse of its medium.

Abu-Assad's imaginative eagerness to incorporate the failures of the medium in which his work is anchored seems to me quite a significant feat, very much in syn with what Espinosa calls "an imperfect art," or with what Rey Chow

---

58. This is, I think, very much in line with what Spivak calls "the uncoercive rearrangement of [the] desires" of the viewers, transforming them, I would add, from passive participants in the spectacle of terror (as a way of being in the world mediated by images) to active dissidents from imperial corporate systems shored up in their name. See Spivak, "Terror," 9.

calls an "ethics of postvisuality."⁵⁹ The camera malfunction undercuts any putative narrative justification of suicide martyrdom and, above all, undermines the spectacular rhetoric of apologetic and pardon-seeking farewell speeches while dealing a severe blow to the video rental business and to the cult of martyrdom and hero worship they profit from and perpetuate. Similarly, Khaled's shopping tips to his mother interrupts the spectacle of martyrdom-heroism, and deflates the seriousness of the matter at hand into a humorous situation, not however in order to undermine it, but in order, in my view, to rediscover it anew and precisely through the humorous attitude, which, at least from a psychoanalytic perspective, not only harshly dramatizes the tensions between the real and the ideal or the everyday and the everlasting (as in the title of the film, *Paradise Now*) but also affirms the subject's mastery over a situation to which he is submitted.⁶⁰

Attentive to the artificiality of its medium, *Paradise Now* seeks not only to break the illusion of mimetic realism, but also the very derealizing effects of the spectacle. By incorporating into its diegesis scenes of a camera malfunction and of Khaled's aside to his mother (regarding where to buy water filters), the film wants to constitute itself on the pyre of the spectacle, enabling itself, in the process, to incorporate (with an ethics of mimetic urgency) very minute details about the everyday lives of Palestinians under siege (Said's photographer's obsession with precision in a historical context of extreme uncertainty beggars the imagination). This puts viewers on the qui vive: mimetic punctiliousness creates a sense of participatory or imaginative immediacy and compels viewers to suspend their judgment and begin the arduous labor of self-reflexivity which might ultimately lead them to the discovery of latent complicity as a

---

59. Espinosa, "Meditations on Imperfect Cinema," 84. In a full article devoted to the theoretical and artistic newness of the internationally acclaimed Chinese film director Zhang Yimou, Rey Chow submits that since in Yimou's work "visuality becomes deconstructed in the process of its own making, its violence ineradicable from its positivistic obviousness and prowess, we will need to imagine a new critical language, something like an ethics of postvisuality." "Toward an Ethics of Postvisuality: Some Thoughts on the Recent Work of Zhang Yimou," *Poetics Today* 25, no. 4 (2004): 687. Nouri Bouzid's *Akir Film* (*Making Of*, 2006) further explores the potentialities of this ethics of postvisuality by blurring the lines between narrative film and metanarrative scenes and by staging, much to the viewer's bafflement, the *making of* a film about the *making of* a suicide bomber. See Nouri Gana, "Powers of Powerlessness: The Politics of Defeat in the Cinema of Nouri Bouzid," *Journal of Visual Culture* 16, no. 2 (August 2017): 253–73.

60. Humor is agentive: it poignantly punctures the spectacle of martyrdom-heroism, exposes the dread of joking about it, and compels the viewer to comprehend the economies of survival and resistance in the West Bank and Gaza. For more on the critical importance of humor, see, for instance, Sigmund Freud, "Humour," in *Art and Literature* ed. James Strachey (London: Penguin, 1990): 425–33.

locus of critique and as a modality of self-reflexivity at the end of which a noncoercive redistribution of their identifications takes place. In this manner, *Paradise Now* invests in the artistic dismantling of the spectacle of violence to shore up the visual anatomy of self-sacrificial resistance and inscribe it in a historical continuum of the secular nationalist aspirations of Palestinians, all the while obstructing the consumption of reel violence by prompting the viewer to contemplate instead the degree of his or her involvement *locally* in the Israeli occupation in Palestine.[61] The film's message remains, however, retrievable only to the extent that the language of Israeli occupation—of state terrorism under the banner of self-defense—becomes no longer intelligible.

Privacy Now

> The horror would appear to be associated with the fact that the attacker dies. Dropping cluster bombs from the air is apparently less repugnant; it is somehow deemed, by the leaders of the Western world at least, to be morally superior. Why dying with your victim should be seen as the greater sin than saving yourself is unclear.
>
> JACQUELINE ROSE[62]

> Suicide is a sin because it is a unique act of freedom, a right that neither the religious authorities nor the nation-state allows. Today, the law requires that a prisoner condemned to death be prevented from committing suicide to escape execution; it is not death but authorized death that is called for.
>
> TALAL ASAD[63]

> To kill yourself with your enemy is a biblical story. The story of Samson already tells us that people prefer to kill themselves together with their enemies rather than accept humiliation.
>
> HANY ABU-ASSAD[64]

The raid on the spectacle of terror and on the culture industry of suicide martyrdom cannot by now be overstated. It constitutes *Paradise Now*'s main

---

61. Hamid Dabashi edited collection of essays on Palestinian film clearly makes the link between narrative nationhood and diasporic Palestinian cinema. See Hamid Dabashi, *Dreams of a Nation: On Palestinian Cinema* (New York: Verso, 2006).

62. Jacqueline Rose, *The Last Resistance* (New York: Verso, 2007), 127.

63. Asad, *On Suicide Bombing*, 67.

64. Abu-Assad, "Dear (),"

aesthetic and critical thrust and is executed in tandem with the narrative unfolding of the story of Said and Khaled. The film offers a double-edged critique of the grand narrative of martyrdom on the one hand and, on the other, of the global discourse of terrorism which Israel has totally coopted to malign all forms of Palestinian resistance to its illegal system of military occupation, all the while condoning grossly disproportionate forms of IDF state terrorism as forms of self-defense. Not only does the global discourse of terrorism mask the asymmetrical military deterrence capabilities between Palestinians and Israelis, but it also displaces and disperses the particular histories of Palestinian struggle for emancipation from the occupation into grotesque threats to justice, freedom, and democracy. No wonder, then, that the overarching concern of the film is to reclaim and reinscribe visually the particular stories of the two childhood friends, and especially the story of Said, since after the mission's failure the first time, the film zeroes in on Said's psychoaffective and sociopolitical struggles as he resolves to go ahead with the mission while Khaled hesitates and is eventually forced back home by Said.

The cover story of *Paradise Now* may be about martyrdom and access to paradise, but the real story is about what it means to live under the Israeli military occupation whose objective is not just to defeat Palestinians and mortgage their future but also to make them internalize defeat and give in to defeatism. Martyrdom is horrifying for sure but only to the extent that it is a testimony to the settler colonial imposition of defeat on an entire nation and an entire people on a diurnal basis. The aim of the Israeli subjugation of Palestinians is not only to make them internalize defeat but also to enlist them as agents that may then self-regulate and self-impose defeat by themselves. In this respect, the reel horror of the film, insofar as Said is concerned, is the erosion of privacy. The image of Palestinian life as overridden with politics is the product of its reception in the outside world, a reception that hinges eventually on national allegories of reading and misreading. I find AbuKhalil's observation here quite pertinent: "Do we really allow the Palestinians to live their lives in the Arab world? I mean, as we represent them, and as we judge their coverage in popular cultures, do we allow them to be entitled to a full life, or do we insist and expect that they engage in struggle, all day long, seven days a week, and all year?"[65] It is not that the lived experience of privacy does not exist anymore, but that the received image of Palestinian life as it travels across the (Arab) world becomes submerged by the politics of resistance to the occupation.

---

65. AbuKhalil, "Paradise Now? Paradise Never."

Apart from this transnational perception of Palestinian privacy, the actual privacy of Palestinians is vanishing beneath the ever-rising flood tide of Israeli intelligence and the panoptic power of the occupation, a reality that Abu-Assad stresses even further in his later film about the indefatigable resistance to and coerced collaboration with the IDF, *Omar* (2013). Still, in *Paradise Now*, the taboo memory of Said's father's collaborative history circulates like an open secret that is transmitted to Said on a daily basis through a multitude of discursive forms and figurative modes of intelligibility, which translate into instances of symbolic violence and acts of shaming, all of which leave Said exposed and unshielded from the disproving public gaze. The general expectation is that Said may become a sellout like his father and meet with the same fate, but he diverges from his father's trajectory and wagers on martyrdom as a means to address and redress the unbearable weight of his father's legacy. Living with a legacy of shame would have been one way of internalizing an imposed defeat. It becomes a sort of self-imposed defeat if Said were to compulsively repeat rather than redress his father's error and become a traitor himself.

The open secret of his father's collaborative past is experienced by Said not only as the ground for societal interpellation but also as a specular judgement on his identity—the son of a collaborator (*mutaʿāwin* or *ʿamīl*). He experiences his father's legacy as an oozing wound, which weighs him down, and compels him in the end to address its root cause. Said's shame slides into guilt: Said's identity (shaped by shame) dissolves into a self-assertive identification (shaped by guilt) with his father. Not that Said comes only vicariously to experience his father's guilt but that he also identifies with it—he feels guilty himself. His guilt, however, is not experienced as a survivor's guilt—Said feels no compulsion to repeat the crime of which his father was guilty, but to settle it, to right the wrong that preceded and precipitated it. Under the duress of the Israeli occupation, Said's guilt is experienced as a failure to act and as an urgent call to set right the injustice to which his father was wrongly subjected. While the Israeli intelligence is shameless about bullying and blackmailing vulnerable Palestinians into becoming informants, the tragic irony in the end is that Palestinians are claimed by guilt whereas Israelis claim innocence. The occupation instrumentalizes and manipulates affect—defusing shamelessness into innocence—while Palestinians are animated by affect to turn shame into a clamor for justice and dignity.

The Israeli occupation relies on a discourse of neoliberal resilience and innocence to wash itself off the everyday crimes it commits with impunity. It consistently displaces and disperses its moral deficit, its diurnal subjugation and indignation of a defenseless population, into peacemaking fantasies with such far-flung fantastical foes as the United Arab Emirates and Bahrain or Morocco. What the Israeli occupiers fail to fathom is that by humiliating Palestinians, they are not subduing them but, at best, fueling their desire to act for fear of the guilt that follows from the failure not to act. It is in this sense that we ought to understand the limited alternatives with which Said has been left in the wake of his father's collaborative history: either involuntary subjection, daily humiliation and servitude to the occupation, or voluntary martyrdom. He chooses to right a wrong, to redress a familial micronarrative in the hope that the national narrative may follow suit despite the full acknowledgement of the colossal challenges it will face. Reclaiming an untarnished family life is no trifling matter but central to Palestinian resistance insofar as the occupation would practically be unenforceable without its systematic undercover infiltration of Palestinian privacy and family ties. For Said, the more relevant title of the film would not be *Paradise Now*, but *Privacy Now*.

Israeli security forces must have recruited Said's father as a native informant during the 1987 intifada. It was around that time that the Palestinian leadership started to execute (alleged) collaborators. Throughout its history but particularly after 1967, Israel conscripted a great number of informants through strict military rule, mass arrests of Palestinians and the use of blackmail or carrot-and-stick method by Shin bet or Shabak, the Israeli General Security Service. Not unexpectedly, Shabak agents "pressure almost every Palestinian who comes into contact with the Israeli authorities for his daily affairs to collaborate."[66] Since Al-Aqsa intifada, recruitment through the permit regime has become systematic, resulting, as Abu-Assad's *Omar* makes patently clear, in the contagious spread of suspicion and paranoia in Palestinian society to the level of becoming a modality of social intelligibility. In such an environment, Said would more likely be seen as a usual suspect or a potential traitor rather than as a trustworthy individual. He therefore is fully justified when he blames the occupation for everything, including of course for confiscating his privacy, condemning him to the social stigma that comes with being a son of a traitor. In the case of Said, "the private is political" is not a slogan—it is a brutal reality.

Said does not seek martyrdom for a divine end or paradisical promise as in the deliberately misleading title of the film (most probably so for counterintuitive pedagogical reasons), but in order to reclaim sovereignty over his confiscated private life. It may sound as if I am privatizing the political here, but the private and the political under occupation are very much indissociable.

---

66. Hillel Cohen and Ron Dudai, "Human Rights Dilemmas in Using Informers to Combat Terrorism: The Israeli-Palestinian Case," *Terrorism and Political Violence* 17 (2005): 233–34.

After all, it was the occupation that turned Said's father into a collaborator and as a result deprived Said of a private life. Said would have preferred to have had a father (private) rather than a collaborator (public, political), given that the latter cast a long shadow on the former, and foreclosed the possibility of privacy. It is these micronarratives, the particular story of Said, and the unquantifiable number of stories that resemble it that constitute the real thrust of *Paradise Now*, all the more so because these kinds of stories are almost always elided as soon as the language of the war on terror kicks in. The resistance to the discourse of the war on terror has always been the first front of the resistance to the occupation. The internalization (*'istibṭān*) of the language of terrorism is as detrimental as the normalization (*taṭbī'*) with the Israeli occupation.

Now that the normalization age is upon us, and that more Arab states are incited to normalize relations with Israel, the settler colonial state may no longer just rely on a network of coerced native informants but also on docile and servile regional state informants. The Israeli occupation in Palestine sought to domesticate itself by mere diplomatic blackmail and the intermediary intimidating force of Trump's America.[67] Enlisting and implicating more and more informants (individuals and nation-states) as agents of its *cause célèbre*, Israel may seem to have reached a state of a *fait accompli* and fulfilled the foundational expectations of a success story—an achieved return to the ancestral land, a materialization of a romantic fantasy of pure origins, and an embodiment of ideological nostalgia: Zionism as atavism, melancholite, and narcissistically regressive, yet fulfilling. Zionists enjoy their symptoms while Palestinians struggle with theirs. What I find tragically ironic here is that while Israeli settler colonialism has almost completely normalized with its melancholite symptoms and recovered the mythically lost loved object (Zion/Palestine), many Arab intellectuals and artists have not yet reckoned with the melancholy disposition that characterizes much of Palestinian and Arab culture in its attachment to the loss of historical Palestine. Perhaps orientalism is to blame since it has already tilted the psychoaffective playing forcefield in favor of melancholite Zionist pride. Abdalla Laroui once painted the double standards that plague the question of Palestine as follows: "the defensive war the Arabs wage is a terrible jihad while Israel's extermination war is legitimate resistance. The attachment of Arabs to the land is a laughable matter while

---

67. I am inspired by Hosam Aboul-Ela's wonderful study of another settler colonial nation-state, the belated disseminator of *domesticatory* discursive practices, the United States. See Hosam Aboul-Ela, *Domestications: American Empire, Literary Culture, and the Postcolonial Lens* (Evanston, IL: Northwestern University Press, 2018).

Jewish tears at the Wailing Wall and celebrations on top of Mount Sinai constitute a rousing scene!! Inverted logic."[68] While it is underarticulated, Laroui points toward the discrepant reception of the overlapping yet divergent melancholy attachments to the same plot of land.

There is a clear clash of melancholies between the Israeli occupiers and the occupied Palestinians. The occupiers are melancholites: they have been and continue to be driven by a narcissistically regressive and fanatically infantile fantasy of omnipotence over historical Palestine, mythologized as ancient Israel. The occupied Palestinians are melancholics: they are attached to the land from which they have been and are being expelled by force. Palestinian melancholia is aligned with a politics of decolonial emancipation and with the pursuit of freedom from injustice while the melancholite pride and "kitsch-consciousness," a sort of angelic blindness to the atrocities of the occupation, is aligned with Israeli nuclear deterrence, superpower dominance and the fulfillment of the fantasy of return to the fatherland—*Kibbutz Galuiot*, or "ingathering of Exiles."[69] The incumbent task for Palestinians and Arabs, as I have stressed throughout this book, is less the liberation from melancholia than the liberation through it. The overall focus on the possibility of overcoming the melancholite proclivities of Islamist movements ought not appropriate all attention away from melancholia's emancipatory and militant potencies.

Would Islamism which makes the exact same gesture of return to an Islamic ideal be seen in the same light as the Zionist fantasy of return to the fatherland? I say "same" in the sense of similarity, not sameness, much less identicalness. In the following chapter, I will examine the less famous yet infamous Islamist fantasy of a return to origins, which may never become a *cause célèbre*, not because it is so different from Zionism but because it has not been successful in the asymmetrical global war of narratives, which is not just about words but more so about a nuclear power to back them up. My case study here will be the psychoanalytic work of Tunisian, Paris-based psychoanalyst, Fethi Benslama, for whom the Islamist movements unanimously profess the return to pure origins at the very top of their foundational agendas. For Benslama, the retrograde project of Islamists foments self-torment and forecloses messianic futurity and must therefore be abandoned in favor of secular modernity. Yet is not Islamism itself a product of secular colonial modernity and, in turn, an immanent movement of resistance against it?

68. Abdalla Laroui, *Khawāṭir al-Ṣabāḥ: Yawmiyyāt: (1967–1973)* (Morning Thoughts: Diaries) (Casablanca: al-Markaz al-Thaqafi al-Arabi, 2001), 20.

69. Gillo Dorfles coined the concept of "kitsch-consciousness" (*Kitschanschauung*). See Malcolm Quinn, *The Swastika: Constructing the Symbol* (London: Routledge, 2005), 135.

6
Melancholy Islam
Jihad, Jouissance, and Female Clairvoyance

Islam is an empty place in the theory of psychoanalysis, *and not at all,
by force of circumstance, in its exercise, in its practice.*
— ABDELKEBIR KHATIBI, "FRONTIERS"

It is impossible to raise the question of psychoanalysis and Islam today, of the commensurability or possible translation of concepts and practices, in philosophical or theological terms, without registering the political charge of the field within which the question has emerged, and without posing, at the same time, the problem of psychoanalysis's reflection on its own politics.
— STEFANIA PANDOLFO, *KNOTS OF THE SOUL*

Psychoanalysis is a symptom.
— JACQUES LACAN, *THE TRIUMPH OF RELIGION*

Psychoanalysis has almost always entertained a contentious relationship with religion, especially since Freud, the founder of the so-called godless science, was not only openly atheist but also unabashedly critical of religion. But while Freud and his followers studied the topic of religion and religious ritual in the West, they have hardly stepped outside the anthropological and intellectual boundaries of Europe and the Judeo-Christian tradition.[1] For decades, Freud's

---

1. This applies not only to Freud, as Said mentions, but also, among others, to Erich Fromm. See Edward W. Said, *Freud and the Non-European* (New York: Verso, 2003) and Erich Fromm, *Psychoanalysis and Religion* (New Haven, CT: Yale University Press, 1978).

quasi-dismissal of Islam in *Moses and Monotheism* acted as an enduring license for later European practitioners of psychoanalysis to thrust Islam into complete oblivion. After propounding that Islam is an "abbreviated repetition" of Judaism, which achieved over a short period of time "great worldly successes," Freud famously surmised that, "the internal development of the new religion soon came to a stop, perhaps because it lacked the depth which had been caused in the Jewish case by the murder of the founder of their religion."[2] The murder of the primordial father described in *Totem and Taboo*, a cornerstone of Freud's theory of psychoanalysis, finds in the murder of Moses (Judaism) and Jesus (Christianity) self-validating analogs but no analog in Islam, only "an empty place," as Khatibi pinpoints.[3] Islam posed a challenge to Freud: it is untranslatable into psychoanalytic language and therefore inassimilable to psychoanalysis unless psychoanalysis transforms itself (in such a way as to accommodate Islam). By the time he wrote *Moses and Monotheism*, toward the end of his life in exile, there was little chance Freud would embark on such a colossal task of revising his theory of psychoanalysis, which by then operated like a well-oiled machine. And since it was too late for Freud to change the theory of psychoanalysis, it must have been too belated for his successors, themselves latecomers and least concerned about Islam, to take seriously its challenge and strike out a new path.[4]

Cartwheeling back and forth in the familiar Judeo-Christian terrain of psychoanalysis and inciting the rest of the world to do the same may have seemed, at least retrospectively, the more convenient approach and guarantor of provincialism with universalist pretensions. At any rate, it was not Freud's view of Islam as a religion that lacks the foundational crime of Oedipal parricide that traveled to the Muslim world but his theories of the unconscious and dream interpretation. Given the Western points of reference of such

---

2. Cited in Fethi Benslama, *Psychoanalysis and the Challenge of Islam*, trans. Robert Bononno (Minneapolis: University of Minnesota Press, 2009), 68.

3. Abdelkebir Khatibi, "Frontiers: Between Psychoanalysis and Islam," trans. P. Burcu Yalim, *Third Text* 23, no. 6 (2009): 691.

4. Could the murder of Hussein, and the birth of Shiism, make Shia Islam assimilable to psychoanalytic theory? Gohar Homayounpour implies that that is the case, even though she doesn't explicitly say so: "We never properly mourned the loss of our glorious past, before it was taken over by Islam. Our melancholic response was to create Shiism, which is a culture of mourning." Homayounpour, *Doing Psychoanalysis in Tehran* (Cambridge, MA: MIT Press, 2012), 56. Interestingly, in his first book, Fethi Benslama attempts to force an unconsciousness of the murder of Cain as a crime that implicates Muslims and therefore makes Islam and psychoanalysis commensurable. See Benslama, *La nuit brisée: Mohammad et l'énonciation islamique* (Paris: Ramsay, 1988).

theories as the Oedipus complex, they did not resonate well with Muslim sensibilities, and only further affirmed the reigning interwar assumption that psychoanalysis is an exotic science, at loggerheads with the Islamic worldview in which Allah exerts immense tutelary power on the everyday lives of Muslims.[5] This view did not change much until the late 1970s, even while it was somewhat debated and steered into more reconciliatory and desirable directions by Malik Badri in his book *Dilemma of Muslim Psychologists*.[6] Apart from intermittent fascination, Freud's work on the interpretation of dreams, on the role of the unconscious in everyday life and on theories of subjectivity writ large proved less contentious, even productive, particularly in bourgeois, elitist, and avant-gardist circles such as the Egyptian school of psychoanalysis.[7]

Freud's tentative view of Islam had never really been taken seriously in the Muslim world until the outbreak of the Iranian revolution (1979) and the emergence of the phenomenon of political Islam or what is also referred to as Islamism at times and Salafism at others. The Rushdie affair (1989)—which started with angry protests against Indian-born British author Salman Rushdie's

---

5. Moroccan psychoanalyst Jalil Bennani argues that, not until recently, the Arab and Muslim world was thought to be a no man's land for psychoanalysis. See Jalil Bennani, "La psychanalyse au Maroc," in *Le sacré, cet obscure objet de désir?* (Paris: Éditions Albin Michel, 2009), 31.

6. Malik Badri, *Dilemma of Muslim Psychologists* (London: NWH London Publishers, 1979).

7. See Omnia El Shakry, "The Arabic Freud: The Unconscious and the Modern Subject," *Modern Intellectual History* 11, no. 1 (2014): 89–118. Between 1954 and 1958, Moustapha Safouan, a disciple of Lacan, practiced psychoanalysis in Cairo. While his contribution to Arab psychoanalysis cannot be gainsaid or slighted—he translated Freud's *The Interpretation of Dreams* into Arabic in 1958—his recollections of his clinical practice in Cairo is clearly elitist, condescending, and orientalist, especially when it comes to Egyptians, "the great majority" of whom, he submits, "continues to live outside the contemporary world, if not seemingly outside time." See Moustapha Safouan, "Five Years of Psychoanalysis in Cairo," trans. Juliet Flower MacCannell, *Umbr(a): Islam* (2009): 35. Jalil Bennani maintains that in the case of Morocco the foundational texts of psychoanalysis remain mostly unavailable in Arabic translation and that clinical practice became the space of psychoanalytic transmission, acculturation, and the tactful integration of the existing traditional maraboutic practices of therapy into the language of psychoanalysis: "Il s'agit non pas de créer de nouvelles spécificités, mais de se réapproprier la tradition en l'insérant dans des valeurs universelles" (It's not a matter of creating new specificities but of re-appropriating tradition by inserting it into universal values). Fifty years or so after Safouan's failed clinical practice in Cairo, Bennani approaches psychoanalysis and traditional modes of therapy comparatively; by delicately managing the playfield of transference, grafting the language of psychoanalysis to the language of maraboutic culture, he founded what sounds like a successful clinical practice, see Jalil Bennani, "La psychanalyse au Maroc," 38.

provocative 1988 novel, *The Satanic Verses*, and reached its apotheosis with his condemnation to death by a Khomeini-issued *fatwa*, or religious decree— fueled the desire to lay down Islam on the analytic couch. It was somewhere between these two events that Fethi Benslama started his project of "psychoanalyzing Islam," thereby following in the footsteps of Freud who most infamously psychoanalyzed Judaism. But while Benslama's model may be Freudian, his methodology is largely Lacanian. Indeed, Benslama mobilizes such Lacanian concepts as desire, lack, and especially (feminine/Other) jouissance in order to deconstruct the question of origins in Islam (partly because of the centrality of such a question to various Islamist movements and partly because it was the topic of both Rushdie's 1988 controversial novel, *The Satanic Verses*, as well as Benslama's own 1988 seminal book, *La nuit brisée / The Shattered Night*). The formidable theoretical challenge that Benslama sets for himself is less to read Freud in the wake of Lacan (after all, it may be impossible to do otherwise) than to read Lacan in the wake of revolutionary or political Islam and vice versa.

Benslama's 2002 book *La psychanalyse à l'épreuve de l'Islam* (later translated into English and published in 2009 as *Psychoanalysis and the Challenge of Islam*) dramatizes both the challenges and insights of translating Islam into Freudian and especially Lacanian psychoanalysis. Along the way, Benslama confesses that he Rushdie affair was somewhat a "rude awakening . . . particularly with regard to the commitment of an intellectual project that led to an investigation of the question of origins of Islam, where psychoanalysis was challenged, both clinically and theoretically, when it found itself transported to a cultural context different from the one in which it had taken shape."[8] Benslama is not unaware of the challenges of applying psychoanalytic theory to Islam, since Islam was not, given Freud's own acknowledgment in *Moses and Monotheism*, a good fit for psychoanalysis. Yet, for Benslama psychoanalysis is partly "culpable" for the present-day "resistance to the intelligibility of Islam" precisely because psychoanalysis did not accord attention to Islam as a topic of analysis, which would have promoted, for better or worse, its intelligibility, and even eventual mainstreaming.[9] Because of this allegedly missed encounter between psychoanalysis and Islam, Benslama's method therefore is not applicative but translational, attempting, as it does, to read Islam and psychoanalysis in tandem. Perhaps Benslama has realized that the issue of the unintelligibility of Islam was nothing more than a red herring. Regardless,

---

8. Fethi Benslama, *Psychoanalysis and the Challenge of Islam*, trans. Robert Bononno (Minneapolis: University of Minnesota Press, 2009), 9.
9. Ibid., 6.

there is no gaining the fact that the unintelligibility of Islam has, quite ironically, been reduced since Freud to the intelligibility of the problem of untranslatability.

This final chapter seeks to shed some critical light on Benslama's deployment of Lacanian psychoanalysis to examine the notion of origins in Islam, given that this notion exerts enormous gravitational pull on so many Islamist movements and given, above all, that the aura of origins constitutes an eternal wellspring of nostalgia and melancholy. The insightful ways in which Lacan's concepts of the real, desire and lack are brought to bear on the construction of origins in Islam and more so on the repression of female/Other jouissance, so central to Benslama's revisionary project of Islam, are admirable feats, generative of cross-cultural critical inquiry and dialogue. In this sense Benslama's book testifies not only to the productive possibility of studying Islam through a psychoanalytic lens but also to the ways in which Lacanian psychoanalysis holds open the promise of worlding psychoanalytic inquiry, reorienting it to the non-Western world at a time when psychoanalysis is agonizing in Euro-America. Yet, as much as there are benefits in compelling Lacan (after Lacan) to travel into uncharted territories, there are also risks and pitfalls, and these may have to do, as it will become clear below, as much with Lacan's brand of psychoanalysis as with Benslama's own deployment of it, especially in light of his avowedly secular ideological leanings. As Stefania Pandolfo astutely puts it, it is impossible for psychoanalysis to intervene in such a politically charged field of inquiry as Islam without first clarifying or interrogating its own politics as well as its own possible entanglement in post-9/11 soft power machinations of secularism to transform Islam.[10] Worse still, psychoanalyzing Islam may be less about secularizing than declaring Islam to be beyond repair and holding it therefore in that same old posture of the eternal nemesis to Western secularism.[11]

The main methodological flaw of Benslama's psychoanalytic engagement with Islam is the tendency to conflate Islamism as a singular-plural political movement, emerging out of specific historical circumstances, with Islam as a

---

10. Stefania Pandolfo, *Knot of the Soul: Madness, Psychoanalysis, Islam* (Chicago: University of Chicago Press, 2017), 128.

11. As Wendy Brown argues: "today, Western secularism is so relentlessly defined through its imagined opposite in Islamic theocracy that to render secularism as generated exclusively through Western Christian European history is to literally eschew the production of ourselves as secular through and against our imagined opposite," see Brown, "Idealism, materialism, secularism," *The Immanent Frame,* October 22, 2007, https://tif.ssrc.org/2007/10/22/idealism-materialism-secularism/.

religion that has a more or less finite core system or structure of belief and ritual despite the numerous internal divergences and different schools of interpretation. It may not be Benslama's own authorial intention, but the constant movements throughout *Psychoanalysis and the Challenge of Islam* from an analysis of Islamism to an analysis of Islam tacitly imply that for Benslama Islamism is (a symptom of) Islam. Obviously, Islamists themselves wouldn't agree with such a conclusion. The enormity of such a risk, though, makes driving a wedge between the two topics—Islam and Islamism—not only urgent but crucial to any project of psychoanalyzing Islam (or, alternatively, Islamism). The attempt to trace Islamism back to Islam without proper and consistent circumstantial differentiations may only further blur the dividing lines between the two, or, worse still, displace and disperse Islamism into Islam. Bearing these concerns in mind, I shall examine how Benslama makes use of Lacanian vocabulary in order first to deconstruct the myth of origin in Islam and the melancholite economy of jouissance that sustains it, and second to reinstate the overlooked role of the female other, not to mention the enigma of female jouissance, in mediating the access to origin in Islam. Women, according to Benslama, are the unacknowledged—if not repressed—midwives of monotheistic and Islamic origin par excellence.

Undoing Origin

> The return to origin should be understood not as a movement of the present toward the past nor as a past that must be made present, but as the return of a past from before the beginning, an anachronic and anarchic antecedence toward the matrical ark of the law. It is a question of being born again into origin from a preorigin. To paraphrase Hamlet, Islam is out of joint.
>
> FETHI BENSLAMA[12]

Inspired by Freud's seminal inquiry into the foundational origins of Judaism in *Moses and Monotheism*, and equipped with a Lacanian poststructuralist method of analysis, Benslama sets himself the task of deconstructing what he calls the "primal fictions of Islam [*fictions originaires de l'Islam*] and the workings of its symbolic system" in order to discern "the kernel of the impossible around which language forms an imaginary shell, a projection of the

---

12. Benslama, *Psychoanalysis and the Challenge of Islam*, 50.

psyche toward the external world."[13] Such a task entails a hermeneutic shift from "metaphysics into metapsychology," or from "the psyche of god to that of the unconscious."[14] The rise of Islamism (a.k.a. Salafism) as a regressive political movement that purports to return to the pure origins of Islam—and to the first Muslim community as an exemplary model on which to refashion the present—provides the circumstantial alibi for Benslama to engage with the ontotheological origins of Islam as the last monotheistic religion whose founder claimed patrilineal descent from Ishmael and Abraham, the founding father of monotheism. "As soon as I began to pay attention to the language of Islamist speech, I realized," Benslama points out, "it was haunted by the question of origins."[15] Islamists conjured up the glorious Muslim past and mobilized the masses around

> the promise of a return to the golden age of the founding of Islam, when the beginning and the commandment were united in a single principle in the hands of, first, the Prophet-founder-legislator, then his four successors. This period was assumed to have been one of ideal justice on Earth, before the fall into the division and internal sedition (*fitna*) that the community would later experience.[16]

Benslama's ultimate goal is quite simply to show to the Islamists that there is no single origin to return to—really, that origin is structured by a void, a constitutive lack that can neither be accounted for nor recreated. Yet, while Benslama achieves a brilliant deconstruction of the myth of origins in Islam, as I will show shortly, he does not inquire much about the historical origins that inform the formation of this fantasy of origins in Islamism itself. Benslama is aware of the traumatic colonial encounter between the Muslim world and Christian Europe, but he takes it as a "form of intellectual imposture" to attribute the causes of Arab Muslim humiliation solely to the West or to the United States. "Victimization by outside forces alone," he contends, "can only deflect attention from internal causes and perpetuate the passivity that characterizes the posture of humility, to the extent that it remains fully wedded to its own desperate collapse."[17] Surely, reducing everything to imperialism is counterproductive but the inverse gesture (i.e., reducing everything to internal

13. Ibid., vii, ix.
14. Ibid., vii, viii.
15. Ibid., 10.
16. Ibid., 4.
17. Ibid., 64.

or intrinsic causes) is no less counterproductive. Clearly, Benslama is just not that interested in the concrete historical grievances of Arabs and Muslims even while he is profoundly aware of the subjective devastation, identificatory crisis and despair of the masses at the World War I loss of the Islamic caliphate, which used to anchor, despite its exponential decline, a conscious or unconscious sense of individual and collective belonging to a community of believers with a past, a present, and a possible future.

I would argue that it was imperialism, and not Islamism, that has blown Muslim time out of joint. Yet, Benslama only focuses on the anachronistic gesture of return to origins that characterizes the Islamists project even while he is, it bears repeating, aware that it is a reactionary gesture, a symptom of Euro-American imperialism par excellence. While treating colonial modernity as more of a foregone conclusion rather than as a cause of the emergence of regressive fundamentalist movements, Benslama concedes that the encroachment of modernity into the Arab Muslim world gave rise to at least two incommensurable desires: there is, on the one hand, the "desire to be an other," which he qualifies as the "most powerful desire that modernity has managed to create," and there is, on the other hand, the "despair of willing to be oneself [*le désespoir où l'on veut être soi*]."[18] Ironically, though, the "desire to be an other" to which Benslama refers has nothing to do with the deconstructive ethical experience of radical alterity, but, rather, with what Badiou calls "*le désir d'Occident*"—i.e., the desire to be as Occidental as the Occidentals, which is, after all, what Benslama admires in the beginning of his book about Habib Bourguiba's project of mimetic modernity in postcolonial Tunisia, a project that was indeed structured by "a desire for the West."[19] The "desire to be an other" is then nothing less than the coercive incitement to conformity exerted by colonial modernity.[20] It is puzzling here to note how in the name of secularity—or of what he calls the "absolute impiety" of Bourguiba, who incited Tunisians not to fast during the holy month of Ramadan—Benslama sanctions the repression of "sacred temporality" and decries the "constitutive repressions" (*refoulement constitutifs*) of religious institutions.[21] In other words, while Benslama seems

18. Ibid., 2, 5, translation modified.
19. The notion of "*le désir d'Occident*" or "desire for the West" is scattered throughout several of Badiou's books and talks; for a more recent example, see Alain Badiou, *The Rebirth of History: Times of Riots and Uprisings*, trans. Gregory Elliott (New York: Verso, 2012), 50.
20. See Talal Asad, "Conscripts of Western Civilization," in *Dialectical Anthropology: Essays in Honor of Stanley Diamond*, vol. 1, *Civilization in Crisis*, ed. Christine Gailey (Gainesville: University Press of Florida, 1992), 333–51.
21. Benslama, *Psychoanalysis and the Challenge of Islam*, 2, vii.

to license the repression of Islam by Bourguiba, he tends to systematically pathologize the reverse repression of modernity by the Islamists. In the meanwhile, both Benslama and Bourguiba as well as the Islamists have accepted the historicist thesis of civilizational retardation and temporal relegation but while Bourguiba and Benslama view modernity as a gift, the Islamists view it as a curse. Yet, as Walter D. Mignolo and Catherine E. Walsh argue, "there is no modernity without coloniality."[22]

European colonizers never considered the peoples they colonized as their contemporaries, or, as Johannes Fabian would say, "coevals."[23] Colonial modernity is, among others, an articulation of Europe's differential politics of identity, yet it created in major segments of the colonized populations a desire for sameness, proximity, and a mimetic politics of identity that verged on despair. Rather than bringing into intimate collision/collusion modernity and despair, Benslama exempts the "desire to be an other" from the despair (of belatedness and exile or alienation from the present) which he reserves for the Islamists (or Salafists writ large in their attempt to recover who they were in the precolonial period). Yet, both the "desire to be an other" (which is also marked by the "*despair* of willing to be an other") and the "despair of willing to be oneself" (which is also marked by the "*desire* to be oneself") are byproducts of colonial modernity and both can be, if excessive, pathological and counterproductive to the same extent. Notwithstanding his tacit secular liberal leanings, Benslama is quite right about his treatment of the "despair of willing to be oneself" as a symptom of exile from the present, in which the immutable temporality of the sacred has come to be violently overshadowed by the encroaching temporality of the secular colonial.[24] The violence and electrifying speed with which modernity entered the Arab Islamic world resulted in a "subjective devastation. The negation of the psychic is a dependent exponential variable of those devastations that are manifested in individual and collective psychoses, in massacre and genocide."[25] What muddied the waters still is that the entry of Arabs and Muslims into the modern world was not mediated by a process of individual and collective mourning, nor were there any cultural reparative works that would have made such a necessary psychoaffective

---

22. Walter D. Mignolo and Catherine E. Walsh, *On Decoloniality: Concepts, Analytics, Praxis* (Durham, NC: Duke University Press, 2018), 4.

23. Johannes Fabian, *Time and the Other: How Anthropology Makes its Object* (New York: Columbia University Press, 2014), 173.

24. For more on Benslama's liberalism, see Joseph A. Massad, *Islam in Liberalism* (Chicago: University of Chicago Press, 2015). See especially chapter 4, titled "Psychoanalysis, 'Islam,' and the Other of Liberalism."

25. Benslama, *Psychoanalysis and the Challenge of Islam*, 54.

process possible in the first place. Benslama speaks of a "modern caesura of identification" with the world of sacred temporality that occurred suddenly and without the necessary and corresponding cultural work (*Kulturarbeit*).[26] In other words, not only have Arabs and Muslims failed to resist the swift meltdown of their life worlds by the encroachment of colonial modernity, but they have also failed to transform themselves from the inside to cope with the transformations dictated and implemented from the outside.

This double failure had thrown the doors wide open for the Islamists' "cry of revolt" and "mass protest" at the loss of a world which used to anchor, consciously or unconsciously, their individual-collective identity (and entire economy of jouissance), and made possible the eventual Islamist recourse to "archaic configurations" as forms of both authentic identification and melancholy resistance to imperial modernity.[27] Islamist despair, Benslama argues, "has been able to produce itself only from an unsustainable exposure to the void of the caesura, to the mass subjective revocation it has brought about, becoming, in response, a headlong quest for truths that restore subjectivity, including the return to the paradise of origin."[28] This melancholite attempt to reclaim the precolonial and premodern world of authentic experience is compounded by the elusiveness of the notion of origin. In the attempt to avoid the void brought about by colonial modernity, Islamists would fall prey to the void of origins brought about by the Quranic revelation. The return to pure origins in Islam is the site of the impossible par excellence even though it feeds on the fantasy of recapturing lost or stolen jouissance, as I will demonstrate further below. Apart from the fact that any such return to origins would not be possible without the mediation of language, the story of origins in Islam is itself marked by the literal intrusion of language. First, Benslama reminds of the Prophet's terrifying childhood vision of an open chest, from which dark flesh was removed and space was cleared for the letter (*al-ḥarf*) of the Quran to be placed. Second, the Quran itself is nothing but a revelation of the hyperoriginary book that had already been written and preserved in a "guarded tablet."[29] In addition to the Prophet's exposure, withdrawal, and agony, the story of origins in Islam invokes accordingly an openness to foreignness and a process of linguistic mediation that goes from grafting to deciphering the letter (*al-ḥarf*) of the Quran. In other words, the story of origins in Islam is the site of piecemeal and processual grafting rather than wholesale gratification: it is

26. Ibid.
27. Ibid., 52, 55.
28. Ibid., 59.
29. Ibid., 13.

marked by that originary hospitality to the stranger (in this case, language)—it is never about an intact purity or "originary plenitude."[30]

The search for authenticity and purity associated with the return to origins is therefore futile, according to Benslama, because of the literal intrusion of language. "The intruder in the heart of man is language," and "whatever assumed the status of 'Islam' acquired its essentiality only from its provenance in the 'Foreign,' which had lodged in this recess of infantile narcissism."[31] The purity of origins has therefore to be measured against the possible impurity of the medium through which origin was mediated in the first place. Moreover, the site of origin in Islam is split between the moment of infantile vision in which the Prophet's chest was opened for the placement of the letter (*al-ḥarf*) and the later moment of reception and reading—indeed, "Read," Gabriel's injunction to the Prophet, constitutes the inaugural gesture of Quranic revelation and the actual beginning of the Muhammadan message. Benslama is right in suggesting here that "the concept of origin in Islam was split between a cut (*entame*) and a beginning (*commencement*)."[32] Yet, this split that distances origin from itself is preceded by an even deeper split or time-lag between the moment of foundation of Islam and its anterior announcement as "a biblical promise."[33] Being the last monotheistic religion, Islam had already been anticipated by the Torah. It is the materialization of god's promise to Hagar after she was driven away with her son, Ishmael, into the desert. The Prophet foregrounded the biblical connection between Abraham and Ishmael as the sources of "a primary monotheistic filiation through the older son, which was prefigured in the scrolls of the Father (*ṣuḥuf 'Ibrāhīm*)."[34] What would the return to the origins of Islam mean if Islam itself was nothing more than a return to origins (i.e., a return to the originary religion of Abraham)?

Islam's positioning as the last monotheistic religion and simultaneously as the originary religion of Abraham opens up the question of singularity of origin to the multiplicity of beginnings. Origin is far from being a self-evident and transparent event in which truth, being, and the absolute collide. Rather, Benslama concludes, "the truth of an event is always compromised by the necessary transition of that event to a text, a work of writing and authorship, and that even if the event is true, its exposition in language pulls it into the realm

30. Ibid., 12.
31. Ibid., 13.
32. Ibid., 14.
33. Ibid.
34. Ibid.

of fiction."[35] There is a considerable time lag between Islam as a biblical promise and the actual beginning of Islam as the last monotheistic religion, not to mention the time lag between the infantile vision of the Prophet and the actual Quranic revelation. These variable time lags make the notion of origin in Islam hardly identical with any clear point of origin. It is rather dispersed and incomplete. At the origin of Islam, then, Benslama concludes in Lacanian fashion, there is a lack of origin.

Notwithstanding his insightful deconstruction of the notion of origin in Islam, Benslama makes it sound as if the lack of origin is indeed what fuels the desire of Islamists to return to origins. While this may be true from a structural Lacanian perspective, in which the fantasy of origin may be seen to mediate an economy of jouissance toward which and by which the Islamist project is driven, it is simply not the case from a historical perspective. It is not the lack of origins in itself that caused the desire to return to origins to arise, but rather the historical encounter with colonialism and the subsequent collapse of the Ottoman caliphate in 1924. Such a historical fact would not be in contradistinction with the Lacanian-inflected insight that the desire to return to origins works from within an economy of jouissance, in which the fantasy of an eventual return offers a form of (traumatic) enjoyment, but it cannot be reduced to it in the way Benslama tends to frame the Islamist torment of origin. Benslama makes a structural argument there where a historical argument would have been more pertinent, at least as the historical backdrop against which particular social movements and collective psychic (or psychopathological and theopathological) formations may emerge. There is tendency in Benslama to reduce what is historical to what is structural or endemic to Muslim societies; the effect is at times more demystifying than illuminating. While this may have in the end to do with Benslama's dependency on Lacanian vocabulary, it does not have to be so if more historical nuancing were to be made. In *Un furieux désir de sacrifice: Le surmusulman* (*A Furious Desire for Sacrifice: The Super Muslim*), Benslama expands his deconstruction of the Islamist obsession with the return to origins by unpacking what I would be calling the melancholite logic—regressive and utilitarian—that sustains its enduring appeal to Muslim youth. The figure of the *surmusulman* is the ultimate embodiment of the despair of being oneself and of the tormenting desire to return to pure Islamic origins as well as of the belief in the redemptive promise of ethereal jouissance that lies in store.

35. Ibid., 15.

Enter the *Surmusulman*

> World-redeeming dreams of ancient greatness arise in peoples in whom the sense of having been left behind by history evokes feelings of impotence and rage.
> ALEXANDER MITSCHERLICH AND MARGARETE MITSCHERLICH[36]

> In principle every colonization is a condemnation to historical death. The old structures, the old habits, the old egoisms rise to the surface of minds and societies, and in misfortune everyone takes refuge in childhood.
> ABDALLAH LAROUI[37]

In *A Furious Desire for Sacrifice*, Benslama sets himself the task of laying down on the analytic couch the Islamist-cum-jihadist figure he calls *"le sur-musulman,"* which literally means a sort of super- or Über-Muslim—a notion immediately reminiscent of Nietzsche's *Übermensch*, if not of the Nazi ideal of racial superiority that capitalized on the concept, as well as of Freud's superego, *das Über-Ich*. While not completely unrelated to the one and the other, the *surmusulman* is simply the name Benslama gives to those Muslims who want to become more Muslim than they actually are. This need for aggrandizement is, furthermore, a symptom of a generalized crisis of subjectivity in Islam, a crisis which must, for Benslama, be overcome by the urgent embrace of secular modernity. The brisk moves that Benslama makes from the diagnosis to the indictment of the *surmusulman* through the prescription of secular modernity leave much to be desired.[38] For one thing, the embrace of secular modernity is not without the kind of shortcomings and ramifications that necessitate analytic intervention. It may be surprising after all that secularism, or *laïcité* more specifically, has not yet constituted a clear topic of psychoanalysis despite its ongoing crisis, especially in the French context, from within which Benslama's interest in Islamism and engagement with the nationwide radicalism debate emerged. Admittedly, the crisis of *laïcité* may be less graphic

---

36. Alexander Mitscherlich and Margarete Mitscherlich, *The Inability to Mourn: Principles of Collective Behavior*, trans. Beverley R. Placzek (New York: Grove Press, 1975), 12.

37. Abdallah Laroui, *The History of the Maghrib: An Interpretive Essay*, trans. Ralph Manheim (Princeton, NJ: Princeton University Press, 1977), 382.

38. Joan W. Scott pinpointed that, while secularism has generally meant the triumph of enlightenment over religion, it has recently "had a simpler referent as the positive alternative, not to all religion but to Islam." Scott, *Sex and Secularism* (Princeton, NJ: Princeton University Press, 2018), 1.

than that of Islamism (especially in the wake of ISIS), yet what beggars the imagination is not only that the crisis of *laïcité* receives short shrift in Benslama's writings but that *laïcité* itself remains the unquestioned ideological framework, under the banner of psychoanalysis, for laying the Islamist figure of the *surmusulman* on the analytic couch. For another, Freudian psychoanalysis may not have abstracted itself from secular modernity either, yet it has long questioned enlightenment rationalism through the concept of the unconscious and has continually reckoned with the limits of its findings beyond ideological, national, or cultural affiliations and exigencies. Besides, and as Alberto Toscano rightly points out, its "methodological atheism is not generative of further political fantasies, illusions of autonomy or cultural superiority."[39]

Regardless of his motives in psychoanalyzing the *surmusulman*, Benslama's mistake throughout much of his work is his tendency to pathologize and melancholize Islamism, and, at least by implication, Islam.[40] Unlike Benslama, while he forcefully traces the melancholy turn of Muslims to the "great crime of all colonization . . . [which] not only stops historical evolution, but obliges the colonized people to regress," Abdallah Laroui ends up deprivatizing and depathologizing, not to say naturalizing, this regression: "in misfortune everyone takes refuge in childhood."[41] Yet there where Laroui naturalizes and universalizes, Benslama privatizes and provincializes. Rather than stop at a geopolitical and sociological understanding of the figure of the *surmusulman*, Benslama ventures into an analytic argument, contrived at the loose nexus of the clinical and the social writ large. Benslama argues that because figures of this sort lose their singularity upon accepting *l'offre jihadiste* or the "jihadist offer" of redemption—and become nothing more than automated robots, exact replicas of each other—they can be analyzed as a homogenous group rather than individually, on a case-by-case or psyche-by-psyche basis.[42] While drawing on his vast clinical experience in northern Paris and on numerous encounters with dozens of patients from the *banlieues* and elsewhere, Benslama does not build a case history (à la Freud) of a given *surmusulman*, but he rather

---

39. Alberto Toscano, *Fanaticism: On the Uses of an Idea* (New York: Verso, 2010), 171.

40. With an eye on Benslama's work, Toscano makes the following pertinent remark: "The idea of transforming psychoanalysis into a secular clinic aimed at diagnosing the phantasmatic impasses that prevent 'Arabs' or 'Muslims' from becoming the properly pathological subjects of modernity (rather than fanatics stuck between crumbling tradition and fear of 'Westoxification') leaves itself open to the accusation that psychoanalysis might constitute yet another stage in that cunning of Christianity which often taken the name of 'secularism.'" See ibid., 165–66.

41. Laroui, *The History of the Maghrib*, 382.

42. Fethi Benslama, *Un furieux désir de sacrifice: Le surmusulman* (Paris: Seuil, 2016), 60.

develops an integrative approach, including so many variable factors, to the prototypical psyche—in a more or less abstract sense—of the *surmusulman*.

Benslama deploys psychoanalysis as a vantage point (or rather supplement, in a Derridean sense, to political science and sociology) from which to make an intervention into a post–November 13, 2015, French public sphere saturated with passionate and incendiary discourses on Islam and Muslims, which seemed to only get worse with every new terrorist attack on French soil. In this generalized atmosphere of fear and mistrust of the Muslim minority, "a dubious new cottage industry has grown up" whose aim is to privately run government-sponsored "de-radicalization" programs, which, as Robert F. Worth observes, resulted in "scores of new outfits and self-proclaimed gurus trumpeting their claims of success."[43] While the aim of these programs was presumably de-radicalization, it was radicalization that gained center stage and became a buzzword in the heavily mediatized French public sphere—most notably dramatized, if not fueled, by the heated national debate-cum-polemic on the roots of radicalization between two of France's most renowned intellectuals and scholars of Islam and the Middle East writ large, Gilles Kepel and Olivier Roy. A classic Orientalist, Kepel adopts a vertical approach to the question of radicalization, claiming that through the hegemony of Salafism—a puritanical Islamic current and leading gateway to jihadist violence—Islam is at the origin of radicalization among French (migrant) youth. For Kepel, Islam is to blame for the violence committed in its name.[44] Between January and November 2015, he wrote *Terreur dans l'Hexagone: Genèse du djihad français*, a book that became a bestseller upon its publication following the November 2015 terrorist attacks. The book discerns the roots of radicalism through three generations of jihadists since the 1980s but focuses mostly on the nefarious transformations of the suburbs from the 2005 *émeutes des banlieues* to the January 2015 Charlie Hebdo terrorist attacks. Since the 2005 large-scale youth riots, Kepel argues, the banlieues have become the breeding ground of hardcore Salafism.

Roy adopts, *pace* Kepel, a horizontal approach, situating jihadist violence in relation to other contiguous forms of extremist violence that just happened

---

43. Robert F. Worth, "The Professor and the Jihadi" *New York Times Magazine*, April 5, 2017, https://www.nytimes.com/2017/04/05/magazine/france-election-gilles-kepel-islam.html.

44. Obviously, and as will become clear, "Islam—or a seventh-century ideal of it—is assumed to possess the unity that eludes the more recent and important influences of colonialism, imperialism, and even ordinary politics." See Edward Said, "Arab, Islam, and the Dogmas of the West," in *Orientalism: A Reader*, ed. Alexander Lyon Macfie (New York: New York University Press, 2000), 105.

to adopt the language of Islamists (and not, for instance, the language of the extreme left of 1970s France). For Roy, radicalization is a nihilist rebellion against society by those same young people whom society had marginalized and rejected in the first place. In other words, for Roy, Islam as a text is a pretext, not a textbook for terror. In his response to *Terror in France*, Roy accuses Kepel of Islamizing radicalism: "Il ne s'agit pas de la radicalisation de l'islam, mais de l'islamisation de la radicalité" (It's not about the radicalization of Islam but the Islamization of radicalism).[45] The French expression therein, *"l'islamisation de la radicalité,"* gained immediate currency, especially on social media, and Kepel was eventually compelled to respond, accusing Roy and his leftist ilk (whom he labels the *"Islamo-gauchistes"*) of liberal naïveté — of failing to understand the nature of the Islamist threat and of acting as if Islam was incidental to the violence committed in its name.[46] A proud member of the commission that helped create France's controversial 2004 law banning Islamic headscarves and other religious symbols and clothing in public schools, Kepel believes that the resurgence of Islam in the French public sphere (the Friday sermons, the theological debates, the issuing of fatwas, and so on) leads not only to the erosion of French state secularism or *laïcité* and to the formation of ethno-social enclaves in the *banlieues* (a.k.a. *communautarisme*) but also, worse by far, to the radicalization of French Muslim youth who come to realize sooner or later at the hands of hardline Islamist ideologues and recruiters that their personal grievances are identical with (and not incidental to) the global plight of the religion they have endorsed, inherited, or adopted.

Roy responded, and the sequence of back-and-forth exchange of arguments and counterarguments went on for quite some time in various media outlets to the point that both Kepel and Roy felt equally compelled to accuse each other of playing into the hands of ISIS. The way the debate veered into a tit-for-tat personal dispute is symptomatic of the profound fracture (also the title of one Kepel's recent books, *La fracture: Chroniques 2015–2016*) of the French public sphere over the Muslim question. Obviously, the sustained (and, needless to say, sensational) press coverage only propelled the polemic forward,

---

45. Oliver Roy, "Le djihadisme est une révolte générationnelle et nihiliste," *Le Monde*, November 24, 2015, http://www.lemonde.fr/idees/article/2015/11/24/le-djihadisme-une-revolte-generationnelle-et-nihiliste_4815992_3232.html. Note that the expression was originally used by Alain Bertho.

46. Sara Daniel, "Gilles Kepel: 'Les islamo-gauchistes, ces charlatans!," *Le Nouvel Observateur*, November 2, 2016, https://www.nouvelobs.com/societe/20161031.OBS0572/gilles-kepel-les-islamo-gauchistes-ces-charlatans.html; Gilles Kepel, "'Radicalisations' et 'islamophobie': Le roi est nu," *Libération*, March 10, 2016, https://www.liberation.fr/debats/2016/03/14/radicalisations-et-islamophobie-le-roi-est-nu_1439535.

but so did the viewpoints of other intellectuals who found themselves wittingly or unwittingly embroiled in what seemed at the time the only debate in le Pays des Lumières. Several public intellectuals were simply summoned to respond to the debate, and while the majority sided either with Roy or Kepel, few came up with a neither-nor approach. Such is the case with the academic and scholar François Burgat, who pointed out that neither Roy nor Kepel had indeed paid enough attention to the geopolitical roots of radicalism and to French colonial legacy, let alone the role of France's current foreign policies, in incubating and instigating the anger of the second generation of Muslims. Implicating non-Muslims, Burgat's historically minded perspective unsettled public opinion and redirected the weight of responsibility on France and French colonial history. No wonder his position has not fared well in displacing the fanaticisms of the moment and the battle cries for stringent anti-immigration measures.

Clearly, though, there are multidirectional approaches to the question of radicalization, each of which seems to foreground one factor over the other in order to be as specific as possible for strategic, pragmatic, and national policy purposes. But if Kepel foregrounds religious fundamentalism, Roy generational nihilism, and Burgat French colonialism, Benslama appropriates attention away from these more or less grand narratives and zeroes in on the psychic origins of the phenomenon of youth radicalization. He points toward the psyche of the marginalized as a malleable entity that may help explain the fascination with the grandeur of assertive acts of defiance and the recourse to suicide martyrdom, or what he calls in a more recent book of the same title *Le saut épique*, "the epic leap."[47] While acknowledging the partial validity of each of the arguments above, Benslama foregrounds the role of psychic permutations in the temptation to radicalize, especially among unassimilated Maghrebi youth or young converts to Islam. In other words, Benslama propounds a psychoanalytic theory of radicalization, arguing broadly that individual and collective psychic injuries and identitarian tribulations may, if they remain unaddressed, find in jihadist violence the dignity of recognition and redress, if not the jouissance of triumphalism and self-accomplishment.

Benslama is widely known as an expert on the study of Islam and psychoanalysis and as a practicing psychoanalyst whose clinical work revolves around the question of migration, exile, and the assimilation of Franco-Maghrebi youth into French society. He has long maintained a clinical practice devoted to child psychiatry in Seine-Saint-Denis, a suburb north of Paris, and is the founder of a counseling center for foreign students at the International

---

47. Fethi Benslama, *Le saut épique, ou le basculement dans le Jihād* (Paris: Actes Sud, 2021).

University of Paris. A Paris-based Tunisian professor of psychopathology at the University of Paris-Diderot, he boasts a vast clinical experience and sociocommunal engagement that cut across the psychoaffective, the socioeconomic, and the theopolitical, and he has paid particular attention in his analytic practice to children, migrants, and foreign students. These three types of patients represent compelling examples of identitarian transformations and trials that could go awry. For Benslama, wherever the sense of identity is in crisis, fragile, or unstable, it is there where Islamist indoctrination may best find its incubatory ground. Islamist indoctrinators and recruiters offer these lost young men and women a sense of belonging to a community of believers (being Muslim), a collective cause (defending Islam), and the means to salvage a lost life and save a future one (martyrdom).

The enormity of the Islamist promise is disarming, especially for those deprived of a sense of identity and belonging, which is why for Benslama the mainstream governmental focus on "*déradicalisation*" is misguided and counterproductive. As a corrective, Benslama contributed to the establishment of the first *centre de réinsertion et de citoyenneté* (center for reintegration and citizenship) in Beaumont-en-Véron (Indre-et-Loire). In an interview with Marie Lemonnier, Benslama conjures up a philological argument about the root meaning of radicalization in Arabic in order to hammer home his denunciation of the de-radicalization strategies: "the fact that the term 'radical' means 'root' is very interesting. Radicalization [*'uṣūliyya*] is an attempt to find a root [*'aṣl*]. And youths caught by radical Islamism are first of all in search of roots."[48] Deradicalization would amount to "de-rooting" again, which would be absurd, as he points out in the same interview:

> It's absurd to propose a new uprooting as treatment; no one would accept to be uprooted, or become an outcast. Rather, the path to follow, on the psychic plane, is to help young people regain their singularity, otherwise lost in automated fanaticisms and fused in group exaltations. The abolition of individual limits in sectarian groups favors autosacrifice. We must therefore embark on the reconstruction work of the kind of subjects that are responsible for themselves and for their own choices.[49]

---

48. Marie Lemonnier, "Le 'surmusulman' et la mort, par Fethi Benslama," *Le Nouvel Observateur*, May 5, 2016, https://bibliobs.nouvelobs.com/idees/20160504.OBS9851/le-surmusulman-et-la-mort-par-fethi-benslama.html.

49. Ibid.

Because of his sensitivity to the identity crisis of young jihadists, Benslama dismisses the "de-identitarian" effort of *"déradicalisation"* in favor of a constructive and pedagogically productive identitarian project of integration and citizenship. In an interview with Marie Barbier and Mina Kaci, Benslama makes it clear that radicalization is at heart an identitarian quest gone awry in the direction of vindictiveness, self-vindication, and contentious politics:

> Those I have encountered in my clinical activity in Seine-Saint-Denis, and who adopted overnight an ultra-Islamist discourse, had the desire to insert [*s'enraciner*] or re-insert [*ré-enraciner*] themselves in a beyond [*un au-delà*] to contend with the status quo. Radicalization can be understood as a symptom of a desire for a contentious enracination [*d'enracinement protestataire*] for those who have no roots or who live as such.[50]

What is important here is that whereas governmental policy and media pundits, as well as the majority of French public intellectuals, see radicalization as a menace that must be eradicated (hence the investment in *"déradicalisation"* programs), Benslama sees it as a "symptom" of a runaway desire on the part of marginalized young people for communal belonging. To see radicalization as a symptom is perhaps Benslama's main contribution in *Un furieux désir de sacrifice* to the debate on radicalization that cast its shadow on the French public sphere for several months after January 2015. It is also a vindication of the psychoanalytic approach, which for Benslama is the more conducive vantage point (compared to sociology and political science) from which to dig into the deep recesses of the psyche, in order to locate the actual psychic problems of which radicalization constitutes a symptomatic manifestation.

Benslama is not unaware of the *extrinsic* socioeconomic and geopolitical circumstances that produce jihadist and *surmusulman* figures, but he refuses to give these factors pride of place, opting instead—in a more or less typical fashion since the publication of *Psychoanalysis and the Challenge of Islam* in 2002—to focus on the *intrinsic* psycho-theological dimension of the jihadist spirit, that is, on the symptoms of the *surmusulman*, or, more precisely, on the *surmusulman* itself as a symptom of something gone awry in Islamic

---

50. Marie Barbier and Mina Kaci, "Fethi Benslama: Le 'surmusulman,' cette figure produite par l'islamisme," *L'Humanité*, November 4, 2016, https://humanite.fr/fethi-benslama-le-surmusulman-cette-figure-produite-par-lislamisme-619723.

civilization from within.⁵¹ The risks of this approach are obvious. They are the risks of psychoanalysis writ large: the tendency to privatize political and ideological agendas determined by broader capitalist and colonial apparatuses. Not that the economic and affective legacies of colonialism are separable— much less that economic disenfranchisement, racism, and postcolonial shame are somehow unrelated—but Benslama fears, and rightly so at times, that placing too much emphasis on the colonial Arab/Muslim past and present might exonerate Arabs and Muslims from their own share of responsibility as agents of their own history. However, it may be difficult to ask of Arabs and Muslims to act independently from the historical condition in which they are caught, for even while this historical condition is not a choice they (can be said to) have made, it nonetheless remains the condition of whatever choice they will make or have already made. In addition to the ritualistic task of condemning violence and condoning nonviolence, it is incumbent upon us to inquire about the kind of tools, if at all, that wronged peoples have at their disposal to combat injustices of various kinds. Here I cannot help but be reminded again and again of C. L. R. James's rephrasing of Marx—"Great men make history, but only such history as it is possible for them to make"—and be tempted to point out in this same vein that Arabs and Muslims will only make the kind of history that is possible for them to make.⁵² The *surmusulman* is one part of that history in the making; it is not its most defining or key aspect, even though it has admittedly garnered much media attention at the expense of the other more productive aspects.

I will not pursue here a symptomatic reading of Benslama's symptomatic reading of the *surmusulman* and reduce the analyst and the analysand to mere symptoms of their own distinct ideological lineaments and lineages. Both analyst and analysand are in the end the products of the same neoliberal dispensation, the same nation-state system, and the same global techno-modernity they promote or resist; neither of them can (be said to) fully claim the moral high ground in their advocacy for or militancy against these hegemonic structures. Benslama's error is that he rarely entertains, let alone maintains, the idea that Islamism is the child of the very secular, nation-state modernity it claims to challenge, and that secular modernity itself has failed in practice to embody the difference and the concern for radical otherness it so claims in

---

51. Benslama, *Psychoanalysis and the Challenge of Islam*, 105.
52. C. L. R. James, *The Black Jacobins: Toussaint L'Ouverture and the San Domingo Revolution* (New York: Vintage Books, 1989), x.

theory to promote and project.⁵³ Similarity, however, does not mean sameness. I agree with Andrea Mura that Benslama's psychoanalytic approach to Islam, especially in *Psychoanalysis and the Challenge of Islam*, "could be enriched with a higher degree of complexity" insofar as "Islamism does not manifest itself as an undifferentiated demand for authenticity, unwilling to find compromises with modernity."⁵⁴ Benslama's recent writings demonstrate an increased sensitivity to questions of economic disenfranchisement, identity politics, and power dynamics, but the risks of essentialism he takes while psychoanalyzing Islam, as Mura points out, are still quite immense.⁵⁵ His unfinished project to lay the jihadi figure of the *surmusulman* on the analytic couch often slides into an attempt to lay Islam itself on the couch, overshadowing his attempts to attend more vigorously than in earlier writings to socioeconomic demarcations and geopolitical differentials.

Jihadi Jouissance

> In the Islamist movement . . . with its belief in the perfection of origin, there is no utopian future, there is no prospect of some new occurrence happening, because the best has already occurred, the apotheosis has already taken place. . . . Melancholy, then, becomes the only stance, aside from terror, to assume while waiting for the last judgment. The Islamist movement should be considered a reversal of messianism: antimessianism as despair over time.
>
> FETHI BENSLAMA⁵⁶

I will focus my critical reading of Benslama's diagnostic appraisal of the *surmusulman* on two concepts that he mentions in passing (and almost takes for granted), but that seem to me of crucial importance to a nuanced and nonessentializing understanding of the furious desire for sacrifice that is said to characterize the *surmusulman*. These two concepts are melancholy and jouissance. While Benslama defines at times what he means by jouissance, especially insofar as the *surmusulman* experiences it as either lost or antici-

---

53. As Wael Hallaq has nuancedly shown, the contradictions of modernity and the nation-state are not easily, let alone neatly, resolvable under the banner of secularity. See Wael B. Hallaq, *The Impossible State: Islam, Politics, and Modernity's Moral Predicament* (New York: Columbia University Press, 2013).

54. Andrea Mura, "Islamism Revisited: A Lacanian Discourse Critique," *European Journal of Psychoanalysis* 1 (2014): 115.

55. Ibid., 107.

56. Benslama, *Psychoanalysis and the Challenge of Islam*, 28.

pated, he hardly explains what he means by *"mélancholie,"* nor does he articulate the form of *"mélancholie"* that best suits and sustains the *surmusulman*. As the preceding quotation from *Psychoanalysis and the Challenge of Islam* shows, he understands melancholy as an alternative to terror: as antimessianic and paralyzing, congealing the movement of the Islamist subject, reducing it to a form of incapacitating stasis or vertigo. Benslama seems to rely on a rudimentary Freudian understanding of melancholy as a negative therapeutic reaction, which in the case of the Islamist or *surmusulman* presents itself as a psychopathological identification with a lost Islamic ideal composed of a historical figure (Prophet Muhammad) and a period of time (the first Muslim community, the mini-state in Medina), as well as a form of Islamic governance (the caliphate), etcetera. There is not a clear-cut object whose loss gives rise to melancholy, but a complete set of attachments, diverse yet cohesive, that structures an entire psychic economy of jouissance (the Islamic ideal or utopia). Melancholy seems to arise here in order to keep in place the psychic economy of jouissance in the event it is upset by the loss of (the aura of) an element of the set or by the impending threat to the entire set, its outright dismissal or reduction to irrelevance by historical developments. Far from being an alternative to terror or violence, as Benslama claims, melancholy exists here on a continuum with violence and nonviolence. After all, is it not melancholy (precisely, the specific form of it I have been calling "melancholite") that sustains the recourse to violence, or the passage to action?

While not unaware of the complexity of the concept of melancholy in Freud, Benslama's concept of *mélancholie* is not specific enough, if not reductive altogether, and needs therefore to be more theoretically corroborated in order to show, pace Benslama, its collusion and alignment with jouissance. For Freud, melancholy is a prolonged psychoaffective, regressive and aggressive reaction to loss because it involves, rather than a common object loss, "a loss of a more ideal kind."[57] The "wounded Islamic ideal" about which Benslama speaks is surely cause enough for melancholy, especially when compounded with the loss of ideals from which most would-be jihadists suffer. The concept has to be nuanced and complicated rather than fixed in the negative. While Mura complicates Benslama's monolithic view of Islamism, he endorses wholesale his regressive view of melancholy: "Far from displaying melancholic or rigid attitudes towards change, many groups continue to preserve the central function of desire, 'positivizing' the very encounter with the real that Benslama preserves as horrifying."[58] Both Benslama and Mura tend

---

57. Freud, "Mourning and Melancholia," 254.
58. Mura, "Islamism Revisited," 116.

to give short shrift to melancholy and approach it as an obstacle to parting ways with the loss of a given object. As Russel Grigg has recently argued, however, melancholy "arises because of the proximity of the object through its failure to have become lost." Given its idealistic character, it may even be the case that "melancholia does not arise from a loss at all, or at least, not from the kind of loss we find in mourning."[59]

Benslama and Mura are misled by mourning, which is fomented by the loss of an object, into thinking negatively about melancholy. They overestimate the loss of the Islamic ideal rather than appreciate its contemporary proximity, especially insofar as its moral dimension is concerned. There are at least two facets of melancholy that can explain, for instance, the difference between, on the one hand, the self-reflexive and soliloquizing Hamlet, and, on the other, the action-prone Hamlet who pounces and kills Polonius impulsively. It bears reiterating here the important difference between the regressive and aggressive facet of melancholy, which I have called melancholite, and the retrospective and productive facet, which I have called melancholic. As I have maintained in the previous chapters of this book, I reserve the *melancholite* variant of melancholy for visceral, reactionary, and often violent reinstatements of the psychic status quo and the *melancholic* variant to the intellectual, creative, and largely nonviolent attitude to the entire question of the psychic economy of jouissance, its governance, distribution, and potential redistribution. Melancholites are driven by melancholy (rage) toward the jouissance that the pain of victimhood permits them to extract, while melancholics or melancholiacs are driven toward melancholy (militancy) by the desire to denounce and overcome the unjust loss of a loved object or ideal. Both melancholites and melancholics decline the affective closure of mourning, which they see as a form of readjustment to injustice, but while melancholites foreground the passage to action, melancholics foreground introspection and intellection prior to action. There is nothing pathological about the ethical attachment to an unjust loss or to an unjustly lost love-object or ideal—it's a political and ethical decision at one and the same time. I will come back to the melancholic variant in the next and last section of this chapter; henceforth, I will focus on the melancholite variant, which is best illustrated by Benslama's construction of the figure of the *surmusulman*.

The *surmusulman* is melancholite precisely because his or her economy of jouissance is sustained by a steadfast attachment to an Islamic ideal that is only

---

59. Russell Grigg, "Melancholia and the Unabandoned Object," in *Lacan on Madness: Madness, Yes You Can't*, ed. Patricia Gherovici and Manya Steinkoler (New York: Routledge, 2015), 144.

mentally conceivable, yet neither obtainable nor abandonable in reality. As Willy Apollon reminds us, jouissance "refers to the upsurge of a pure mental representation that provokes an effraction in the living being that disregards the limits of pleasure and reality. Or better, jouissance is the insistent work of this effraction, which subverts the conditions of conscious perception, pushing beyond the limits of reality and pleasure."[60] What strengthens the melancholite attachment and intensifies the jouissance even further is the secular injunction that it be given up, since, as Apollon further reminds us, "a being, as the object of a censored jouissance, becomes the subject of a desire and a speech that would evoke this jouissance."[61] Melancholy and jouissance may seem *prima facie* divergent psychoaffective motor forces but they actually converge around the notion of the promise. While melancholy (especially the melancholite variant) is characterized by the backward movement toward a lost ideal object or a past utopian experience, jouissance is characterized by a presentist concern or even more so by the futuristic resurrection of the object of melancholite identification. It may be said, I submit, that the melancholite adhesion to the object as a symptom is itself mediated by jouissance, since it involves the kind of psychopathological regression into individual or group narcissism from which the *surmusulman* derives ecstatic pleasure. At any rate both melancholy and jouissance coalesce under the sign of the promise, the promise of resurrecting a utopian past and earning a ticket to eternal paradise, a promise that Benslama calls "anticipated jouissance" (*la jouissance anticipée*).[62]

Note here that jouissance itself, and insofar as it is attached to the first Muslim community or the primal scene of Islam, becomes the very object of melancholite jihad. The economy of jouissance structures the furious desire for self-sacrifice because it holds open the promise of everlasting or "absolute" jouissance (*la "jouissance paradisiaque absolue"*).[63] As Bruce Fink reminds us, there is something idealistic about jouissance beyond the paltry phallic function:

> we think that there must be something better, we say that there must be something better, we *believe* that there must be something better. By saying it over and over, whether to ourselves, to our friends, or to our analysts, we give a certain consistency to this other satisfaction,

---

60. Willy Apollon, "The Untreatable," trans. Steven Miller, *Umbr(a)* 1 (2006): 30.
61. Ibid., 32.
62. Benslama, *Un furieux désir de sacrifice*, 62.
63. Ibid., 57.

this Other jouissance. In the end, we wind up giving it so much consistency that the jouissance we do in fact obtain seems all the more inadequate. The little we had diminishes further still. It pales in comparison with the ideal we hold up for ourselves of a jouissance that we could really count on, that would never let us down.[64]

The melancholite return to origins is driven by and toward a jouissance that never fails, an infallible and unfailing jouissance. The assumption that the Euro-colonial Other withholds or blocks the path toward recapturing lost jouissance and plenitude further foments the fantasy to take stock of it (except that this fantasy keeps stumbling against the intractability of the real). Ironically, though, the object of jouissance, because irreducible and unyielding, is eventually displaced by the very ideology—here, Islamism—that purports to recover it.

The Euro-colonial Other repudiates the *surmusulman*'s melancholite and precolonial jouissance of grandeur and plenitude, reinforcing thusly its lethal symptoms. The inaugural moment in the birth of the *surmusulman* is evidently historical. In his quasi-genealogical remapping of the historical background of the present subjective impasses that the *surmusulman* comes to represent, Benslama singles out the fall of the Ottoman caliphate in 1924 as a defining moment, given that four years afterwards the Muslim Brotherhood was founded in Egypt under the leadership of Hassan al-Banna. For Benslama such historical traumas as the dissolution of the caliphate have been used strategically by ideologues and fundamentalists to install a sort of melancholy haunting in the collective psyche of the Muslim community rather than to incite them to embark on the necessary task of mourning occasioned by the loss of the caliphate.[65] Be that as it may, Benslama is primarily interested in the *surmusulman* as the byproduct of a wide-ranging historical process of Islamist mobilization of Muslims around the task of redressing the injuries inflicted upon the Islamic ideal, and which have only multiplied and grown since the beginning of the twentieth century.[66] In other words, the phenomenon of the *surmusulman* is the product of a historical process of change internal to Islam. Benslama may be, it bears repeating here, underestimating the devastating effects of the imperial encounter between the European West and the Arab East, but the Islamists themselves did not, according to Benslama,

64. Bruce Fink, "Knowledge and Jouissance," in *Reading Seminar XX: Lacan's Major Work on Love, Knowledge, and Feminine Sexuality*, ed. Suzanne Bernard and Bruce Fink (Albany: SUNY Press, 2002), 35.
  65. Benslama, *Psychoanalysis and the Challenge of Islam*, 52.
  66. Benslama, *Un furieux désir de sacrifice*, 96, 98.

accord it too much attention either. It is in fact ironic that some of the post-caliphate Islamists have come to perceive the imperial encroachments in the region as a form of deserved divine punishment modern-day Muslims incurred for having strayed away from the path of God.

The early Islamist movements, Benslama pinpoints, did not ask why God has abandoned Muslims to their miserable fate, but why Muslims have abandoned God, and concluded that the only way back to God passes through jihad: "L'islamisme ne s'est pas demandé pourquoi Dieu a abandonné les musulmans . . . mais pourquoi les musulmans ont abandonné Dieu et comment en retrouver le chemin, qui n'est autre que celui du jihad" (Islamism did not ask why God abandoned Muslims . . . but why Muslims had abandoned God and how they can find their path back to Him, which is nothing but that of jihad).[67] I would be remiss not to mention here that the notion of jihad itself has undergone over the years a serious turn until it has become no longer about the risk of death in the battlefield (hence martyrdom), but, rather, about the proactive instigation of a guaranteed death, a sort of will-to-death through self-sacrifice (*l'autosacrifice*).[68] Death is no longer a risk to be taken by a combatant or "warrior-martyr" who eventually wants to remain alive but a final destination, actively and furiously sought by the "martyr-martyr" (now called *al-'istishhādī*, the one who is in pursuit of martyrdom).[69]

It may be the case, I would argue, that the desire for being more than Muslim is the product of the failure and guilt of not having been Muslim enough, not having been pious enough or, above all, not having satisfied the requirements of the greater jihad, the kind of jihad that involves an investment in pious behavior, self-exertion, and inward contemplation and purification of the self/soul from satanic temptation. Such greater jihad (or *al-jihād al-akbar*) is even for the likes of Sayyid Qutb a prerequisite for the involvement in the smaller jihad (or *al-jihād al-asghar*), which entails the use of brute force. As Qutb states:

> Before a Muslim steps into the battlefield, he has already fought a great battle within himself against Satan [*ma'rakit al-jihād al-akbar fī nafsihi ma'a al-shaytān*], against his own desires and ambitions, his personal interests and inclinations, the interests of his family and of his nation; against [that] which is not from Islam; against every obstacle

---

67. Ibid., 98.
68. Ibid., 104.
69. For a short history on the turn from "warrior-martyr" to "martyr-martyr" in the interpretation of jihad in Islamic thought and practice, see Fethi Benslama, "Dying for Justice," trans. Roland Végsö, *Umbr(a): Islam* (2009): 13–23.

which comes into the way of worshipping Allah Almighty and the implementation of the Divine authority on earth, returning this authority to Allah Almighty and taking it away from the rebellious usurpers.[70]

Could it be that the furious desire for sacrifice, this fanatic zeal for *"le passage à l'acte"*—or acting out, this kind of flight into the future (*la fuite en avant* or *al-hurūb 'ilā al-'amām*) through the engagement in the smaller jihad—could it be in the end nothing but a compensatory gesture for the failure to go through the greater jihad, *jihād al-nafs* (the struggle within the psyche/soul/self against Satan)? It may very well be so given that the dissolution of the body in the act of suicide martyrdom, for instance, is generally perceived as the ultimate form of purification, in fact the testament to the fulfillment of the purification process.[71]

Moreover, and as Stefania Pandolfo shows in her crucially important work on Quranic cure in Morocco, *jihād al-nafs* bespeaks a fierce duel between Allah and Satan that takes place in the battlefield of the psyche, and at the risk of madness or blasphemy, but not without the prospect of an eventual affirmation of faith.[72] Quranic cure may possibly serve the purposes of the greater jihad, but the extent to which it may nullify the temptations of the jihadist offer remains shrouded in mystery.

The jihadist offer seems to play the sense of guilt of potential jihadists against the promise of salvation, rendering the desire for self-sacrifice not only a form of necessary psychic compromise but also of expiation and atonement. When compounded by the sense of guilt of having abandoned Islam and lived in the modern-day *Jāhiliyya* (which is a reference to the pre-Islamic age of oblivion and ignorance), the reconversion to Islam takes the shape of a hyperidentification (*suridentification*) and exerts enormous psychological pressure, especially on the newly converted, to become more Muslim than other Muslims, which entails an endless process of demonstration of piety and willingness to pay the ultimate price for the promise of salvation.[73] The *"surmusulman* is a diagnosis of the psychic life of Muslims impregnated by Islamism, haunted by guilt and sacrifice." (Le surmusulman est un diagnostic sur la vie psychique

---

70. Sayyid Qutb, *Milestones*, ed. A. B. Al-Mehri (Birmingham: Maktabah, 2006), 71; *Ma'ālim fi al-Ṭarīq* (Cairo: Dār al-Shurūq, 1979), 75.

71. Qutb, *Milestones*, 57.

72. Stefania Pandolfo, "'Soul Choking': Maladies of the Soul, Islam, and the Ethics of Psychoanalysis," *Umbr(a): Islam* (2009): 86.

73. Benslama, *Un furieux désir de sacrifice*, 102.

de musulmans imprégnés par l'islamisme, hanté par la culpabilité et le sacrifice).[74]

Although the initial gesture of the *surmusulman* may be simple—to relinquish the position of being or having been a bad Muslim—the open-endedness of the pursuit may confront the subject eventually with the feeling of their inadequacy in front of the task at hand. Steadily this feeling of not having done enough translates into ever-excessive acts of piety (and, as Benslama propounds, of violence and terror). It is at the nexus of excess and inadequacy, then, that the drama of the *surmusulman* plays itself out. The compensatory and redemptive power of the former (excess) cannot be understood separately, I believe, from the guilt-ridden force of the latter (inadequacy). In this sense, Benslama maintains that humility is the essence of being Muslim, but pride is that of being super-Muslim. Similarly, while the expression *Allah akbar* (God is great) should normally mark one's smallness in front of God, it has become a source of infinite power and incitement to commit atrocities (hence, killing is always accompanied by the repetition of *Allah akbar*). The stakes of jouissance involved in the injury of the Islamic ideal, the dissolution of the caliphate, the humiliation of Muslims, all combine to produce the *surmusulman* as a sacrificial-cum-vindictive figure. The fantasy of a utopian Muslim past becomes the object of unbearable waiting, from which emerges the darkest aspiration to death as the means for a mystical fusion with origin. The smaller jihad becomes precisely a form of melancholite jouissance that governs the relation to and distance from this ideal and utopian past of grandeur, glory, and infinite rapture.

As is the case with any reactionary figure, the *surmusulman* ends up destroying the very object—Islam—it wants to resurrect, reclaim, and reassert. In *Psychoanalysis and the Challenge of Islam*, Benslama argues that "the failure to create new modes of subjectivization through which a more appropriate distribution of limits might take place has led to the appearance of morbid and cruel forces."[75] It should be clear by now that Benslama's project of putting the *surmusulman* on the couch mobilizes psychoanalysis to validate a predetermined condemnation of the *surmusulman* on licensed grounds. Unlike Freud's, Benslama's analysis is terminable before it even starts. He hardly allows any intellectual skepticism in his methodological approach, let alone the slightest possibility to treat Islamist jihadists on their own terms. And why should he? "The jihadi fighter is" after all, and as Darryl Li has recently argued, "a *universal* enemy . . . not due to an implacable hostility to

---

74. Ibid., 93.
75. Benslama, *Psychoanalysis and the Challenge of Islam*, 51.

humanity on his part, but because he has been declared as such by those whose right to speak in the name of the universal is often taken for granted."[76] This new universal image was painted mostly after 9/11 and not, mind you, during the decade-long, Euro-American-backed Afghani Muslim jihad against the Soviet intervention in Afghanistan (1979–1989).

Since the *surmusulman* is the figure of a subjective impasse *par excellence*, let me now examine Benslama's implied ideal figure of subjectivization, a figure who effected a return to Islam only to secularize it—ironically, through a call for jihad. Habib Bourguiba (1903–2000), Tunisia's first post-independence president, serves as the figure of what I call *l'altermusulman* or the alternative Muslim. Benslama does not use the word *altermusulman*, but it is encoded in his passing invocations of an alternative to the *surmusulman*. Benslama wagers on the kind of radical transformation of society that social and political actors like Bourguiba, and not theologians and their endless reforms to Islam since the nineteenth century, can bring about as the more viable solution to the subjective impasse of the *surmusulman*. Yet, since the *surmusulman* and the *altermusulman* lie at opposite ends of the spectrum of subjectivity, Benslama can be said to have laid (to rest) on the psychoanalytic couch an extreme figure, only to offer yet another extreme figure at the opposite side as a model subject.

As I discussed in chapter 4, Bourguiba embraced a top-down, state-led project of modernity that soon crystallized into an all-out campaign to diminish the role of Islam in society. He targeted two out of the five pillars of Islam, the hajj to Mecca and the holy month of Ramadan. One of the most infamous episodes in his three decades in office occurred in a public rally in 1964 during the first day of Ramadan: Bourguiba reached out for a glass of juice and broke the fast in broad daylight, to the surprise and perplexity of all his supporters. Although several sources maintain that the episode was aired on national TV to the wonder and amazement of the Tunisian public, I have neither found nor seen the video myself. At any rate, given the historical record of his outspoken campaign against Ramadan since the 1960s, Bourguiba could have sought to set an example or act in a shock therapy style, even at the risk of fomenting a public scandal, all the more so since Bourguiba thought he was mainly following the lead of Prophet Mohammad who had once commanded his combatant companions to break their fasts during the exhausting conquest of Mecca (*ghazwat Mecca*) so that they could garner enough strength and energy to defeat their enemies, reiterating to them: "Fortify yourselves for your enemies" (*Afṭirū litaqwuū 'alā mulāqāti 'aduwikum*).

---

76. Darryl Li, *The Universal Enemy: Jihad, Empire and the Challenge of Solidarity* (Stanford, CA: Stanford University Press, 2020), 3.

When some of his companions proved reluctant to obey his orders, the Prophet asked for a glass of water, raised it until his companions saw it, and then drank it. It is said that the Prophet stopped fasting for the remainder of the month and the entire episode resulted in the emergence of one of the earliest rulings regarding the breaking of the fast, which absolves from fasting those waging a holy war in the path of God—or a *jihād fī sabīl Allah*. This episode in the *sīra nabawiyya* or life of the Prophet constituted for Bourguiba—who not surprisingly regarded himself as a modern-day prophet—a sufficiently robust precedent for him to call a halt to the observance of Ramadan, not because Tunisia was at war with another country but because it was, he persistently professed, at war against poverty, backwardness, and underdevelopment.

Making use of *ijtihād*, or independent reasoning, Bourguiba concluded that the jihad against underdevelopment is as toilsome and demanding as the jihad against the unbelievers of Quraysh. Making use of the heuristic of *qiyās*, or analogy, Bourguiba proclaimed: "I repeat again and again that our struggle to raise this Moslem nation from the underdevelopment it had inherited from the periods of decadence is of no less value than the Jihad, or armed struggle in a holy cause."[77] Not only that—Bourguiba went even further and considered the jihad against poverty, disease, and backwardness a form of *al-jihād al-akbar* or the greater *jihad* and crowned himself with the fittingly honorific title of the supreme combatant (or *al-mujāhid al-akbar*): "Al-jihād al-akbar huwa al-jihād ḍidda al-faqr wal-maraḍ wa-takhalluf wal-'ilm wal-'amal humā bawwabatunā naḥwa al-ḥadātha wa al-taṭawur" (Al-jihad al-akbar is the jihad against poverty, disease and backwardness; science and work are our gateway to modernity and progress).[78] Instead of fasting and cutting the working day hours in half, dropping production and productivity, increasing consumption and waste, Bourguiba called for restraint and more commitment to work or what he called: "Productive, rational and methodically organized work, undertaken to create new wealth and cause an upheaval comparable to what the Arabs achieved in passing from the pre-Islamic to the Islamic era."[79] What good would Ramadan and Islam make for us, Bourguiba argued, if we remained forever backward, degenerate, and dependent on others for the slightest piece of machinery?

Religious scholars such as Tahar Ben Achour and Abdelaziz Djait, whom Bourguiba claimed to have consulted, rebuked his deviation-cum-innovation.

---

77. Habib Bourguiba, "For Ramadan Reform," in *The Contemporary Middle East: Tradition and Innovation*, ed. Benjamin Rivlin and Joseph S. Szyliowicz (New York: Random House, 1965), 173.

78. Ibid., 170.

79. Ibid.

Djait, then grand mufti, issued a fatwa urging people to work hard and not to stay out late at night, and insisted that Ramadan be observed. Even though Djait tried to delicately distance himself from Bourguiba without alienating him, he implied that whoever does not observe Ramadan commits blasphemy (not exempting Bourguiba himself).[80] In characteristically undemocratic style, Bourguiba dismissed both Ben Achour and Djait and maintained that Islam is not "a doctrine of intellectual asphyxia," but is amenable to the kind of rational arguments he made for the suspension of Ramadan, not least as these were in keeping with the bold inventiveness and creativity of the first leaders of Islam.[81] Or is it that the gate of *ijtihād* was indeed forever closed? For Benslama, like Bourguiba before him, that gate is surely still wide open. But it is up to political and social actors to bring about the kind of societal change that will force into being a contingent and geopolitically prudent understanding of jihad. Only then, Benslama suggests, can the impasses of subjectivity that the psychopathology of radicalization presents us with be redirected toward new projects of subjectivization.

While elsewhere he cautioned against wholescale societal changes without the necessary and corresponding cultural groundwork, Benslama seems to exempt Bourguiba's modernity from such a recommendation.[82] Commenting on this same episode, Albert Memmi lamented: "Bourguibism was an unexpected opportunity for Tunisia and a possible model for the Arab world, but Bourguiba was no more than a flash in the pan, the resistance too strong." In his tirade against postcolonial North Africans, Memmi went as far as to bemoan the fact that Tunisia "did not fail to write into Article 1 of its constitution that it was a Muslim state. Too bad for the minorities."[83] He forgot to add that Bourguiba, his idol, was the undisputed architect of Article 1, the "spinal cord" of the 1959 constitution.[84] Above all, he missed to add to his portrait that, while he decries the inclusion of Islam in the Tunisian constitution, he wholly supports the exclusively Jewish character of the Zionist state of Israel and thinks that Israeli apartheid is best for minorities and Palestinians alike. For someone like Memmi whose *The Colonizer and the Colonized* was a mag-

---

80. See Chokri Mabkhout, *Tārīkh al-takfīr fī Tūnis* (Tunis: Miskiliani, 2018), 287–88. Mabkhout contends that Bourguiba failed to convince Tunisians to give up fasting Ramadan because he sought to justify his nonreligious reasoning from within Islam rather than in opposition to it, 241.

81. Ibid.

82. Benslama, *Psychoanalysis and the Challenge of Islam*, 54.

83. Albert Memmi, *Decolonization and the Decolonized*, trans. Robert Bononno (Minneapolis: University of Minnesota Press, 2006), 45.

84. Samy Ghorbal, *Orphelins de Bourguiba et héritiers du prophète* (Tunis: Cérès, 2012), 24.

isterial scrutiny of colonial double standards, it is hard to fathom the ironically tragic or farcical reversal of his late style.[85]

Memmi's and Benslama's admiration notwithstanding, Bourguiba's secularization of jihad and annulment of Ramadan partake of the same melancholite logic that holds the *surmusulman* steadfast to the lost Islamic ideal. It hardly occurs to Benslama that Bourguiba's laicist project of subjectivization is very much reactionary and melancholite because it requires the abandonment of tradition, identity, and two pillars of Islam—Ramadan and hajj—in order to ensure access to secular capitalist modernity, all the more so since Islam was not so long ago instrumental to Bourguiba in mobilizing everyday Tunisians gathered in mosques and Sufi shrines against French cultural colonialism. As Fanon notes in his 1961 letter to the Iranian Islamist and Marxist scholar Ali Shariati, "Islam has fought against the west and colonialism more than all Asia and all Africa."[86] It was in this spirit that Bourguiba supported the wearing of the veil in 1929 and the fatwa of Bizerte's mufti against the burial of naturalized French Tunisians in Islamic cemeteries. Bourguiba was then, though, less interested in fortifying Islam than in defeating the French, and he embarked therefore on a reverse campaign in the wake of independence, mobilizing Tunisians to give up a number of traditional Islamic practices and urging them to concentrate their efforts on the fight against underdevelopment.

Ironically, Benslama does not melancholize Bourguiba, not because he is less melancholite than the *surmusulman* but because Benslama's rudimentary concept of melancholy is monolithic and targets only those subjects who maintain attachments that cannot be given up (the *surmusulman*), while it discounts or exempts subjects who prescribe that some attachments be given up (*l'altermusulman*). If Islamists would want to go back to a Golden Age of Islam, one wonders why Benslama does not call them romantics (much like the romantic Zionists who embarked on a settler colonial invention of ancient Israel). It is as if subjects who want to claim a new identity are not as melancholite in the end as those who want to reclaim an old one. The latter resist the

---

85. I am echoing Gil Hochberg's remark, "what it takes for such a brilliant writer and astute political mind, to stay blind to Zionism's detrimental racist and colonial implications." See Hochberg, "An anti-colonial Zionist? Remembering Albert Memmi," *Mondoweiss*, June 25, 2020, mondoweiss.net/2020/06/an-anti-colonial-zionist-remembering-albert-memmi. David Lloyd insightfully uses Memmi's own theoretical insights to understand his "rightward turn" as an instance of the "colonizer who accepted," See Lloyd, "Albert Memmi: Contradictions of the Colonial Condition," *Mondoweiss*, June 25, 2020, https://mondoweiss.net/2020/06/albert-memmi-contradictions-of-the-colonial-condition/.

86. Frantz Fanon, *Alienation and Freedom*, ed. Robert Young and Jean Khalfa, trans. Steven Corcoran (London: Bloomsbury, 2018), 668.

deprivation of identity while the former require the deprivation of identity in anticipation of a future modern identity. If the entry into secular modernity requires that certain attachments (to Ramadan in particular and to Islam in general) be given up, then such entry is clearly melancholite.[87] All the more so given that Bourguiba failed to embody the political entailments of the very promise of secular modernity with which he so forcefully identified. Secular modernity is aggressively homogenizing but it is not without its contradictions, namely that it conscripts subjects whom it fundamentally rejects. It is tragically ironic that Bourguiba identified with a tyrannical project that rejected him in the colonial period and that he in turn failed to embody in the postcolonial era, and not for lack of trying. For better or worse, Benslama's *altermusulman* may need to be laid on the analytic couch as well.

Gendering Origin

It is insofar as her jouissance is radically Other that woman has more of a relationship to God than anything that could have been said in speculation in antiquity following the pathway of that which is manifestly articulated only as the good of man.

JACQUES LACAN[88]

Hagar is the origin that has been repudiated in order to preserve filiation in accordance with the imaginarized impossible. The imaginarized impossible is the foundation of the origin in metaphysics. The concept of the father in originary monotheism entails the repudiation of the foreigner and the phallic choice of the proper.

FETHI BENSLAMA[89]

Both the *surmusulman* and the *altermusulman* are melancholites, neither aberrations nor exemplars of the melancholy disposition I have been painting throughout this book. I would like to come back to the more productive

---

87. In this sense, one may even be justified in suggesting, following Toscano, that "psychoanalysis could find itself as the midwife of secularism—in other words, as an institution that takes the parameters of acculturation (and pathology, anomaly and dislocation) provided by Western Christendom and its secular inheritance as somehow normative," Toscano, *Fanaticism*, 162.

88. See Jacques Lacan, *The Seminar of Jacques Lacan, Book XX: Encore: On Feminine Sexuality, the Limits of Love and Knowledge, 1972–1973*, ed. Jacques-Alain Miller, trans. Bruce Fink (New York: Norton, 1988), 83.

89. Benslama, *Psychoanalysis and the Challenge of Islam*, 96.

dynamic of melancholy Islam, that is, to the melancholic rather than melancholite variant which is subtly at work in *Psychoanalysis and the Challenge of Islam,* and in which Benslama himself embodies the role of the melancholic intellectual and analyst *par excellence*: he returns to the archive of Islamic texts in an effort not only to discern and retool Sufism as a corrective to Salafism, but also to deconstruct and reclaim the crucial role of feminine clairvoyance/jouissance in the story of Islamic and monotheistic origins. This recuperative retrieval which renders justice to the female contribution to monotheism is, as will become clear, a solid example of melancholic critique (and, I should add, of what the *melancholicization* rather than the more routine, virulent, and hegemonic *melancholization* of Islam should look like).

Monotheism could have possibly done without Hagar and started with Sarah *tout court*. In Benslama's words, "it would have been possible for the absolute god of monotheism to offer the gift of a single origin, within a united family."[90] Yet, god did not. The gift of origin was initially withheld from Sarah and granted to Hagar who gave birth to Ishmael and established the biological paternity of Abraham. This purely human patrilineal modality of descent, which would later establish Islam as the only truly Abrahamic monotheistic religion, proved to be, according to Benslama, only "a bastard beginning."[91] Therefore, it isn't until the last moment, Benslama observes, "that a purer, nobler, more spiritual beginning is produced, one satisfied with being not merely the gift of a child but the gift as the impossible. Sarah's conception is that of the miracle of the dead body that suddenly comes to life, contradicting the laws of human procreation."[92] The birth of Isaac renders Abraham a "father by proxy," just like Joseph in relation to Jesus.[93]

What complicates the notion of origin in Islam is the fact that the origin of monotheism itself is marked by the lack of a single origin. Instead, there are two divergent principles of origin, each quite distant from the other, one paternal, the other divine—"One, originating in Hagar, is the principle of the flesh, or the gift of the possible; the other, coming through Sarah, is that of the spirit or the gift of the impossible."[94] It is origin through the sexual insemination of Hagar by Abraham, as Benslama notes, that has been repudiated in favor of origin through Sarah, in which Abraham serves as "a

---

90. Ibid., 80.
91. Ibid., 88.
92. Ibid.
93. Ibid., 86.
94. Ibid., 89.

father by proxy," a mere "representation of the real father."[95] It is as if beginning through Abraham-Hagar-Ishmael proved too mundane and not worthy of monotheistic origins as such; it was more of an impasse of beginning rather than a proper beginning, especially given that Hagar was a bondwoman, a slave gifted to Sarah by Pharaoh (indeed, Hagar was a countergift to Sarah, who was Abraham's initial gift to Pharaoh). But while Hagar was pushed aside in the story of monotheistic origin, she remains not only "the disturber of originary paternity and its triumvirate conception," but also the locus of Other jouissance—the recipient of God's covenant following their mystical encounter in the desert.[96]

Hagar was initially brought up as some sort of a solution to Sarah's infertility; once Sarah realized that the God of Genesis had denied her the gift of origin, she offered her slave Hagar to Abraham as a surrogate womb to offer him the gift of a son and the gift of origin at one and the same time. At stake in the arrival of the son is the very arrival of the father; without the son, Abraham cannot become father, much less the father of monotheism. Needless to say, withholding the son in Genesis is tantamount to holding both the father and monotheistic origin in suspense: "In the beginning is 'that which withholds.' In other words, there is that there-is-not [*Il y a qu'il n'y a pas*]. We cannot push origin further back than this."[97] "Monotheism," Benslama rightly concludes, "is initially presented as faith in this impossible that is the lack of the father in the world, or the imaginary lack of origin."[98] Both father and son are lacking yet forthcoming. From this clearly Lacanian perspective, origin is structured by lack or, as Benslama has it, by the "void of interval" between *entame*/cut and *commencement*/beginning.[99] This lack may have preceded the arrival of Sarah and Hagar, but it comes to structure their relationship and later rivalry and fuel the desire of each one of them to overcome it.

Understandably, all Sarah wanted is to "overcome the lack of god in herself" by way of Hagar; yet through her act, Benslama observes, "Genesis makes the transition from the initial lack of origin to the question of female *jouissance* in its relation to the establishment of the father."[100] In other words, "the woman who commands [Sarah] does not begin, leaving the primacy of the

95. Ibid., 86.
96. Ibid., 78.
97. Ibid., 92.
98. Ibid.
99. Ibid., 123.
100. Ibid., 80.

gift of the father to the woman who engenders through the flesh [Hagar]."[101] Sarah sought to overcome the lack of origin in her by the proxy womb of Hagar. The transfer of the gift of origin from Sarah to Hagar entails therefore the tacit endowment of Hagar with female jouissance (and with Other jouissance following the mystical encounter with God). At the origin, there is therefore female (and not solely phallic) jouissance—there is, in other words, Hagar's overcoming the lack of origin in Sarah and establishing Abraham as father. As Lacan intimates, female jouissance involves a relationship to God that is neither phallic nor knowable outside of experience.[102] For Benslama, Hagar's encounter with the God of Genesis gives her access to this excess jouissance or radically Other jouissance.

The overarching goal of Benslama's *Psychoanalysis and the Challenge of Islam* is to "formulate a structural function of the feminine at the moment of origin, which conditions the genealogical establishment of the father."[103] This is all the more so given that "Hagar's story is one of repudiation at monotheism's origin, which became disavowal when Islam began."[104] For instance, Benslama underlines the following fact about Hagar's elision from the Quran: "Although Ishmael is cited a dozen times in the Koran, and Abraham seventy-eight, Hagar is nowhere to be found."[105] Similarly, the Quran refers to Isaac's birth and blesses Sarah as "the wife of Abraham," but refers to Hagar only indirectly when relating the episode about her exile with her son Ishmael, her distress and frantic search for water in the desert.[106] Interestingly enough, it is during this episode, when Hagar and Ishmael were abandoned in the desert, that the God of Genesis hears her suffering, and promises to make her "the origin of descendants beyond number."[107] With the founding of Islam, this promise to Hagar was somewhat fulfilled, except that Islam staked a genealogical claim to Abraham and Ishmael to the detriment of Hagar: "The return to Abraham was the key element in the Muhammedan refounding, a return that saw itself as the culmination of monotheism, binding its origin to its end."[108] While deconstructing the notion of origin,

---

101. Ibid., 95.
102. See Jacques Lacan, *The Seminar of Jacques Lacan, Book XX: Encore: On Feminine Sexuality, the Limits of Love and Knowledge, 1972–1973*, ed. Alain Miller, trans. Bruce Fink (New York: Norton, 1988), 83.
103. Ibid., 97.
104. Ibid., 110.
105. Ibid., 120.
106. Ibid., 102–4.
107. Ibid., 81.
108. Ibid., 69.

Benslama does not do away altogether with the gesture of return and offers instead a corrective to the established patriarchal and phallic theological narrative of origins in Islam.

The *recovery from* the myth of a pure Islamic (or monotheistic, for that matter) origin is as important as the *recovery of* how origin was en*gendered* in the first place. In this sense, the eradication of Hagar from the story of monotheistic-Islamic origins is symptomatic of a more structural gesture that sought to gender origin at the outset by excluding or eliding the role of the feminine and the excessive jouissance that comes with it. The need to recover and reinscribe the role of the female and foreign other in the story of origin is therefore a salutary melancholic endeavor; all the more so if, as Benslama claims, "Islam had recourse to a stream of proscriptions to reduce, dismantle, then deny that Other *jouissance*, so as to gradually establish the sovereignty of a phallic, juridical, and ethical order congruent with the formation of the state."[109] It is quite misleading, however, to seek to establish, as Benslama propounds, an allegorical correspondence between the marginalization of the female other in the monotheistic-Islamic story of origins and the contemporary "condition of women in Islamic societies."[110] Such an analogical ruse not only exempts the other monotheistic religions from this same problem but also excludes the circumstantial dynamics of history and geopolitics that continue to produce and reproduce the so-called contemporary condition of women in Islamic societies. Finally, it replicates—really, ratifies—the anachronistic Islamist gesture, which wants to refashion the present in the image of the past (in which case Benslama's suggestion—that the current condition of women in Islamic societies corresponds to the exclusion of the feminine in the story of monotheistic-Islamic origins—sanctions the same anachronism it seeks to deconstruct in relation to Islamist puritanical rhetoric).

It is incumbent therefore to reclaim and reinscribe the particular roles played by a number of illustrious women in the story of monotheistic-Islamic origins and, simultaneously, to resist the temptation to recast the systemic repression of the female other in that story as a timeless framework for the analysis of the contemporary condition of women in Muslim societies. Bearing this in mind, I will now examine the important role that two other women (in addition to Hagar) played in Islam's story of origin. The aim here is to further explore (and not to entirely map) the elements of what would constitute an alternative female spiritual path to the phallocentric story of foundation in Islam. Little wonder that this alternative spiritual path is anchored in

---

109. Ibid., 149.
110. 109.

feminine/Other jouissance. It is as if the gendering of origin in Benslama must pass through the gendering of jouissance in Lacan: "There is a jouissance that is hers about which she herself perhaps knows nothing if not that she experiences it—that much she knows. She knows it, of course, when it comes (*arrive*). It doesn't happen (*arrive*) to all of them."[111] Not unlike Lacan and his followers, including Bruce Fink, Benslama does not explain why this unspeakable jouissance should be structured along gender lines, especially that much of Benslama's analytical innovations hinge on the hermeneutical insights of Ibn Arabi, whose work interweaves neatly philosophy, theology, and Sufism. Paul Verhaeghe may be right to observe that the "post-Lacanian hype about 'feminine jouissance' is nothing more than a hysterical attempt to recuperate something that cannot be recuperated, owing to its very nature."[112] However, what sets Benslama's recuperative historiography apart from other Lacanian critics is that it expands Lacan's repertoire of female examples beyond Hadewijch of Antwerp and Saint Teresa and maps a stellar assemblage of diverse female figures whose supplementary experiences of Other jouissance has been elided in the monotheistic-Islamic story of origins. Benslama contends that "Islam, ever since the originary repudiation, has been haunted by the other woman, who has threatened to capture the son, making him an illegitimate bastard."[113] Benslama has in mind here not only Ishmael in relation to Hagar, but also, as will become clear, Ruqayya in relation to Prophet Muhammad; it was Ruqayya who wanted to entice Abdallah (who would become the father of Prophet Muhammad) to have sex with her and give her access to the phallic jouissance that would enable her to capture the founding son, and reach the status of woman of the Other.

The role of the other woman in the story of monotheistic-Islamic origins cannot be overstressed. Hagar was not only the recipient of God's promise but also the only woman in biblical narrative to have seen God without dying.[114] Insofar as Islam is a biblical promise, the promise was made to Hagar and not to Abraham. Without the coming of Prophet Muhammad, however, Islam would have remained a biblical promise in search of a founding son. The story of the procreation of Prophet Muhammad is therefore central to the foundation of Islam, all the more so since it involved yet another tale of female rivalry, not unlike the rivalry between Hagar and Sarah, which denied

---

111. See Lacan, *Seminar XX: Encore*, 74.
112. Paul Verhaeghe, "Lacan's Answer to the Classical Mind/Body Deadlock: Retracing Freud's *Beyond*," in Bernard and Fink, *Reading Seminar XX*, 113.
113. Benslama, *Psychoanalysis and the Challenge of Islam*, 116.
114. Ibid., 123.

monotheism the benefit of a single origin. While Amina was the actual mother of Prophet Muhammad, Ruqayya is the name of the other woman who saw the sign of the forthcoming son (the glow between the eyes of Abdallah, the father of the Prophet), and who wanted to capture the seed of origin from Abdallah (ironically, Abdallah was somewhat the oblivious bearer of the seed of the son and as such the *bearer* of the object of Ruqayya's desire but not the object of that desire per se). Ruqayya, according to Benslama, "enjoys a knowledge about light and the body, about the body of light of infantile origin, that is invisible to the father who carries it."[115] Like Hagar before her, Ruqayya emerges as the other woman who threatens to capture the son from the rightful mother Amina. In short, "both Hagar and Ruqayya possess an arrogant power of clairvoyance that enables one of them to see god without dying and name him with the name of that vision, and the other to perceive the glow of sanctity and want to capture it."[116]

The clairvoyant power of the other woman, which haunts the fiction of monotheistic-Islamic origins, cannot be understood from within the prisms of phallic jouissance alone. The other woman's access to the phallic absolute supplements and surpasses the procreative realm of phallic jouissance and overflows into the mystical realm of absolute alterity and of Other jouissance. For, as Lacan surmises, "it is in the opaque place of jouissance of the Other, of this Other insofar as woman, if she existed, could be it, that the Supreme Being is situated."[117] The rivalry between Ruqayya and Amina revolves "not so much around the man as sexual object as around access to the status of woman of the Other and to the phallic *jouissance* that access confers, that is, the supreme power of engendering the son who will become the founding father."[118] Female jouissance is a central asset that endows women with the capacity to recognize the foundation of truth in Islam. No wonder, then, it had taken one woman to recognize and try to capture the seed of the founding son of Islam (Ruqayya) and yet another (Khadija) to discern and establish the truth of Quranic revelation. Indeed, it was his first wife Khadija who was able to reassure Prophet Muhammad that the larger-than-life being that appears to him every now and then is not a demon but an angel. Benslama relates the compelling story of the encounter between the Prophet, the archangel Gabriel, and Khadija and how the archangel disappeared as soon as Khadija unveiled herself. While unable to see the angel herself, Khadija concluded thenceforth

---

115. Ibid., 115.
116. Ibid., 131.
117. Lacan, *Seminar XX: Encore*, 82.
118. Benslama, *Psychoanalysis and the Challenge of Islam*, 115.

that had it been a demon, it would have possibly not been unsettled by female immodesty and withdrawn itself immediately from the scene and the sight of the Prophet. Benslama does not make light of this story, a primal scene of sorts, regardless of its historical veracity; on the contrary, he accords it a great deal of analytical and critical attention and teases out a number of conclusions that underline the central importance of female clairvoyance to the story of foundation in Islam. Benslama had ruminated before on this very scene in his 1988 *La nuit brisée*, following perhaps in the footsteps of Abdelkebir Khatibi who suggested that Khadija "deciphered certain signs of prophecy on her own body and on that of her husband. She read, in a way, on the imaginary body of Islam where, illegible to Mohammad himself, the prophetic message becomes apprehensible by the feminine body."[119] Other jouissance for Benslama becomes the locus of the Tiresias-like clairvoyance of Khadija.

Benslama pays particular attention to the contradictions of this scene and to the paradoxes of the moment of foundation in general. For one thing, Khadija's unveiling reveals and simultaneously conceals the truth, given that the angel disappears at the sight of Khadija's hair; yet, "the concealment of truth is the verification of truth."[120] For another, the founder of truth does not recognize the revelation of the truth, which "inevitably leads toward the conclusion that man, if he is to believe in god, must rely upon belief in a woman, one who has access to a knowledge of truth that precedes and exceeds the knowledge of the founder himself. She verifies the founder's truth."[121] She has access to the truth of the Other precisely because of her position as eternal Other. Benslama translates Lacan here in more concrete terms: "The Other is not simply the locus in which truth stammers. It deserves to represent that to which woman is fundamentally related. . . . Being the Other, in the most radical sense, in the sexual relationship, in relation to what can be said of the unconscious, woman is that which has a relationship to that Other."[122] Far from being a disadvantage, Otherness here becomes something "extra (*en plus*)."[123] Otherness gives access to the experience of Other jouissance, the experience of this quasi-prophetic insight that Khadija becomes privy to but is incapable of giving an account of it. Perhaps, as Fink claims following Lacan, "the idea here seems to be that one can experience this Other jouissance, though one cannot say anything about it because it is ineffable; just because it does not

119. Khatibi, "Frontiers," 692.
120. Benslama, *Psychoanalysis and the Challenge of Islam*, 134.
121. Ibid.
122. Ibid., 81.
123. Ibid., 77.

exist does not mean one cannot experience it: one's experience of it simply ex-sists."[124]

Given that Khadija was the first person to believe in the Prophet, she became the first Muslim. Arguably, without her mediation, the Prophet would not have himself believed in God's messenger (archangel Gabriel) as well as in himself as messenger of God. Benslama is right here in perceiving of Khadija as "the intermediary between intermediaries."[125] Undoubtedly, her role cannot be overestimated. However, Benslama claims that she became "the antiorigin upon which the initial faith in origin resided."[126] He goes on to suggest that woman went through "three stages in the female operation of theology: initially veiled, unveiled to demonstrate originary truth, then reveiled by order of the belief in that truth of origin. For, once established, truth aspires to conceal the nothingness through which it has passed."[127] While the act of veiling plays an important role in the revelation of the truth here, Benslama chooses to privilege unveiling and to look unfavorably at veiling even though Khadija was veiled before the revelation of truth. In addition, what I find of particular interest here is that Khadija wore the veil in the privacy of her home; had she not been wearing the veil in the privacy of her home, though, the archangel might not have been revealed to the Prophet. Khadija's modesty must have had no bounds already, and before Islam—or is it that modesty/veiling was always about revelation, a spiritual relation? Ironically, but not surprisingly, Benslama Islamizes veiling there where he should have historicized it.

The scene of origins is the scene of contradictions and contingencies par excellence. Khadija "founds the truth of the founder,"[128] even while she has no direct access to that truth herself and even though her act of unveiling amounted to nothing less than an assault on the modesty of God's messenger. In other words, the one who can identify the truth of revelation (Khadija) does not see it and the one who can see it (Prophet Muhammad) cannot identify it. The story of origin is decentered. The paternal and maternal play equal roles in its dispersed formation. The fact that it was gendered in monotheistic history is not enough alibi to regender it here and reproduce the inverse yet same essentialist gesture. That said, I cannot agree more with Benslama in his reproach of European psychoanalysts "who overlooked the existence of a

---

124. Fink, "Knowledge and Jouissance," 40.
125. Fethi Benslama, "The Veil of Islam," S: Journal of the Circle for Lacanian Ideology Critique 2 (2009): 19.
126. Benslama, Psychoanalysis and the Challenge of Islam, 135.
127. Ibid.
128. Ibid., 18.

feminine spiritual path that the original monotheism glimpses but rejects."[129] His psychoanalytic project entails a *melancholic return* and rescue of this feminine spiritual path, while that of the Islamists is more of a *melancholite return*: a reactionary attempt that aims in the end to resurrect and perpetuate the phallocentric fictions or established theological order of origin. It bears reiterating, though, that such melancholite returns ought to be carefully nuanced, especially when approached from within Euro-American identity politics and the war on terror discourse which have habitually found in the demonization of Islam a measure of redemption as well as a convenient strategy of continual colonial domination.

Psychoanalysis cannot afford to give short shrift to the differential grievances of melancholites even while they embark on a theopathological return to origins and stake claims to an otherwise nonexistent originary purity. Benslama's melancholizing (and depoliticizing) diagnosis leaves much to be desired, for sure, but what is salutary is his revisionary return to origins to rescue the repressed figure of the feminine as key to a nonpatriarchal and nonpatrilineal understanding of monotheistic origins. For Benslama, Islam lacks a finite point of reference identical with origin. While it may seem that Benslama reproduces as he reverses the gender biases at the origin of monotheistic and Islamic history, it is understandable that his melancholic gesture is more recuperative than essentialist. After all, the foundation of the last monotheistic religion came about through different installments over time, ranging from the biblical promise to Hagar by the God of Genesis to the revelation of the Quran to the Prophet Muhammad by the archangel Gabriel. The challenge is to steer clear of the phallocentric story of Islamic origin and to unveil in the process the female spiritual itinerary which it has left out of the account. This is perhaps the more worthwhile challenge in the title of Benslama's book, *Psychoanalysis and the Challenge of Islam*, rather than the highly mediatized and sensationalized challenge of Islamism.

---

129. Fethi Benslama, "Islam in Light of Psychoanalysis," in *Psychoanalysis, Monotheism and Morality: Symposia of the Sigmund Freud Museum 2009–2011*, ed. Wolfgang Müller-Funk, Ingrid Scholz-Strasser, and Herman Westerink (Leuven: Leuven University Press, 2013), 16.

Epilogue
Melancholy Critique

Much of my concern in the last chapter and throughout the book has been over the slippages between historical contingencies or actualities and structural exigencies or determinacies. As a comparatist, what I find most compelling about psychoanalysts from Freud to Benslama through Lacan is the constancy and dexterity with which they straddle the archeological and philological inquiry into the psyche. Perhaps Lacan's most famous aphorism that the unconscious is structured like a language best captures this psychoanalytic disposition toward philology. What I find puzzling in Benslama's work though is that at times for him the unconscious is structured *by* language rather than *like* a language. Not that it is not, especially if it does not resist symbolization, but I mean this in a specific way. In "L'agonie pour la justice" (Dying for Justice), Benslama sets himself the challenging task of constructing a genealogy of the phenomenon of self-sacrifice, *l'autosacrifice*. After a meticulous probing of the well-known work of Ernst H. Kantorowicz and the secularization of martyrdom in medieval Europe, Benslama wonders why the National Liberation Front (FLN) never had recourse to suicide attacks despite the systematic oppression, torture, and humiliation to which Algerians were subjected by the French settler colonial regime, especially in the wake of the Sétif massacre in May 1945.

The historical circumstances were not compelling or sufficient enough as an explanation for the emergence of suicide attacks in the decolonial era, nor were the theological texts that contain passages which would have justified the recourse to suicide attacks. What was missing, Benslama argues, was a *linguistic* operation:

> Around the middle of the 1980s an important event took place, an event in the order of discourse in the Arabic language . . . it is the invention of a new term that did not exist before and that did not have any currency during the fourteen centuries of the history of Islam. . . . Based on the root "sh.h.d," the term "'*istishhādī*" will be forged, a term constructed in such a way that it corresponds in the canons of the language to what is called "the urgent demand for something." To put it differently, what is invented through this name is the "candidate for martyrdom" [*le demandeur de martyre*]. There is a historical turning point which transforms the world of meaning of "shahīd" from the order of the passive subject, suffering his fate accidentally, to that of an agent in quest of death, under the mode of wanting to kill and be killed at the same time. . . . By making possible in the world of discourse and in the Arabic language the urgent demand for martyrdom, a "niche" of deadly address opens up toward which certain subjects will orient themselves.[1]

Benslama suggests here that as soon as a new word in the Arabic language was coined to label the agent of a martyrdom operation, a new sphere of symbolic action opened up. What I find quite puzzling is Benslama's underlying assumption that Arabs and Muslims must have been insulated from the world around them (or that they were simply immune to the contagious potential of, for instance, the Japanese kamikaze pilots during World War II and the suicide attacks of the Tamil Tigers in Sri Lanka since 1972, or, for that matter, the biblical story of Samson, "arguably the first suicide killer," according to Jacqueline Rose); they were waiting for the creation of the neologism '*istishhādī* to embark on a series of martyrdom operations.[2] In other words, for Benslama, '*istishhādī* operations could not have started avant la lettre. This overemplotment of the Arabic language (which is not uncommon among Arab Lacanians, including most notably Moustapha Safouan) may be in the end nothing more than a projection of the linguistic inauguration of Islam and the miracle of Quranic language on the messy formation and contagious circulation of historical phenomena such as suicide militancy after World War II.[3]

---

1. Fethi Benslama, "Dying for Justice," trans. Roland Végsö, *Umbr(a): Islam* (2009): 18–19.
2. Jacqueline Rose, *The Last Resistance* (New York: Verso, 2007), 126.
3. While one cannot underestimate the actantial and agentive value of language, Benslama's exaggeration of the significance of the word '*istishhādī* here reeks of Orientalist reflexes: "The exaggerated value heaped upon Arabic as a language permits the Orientalist to make the language equal to mind, society, history, and nature." See Edward Said, "Shattered Myths," in *Orientalism: A Reader*, ed., Alexander Lyon Macfie (New York: New York University Press,

Regardless, Benslama is not specific as to when exactly the neologism *'istishhādī* entered the Arabic lexicon ("the middle of the 1980s," he says), but in all probability it succeeded rather than preceded the phenomenon of deliberate martyrdom operations.[4] As Benslama is well aware, the first kamikaze attack took place on May 30, 1972, in the Lod Airport in Tel-Aviv and was committed by the Japanese Red Army. In June 1982, and in the wake of the 1982 Israeli invasion of Lebanon, Hezbollah was created, and in 1983 it orchestrated its first martyrdom operation. Sensing the impasse of his linguistic hypothesis, Benslama falls back on the default position of Islam. He factors in the connection between Hezbollah, Shiite Islam, and the influential theoretical work of Islamist-Marxist Iranian scholar Ali Shariati. It was Shariati who reinterpreted the martyrdom of Hussein and qualified him not as a "warrior-martyr" (*shahīd*), an involuntary martyr, but as a "martyr-martyr" (*'istishhādī*), as someone who voluntarily and proactively sought his own martyrdom.[5] In the first version of the article published in 2008, Benslama implies that Hezbollah transported the concept and practice of voluntary martyrdom to the Arab world.[6] In a 2014 collection of essays, *La guerre des subjectivités en Islam* (The War of Subjectivities in Islam), Benslama reprints the same 2008 article with an addendum.[7] The added section is devoted to an exploration of the transmission of voluntary martyrdom from Shiite to Sunni Islam. Enter Palestine!

While in the earlier version of the article he gave short shrift to anticolonial struggles, particularly the Algerian war of independence, in the later supplement to that same article the Palestinian struggle for self-determination gains pride of place in the importation and appropriation of voluntary martyrdom operations. The supplement supplants Benslama's earlier thesis about the genealogy of voluntary martyrdom, which he locates first in the Arabic language and then in Hezbollah and Shiite Islam—all the more so since Hezbollah had not had recourse to orchestrated martyrdom operations since the Israeli withdrawal from Lebanon in May 2000. *Islam proposes, history disposes*: even while Shariati-inflected Shiite Islam authorizes martyrdom operations,

---

2000), 100. This Orientalist attitude toward the Arabic language is in full display in Moustapha Safouan, *Why Are the Arabs Not Free? The Politics of Writing* (Oxford: Wiley-Blackwell, 2007).

4. Regardless of the new meaning—seeking martyrdom—it has acquired, *istishhād* is a commonly used word in Arabic which means furnishing concrete and reliable evidence, that is, documented and backed up evidence which can serve in court.

5. Benslama, "Dying for Justice," 20.

6. Fethi Benslama, "L'agonie pour la justice," *Topiques* 1, no. 102 (2008): 71–82.

7. Fethi Benslama, "L'agonie pour la justice," in *La guerre des subjectivités en Islam* (Tunis: Cérès, 2014), 43–64.

it is particular historical junctures that determine their deployment. In fact, the first martyrdom operations orchestrated by Hamas in the spring of 1994 were referred to as *'amaliyyāt fidā'iyya* (self-sacrificial operations) and *'amaliyyāt 'istishhādiyya* (martyrdom operations) by local media and by Hamas officials respectively.[8] They were, it bears repeating, prompted by an act of state-sanctioned terrorism: the killing of twenty-nine praying Palestinian Muslims in the Mosque of the Patriarch in Hebron by Zionist settler Baruch Goldstein on February 25, 1994. While Islam is still instrumental to the culture of militant martyrdom, it is the diurnal terrorization and continual dispossession of Palestinians that is at the origin of its historical formation and development, and it is the nationalist struggle against the Israeli occupation that is the purpose and object of acts of voluntary martyrdom.[9] The logic of the global war on terror and the neoliberal identity politics that sustain it hinge on the repudiation of the "suicide bomber" rather than on the recognition of the *shahid*, *fidā'ī*, the martyr, the political agent of the struggle against Zionism. Yet, as Talal Asad argued, the so-called suicide bombers do, in fact, "tell us more about liberal assumptions of religious subjectivities and political violence than they do about what is ostensibly being explained."[10]

There is still no clear genealogy of voluntary martyrdom in the new 2014 version of the article, but what I find intriguing about Benslama's long-term reflection on such a genealogy is that while he initially discounted history, he later foregrounded it. Why did Benslama change his mind between 2008 and 2014? What intervened is the Tunisian Revolution of Freedom and Dignity,

---

8. Nasser Abufarha, *The Making of a Human Bomb: An Ethnography of Palestinian Resistance* (Durham, NC: Duke University Press, 2009), 8. The *fidā'ī* is the militant figure of secular self-sacrifice *par excellence* because he gives his own life for the sake of the homeland (*fidā'an-lil-waṭan*). The *fidā'ī*, or militant fighter, had become the *mot du jour* in Palestine and the Arab world since the victory of PLO factions over the Israeli army in the Karama battle in Jordan in 1969. It continued to be the dominant iconic figure of cross-border operations against the Israeli army in the 1970s until it was almost completely displaced by the *'istishhādī* figure of the second intifada. Hamas leaders sought to attach a religious meaning to the otherwise nationalist purpose of the act of *'istishhād* or self-sacrifice to "alleviate the intentionality of martyrdom as an act of heroism" (10).

9. Robert A. Pape compiled and studied 315 suicide attacks around the globe from 1980 to 2003 and concluded that "what nearly all suicide attacks have in common is a specific secular and strategic goal: to compel modern democracies to withdraw military forces from territory that the terrorists consider to be their homeland. Religion is rarely the root cause, although it is often used as a tool by terrorist organizations in recruiting and in other efforts in service of the broader strategic objective." Pape, *Dying to Win: The Strategic Logic of Suicide Terrorism* (New York: Random House, 2005), 4.

10. Talal Asad, *On Suicide Bombing* (New York: Columbia University Press, 2007), 42.

and particularly the self-immolation of Bouazizi, a form of suicide so uncommon in North Africa and for which Benslama found no origin in Islam: "Self-sacrifice is a terrible response to an injustice whose enormous subjective, political, and anthropological dimensions remain yet to be known".[11] While he wrote *Psychoanalysis and the Challenge of Islam* in the wake of 9/11 and *A Furious Desire for Sacrifice* in the wake of the series of coordinated terrorist attacks that took place on November 13, 2015, in Paris, Benslama wrote *Soudain la revolution!* right after the Tunisian revolution. The self-immolation of Bouazizi garnered much of Benslama's psychoanalytic acumen; he capitalized on it as a breakthrough act lodged between two alternative modalities of nonexistence under the authoritarian regime of Ben Ali: total "desensitization to despair" (*désensibilization au désespoir*) alternating with the promise of total reparation in the Hereafter. The "flight into self-sacrifice" (*l'échappatoire dans l'autosacrifice*) is prompted by a sudden rediscovery/recovery of one's "sensitivity to despair" (*sensibilité au désespoir*).[12]

Benslama conceives of Bouazizi's "immanent martyrdom" as a transformational generative act: it enabled the formation of forms of political subjectivization and a nonviolent movement of emancipation. All of these are promissory developments in Benslama's own sensitivity to the actual sociopolitical impasses of Arab subjectivity and toward an emancipatory rather than self-validating practice of psychoanalysis, which he himself calls in the subtitle to the book, following Derrida, "a geopsychoanalysis of an uprising." Still, however, Benslama cannot just curb the lure to generalize about the despair that prompted Bouazizi to engulf himself in flames: "ce n'est plus la verité du bien et du mal, du paradis et de l'enfer, de la fusion dans le corpus mysticum de la Oumma dont il s'agit, mais la verité immanente de la condition humaine, celle de la détresse et de l'abandon au désespoir à l'origine de l'humain" (It is no longer the truth of good and evil, nor of paradise and hell, or of the fusion into the *corpus mysticum* of the Umma, but of the immanent truth of the human condition, the distress and the abandonment to despair at the origin of the human).[13] While it may seem generous to confer the mantle of the universal upon Bouazizi's protestant despair, such a gesture would entail the abstraction and emptying of Bouazizi's particular experience of despair into the universal despair that is constitutive of the human condition (and that can be found in abundance in continental existential philosophy from Kierkegaard to Camus through Heidegger). Wittingly or unwittingly, Benslama reduces to

---

11. Benslama, "L'agonie pour la justice," 62.
12. Benslama, *Soudain la révolution! Géopsychanalyse d'un soulèvement* (Tunis: Cérès, 2011), 47.
13. Ibid., 77.

the structurally undifferentiated ontological condition of the human psyche Bouazizi's historically specific experience of despair and *hoqra* or *hogra* (which condenses a spectrum of psychoaffective differentials that the ruling elites excite in the masses, ranging from feelings of indifference, infantilization, and indignation to contempt and humiliation through an overall sense of injustice and disenfranchisement).

Framing it in the transhistorical and universal terms of the existential condition of being human, Benslama relativizes and dehistoricizes Bouazizi's actual Tunisian experience of despair and entrapment following the demeaning treatment he received from the officials. He abandons one structural interpretation for another: if it's not Arabic, or Islam or the Umma, it's the universal human condition. Such displacements from the particular to the universal have grave political implications in that they cancel out concrete history and reduce the differential potential of political agency to a mere function within an overdetermining existential condition (marked at the outset by despair, abandonment, or what Heidegger would call "thrownness" into the world).[14] Worse still, such displacements encourage the assimilation of Bouazizi's singular grievances into the ahistorical consumerism that is basic to the resilience of global capitalist hegemony and neoliberal authoritarianism in the Arab world. True, the Tunisian revolution has loosened Benslama's commitment to reductionism; yet it has not transformed his rudimentary and disempowering understanding of the concept of melancholy. In *Soudain la revolution!* Benslama comes very close to conceiving of melancholy as an empowering affect with insurrectionary potential: "il a bien fallu éprouver un puissant sentiment de déchéance pour que quelqu'un soit précipité dans la mélancolie autodestructrice" (An intense feeling of worthlessness must have precipitated Bouazizi's self-destructive melancholy).[15]

Though the point is understated, there is a considerable overlap between conceiving of Bouazizi's self-immolation as, at one point, "self-destructive melancholy" and, at another, as a "sensitization to despair," which implies that Benslama is here holding in tandem melancholization and sensitization (i.e., melancholicization). That is the closest Benslama comes to conceiving of Bouazizi's self-immolation as a melancholy act, a suicidal protest (*suicide protestataire par le feu*)—a denunciation of indignity and *hogra*. Karima Lazali's critically acclaimed 2018 book *Le trauma colonial* does not offer much of an improvement on Benslama's rudimentary concept of melancholy, even though

---

14. See Martin Heidegger, *Being and Time*, trans. Joan Stambaugh (Albany: SUNY Press, 1996), 262.

15. Benslama, *Soudain la révolution*, 20.

Lazali foregrounds colonial history there where Benslama would foreground Arabic, Islam, or Islamism. For Lazali, and as I mentioned in the introductory chapter, thirteen decades of French colonialism resulted in a complete melancholization (*mélancolisation*) of Algerian society.¹⁶ It is at the level of the "unconscious" that traumatic colonialism in Algeria is still alive and well in the absence of adequate political reckoning (*recevabilité par le politique*).¹⁷ Yet, while she devotes much of her discussion toward the end of the book to Fanon, Lazali does not attend to the decolonializing twists that Fanon incubates into psychoanalytic concepts such as trauma, the unconscious, and especially melancholy. Even if she foregrounds the role of the literary in challenging the indisposition of the political to make reparations, what Lazali's thesis fails to account for is the immanent capacities of Algerian melancholy to induce insurrectionary acts of defiance and revolt against colonial injustice.

As I have demonstrated throughout the book, Arabic novelists, poets, and artists have produced a plethora of examples that evoke the empowering swerves of the disposition toward melancholy. The idiomatic stability of the Arabic language, which for Benslama is tantamount to worldmaking, has been routinely challenged and opened up to host the urgency of historical convulsions. The idiomatic innovations that Mahmoud Darwish has been exploring are a case in point, and I will briefly engage with one final example to recapitulate what I mean by a melancholy swerve. In the titular section of *Diaries of Ordinary Sadness* (يوميّات الحزن العادي), an unclassifiable collection of texts that chronicles Palestinian everydayness under occupation, Darwish starts fragment number seventeen as follows: "أحيانا يلقون عليك القبض وأنت ترتكب الحلم" Literally, this means in English: "They sometimes arrest you while you're committing the dream."¹⁸ In Arabic as in English the expression "ارتكب الحلم" or "to commit the dream" is just not fluent enough—in fact, it is unidiomatic. The right idiomatic expression would be, for instance, "ارتكب جريمة أو خطأ"—that is—"to commit a crime or an error." The particular poetic venture of Darwish, as I see it, consists less in a quixotic rebelliousness against the transhistorical stability of the Arabic idiom as in an imaginative attempt to confront it with the mutability, malleability, and extreme precarity of Arab and Palestinian contemporaneity. His wide-ranging surgical operations on the Arabic idiom seek therefore to transplant it in the Arab and Palestinian present—that is, to

---

16. Karima Lazali, *Le trauma colonial: Une enquête sur les effets psychiques et politiques contemporains de l'oppression coloniale en Algérie* (Paris: La Découverte, 2018), 263.
17. Ibid., 9.
18. Mahmud Darwish, *Yawmiyāt al-ḥuzn al-ʿādī* (Beirut: Riad El-Rayyes Books, 2007), 77.

locate it in and simultaneously open it up to its fierce historical and political reality.

Darwish's poetry stages an ambitious and steady transfiguration and reconfiguration, expropriation, and appropriation of the Arabic idiom in the service of inscribing and articulating history in and through language. This idiomatic neologism, a catachresis of sorts, is undergirded by a poesis and a "poetics of the swerve," in Joan Retallack suggestive expression, which serves not only to unsettle the normative intelligibility of the Arabic idiom but also to inaugurate what Retallack calls "the kind of dynamic present-tense poetics of human rights that might swerve minds out of intractable gridlock."[19] It is no exaggeration to suggest that the suddenness with which the novelty of an idiomatic expression is recognized verges truly on the epiphanic. In "ارتكب الحلم" ("to commit the dream"), for instance, which is, as I mentioned earlier, an idiomatic pun on "ارتكب الجريمة" ("to commit the crime"), the sudden cognizance that this idiomatic neologism departs from the idiom's standard configuration occurs *simultaneously* with the empathic cognizance of the extreme vulnerability of the dispossessed Palestinian whose very ordinary dreams have become incriminating. The epiphany of the idiomatic neologism can potentially inspire not only empathy and solidarity with Palestinians but also empower their will to justice. The melancholy swerve of the new idiom from the dramatization of injustice to the encoded mobilization against it hinges on the empathic jolt of anagnorisis and its generative agentive potentialities.[20]

The haunting resonance of the new idiom, its exposure of the incrimination of Palestinian dreams, may be seen to exacerbate a sense of helpless melancholy, but what I have been driving at throughout this book is that such a conclusion is incomplete because it fails to account for the new idiomatic expression as a melancholy act that incorporates a claim to territorial legitimacy and a restorative project for political agency. The sweeping melancholization without differentiation of Arab culture that has been a staple of orientalist discourse—with the presumption that melancholy is stationary, regressive, and pathological—has done an enormous disservice to a culture that has overall attempted to reroute the political crisis and impotence of Arab contempora-

19. Joan Retallack, *The Poethical Wager* (Berkeley: University of California Press, 2003), 9.
20. I have called this hybrid experience of empathy and epiphany in the related context of Joyce's postcolonial Ireland "empiphany," the recognition of the other at the very moment of his revelation. See Nouri Gana, *Signifying Loss: Toward a Poetics of Narrative Mourning* (Lewisburg, PA: Bucknell University Press, 2014), 66.

neity into literary and artistic projects of investiture and transformative futures. I found myself wondering, perplexedly at times, why a geopolitical region like the Arab world, which has incurred one humiliating colonial defeat after another throughout the twentieth and into the twenty-first century, should be so misconstrued as impotent when it is only experiencing the kind of psychoaffective turmoil that is called for by the seriality of defeats it experienced. Apart from their direct and collateral human toll or material and economic ravages, these repeated colonial assaults resulted in a melancholy disposition whose manifestations range from grief and inconsolability through self-loathing and narcissistic omnipotence, to a melancholy commitment to fallen ideals and lost causes as well as to solidarity with collectively punished and vanquished populations. Unless Arabs are expected to emerge out of these catastrophic defeats totally unscathed, which would be unrealistic, not to say disingenuous, there is a deliberate interest in melancholizing them. Melancholization is not just a passing judgment on the character of Arabs but also a baseless charge that serves both to legitimize Israeli and Euro-American hegemony in the region and to delegitimatize *a priori* any form of resistance to it. Perhaps orientalism is to blame, as it has rigged the discursive playing field at the outset, but the fact is that even sophisticated Arab intellectuals of the postcolonial period have somewhat failed to locate the empowering swerves or potentialities of the corrosive melancholy they noticed about Arab culture, at least since 1967.

This applies not only to Benslama, Lazali, Tarabishi, and Bennabi, whom I discussed before, but also to Abdalla Laroui, whose verdict on Arab nations and Morocco in particular in terms of melancholy belatedness is accurate but incomplete. Laroui's bleak verdict does not hold open a space of enablement or transformation, the kind of space from within which he writes—and melancholically so, I must add: "plus une nation arrive au monde moderne en retard, plus ells vit dans un paysage décoloré . . . sur le mode de la mélancolie" (the more a nation arrives late to the modern world, the more it lives in a dull landscape . . . in the mode of melancholy).[21] Accordingly, Morocco's future will always be France's past. Any proactive catch-up work will only affirm the despondency of Moroccans in the prison house of retardation and belatedness. "Anguished and enraged by what he sees as a predicament of subjugation and impasse, Laroui does not explore," as Stefania Pandolfo aptly pinpoints, "the revolutionary possibilities of the melancholic subject he describes: a subject born from the incorporation of loss, who creates and recreates new worlds in

---

21. Abdalla Laroui, *L'ideologie arabe contemporaine* (Paris: François Maspero, 1982), 49.

a space of unresolvable mourning."[22] Melancholy is bound up with the colossal legacy of colonial injustice, yet Laroui melancholizes (pathologizes) rather than melancholicizes (politicizes) the Arab subject. In other words, rather than seizing upon the vantage point of melancholicizing over loss to inquire about its actantial potential to inform future-oriented subject positions and common decolonial struggles for freedom from colonial injustice, an agenda to which he would surely subscribe, Laroui falls into the melancholizing orientalist trap that reduces melancholy to the *fichue position* of crippling belatedness.

Melancholization may, as is surely the case with Laroui, stem from goodwill (insofar as feelings of indignation, disenchantment, and resentment may serve as incitements to insurrection and revolt), yet it is hard to overestimate its distortive and demoralizing effect. At best, as in the case of Hisham Sharabi, for instance, it may relay a counterintuitive commitment to change: "What is the cause of this abject helplessness, this hopeless disunity, this global collapse? Is it just Zionism, colonialism, imperialism? Or is it something else, something at the heart of the society, some invisible disease eating at the center?"[23] That "disease" is what Sharabi calls "neopatriarchy," the distorted appropriation of modernity, but he forgets to add that neopatriarchy is not the cause of the crisis of Arab contemporaneity but the result of colonial modernity. The "festering cancer is structural," for sure, but neopatriarchy is its symptom.[24] Indeed, neopatriarchy is a symptom and a form of psychopolitical compromise with the disease—colonial modernity. A proverbial oxymoron, colonial modernity in the Arab world is the generative structural origin of all later degenerative distortions. Sharabi's insights here, like Laroui's and Benslama's, fail to paint a full picture and find in reductionist scenarios less troublesome exit strategies. Perhaps in their variedly impatient pursuits to hold Arab intellectuals, language, or religion accountable, they opted in favor of targeted essentialist criticisms rather than in favor of more elaborate and imaginative forms of melancholic critique. They failed to look for rhetorically inflected twists and swerves of melancholy empowerment in the Arab discourse of crisis, but an argument could surely be made

22. Stefania Pandolfo, "The Thin Line of Modernity: Reflections on Some Moroccan Debates on Subjectivity," in *Questions of Modernity*, ed. Timothy Mitchell (Minneapolis: University of Minnesota Press, 2000), 126.

23. Hisham Sharabi, *Neopatriarchy: A Theory of Distorted Change in Arab Society* (New York: Oxford University Press, 1988), viii.

24. See Stephen Sheehi, "Failure, Modernity, and the Works of Hisham Sharabi: Towards a Postcolonial Critique of Arab Subjectivity," *Critique* 6, no. 10 (1997): 40.

that they have reproduced the swerves rather than articulated them, that they are the swerve.[25]

Bouazizi's melancholy fury, resentment and swerve would prove contagious and give rise to a nationwide uprising that permitted his belated identification as a *shahid*. Similarly, his act of self-burning, which recalls the self-immolation acts of social protest by Buddhist monks and nuns against the Diem regime in Vietnam and the Chinese government in Tibet, has been reframed as an act of self-sacrifice and martyrdom rather than a suicide (*intiḥār*). Suicide is forbidden in Islam, and many religious clerics aligned with Arab authoritarian regimes quickly issued fatwas to that effect, but others begged to differ or were simply called upon to confirm what the protestors have already decided: anyone who dies in the mass protests against dictatorship is immediately labeled as a *shahid*—a honorific, redemptive, and celebratory epithet. Today, in several countries across the Arab world, anyone who succumbs to an unjust death is declared a *shahid* by the authorities or by the public sphere, in total disregard of religious decrees or lack thereof. Bouazizi's melancholy act of sociopolitical protest was, *grosso modo*, favorably received worldwide, especially that it started a nationwide revolution which ousted a local dictator but may have already exhausted the critical edge of its spectacular atrocity aesthetics. The melancholy acts I have been concerned with in much of this book will probably never receive such worldwide recognition, even while, as I have argued, they constitute the cultural and critical cumulative groundwork on which mass protests hinge.

The challenge I have set myself in this book is to demonstrate how Arab contemporaneity (insofar as it is visible in Arabic literature and culture) is informed by a psychoaffective disposition toward melancholy—a melancholy from which and, paradoxically, through which it tries to decolonize itself and inspire viable futures. The coercive forces of Zionism and global neoliberal imperialism continue to produce and reproduce almost all aspects of Arabic literature and culture not only by inflicting on the Arab psyche unquantifiable pain and suffering but also by setting insurmountable constraints on the creative imagination. Not unlike everyday Arabs, Arab littérateurs and artists find themselves caught in such a finite psychic economy in which the full recovery *from* melancholy is seemingly as impossible as recovery *through* it. They dramatize *by* and *through* their works melancholy acts, playing the impossibility of bringing about change against their enduring commitment to change and "the profound hopelessness of the struggle" against "the still more

---

25. This is indeed the topic of a related book project in progress, tentatively titled *Arab Melancholia*.

profound hopelessness of its abandonment."[26] I have found nothing better to approximate the diversity of the psychoaffective forcefields and fecundity of feelings from within which much works of literature and culture are produced other than the concept of melancholy precisely because it is a capacious concept that best accounts for intellectual and creative ambivalence and for enduring cultural and political resistance as much as for the visceral vicissitudes into fantasies of omnipotence, madness, and suicide, all of which continue to cast the concept of melancholy with visions of gloom and morbid apprehensions. Covering a spectrum of affective differentials, melancholy assumes discrepant postures and psychopolitical *force-feelings* that range from solipsistic self-loathing and narcissistic omnipotence through reactionary leaps into (suicidal) violence, to the introspective and retrospective critical dimensions with which I have been largely preoccupied throughout this book, and without which no grand artistic achievement is conceivable in the contemporary Arab world, or, for that matter, a decolonial project of emancipation.

To attend to the complexity and multiplexity of Arabic literature and culture today we need a composite and multipronged concept of critique— *melancholy critique*—that can travel the distance between an attention to the empowering particularities of poetic and visual form and an interrogation of local authoritarian and foreign imperial hegemony as well as a scrupulous scrutiny of cultural fantasies of past and future omnipotence, theirs and ours, no matter how unconscious and anachronistic they may or can be. After all, and as I have suggested in my reflections on Darwish's idiomatic neologisms (for instance, "*tuṣbiḥūna ʿalā waṭan*" or "May you wake up to a homeland"), melancholy critique is not beholden to national allegory because of its claim for freedom from injustice, but holds open, above all, an allegory of becoming, a decolonial allegory that may do away with the nationalist imaginary *once* it is achieved. Unlike the "melancholy pride" that has inaugurated and anticipated the fulfillment of the Zionist project of capturing Palestine and dispossessing Palestinians, melancholy critique boasts no such pride except in its commitment to the discernment and exposure of the injustices the Zionist project committed, disavowed, or assimilated in the process of its settler colonial state formation.[27]

---

26. Georg Lukács, *The Theory of the Novel*, trans. Anna Bostock (Cambridge, MA: MIT Press, 1971), 86.

27. In Mark Gelber's *Melancholy Pride*, there is a sense in which German cultural Zionism projected a discourse of melancholy and nostalgia for the would-be-left-behind European Jewish homeland that nevertheless found immediate consolation in the much-anticipated possession of the newfound Oriental land. This melancholy discourse not only propelled at the outset

EPILOGUE: MELANCHOLY CRITIQUE

The melancholy disposition, by no means monolithic or homogenous, that I have examined in Arabic literature and culture has not so far garnered the attention of critical work or constituted the object of any given theoretical inquiry into Arab contemporaneity even while it is quite visible at the level of cultural and literary production, nonfictional discursive practices, and even everyday language. It is as if by dismissing melancholy *a priori* as corrosive and narcissistically regressive, critics assume they have conjured it away, that they don't have to deal with it anymore, or that it no longer exists. Yet, this melancholy disposition has continually exerted enormous pressures on the creative imagination such that to attend to it one has to read as it were *melancholically*—that is, to read scrupulously with an eye for what is lost and what remains and for what is silent, inarticulate, or opaque, and to discern meanwhile the kernel of theoretical impasses, the tactical swerves of resistance, and the clamor for freedom from injustice as well as the staggering fidelity to agentive possibility in the midst of poetic fragility and invisible pain. Consider, for instance, the kind of poetic fidelity and fragility that the late Mourid Barghouti dramatizes when he asserts quite melancholically: "I see a wonderful dream collapse but I do not abandon it" (أبصرُ موت حُلمٍ رائع وأواصله).[28] It is this persistent attachment to a dream that for Darwish had become incriminating that bespeaks a poesis and a poetics of ethical and political responsibility, "with the courage of the swerve."[29]

It is as if hope had become the psychopolitical locus of a cruel commitment *par excellence*, the unyielding commitment to continuing the dream from within the harsh consciousness of its collapse. For, after all, and in Wannous's memorable aphoristic and aporetic formulation: "We are condemned to hope and what is happening today cannot be the end of history" (إننا محكومون بالأمل.وما يحدث اليوم لا يمكن أن يكون نهاية التاريخ).[30] Note here the polysemy of Wannous's

---

the settler colonial impulse of the Zionist project, but it also made the occupation of Palestine the very condition for Zionism to achieve emotional closure. See Mark H. Gelber, *Melancholy Pride: Nation, Race, and Gender in the German Literature of Cultural Zionism* (Tübingen: Max Niemeyer Verlag, 2000), 276. This goes to say, in turn, that Zionist manipulation of grief and victimhood is not a post-Holocaust phenomenon but a foundational principle of Zionism and that grief, while an indispensable human affect, was aligned in this case with settler colonialism in as much as it is aligned nowadays with consumerist culture and the commodification of emotional resilience and exchange.

28. Mourid Barghouti, *Ṭāla al-Shatāt* (No End to the Diaspora) (Beirut: Dar al-Kalima, 1987), 105.

29. Retallack, *The Poethical Wager*, 3.

30. Saadallah Wannous, "Al-Jūʻ ilā al-ḥiwār" (The Hunger for Dialogue), *Al-Aʻmāl al-Kāmila* (Damascus: Al-Ahālī, 1996), 1:19.

maḥkūmūn, whose three-letter root *ḥa-ka-ma* could mean "sentence," "rule," or "referee," and any of these root-meanings would make sense as a translation. But given his Sartrean existentialist politics, and Sartre's assertion that "man is condemned to be free," it is best to translate *maḥkūmūn* as "condemned."[31] We can only wonder though about the measure of Wannous's melancholic attachment to hope given that he was terminally ill when he reiterated twice this statement in a poignant 1996 UNESCO World Theater Day Message, one year before his passing, and given that less than twenty years earlier he had seriously attempted suicide by overdose following Sadat's visit to Israel on November 19, 1977, in preparation for what would become the 1978–79 Camp David Accords between Egypt and Israel. Wannous, who can be said to have journeyed between both ends of the spectrum of melancholy, best knows the extent to which this psychoaffective disposition has become a condition of subjective and collective empowerment or disempowerment in the Arab world (to the extent that liberation from melancholy may be less feasible than liberation through it). My contentment in this book is that the melancholy psychic apparatus is a psychopolitical formation that is historically produced and that, without sensitivity to this stark fact of which the colonial Arab present is an extension, we may be able to neither better appreciate its empowering apertures nor contain its disempowering vicissitudes.

A comprehensive or nationally specific theory arising out of the disjuncture between the political impoverishment and cultural proliferation of the Arab world cries out for elaboration. *Melancholy Acts* will only partly fill this void in the theoretical engagement with the conflictual forces that propel Arabic literary and cultural production. The notion of defeat that has come to mark and define an entire region has in the meanwhile elided a rich cultural history of critique and painful struggle to defeat the very hold of defeat itself, to decolonize the mind and psyche which have been numbed by the disarming specter of unmitigated defeat. What is proposed here is by no means a master theory that is detailed enough to reflect the oftentimes breathtaking untidiness and twisted operations of Arab culture. Throughout the book, I pull together multiple connections between different genres of literary and cultural production, but I also devote entire chapters to specific works of particular national literatures and cultures in order to dig deeply into particular issues. Most of the findings are generalizable, but that is a project for others to take over if they so wish to do. My goal has never been to be exhaustive but rather illustrative, and to highlight an eclectic yet cohesive set of case studies that

---

31. Jean-Paul Sartre, *Existentialism as Humanism*, trans. Carol Macomber (New Haven, CT: Yale University Press, 2007), 29.

EPILOGUE: MELANCHOLY CRITIQUE

cut across a plethora of topics, genres, and discursive practices. Yet, one cannot help but be struck by the zeal whereby Arab culture never ceased to assert itself, to draw attention to itself, to defy and to dissent from dominant political trends and hegemonies. The dynamics of this culture far exceed the many policies and regulations by which it is produced and overseen. It is my hope that such an approach will prove productive and encourage multiple other engagements with the poorly understood valences of the melancholy disposition in Arabic literature and culture.

Acknowledgments

This book has been several years in the making. It evolves out of my first book, *Signifying Loss: Toward a Poetics of Narrative Mourning* (2011), in which I call for a geopolitics of mourning capable of attending to the sociohistorical, psychocultural, and circumstantial particularities in which mourning and melancholia arise and continue to arise or fail to arise and continue to fail to arise. *Melancholy Acts* is the closest I have come to elaborating a geopolitics of affect in the complex postcolonial colonial context of the Arab world from the Nakba (1948) to the Naksa (1967) and beyond. I have come to realize throughout that what I am after is a comparative ethics of reading the narrative temporalities of the psyche at the crossroads of geopolitics and poetic form. Affect is a cause!

Throughout the various stages of the process, from conception to completion, I have incurred numerous debts that I would like to acknowledge, however inadequately. While revising and preparing the final manuscript for submission to the press, I have benefited immensely from the incisive comments and invaluable feedback that Samera Esmeir, Hala Halim, Stefania Pandolfo, and Soraya Tlatli generously offered on different chapters of the book. I am very grateful for the many supportive and fruitful conversations I have had in person or over the phone with many friends and kindred spirits: Hosam Aboul-Ela, Samera Esmeir, Hala Halim, Nizar Hermes, Efraín Kristal, Kirstie McClure, Nabil Matar, Waïl Hassan, Adnan Husain, Firat Oruc, Stefania Pandolfo, Jeff Sacks, Stephanie Bosch Santana, and Soraya Tlatli.

I am fortunate to have had the opportunity to present draft portions of the book-in-progress in invited talks, workshops, and conferences at, among others, UC, Berkeley; UC, Riverside; UC Santa Cruz; NYU; NYU, Abu Dhabi;

University of Georgetown, Qatar; University of Michigan, Ann Arbor; University of Wisconsin, Milwaukee; Arizona State University, Tempe; University of Virginia; University of Perugia, Italy; and University of Manouba, Tunisia. I am very thankful to the organizers of these events for their invitations and hospitality and to the participants for their challenging questions and feedback. I especially want to thank Jeff Sacks for inviting me to UC Riverside more than once.

I am grateful to my students and mentees, my most inspiring interlocutors, for the many rigorous intellectual discussions we have had over the last dozen years. I wish I could thank you each individually but I must thank you en masse. I am sure some of the ideas that crystallized in my mind during these productive engagements inside and outside seminar rooms and lecture halls must have found their way into *Melancholy Acts* in ways that I can neither discern nor account for. For providing a sense of belonging to a vibrant intellectual community, I am particularly grateful to my colleagues at UCLA: Whitney Arnold, Domenico Ingenito, Eleanor Kaufman, Efraín Kristal, Kathleen L. Komar, Tamara Levitz, Kirstie McClure, David MacFadyen, Aamir Mufti, Anjali Prabhu, Michael Rothberg, Shu-mei Shih, Stephanie Bosch Santana, and Zrinka Stahuljak.

I am indebted to the anonymous press referees for their thorough reports and constructive criticisms which helped steer my final revisions of the manuscript. I also benefited a great deal from the insightful commentaries on my work by the anonymous reviewers (you know who are!) of my research and promotion file for UCLA. Warm thanks to the production and editorial staff at Fordham University Press particularly to Eric Newman who shepherded the project through the various stages of the process during challenging times. I especially want to thank Thomas Lay for his instinctive faith in the value of the project. Profuse thanks to Haitham Khatib for providing multiple shots of the cover art and to Mark Lerner for the design of the book cover. I owe special thanks to Omar Khalifah for helping me connect to the artist whose artwork graces the front cover of this book.

Short and significantly different versions of the six chapters of the book appeared at various points in time over the last decade in the following peer-reviewed journals: *Representations* 143 (2018); *Psychoanalysis and History* 20.3 (2018); *The Journal of North African Studies* 15.1 (2010); *Public Culture* 22.1 (2010), and *Comparative Studies of South Asia, Africa and the Middle East* 28.1 (2008). An earlier version of chapter 3 appeared in the *MLA Approaches to Teaching the Works of Naguib Mahfouz* (2012), edited by Waïl S. Hassan and Susan Muaddi Darraj, and a short section of chapter 6 appeared in *After Lacan* (2018), edited by Ankhi Mukherjee. I am grateful to the editors of these two volumes and to all the anonymous readers of the journals for their trenchant criticisms and to the publishers for their kind permission to incorporate copyrighted material into *Melancholy Acts*. All these previously published versions have been either entirely rewritten and reconfigured or thoroughly revised and expanded prior to inclusion into the book.

The Unsheltering Sky: A Note on the Cover Art

The cover image is of a sculpture representing twelve-year-old Palestinian boy, Muhammad al-Durrah, and his father, Jamal al-Durrah. The photographer and sculptor, Haitham Khatib, is an activist, artist, freelance photojournalist, and documentary filmmaker, based in the West Bank. Khatib made the sculpture by bending, twisting, binding, and cutting recycled metal wires into the shape of Muhammad and Jamal al-Durrah to mark the murder of the fifth grader by the Israeli Defense Forces (IDF) on September 30, 2000, the second day of the Second Intifada (aka, al-Aqsa Intifada, 2000–2005). The sculpture is based on a still from a live video shot on Saladin Road, south of Gaza City, by freelance cameraman, Talal Abu Rahma, and aired on France 2 with a voiceover by Charles Enderlin, the France 2 bureau chief in Jerusalem.

The 59-second-video footage shows the father and son hunkering down and taking cover behind a concrete cylinder to avoid an avalanche of gunfire coming from across the Netzarim junction, where the two-story outpost of the IDF is located; the terrified son can be seen wailing and clinging to his father who is trying to protect him with his right hand while waving and screaming for help; the final segment shows, once the bloodletting has subsided, the father sitting upright, dizzied and injured, and the boy lying down motionless in his lap. He was fatally shot with an explosive bullet in the abdomen. The father survived the shooting but was critically wounded by nine bullets.

The graphic video footage went viral, and Muhammad al-Durrah became a symbol of the Second Intifada and a transnational rallying cry for mobilizations against the occupation. Israel initially issued a statement accepting IDF responsibility for the murder but retracted it in 2005 and sought instead to cast doubt on the veracity of the raw video footage. Israel's default alibi for targeting children has always been that Palestinians use children as human shields. Both father and son were coming from a car auction and were passing by the junction after getting off a cab; they were neither demonstrators, nor human shields in the unsheltering skies of Gaza. The video captures the gnawing disparity between Israel's global image as a refuge for world Jewry from persecution and its bleak reality as a settler colonial and ethnocidal apartheid state.

The raw footage resonated worldwide because it unmasked, for probably the first time since the 1987 Intifada, the ruthlessness of IDF violence against defenseless civilians and children. Khatib's sculpture dramatizes the eloquent helplessness and selflessness of a father as he tries to shield his son with his right arm from the raging gunfire. According to Khatib, the sculpture immortalizes al-Durrah and inspires an enduring sense of collectivity and solidarity across time and space. Its uncanny aesthetic poignancy evokes the ingenuity of artistic commitment while its intricately interwoven wire fabric enacts the spiraling struggle against erasure and the melancholic longing for freedom from injustice in Palestine.

Bibliography

Abdelkader, Bouarfa. *Malek Bennabi: Une vie, une oeuvre, un combat*. Casablanca: Centre Culturel du Livre, 2019.
Abdel-Malek, Anouar. *The Army Regime, The Left, and Social Change under Nasser*. Translated by Charles Lam Markmann. New York: Random House, 1968.
Aboul-Ela, Hosam. *Domestications: American Empire, Literary Culture, and the Postcolonial Lens*. Evanston, IL: Northwestern University Press, 2018.
Abufarha, Nasser. *The Making of a Human Bomb: An Ethnography of Palestinian Resistance*. Durham, NC: Duke University Press, 2009.
Abu-Assad, Hany, dir. *Paradise Now* (Al-Jannah-tul-'Ān). Burbank, CA: Warner Home Video, 2006.
Adonis. *An Introduction to Arab Poetics*. Translated by Catherine Cobham. London: Saqi Books, 1990.
———. *Sufism and Surrealism*. Translated by Judith Cumberbatch. London: Saqi, 2016.
Adorno, Theodor. "Commitment." In *Aesthetics and Politics*, edited by Ronald Taylor, 177–195. New York: Verso, 1980.
———. "The Meaning of Working Through the Past." In *Critical Models: Interventions and Catchwords*, translated by Henry W. Pickford, 89–103. New York: Columbia University Press, 1998.
———. *Minima Moralia*. Translated by E. F. N. Jephcott. London: Verso, 1984.
———. *Negative Dialectics*. Translated by E. B. Ashton. New York: Continuum, 1973.
———. *Prisms*. Translated by Samuel Weber and Shierry Weber. Cambridge, MA: MIT Press, 1988.
Agamben, Giorgio. *Stanzas: Word and Phantasm in Western Culture*. Translated by Ronald L. Martinez. Minneapolis: University of Minnesota Press, 1993.
Ahmed, Leila. *Women and Gender in Islam: Historical Roots of a Modern Debate*. New Haven, CT: Yale University Press, 1992.

Ahmed, Sara. "Happy Objects." In *The Affect Theory Reader*, edited by Melissa Gregg and Gregory J. Seigworth, 29–51. Durham, NC: Duke University Press, 2010.

Al-Attabi, Qussay. "The Polemics of Iltizām: *Al-Ādāb*'s Early Arguments for Commitment." *Journal of Arabic Literature* 52 (2021): 124–146.

Amin, Qasim. *The Liberation of Women and the New Woman: Two Documents in the History of Egyptian Feminism*. Translated by Samiha Sidhom Peterson. Cairo: American University in Cairo Press, 2001.

Anderson, J. N. D. "The Tunisian Law of Personal Status." *International and Comparative Law Quarterly* 7, no. 2 (1958): 262–79.

Apollon, Willy. "The Untreatable." Translated by Steven Miller. *Umbr(a): The Journal of the Unconscious* 1 (2006): 23–39.

Armes, Roy. *Postcolonial Images: Studies in North African Film*. Bloomington: Indiana University Press, 2005.

Asad, Talal. "Conscripts of Western Civilization." *Dialectical Anthropology: Essays in Honor of Stanley Diamond*, vol. 1, *Civilization in Crisis*, edited by Christine Gailey, 333–51. Gainesville: University Press of Florida, 1992.

———. *On Suicide Bombing*. New York: Columbia University Press, 2007.

Atzmon, Gilad. *The Wandering Who? A Study of Jewish Identity Politics*. Washington, DC: Zero Books, 2011.

Ayeb, Habib, and Ray Bush. *Food Insecurity and Revolution in the Middle East and North Africa*. London: Anthem Press, 2019.

Badawi, M. M. "Commitment in Contemporary Arabic Literature." In *Arabic Literature and the West*, edited by M. M. Badawi, 1–25. London: Ithaca Press, 1985.

Badiou, Alain. *Infinite Thought: Truth and the Return to Philosophy*. London: Continuum, 2005.

———. *The Rebirth of History: Times of Riots and Uprisings*. Translated by Gregory Elliott. New York: Verso, 2012.

Badri, Malik. *Dilemma of Muslim Psychologists*. London: NWH London Publishers, 1979.

Bal, Mieke. "The Story of W." In *A Mieke Bal Reader*, 40–67. Chicago: University of Chicago Press, 2006.

Barakat, Halim. *The Arab World: Society, Culture, and State*. Berkeley: University of California Press, 1993.

Barghouti, Mourid. *Tāla al-Shatāt* (No End to the Diaspora). Beirut: Dar al-Kalima, 1987.

Barthes, Roland. *The Neutral: Lecture Course at the Collège de France (1977–1978)*. Translated by Rosalind E. Krauss and Denis Hollier. New York: Columbia University Press, 2005.

———. *Writing Degree Zero*. Translated by Annette Lavers and Colin Smith. New York: Hill & Wang, 1968.

Bayat, Asef. *Life as Politics: How Ordinary People Change the Middle East*. Stanford, CA: Stanford University Press, 2010.

Beinin, Joel. *Was the Red Flag Flying There? Marxist Politics and the Arab-Israeli Conflict in Egypt and Israel, 1948–1965*. Berkeley: University of California Press, 1990.

Beinin, Joel, and Zachary Lockman. *Workers on the Nile: Nationalism, Communism, Islam, and the Egyptian Working Class, 1882–1954*. London: IB Tauris & Co., 1988.

Béji, Hélé. *Désenchantement national: Essai sur la décolonisation*. Paris: François Maspero, 1982.

Benda, Julien. *The Treason of the Intellectuals*. Translated by Richard Aldington. New Brunswick, NJ: Transaction Publishers, 2009.

Benjamin, Walter. *Illuminations: Essays and Reflections*. Translated by Harry Zohn. New York: Schocken Books, 1969.

———. "Left-Wing Melancholy." In *Selected Writings: Volume 2: 1927–1934*. Edited by Michael W. Jennings. Cambridge, MA: Belknap Press, 1999.

———. *The Origin of German Tragic Drama*. Translated by John Osborne. New York: Verso, 1998.

———. *Origin of the German Trauerspiel*. Translated by Howard Eiland. Cambridge, MA: Harvard University Press, 2019.

Bennabi, Malek. *Vocation de l'Islam*. Algiers: Edition ANEP, 2006.

Bennani, Jalil. *Le sacré, cet obscure objet de désir?* Paris: Éditions Albin Michel, 2009.

Bensaïd, Daniel. *An Impatient Life: A Memoir*. Translated by David Fernbach. London: Verso, 2014.

———. *Le pari mélancolique: Métamorphoses de la politique, politique des métamorphoses*. Paris: Fayard, 1997.

Benslama, Fethi. "Dying for Justice." Translated by Roland Végsö. *Umbr(a)*: Islam (2009): 13–23.

———. "L'agonie pour la justice." *Topiques* 1, no. 102 (2008): 71–82.

———. "L'agonie pour la justice." In *La guerre des subjectivités en Islam*, 43–64. Tunis: Cérès, 2014.

———. *La nuit brisée: Mohammad et l'énonciation islamique*. Paris: Ramsay, 1988.

———. *Psychoanalysis and the Challenge of Islam*. Translated by Robert Bononno. Minneapolis: University of Minnesota Press, 2009.

———. *Soudain la révolution! Géopsychanalyse d'un soulèvement*. Tunis: Cérès, 2011.

———. *Un furieux désir de sacrifice: Le surmusulman*. Paris: Seuil, 2016.

Berkley, Anthony R. "Respecting Maya Language Revitalization." *Linguistics and Education* 12, no. 3 (2001): 345–66.

Best, Stephen, and Sharon Marcus. "Surface Reading: An Introduction." *Representations* 108, no. 1 (2009): 1–21.

Bitton, Simone, dir. *Mahmoud Darwish: As the Land Is the Language/Et la terre comme la langue*. Seattle: Arab Film Distribution, 1997.

Borowiec, Andrew. *Modern Tunisia: A Democratic Apprenticeship*. Westport, CT: Praeger, 1998.

Borradori, Giovanna. *Philosophy in a Time of Terror: Dialogues with Jürgen Habermas and Jacques Derrida*. Chicago: University of Chicago Press, 2003.
Botman, Selma. *The Rise of Egyptian Communism, 1939–1970*. Syracuse, NY: Syracuse University Press, 1988.
Boughedir, Férid, dir. *Halfaouine: Boy of the Terraces*. Paris and Tunis: Ciné Télé Tilms & Scarabée Films, 1990.
Bouhdiba, Abdelwahab. *Sexuality in Islam*. Translated by Alan Sheridan. London: Routledge, 1985.
Bourdieu, Pierre. *The Masculine Domination*. Translated by Richard Nice. Stanford, CA: Stanford University Press, 2001.
Bourguiba, Habib. "For Ramadan Reform." In *The Contemporary Middle East: Tradition and Innovation*, edited by Benjamin Rivlin and Joseph S. Szyliowicz, 169–73. New York: Random House, 1965.
———. *Ma vie, mes idées, mon combat*. Tunis: Ministère de l'Information, 1977.
———. "The Tunisian Way." *Foreign Affairs* 44, no. 3 (1966): 480–88.
Bouzid, Nouri, dir. *Man of Ashes*. Tunis and Paris: Ciné Télé Films & La Médiathèque des Trois Mondes, 1986.
———. "New Realism in Arab Cinema: The Defeat-Conscious Cinema." Translated by Shereen el Ezabi. *Alif: Journal of Comparative Poetics* 15 (1995): 242–50.
———. "On Inspiration." In *African Experiences of Cinema*, edited by Imruh Bakari and Mbye B. Cham, 48–59. London: British Film Institute, 1996.
Brown, Wendy. *Politics out of History*. Princeton, NJ: Princeton University Press, 2001.
———. "Resisting Left Melancholia." In *Loss: The Politics of Mourning*, edited by David L. Eng and David Kazanjian, 458–65. Berkeley: University of California Press, 2003.
Butler, Judith. *Precarious Life: The Powers of Mourning and Violence*. New York: Verso, 2004.
———. *The Psychic Life of Power: Theories in Subjection*. Stanford, CA: Stanford University Press, 1997.
———. *Undoing Gender*. New York: Routledge, 2004.
Camau, Michel, and Vincent Geisser. *Le syndrome autoritaire*. Paris: Presses de Sciences Po, 2003.
Camus, Albert. *The Myth of Sisyphus*. Translated by Justin O'Brien. New York: Penguin, 1979.
Chow, Rey. *Primitive Passions: Visuality, Sexuality, Ethnography, and Contemporary Chinese Cinema*. New York: Columbia University Press, 1995.
———. *The Protestant Ethnic and the Spirit of Capitalism*. New York: Columbia University Press, 2002.
Colla, Elliott. "Badr Shākir al-Sayyāb, Cold War Poet." *Middle Eastern Literatures* 18, no. 3 (2015): 247–63.
Curtiss, R. H. "Women's Rights: An Affair of State for Tunisia." *Washington Report on Middle East Affairs* 12, no. 3 (September/October 1993): 50–51.

Dabashi, Hamid. *Dreams of a Nation: On Palestinian Cinema*. New York: Verso, 2006.
Darraj, Faisal. "The June War and the Foundation of Generative Defeat." *Majallat al-Dirasat al-Filastiniyya* 111 (2017): 47–50.
Darwish, Mahmoud. *The Butterfly's Burden: Poems by Mahmoud Darwish*. Translated by Fady Joudah. Port Townsend, WA: Copper Canyon Press, 2007.
———. *Dhākira lil-nisyān* (Memory for Forgetfulness). Beirut: Riad El-Rayyes, 2007.
———. *Ḥayrat al-ʿāʾid* (The Hesitant Homecomer). Beirut: Riad El-Rayyes, 2007.
———. *Ka-zahr al-Lawz aw abʿad* (Like Almond Flowers or Further). Beirut: Riad El-Rayyes, 2005.
———. *In the Presence of Absence*. Translated by Sinan Antoon. New York: Archipelago Books, 2011.
———. *Memory for Forgetfulness*. Translated by Ibrahim Muhawi. Berkeley: University of California Press, 1995.
———. *A River Dies of Thirst: Journals*. Translated by Catherine Cobham. New York: Archipelago Books, 2009.
———. *Ward Aqall* (Fewer Roses). Beirut: Almu'assassa Al-ʿArabiyya Lildirāsāt wa Al-nashr, 1987.
———. *Yawmiyāt al-ḥuzn al-ʿādī*. Beirut: Riad El-Rayyes Books, 2007.
Debord, Guy. *The Society of the Spectacle*. Translated by Donald Nicholson-Smith. New York: Zone Books, 1995.
Deleuze, Gilles. *Difference and Repetition*. Translated by Paul Patton. New York: Columbia University Press, 1995.
Deleuze, Gilles, and Felix Guattari. *Anti-Oedipus: Capitalism and Schizophrenia*. Translated by Robert Hurley, Mark Seem, and Helen R. Lane. Minneapolis: University of Minnesota Press, 1983.
Derrida, Jacques. *Acts of Religion*. Edited by Gil Anidjar. New York: Routledge, 2002.
———. *Demeure: Fiction and Testimony*. Translated by Elizabeth Rottenberg. Stanford, CA: Stanford University Press, 2000.
———. *Rogues: Two Essays on Reason*. Stanford, CA: Stanford University Press, 2005.
———. *A Taste for the Secret*. Translated by Giacomo Donis. Edited by Giacomo Donis and David Webb. Cambridge: Polity Press, 2001.
———. *The Work of Mourning*. Edited by Pascale-Anne Brault and Michael Naas. Chicago: University of Chicago Press, 2001.
Djebar, Assia. *A Sister to Scheherazade*. Translated by Dorothy S. Blair. Portsmouth, NH: Heineman, 1987.
Dubiel, Helmut. "Beyond Mourning and Melancholy on the Left." *Praxis International* 10, nos. 3–4 (1990–91): 241–49.
Dürrenmatt, Friedrich. *The Visit: A Tragicomedy*. In *Selected Writings: Volume 1, Plays*. Translated by Joel Agee. Edited by Brian Evenson, Kenneth J. Northcott, and Theodore Ziolkowski. Chicago: University of Chicago Press 2006.

El Shakry, Omnia. "The Arabic Freud: The Unconscious and the Modern Subject." *Modern Intellectual History* 11, no. 1 (2014): 89–118.
Eliot, T. S. *The Complete Poems and Plays 1909–1950*. New York: Harcourt, 1971.
Esmeir, Samera. *Juridical Humanity: A Colonial History*. Stanford, CA: Stanford University Press, 2012.
———. "1948: Law, History, Memory." *Social Text* 21, no. 2 (2003): 25–48.
Espinosa, Julio García. "Meditations on Imperfect Cinema . . . Fifteen Years Later." In *New Latin American Cinema: Theory, Practices and Transcontinental Articulations*, translated by Michael Chanan and edited by Michael T. Martin, 83–85. Detroit, MI: Wayne State University Press, 1997.
Fabian, Johannes. *Time and the Other: How Anthropology Makes Its Object*. New York: Columbia University Press, 2014.
Fanon, Frantz. *Alienation and Freedom*. Edited by Robert Young and Jean Khalfa. Translated by Steven Corcoran. London: Bloomsbury, 2018.
———. *A Dying Colonialism*. Translated by Haakon Chevalier. New York: Grove Press, 1965.
———. *The Wretched of the Earth*. Translated by Constance Farrington. New York: Grove Press, 1963.
Fares, Nadia, dir. *Honey and Ashes*. Zürich and Tunis: Dschoint Ventschr AG and CTV Services, 1996.
Felski, Rita. *The Limits of Critique*. Chicago: University of Chicago Press, 2015.
Fink, Bruce. "Knowledge and Jouissance." In *Reading Seminar XX: Lacan's Major Work on Love, Knowledge, and Feminine Sexuality*, edited by Suzanne Bernard and Bruce Fink, 21–46. Albany: State University of New York Press, 2002.
Flatley, Jonathan. *Affective Mapping: Melancholia and the Politics of Modernism*. Cambridge, MA: Harvard University Press, 2008.
Foucault, Michel. *Dits et Ecrits II, 1976–1988*. Paris: Gallimard, 2001.
Freud, Sigmund. *Art and Literature*. London: Penguin, 1990.
———. *On Metapsychology: The Theory of Psychoanalysis*. Translated by J. Strachey. Edited by A. Richards. London: Penguin, 1991.
Frey, Hans-Jost. *Interruptions*. Albany: State University of New York Press, 1996.
Fromm, Erich. *Psychoanalysis and Religion*. New Haven and London: Yale University Press, 1978.
Gabriel, Teshome H. *Third Cinema in the Third World: The Aesthetics of Liberation*. Ann Arbor, MI: UMI Research Press, 1982.
Gana, Nouri. "Introduction: Collaborative Revolutionism." In *The Making of the Tunisian Revolution: Contexts, Architects, Prospects*, edited by Nouri Gana, 1–31. Edinburgh: Edinburgh University Press, 2013.
———. *Signifying Loss: Toward A Poetics of Narrative Mourning*. Lewisburg, PA: Bucknell University Press, 2014.
———. "Sons of a Beach: The Politics of Bastardy in the Cinema of Nouri Bouzid." *Cultural Politics* 13, no. 2 (2017): 177–193.

Gauch, Suzanne. *Liberating Shahrazad: Feminism, Postcolonialism, and Islam.* Minneapolis: University of Minnesota Press, 2007.
Geer, Benjamin. "Prophets and Priests of the Nation: Naguib Mahfouz's *Karnak Café* and the 1967 Crisis in Egypt." *International Journal of Middle East Studies* 41 (2009): 653–69.
Gelber, Mark H. *Melancholy Pride: Nation, Race, and Gender in the German Literature of Cultural Zionism.* Tübingen: Max Niemeyer Verlag, 2000.
Genet, Jean. "Four Hours in Shatila." Translated by Daniel R. Dupêcher and Martha Perrigaud. *Journal of Palestine Studies* 12, no. 3 (1983): 3–22.
Ghorbal, Samy. *Orphelins de Bourguiba et héritiers du prophète.* Tunis: Cérès, 2012.
Gilroy, Paul. *Postcolonial Melancholia.* New York: Columbia University Press, 2004.
Ginat, Rami. *Egypt's Incomplete Revolution: Lutfi Al-Khuli and Nasser's Socialism in the 1960s.* London: Frank Cass, 1997.
Glissant, Edouard. *Caribbean Discourse.* Translated by J. Michael Dash. Charlottesville: University Press of Virginia, 1992.
Grigg, Russell. "Melancholia and the Unabandoned Object." In *Lacan on Madness: Madness, Yes You Can't*, edited by Patricia Gherovici and Manya Steinkoler, 139–58. New York: Routledge, 2015.
Haddad, Tahir. *Imra'atuna fi-l-shari'a wa-l-mujtama'* (Our Woman in Islamic Law and Society). Sousse: Dar al-Ma'arif, 1930.
Hage, Ghassan. "'Comes a Time We Are All Enthusiasm': Understanding Palestinian Suicide Bombers in Times of Exighophobia." *Public Culture* 15, no. 1 (2003): 65–89.
Hallaq, Wael B. *The Impossible State: Islam, Politics, and Modernity's Moral Predicament.* New York: Columbia University Press, 2013.
Heidegger, Martin. *Being and Time.* Translated by Joan Stambaugh. Albany: SUNY Press, 1996.
Hochberg, Gil. "National Allegories and the Emergence of Female Voice in Moufida Tlatli's *Les Silences du palais*." *Third Text* 14, no. 50 (2000): 33–44.
Hoffman, Eva. *Lost in Translation: A Life in a New Language.* New York: Dutton, 1989.
Holt, Elizabeth M. "'Bread or Freedom': The Congress for Cultural Freedom, the CIA, and the Arabic Literary Journal *Hiwār* (1962–67)." *Journal of Arabic Literature* 44 (2013): 83–102.
Homayounpour, Gohar. *Doing Psychoanalysis in Tehran.* Cambridge, MA: MIT Press, 2012.
Hopwood, Derek. *Habib Bourguiba of Tunisia: The Tragedy of Longevity.* London: Macmillan, 1992.
Horkheimer, Max, and Theodor W. Adorno. *The Dialectic of Enlightenment.* Translated by John Cumming. New York: Continuum, 1989.
Hussein, Taha. "Al-Adab bayna al-Ittiṣāl wal-Infiṣāl." *Al-Kātib al-Maṣrī* 3, no. 11 (1946): 373–88.

———. "Fil-Adab Al-Firansī: Jean-Paul Sartre wal-Sīnemā." *Al-Kātib al-Maṣrī* 7, no. 26 (1947): 179–202.
———. "Mulāḥẓāt." *Al-Kātib al-Maṣrī* 6, no. 21 (1947): 9–21.
Ibn Manzur, Abul Fadl Djamal al-Din Muhammad ibn Makram. *Lisan al-'Arab*. Beirut: Dar Al-Jeel, 1988.
Ibrahim, Sonallah. *67*. Cairo: Dār al-Thaqāfa al-Gedīda, 2017.
———. *That Smell and Notes from Prison*. Translated by Robyn Creswell. New York: New Directions, 2013.
Idriss, Suhail. "Risālat al-Adab" (The Message of al-Adab). *Al-Adab* 1, no. 1 (1953): 1–2.
James, C. L. R. *The Black Jacobins: Toussaint L'Ouverture and the San Domingo Revolution*. New York: Vintage Books, 1989.
Jameson, Frederic. *The Political Unconscious: Narrative as a Socially Symbolic Act*. New York: Routledge, 1983.
———. *Postmodernism, or, The Cultural Logic of Late Capitalism*. Durham, NC: Duke University Press, 1991.
———. "Third-World Literature in the Era of Multinational Capitalism." *Social Text* 15 (1986): 65–88.
Jankowski, James. *Nasser's Egypt, Arab Nationalism, and the United Arab Republic*. Boulder, CO: Lynne Rienner, 2001.
Joseph, Suad, ed. *Intimate Selving in Arab Families*. Syracuse, NY: Syracuse University Press, 1999.
Joyce, James. *Ulysses*. Edited by Declan Kiberd. New York: Penguin, 1992.
Kanafani, Ghassan. *Al-Adab al-Filastini al-Muqawim taht-al-Ihtilal, 1948–1968* (Palestinian Resistance Literature under Colonial Occupation). Beirut: Institute for Palestine Studies, 1986.
———. *Al-Bāb* (The Door). Nicosia, Cyprus: Dār Manshūrāt al-Rimāl, 2013.
———. "Letter from Gaza." In *Men in the Sun and Other Palestinian Stories*, translated by Hilary Kilpatrick, 111–15. Boulder, CO: Lynne Rienner, 1999.
———. *Men in the Sun and Other Palestinian Stories*. Translated by Hilary Kilpatrick. Boulder, CO: Lynne Rienner, 1999.
———. *Palestine's Children: Returning to Haifa and Other Stories*. Translated by Barbara Harlow and Karen E. Riley. Boulder, CO: Lynne Rienner, 2000.
———. *Returning to Haifa*. In *Palestine's Children*, 149–96. Translated by Barbara Harlow and Karen E. Riley. Boulder, CO: Lynne Rienner, 2000.
———. "Waraqa min Gaza." In *Al-Athār al-Kāmila: Al-qisas al-qasīra*, 2:341–50. Beirut: Mu'assisat al-Abḥāth al-'arabiyya, 1987.
———. "Waraqa min Gaza." In *Arḍ al-burtuqāl al-hazīn* (The Land of Sad Oranges), 63–71. Nicosia, Cyprus: Manshūrāt al-rimāl, 2013.
Kassir, Samir. *Being Arab*. Translated by Will Hobson. New York: Verso, 2006.
Kermode, Frank. *The Sense of Ending*. New York: Oxford University Press, 2000.
Khanna, Ranjana. *Dark Continents: Psychoanalysis and Colonialism*. Durham, NC: Duke University Press, 2003.

Khatibi, Abdelkebir. "Frontiers: Between Psychoanalysis and Islam." Translated by P. Burcu Yalim. *Third Text* 23, no. 6 (2009): 689–96.
Klein, Naomi. *The Shock Doctrine: The Rise of Disaster Capitalism*. New York: Metropolitan Books, 2007.
Klemm, Verena. "Different Notions of Commitment (*Iltizām*) and Committed Literature (al-Adab al-Multazim) in the Literary Circles of the Mashriq." *Arabic and Middle Eastern Literatures* 3, no. 1 (2000): 51–62.
Koselleck, Reinhart. *The Practice of Conceptual History: Timing History, Spacing Concepts*. Translated by Todd Presner, Kerstin Behnke, and Jobst Welge. Stanford, CA: Stanford University Press, 2002.
Krichen, Aziz. *Le syndrome Bourguiba*. Tunis: Cérès Productions, 1992.
Kristeva, Julia. *Black Sun: Depression and Melancholia*. Translated by Leon S. Roudiez. New York: Columbia University Press, 1989.
Lacan, Jacques. "The Mirror Stage as Formative of the *I* Function as Revealed in Psychoanalytic Experience." In *Écrits*, 75–81. Translated by Bruce Fink. New York: Norton, 2006.
———. *The Seminar of Jacques Lacan, Book XX: Encore: On Feminine Sexuality, the Limits of Love and Knowledge, 1972–1973*. Edited by Jacques-Alain Miller. Translated by Bruce Fink. New York: Norton, 1988.
———. "The Signification of the Phallus." In *Écrits*, 575–84. Translated by Bruce Fink. New York: Norton, 2006.
———. *The Triumph of Religion*. Translated by Bruce Fink. Malden, MA: Polity, 2013.
LaCapra, Dominick. *Writing History, Writing Trauma*. Baltimore, MD: Johns Hopkins University Press, 2014.
———. "Trauma, Absence, Loss." *Critical Inquiry* 25 (1999): 696–727.
Lang, Robert, and Maher B. Moussa. "Choosing to Be 'Not a Man': Masculine Anxiety in Nouri Bouzid's *Rih Essed/Man of Ashes*." In *Masculinity: Bodies, Movies, Culture*, edited by Peter Lehman, 81–94. New York: Routledge, 2001.
Laplanche, J., and J. B. Pontalis. *The Language of Psycho-analysis*. Translated by Donald Nicholson-Smith. New York: Norton, 1973.
Laroui, Abdallah. *The Crisis of the Arab Intellectual: Traditionalism or Historicism?* Translated by Diarmid Cammell. Berkeley: University of California Press, 1976.
———. *The History of the Maghrib: An Interpretive Essay*. Translated by Ralph Manheim. Princeton, NJ: Princeton University Press, 1977.
———. *Khawāṭir al-Ṣabāḥ: Yawmiyyāt: (1967–1973)* (Morning Thoughts: Diaries). Casablanca: Al-Markaz al-Thaqafi al-Arabi, 2001.
———. *L'ideologie arabe contemporaine*. Paris: François Maspero, 1982.
Lazali, Karima. *Colonial Trauma: A Study of the Psychic and Political Consequences of Colonial Oppression in Algeria*. Translated by Matthew B. Smith. Cambridge: Polity, 2021.
———. *Le trauma colonial: Une enquête sur les effets psychiques et politiques contemporains de l'oppression coloniale en Algérie*. Paris: La Découverte, 2018.

Lazreg, Marnia. *The Eloquence of Silence: Algerian Women in Question.* New York: Routledge, 1994.
Lear, Jonathan. *Radical Hope: Ethics in the Face of Cultural Devastation.* Cambridge, MA: Harvard University Press, 2006.
Li, Darryl. *The Universal Enemy: Jihad, Empire and the Challenge of Solidarity.* Stanford, CA: Stanford University Press, 2020.
Lukács, Georg. *The Theory of the Novel.* Translated by Anna Bostock. Cambridge, MA: MIT Press, 1971.
Maasri, Zeina. *Cosmopolitan Radicalism: The Visual Politics of Beirut's Global Sixties.* London: Cambridge University Press, 2020.
Mabkhout, Chokri. *Eṭṭaliyānī.* Tunis: Dār et-Tanwīr, 2014.
———. *The Italian.* Translated by Karen McNeil and Miled Faiza. New York: Europa, 2021.
———. *Tārīkh al-takfīr fī Tūnis.* Tunis: Miskiliani, 2018.
Macherey, Pierre. "Out of Melancholia: Notes on Judith Butler's *The Psychic Life of Power: Theories in Subjection.*" *Rethinking Marxism: A Journal of Economics, Culture and Society* 16, no. 1 (2004): 16–17.
MacKinnon, Kenneth. *Love, Tears, and the Male Spectator.* Madison, NJ: Fairleigh Dickinson University Press, 2002.
Mahfouz, Naguib. *The Beggar, The Thief and the Dogs, Autumn Quail.* Translated by Nancy Roberts. New York: Anchor Books, 2000.
———. *The Karnak Café.* Translated by Roger Allen. New York: Anchor Books, 2007.
Marcuse, Herbert. "Repressive Tolerance." In *A Critique of Pure Tolerance*, edited by R. P. Wolff, B. Moore Jr., and H. Marcuse, 81–117. Boston: Beacon Press, 1965.
Marriott, David. *Wither Fanon? Studies in the Blackness of Being.* Stanford, CA: Stanford University Press, 2018.
Marx, Karl. "The Eighteenth Brumaire of Louis Bonaparte." In *The Marx-Engels Reader*, edited by Robert C. Tucker, 594–617. New York: Norton, 1978.
Massad, Joseph. *Islam in Liberalism.* Chicago: University of Chicago Press, 2015.
———. *The Persistence of the Palestinian Question: Essays on Zionism and the Palestinians.* London: Routledge, 2006.
———. "Re-Orienting Desire: The Gay International and the Arab World." *Public Culture* 14, no. 2 (2002): 361–85.
Mbembe, Achille. "Necropolitics." *Public Culture* 15 (2003): 11–40.
McEleney, Corey. "The Resistance to Overanalysis." *Differences* 32, no. 2 (2021): 1–38.
McGowan, Todd. *Enjoying What We Don't Have: The Political Project of Psychoanalysis.* Lincoln: University of Nebraska Press, 2013.
Memmi, Albert. *The Colonizer and the Colonized.* Translated by Howard Greenfeld. Boston: Beacon Press, 1991.
———. *Decolonization and the Decolonized.* Translated by Robert Bononno. Minneapolis: University of Minnesota Press, 2006.

Mernissi, Fatima. *Scheherazade Goes West: Different Cultures, Different Harems.* New York: Washington Square Press, 2001.
Mignolo, Walter D., and Catherine E. Walsh. *On Decoloniality: Concepts, Analytics, Praxis.* Durham, NC: Duke University Press, 2018.
Mitchell, W. J. T. "The Commitment to Form; Or, Still Crazy after All These Years." *PMLA* 118, no. 2 (2003): 321–25.
———. "The Unspeakable and the Unimaginable: Word and Image in a Time of Terror." *ELH* 72, no. 2 (2005): 291–308.
Mitscherlich, Alexander, and Margarete Mitscherlich. *The Inability to Mourn: Principles of Collective Behavior.* Translated by Beverley R. Placzek. New York: Grove Press, 1975.
Moore, C. H. *Tunisia since Independence: The Dynamics of One-Party Government.* Westport, CT: Greenwood Press, 1965.
Moore, Lindsey. *Arab, Muslim, Woman: Voice and Vision in Postcolonial Literature and Film.* New York: Routledge, 2008.
Mura, Andrea. "Islamism Revisited: A Lacanian Discourse Critique." *European Journal of Psychoanalysis* 1 (2014): 107–26.
Muruwwa, Hussein. *Kalimāt Ḥayya* (Live Words). Beirut: Dar Al-Farabi, 2012.
Naaman, Dorit. "Woman/Nation: A Postcolonial Look at Female Subjectivity." *Quarterly Review of Film and Video* 17, no. 4 (2000): 333–42.
Nancy, Jean-Luc. "Consecration and Massacre." *Postcolonial Studies* 6, no. 1 (2003): 47–50.
Newton, Huey P. *Revolutionary Suicide.* New York: Harcourt Brace Jovanovich, 1973.
Nietzsche, Friedrich. *Unfashionable Observations.* Translated by Richard Gray. Stanford, CA: Stanford University Press, 1995.
Pandolfo, Stefania. *Knot of the Soul: Madness, Psychoanalysis, Islam.* Chicago: University of Chicago Press, 2017.
———. "'Soul Choking': Maladies of the Soul, Islam, and the Ethics of Psychoanalysis." *Umbr(a): Islam* (2009): 71–104.
Pappe, Ilan. *The Ethnic Cleansing of Palestine.* Oxford: One World, 2007.
Perkins, Kenneth. *A History of Modern Tunisia.* New York: Cambridge University Press. 2004.
Qabbānī, Nizār. "Hawāmish 'alā daftar al-naksa" (Marginal Notes on the Book of Defeat). In *Qaṣā'id Nizār Qabbānī* (Poems of Nizār Qabbānī). Edited by Nawāl Al-Khālidī. Ammān: Dār Osāma li-l-nashr wa-ettawzī', 2005.
———. *Qaṣīdat Balqīs* (The Poem of Balqīs). Beirut: Manshourāt Nizār Qabbānī, 1982.
The Quran. Translated by M. H. Shakir. New York: Tahrike Tarsile Qur'an, 2002.
Qutb, Sayyid. *Ma'alim fi al-Tariq.* Beirut and Cairo: Dar al-shourouk, 1979.
———. *Milestones.* Edited by A. B. Al-Mehri. Birmingham: Maktabah Booksellers and Publishers, 2006.

Rastegar, Kamran. *Surviving Images: Cinema, War, and Cultural Memory the Middle East*. New York: Oxford University Press, 2015.
Retallack, Joan. *The Poethical Wager*. Berkeley: University of California Press, 2003.
Rogan, Eugene. *The Arabs: A History*. New York: Basic Books, 2009.
Rose, Jacqueline. *The Last Resistance*. New York: Verso, 2007.
Rothberg, Michael. *Traumatic Realism: The Demands of Holocaust Representation*. Minneapolis: University of Minnesota Press, 2000.
Ruoff, Jeffrey. "The Gulf War, the Iraq War, and Nouri Bouzid's Cinema of Defeat: *It's Scheherazade We're Killing* (1993) and *Making of*." *South Central Review* 28, no. 1 (2001: 18–35.
Sacks, Jeffrey. *Iterations of Loss: Mutilation and Aesthetic Form, Al-Shidyaq to Darwish*. New York: Fordham University Press, 2015.
Safouan, Moustapha. "Five Years of Psychoanalysis in Cairo." Translated by Juliet Flower MacCannell. *Umbr(a): Islam* (2009): 36–40.
——. *Why Are the Arabs Not Free? The Politics of Writing*. Oxford: Wiley-Blackwell, 2007.
Said, Edward. *After the Last Sky: Palestinian Lives*. Photographs by Jean Mohr. New York: Columbia University Press, 1999.
——. "Arabic Prose and Prose Fiction After 1948." In *Reflections on Exile and Other Essays*, 41–60. Cambridge, MA: Harvard University Press, 2003.
——. *Freud and the Non-European*. New York: Verso, 2003.
——. *Humanism and Democratic Criticism*. New York: Columbia University Press, 2004.
——. "Permission to Narrate." *Journal of Palestine Studies* 13, no. 3 (1984): 27–48.
Salem, Sara. *Anticolonial Afterlives in Egypt: The Politics of Hegemony*. New York: Cambridge University Press, 2020.
Salih, Arwa. *Saraṭān al-Rūḥ* (Cancer of the Soul). Cairo: Dar al-Nahar, 1998.
——. *The Stillborn: Notes of a Woman from the Student-Movement Generation in Egypt*. Translated by Samah Selim. New York: Seagull, 2017.
Salloum, Jacqueline Reem, dir. *Slingshot Hip-Hop*. Ramallah, Palestine: Fresh Booza DVD, 2008.
Samak, Qussai. "The Politics of Egyptian Cinema." *MERIP Reports* 56 (April 1977): 12–15.
Santner, Eric. *Stranded Objects: Mourning, Memory, and Film in Postwar Germany*. Ithaca, NY: Cornell University Press, 1990.
Sartre, Jean-Paul. *Being and Nothingness: A Phenomenological Essay on Ontology*. Translated by Hazel Barnes. New York: Washington Square, 1956.
——. *Existentialism Is a Humanism*. Translated by Carol Macomber. New Haven, CT: Yale University Press, 2007.
Schivelbusch, Wolfgang. *The Culture of Defeat: On National Trauma, Mourning and Recovery*. Translated by Jefferson Chase. New York: Picador, 2003.
Schwenger, Peter. *The Tears of Things: Melancholy and Physical Objects*. Minneapolis: University of Minnesota Press, 2006.

Scott, David. *Omens of Adversity: Tragedy, Time, Memory, Justice*. Durham, NC: Duke University Press, 2014.
Scott, Joan W. *Sex and Secularism*. Princeton, NJ: Princeton University Press, 2018.
Sedgwick, E. K. "Gosh, Boy George, You Must be Awfully Secure in Your Masculinity." In *Constructing Masculinity*, edited by Maurice Berger, Brian Wallis, and Simon Watson, 11–20. New York: Routledge, 1995.
Shabad, Peter. "The Most Intimate of Creations: Symptoms as Memorials to One's Lonely Suffering." In *Symbolic Loss: The Ambiguity of Mourning and Memory at Century's End*, edited by Peter Homans and Julia Stern, 197–212. Charlottesville: University Press of Virginia, 2000.
Shafik, Viola. *Arab Cinema: History and Cultural Identity*. Cairo: American University in Cairo Press, 1998.
Shaheen, Jack. *Guilty: Hollywood's Verdict on Arabs after 9/11*. Northampton, MA: Olive Branch, 2008.
Sharabi, Hisham. *Neopatriarchy: A Theory of Distorted Change in Arab Society*. New York: Oxford University Press, 1988.
Shehadeh, Raja. *Strangers in the House: Coming of Age in Occupied Palestine*. London: Profile Books, 2009.
Sherzer, Dina. "Remembrance of Things Past: *Les silences du palais* by Moufida Tlatli." *South Central Review* 17, no. 3 (2000): 50–59.
Shohat, Ella. *Taboo Memories, Diasporic Voices*. Durham, NC: Duke University Press, 2006.
Slawy-Sutton, Catherine. "*Outremer* and *The Silences of the Palace*: Feminist Allegories of Two Countries in Transition." *Pacific Coast Philology* 37 (2002): 85–104.
Spargo, Clifton. *The Ethics of Mourning: Grief and Responsibility in Elegiac Literature*. Baltimore, MD: Johns Hopkins University Press, 2004.
Spivak, Gayatri C. *Death of a Discipline*. New York: Columbia University Press, 2003.
———. "Subaltern Studies: Deconstructing Historiography." In *Selected Subaltern Studies*, edited by Ranajit Guha and Gayatri C. Spivak, 3–32. Delhi: Oxford University Press, 1988.
———. "Terror: A Speech after 9/11." *Boundary 2* 31 (2004): 81–111.
Stollery, Martin. "Masculinities, Generations, and Cultural Transformation in Contemporary Tunisian Cinema." *Screen* 42, no. 1 (2001): 49–63.
Tarabishi, George. *Al-Muthaqqafūn al-'Arab wa al-Turāth* (Arab Intellectuals and Tradition). London: Riad El-Rayyes Books Ltd, 1991.
———. *Allah fi rihlat Naguib Mahfouz al-ramziya*. Beirut: Dar al-Tiba'a wa-nashr, 1988.
Tlatli, Moufida. "Moufida Tlatli Showcases the Inner World of Women's Emancipation." *Magharebia: The News & Views of the Maghreb*, 2005.
———, dir. *The Season of Men*. Paris and Tunis: Les Films du Losange and Maghreb Films Carthage, 2000.

———, dir. *The Silences of the Palace*. Tunis and Paris: Ciné Télé Films and Mat Films, 1994.

———. "Une affaire de femmes/Stories of Women." *Ecrans d'Afriques* 8, no. 2 (1994): 8-11.

Toscano, Alberto. *Fanaticism: On the Uses of an Idea*. New York: Verso, 2010.

Traverso, Enzo. *Left-Wing Melancholy: Marxism, History and Memory*. New York: Columbia University Press, 2016.

Turki, Fawaz. "Meaning in Palestinian History: Text and Context." *Arab Studies Quarterly* 3, no. 4 (1981): 371–83.

Wannous, Saadallah. "Anā al-Janāza wal-mushayyi'ūn" (I Am the Funeral and the Funeral-Goer). In *Al-A'māl al-Kāmila*, 3:439–43. Damascus: Al-Ahālī, 1996.

———. *Haflat Samar min ajl al-Khāmis Ḥuzayrān* (An Evening Entertainment for the Fifth of June). Beirut: Dār al-Adāb, 1980.

———. *Sentence to Hope: A Saadallah Wannous Reader*. Translated by Robert Meyers and Nada Saab. New Haven, CT: Yale University Press, 2019.

Warschawski, Michel. *Toward an Open Tomb: The Crisis of Israeli Society*. New York: Monthly Review Press, 2004.

White, Hayden. "The Value of Narrativity in the Representation of Reality." *Critical Inquiry* 7, no. 1 (1980): 5–29.

Yusuf, Hasan. *Al-Mufakkir Al-Ishtiraki fi fikr Naguib Mahfouz*. Cairo: Dar Al-'Alim Al-Thalith, 2005.

Ziarek, Ewa Plonowska. *Feminist Aesthetics and the Politics of Modernism*. New York: Columbia University Press, 2012.

Žižek, Slavoj. *Enjoy Your Symptom*. New York: Routledge, 2008.

———. *In Defense of Lost Causes*. New York: Verso, 2008.

———. "Melancholy and the Act." *Critical Inquiry* 26, no. 4 (2000): 657–81.

———. *Welcome to the Desert of the Real: Five Essays on September 11 and Related Dates*. New York: Verso, 2002.

Index

abandonment, 60, 144, 281–82, 288
Abdelkader (Abd al-Qādir), Emir, 14–15, 145
Abraham, 240, 244, 267–69, 271
act, 3, 10, 28, 34, 37–38, 91, 118, 121, 127, 192, 200, 208, 214, 250, 260–61, 274, 281; decolonial, 28; ethical, 35; melancholy, 1, 2, 11, 22, 39, 41–42, 55, 214, 222, 226, 282, 287, 290; perfunctory, 28; selfless, 24; sovereign, 22; suicidal, 22
acting out, 177, 210, 260
aesthetic, 52, 57–58, 71, 91, 203; autonomy, 77, 90fn1; burden, 203; commitment, 90fn1; dramatization, 87; embodiment, 72; form, 87; ideal, 72; judgment, 204; praxis, 75; protest, 87; value, 204; thrust, 229; schism, 4; standards, 115; transaction, 191
aestheticization, 31, 41; aestheticizing failure, 19; of atrocity, 195
aesthetics: of defeat, 52, 59; of failure, 41; of redemption, 121
affective, 201; ambiguity and ambivalence, 27; ambivalence, 143; apparatus, 168; closure, 61, 102, 256; corollary, 15; corollary, 16; correlative, 15; currents, 16; detachment, 15; differentials, 28, 288; disposition, 3, 48; economies, 130; flatness, 68; legacies, 253; map, 5; mass appeal, 61; movements, 21; politics, 16; response, 143; tie, 26; turmoil and disarray, 61, 148. See also psychoaffective
affect(s), 2, 4, 19, 20, 21, 28, 39, 60, 68, 69, 230, 282, 288–89n27; colonial, 18; foreclosure of,

61; question of, 69; pseudo-European, 73; spectrum of, 143
affectlessness, 60, 67, 69; affectless withdrawal, 15, 60
afteraffect(s), 7, 8, 31
affectual, 34; commitments, 35; indifference, 61; revolt, 36
agentive, 28–29, 224–25, 227n60, 278n3, 289
aggression, 2–3, 5–6, 23, 29, 122, 179, 211n27; autoimmunitary, 223
aggressivity/aggressive, 18–21, 94n8, 156, 223, 266; compulsive, 20
Algerian melancholy, 18, 20–1
allegory/allegories/allegorical, 4, 43, 50–52, 55, 60, 69, 76, 78–79, 82–83, 96, 172n26, 190, 207, 213, 229, 270, 288
allegorize/allegorizing/allegorization, 40, 49, 51, 55, 80–81, 83
altermusulman, 262, 265–66. See also *surmusulman*
'amaliyyāt 'ishtishhadiyya (martyrdom operations), 202, 221, 278. See also martyrdom
amnesia, 14, 158, 220; sanctioned, 159
anagnorisis, 58, 284
Andalus (Andalusia), 108, 113. See also post-Andalusian
anxiety, 60, 62, 68, 81, 87, 102, 109, 185; settler, 87
Arabic, 23, 27, 37, 39, 52, 54, 62, 67, 70–71, 75, 88, 91, 92n5, 95, 97–99, 101, 110, 113–14, 120–21, 158, 160–61, 199, 214n36, 220–21, 236n7, 251, 278–79, 278n3, 282–84, 287–89, 291

Arab psyche, 5, 8, 9, 11, 103, 287. *See also* subjectivity
Arafat, Yasir, 213
atrocity, 15, 90–91, 195; aesthetics, 91fn4, 287
authentic/authenticity, 3n4, 6, 20, 243–44, 254
autocritique, 58
autodestructrice, 282. *See also* autodestructive
autodestructive, 18, 14, 18, 222, 222n51, 224, 282
autoimmunitary, 209, 223–24, "autoimmunitary aggression," 223
autoimmunize, 223, 225
autosacrifice, 251, 259, 277, 281–82
Ayouch, Nabil, 202

barbarism/barbaric, 20, 39, 89, 90, 92–93, 100, 103, 107, 110, 117–18, 203
Battle of Algiers (1954–57), 45; film, 193, 202
belated/belatedness, 2n2, 6, 9, 25, 32, 48, 96, 104, 117, 148, 151, 157, 190, 232n67, 235, 242, 285, 287
Ben Achour, Tahar, 263–64
Ben-Gurion, David, 22–23, 84
Ben M'Hidi, Larbi, 45–47, 193
Bouazizi, Mohamed (street vendor), 1–3, 5, 10, 11, 281–82, 287
Bourguiba, Habib, 40, 51, 156, 161, 163, 165–68, 173, 178, 183, 190, 241–42, 262–66

castration, 6, 51–52, 65, 191, 192
collaborative, 3, 176, 210, 221, 230–31
collective, 2–3, 10–11, 13, 21, 25, 28, 37, 47, 50–51, 73, 84, 103, 166–67, 171, 241–43, 245–46, 250–51, 290; consciousness, 26, 162, 192; continuum, 78; disposition, 11, 48; neurosis, 6; psyche, 8, 14, 258; salvation, 24, 33; shame, 8; solidarity, 192; unconscious, 168, 183; woes, 26
collectivity, 27, 32, 158
colonial, 2–4, 5n7, 6, 8, 10–18, 21, 23, 28, 31, 37–38, 41, 47, 49, 94n8, 123, 127, 157, 160, 165–68, 173–74, 190–91, 203, 205n18, 250, 253, 265, 275, 283, 285–86, 290; modernity, 40, 161, 241–43, 286; shame, 180
colonialism, 10, 12, 16–21; postcolonial colonialism, 27; settler, 3–5, 8, 10, 12, 19
coloniality, 159, 242; of power, 12, 17
colonisabilité (colonisability), 16
commitment, 3n4, 4, 9, 24, 33, 35, 37–38, 49, 50, 58–70, 73–79, 81–82, 88, 90n1, 92, 93n6, 99, 128, 139, 143–44, 175, 167, 194, 199, 237, 282, 285–87, 289. See also *iltizām*

compulsion, 214, 223; to repeat, 12, 95fn9, 154, 230
compulsive, 21, 30, 66, 95n9, 222; aggressivity, 20, 21, 30, 179; compulsive repetition, 66, 178, 198, 223
compulsory, 21, 126, 163, 222
congenital, 18, 48, 207
continuum, 3, 47, 51–52, 57, 59, 66, 78, 90, 96, 228, 255
counterelegy, 101–2. *See also* postelegiac

decolonial, 7, 15–16, 19–21, 23, 25–28, 37, 39, 46–48, 58, 70, 72–74, 88, 124, 127, 134, 161, 168, 233, 277, 283, 286, 288
defeat, 4, 22, 26, 30, 35–36, 45, 48, 51–54, 58–62, 73, 97, 155, 191, 229, 230, 262, 290; of 1967, 5, 7–9, 11, 28, 38–39, 47, 50, 55–56, 61–63, 66–67, 82, 86, 88; culture of, 16, 53; ethics of, 57; odor of, 23; politics of, 57. *See also* aesthetics
defeatism, 55, 60, 82, 192, 229; defeatist, 9, 60
dehumanize/dehumanizing/dehumanization, 193, 203–5, 207
denial/denialism, 12–13, 59, 60, 87, 206
depathologize, 247
depoliticize, 17–18
deradicalization, 248, 251
derealizing/derealization, 15, 31, 33, 78, 81, 110, 112, 207, 227
destructive, 19; auto-, 18, 222; hetero-, 14, 18, 20, 22, 222, 236; self-, 282
disaffection, 54, 67
disappearance, 12–13, 84; practices of, 15
disempowering, 2, 213, 282, 290. *See also* empowering
disgust, 2
discontent, 2, 79, 164
disposition, 27, 125–26, 170, 207, 277, 290; collective, 2, 11; decolonial, 16; melancholite, 183, 187; melancholy, 2, 14, 11, 15, 16, 37, 39, 48, 55, 73, 266, 283, 285, 287, 289, 291; psychopolitical, 4; saturnine, 50
dissent, 2n1, 28, 37, 65, 113, 291
Djait, Abdelaziz, 263–64
Doueiri, Ziad, 202

ecstasy (Sufism), 124, 130, 141, 145–50, 152–53, 155
elegiac, 47, 59, 88, 97–98; rhetorical modes, 88; tradition, 21. *See also* postelegiac
elegy, 99–101, 109–11, 120

INDEX

315

embodiment, 3, 24, 25, 42, 60, 68, 72, 170, 220, 245
empathy/empathic, 24, 30, 151, 171, 187, 189, 192, 198, 226, 284, 284n20
empiphany, 24–25, 284n20
empowering, 1–2, 55, 73, 97, 116–17, 126, 128–39, 153, 283, 285, 288, 290. See also disempowering
enact, 25, 34, 38, 126, 185, 216
enracinement protestaire, 252
epiphany/epiphanic, 24, 26, 36, 129, 151, 284, 284n20
esteem as in self-esteem, 31, 37, 133
ethical, 27–33, 35–37, 79, 88, 91–92, 101–2, 110, 112, 186, 241, 256, 270, 289; imperative, 32; swerve, 33; vacuum, 32
ethics, 25, 32, 78–79, 102, 109, 227; of melancholicization, 27, 32; of solidarity, 32; of defeat, 57
ethnocidal, 215
European melancholy, 20–21

fanatic/fanaticism, 201, 205n18, 233, 247n40, 250–51, 260
fantasies, 31, 36–37, 56, 188, 230, 247, 288; of necromnipotence, 224; of omnipotence, 7n9, 288
fatwa, 164n10, 237, 249, 264–65, 287
female jouissance, 238–39, 267, 269, 270–73
flight, 13, 32, 125, 145–46, 260, 281; the desire for, 25–26; into illness, 151
foreclosure of, 15, 61, 90, 187, 189, 198
foundational melancholia, 128–29, 143, 153
fedayeen, 23, 85–86
flagellation as in self-flagellation, 29, 61
Front de Libération Nationale (FLN), 45–46, 193, 205n18, 277

grandeur, 31, 250, 258, 261
grand narrative, 60, 69, 190, 209, 229, 250; artistic achievement, 288
grief, 4–5, 26–28, 36, 57, 101, 122, 182, 285, 289n27
grievance, 1, 4–5, 14, 16, 25, 27–28, 55, 74, 103, 207n20, 241, 249, 282
glory: Arab, 7; Arab Islamic, 7, 261; Bourguiba, 165; Israeli, 31; Nasserite, 60
Golden Age, 240, 265
Golden Globe, 202

Habash, George, 22
Hagar, 244, 266–72, 275
Hawi, Khalil, 2–3, 5, 10, 11, 15
hazīma, 47. See also defeat
heteroimmunitary, 187, 187n42, 192
hogra, 282
hope, 9, 11, 39, 76, 85–86, 114, 136, 174, 196, 209, 214, 218, 231, 289, 291
hopeless/hopelessness, 8–9, 177, 192, 197, 210, 214n34, 286–88
human, 57, 84, 106, 130, 153, 204, 217, 267; affect, 289n27; agency, 46; attributes, 160; call, 25; causes, 10; concerns, 74; dignity, 26; defenselessness, 182; exposure, 57; fragility, 59, 60, 110; impulse, 114; intervention, 164; procreation, 267, 281–82; psyche, 282; recognition, 171; responsibility, 59; rights, 5, 156, 174, 212, 231n66, 284; solidarity, 187; vulnerability, 177; will, 193; toll, 285
humane, 17. See also inhumane
humanist, 17
humanitarian, 212
humanity, 41, 70, 81, 110, 114, 262; crimes against, 12
humanize/humanization, 41, 57, 81, 203, 205–7. See also dehumanize

identification, 12, 17, 29, 31, 60, 139, 144, 179, 187, 190; identificatory, 28
ijtihād (independent reasoning), 164n10, 264
iltizām, 38, 70–74, 76–79, 99. See also commitment
immune/immunity, 178, 225
immunize, 60, 80, 182, 278
immunopoetic practices, 224
implication, 9, 17, 39, 51, 53, 64, 79, 84, 112, 189, 217, 247; colonial, 265n85; grave, 16; pathological, 15; political, 282
incitement, 19, 29, 71, 81, 149, 185, 187, 241, 261; to action, 17; to dissidence, 69; to insurrection, 286; to militancy, 19; to poetic insurgency, 93; to rebellion, 77
inconsolable/inconsolability, 22, 28, 92, 101, 179, 185, 285
indictment, 3, 32, 55, 61, 66, 69, 70, 77, 81, 90n1, 91, 93n6, 147, 189, 246
indifference, 8, 60–61, 153, 282
indignation, 2, 49, 230, 282, 286
indignity, 282; of defeat, 98
indisposition, 5, 283
inhizāmiyya, 59. See also defeatism

inhumane, 199
injustice, 2, 8, 10, 14–15, 26, 32–33, 35–38, 48–49, 64, 74, 92, 96, 171, 191, 230, 233, 253, 256, 281, 283–84, 286, 288, 289
insurrection/insurrectionary, 3, 12, 14, 17, 21, 127, 138, 189n45, 282, 286
internalize/internalization, 13–14, 16, 94n8, 161–62, 174, 176, 176n30, 229, 230, 232
introspective/introspection, 14, 21, 29, 73, 188, 256, 288
invulnerability, 178, 183, 192, 225; fantasy of, 187; illusion of, 223
Isaac, 267, 269
Ishmael, 240, 244, 267–69, 271
Islamization of radicalism, 42, 249
'istishhādī (seeker of martyrdom), 259, 278–79, 280n8. See also martyr

Jesus, 151, 235, 267
jihad, 164, 164n10, 232, 261–65
jihadist, 42, 247–48, 250, 252, 254–55, 259, 261; offer, 260
jihad akbar (greater jihad), 259, 260
jihad asghar (smaller jihad), 259, 260
jolt as in empathic jolt, 284
jouissance, 158, 239, 245, 250, 254–58; compensatory, 20, 42; stolen, 243. See also Other jouissance
jouissance anticipée (anticipated jouissance), 257
jouissance paradisiaque absolue (absolute jouissance), 257

Khadija (wife of prophet Muhammad), 272–74

laïcité (laicism), 58, 165, 249, 265
left melancholy, 35, 126, 129, 144–45, 153–54
liberation, 37, 54, 56, 66, 68, 122, 172n26, 173, 199, 208–9, 224, 233, 290. See also national liberation
licensed chaos, 140
licensed grounds, 41, 261; premises, 208
license: to cynicism, 92; to forgetting, 111; to suffering, 147

marthiyya (elegy), 101–2, 121. See also elegy
martyr, 74, 116, 199, 213, 216–71, 221, 224–25, 259, 279, 280
martyrdom, 22, 203, 208, 220, 224, 229, 231, 251, 259; acts, 192; missions, 202, 210, 224; operations, 2, 42, 59, 192, 194, 198–99, 202, 217, 221, 278–79

matereality, 209, 223–26
materialization, 2, 11, 28, 127, 144, 232, 244
melancholia of the oppressed, 27, 30–31. See also postcolonial melancholy
melancholic, 9, 14, 18, 20, 22, 25–26, 28–29, 31–33, 35–37, 46, 82, 84, 87–88, 98, 101, 104, 125, 129, 139, 143–44, 149, 171, 175, 180, 188–89, 191–92, 199, 221–22, 233, 255–56, 267, 270, 282, 285–86, 289–90. See also disposition
melancholite, 9, 26, 29, 31, 42, 59, 68, 125, 128, 143, 150, 155, 168, 174–75, 178, 180, 182–83, 186–88, 190–92, 232–33, 239, 243, 255–58, 265–66, 275
melancholizing/melancholization, 4, 8–9, 11–17, 21, 19, 23–27, 29–32, 73–75, 80–81, 157, 191, 217, 265, 267, 275, 282, 284, 286
mélancolie/mélancolique, 39, 123, 144, 255, 285
mélancolisation, 13. See also melancholizing
mobilizing/mobilization, 1, 2n1, 14, 18, 25n50, 30, 71–72, 138, 161, 190, 197, 209, 237, 240, 258, 261, 265, 284
Mohammad, 262, 273
monotheism, 240, 266, 267, 268, 275; monotheistic, 43, 239, 240, 244–45, 268, 270–71, 274–75
Moses, 235
Moses and Monotheism, 235, 237, 239
mourning, 8, 10, 15, 28, 33, 37, 60, 61, 69, 91, 98, 100–2, 109, 110–11, 121, 125, 127, 141, 143–44, 183, 189, 221n49, 224, 242, 256, 286; experience of, 183; normative structures of, 28; practices of, 171; process of, 182; rituals of, 221; spectacle of, 182; task of, 125, 258; work of, 125, 187
"Mourning and Melancholia," 5n7, 125

nahḍa, 6–7, 160, 167
nakba (1948 Catastrophe), 4, 10, 21, 23, 26, 31, 33, 39, 49, 80–81, 84, 87–88, 92–93, 95–97, 121–22, 202
naksa (1967 Six Day War), 5–6, 8–9, 11, 21, 28, 31, 33, 38–39, 45, 47–48, 50–51, 53–54, 60–61, 69, 72–73, 82–83, 92, 97–98, 103, 113, 121–22, 161, 199
nashwa (ecstasy), 145–47, 152. See also ecstasy
nationalism, 7, 9, 93n7, 94, 94n8, 159, 166; Arab, 5, 7, 38, 52, 59, 70, 98, 133, 135, 190; German, 94n8; homonationalism, 188n43
nationalist, 4, 7, 54, 69, 103, 124, 130–31, 136, 156, 161, 173–74, 228, 280, 288

INDEX 317

national liberation, 2, 8, 19, 27, 31, 33, 39, 41, 46–48, 66, 70, 92, 131, 172, 208; sovereignty, 5, 8, 26, 69
narcissism, 4, 8, 28, 37, 56, 244, 257
narcissistic, 8, 9, 20, 29, 31, 68, 96, 125, 182, 222, 232–33, 289; attachment, 144, 171; omnipotence, 285, 288; regression, 147
Nasser, Gamal Abdel, 5–8, 38, 40, 52, 60–63, 66–69, 122–23, 130, 132–39, 154
necromnipotence (as in *fantasies of necromnipotence*), 224
necropower, 223, 223n52
necropolitical, 223–24
necropolitics, 95n10
Nehru, 133
neocolonial, 15, 47, 70, 127, 156, 165, 190
neopatriarchy, 40, 157, 159, 167–68, 170–72, 175, 183, 190, 286
neurosis, 6; neurotic, 187

oriental despotism, 5
orientalism, 232, 248, 284–85
orientalist, 4–5, 30, 107, 202n13, 236n7, 278n3, 284
origin(s), 6, 42–43, 81, 155, 173, 190, 208, 232–33, 237–41, 243–45, 250, 254, 258, 261, 266–72, 274–75, 280–81, 286; myth of, 42, 240
originary, 25–26, 129, 140, 143, 153, 244,
Oscars, 202
Oslo Accords, 202
Other jouissance, 238, 258, 268, 270–73

passage à l'acte, 260. *See also* acting out
pathologize/pathologization, 9, 16, 30, 43, 73, 217, 242, 247, 286. *See also* depathologize
pathology/pathological, 5, 14, 16–17, 18, 21n43, 31, 37, 73, 94, 153, 188, 222n51, 242, 247n40, 256, 266n87, 284; quasi-, 8
precarious, 83, 88, 92n5, 95n11, 127, 134, 185, 209; precariousness, 219
precarity, 16, 27, 32, 36, 48, 88, 283
poetry after, 92, 100, 121; Auschwitz, 39, 89, 90n1, 90n2, 91, 93, 93n6, 95–96, 117, 121; Iraq, 89, 96, 111, 117, 120–21; the Nakba, 93–96, 121; the Naksa, 97, 121
Pontecorvo, Gillo, 45, 193, 202
Popular Front for the Liberation of Palestine (PFLP), 22, 82
post-Andalusian, 16–17, 107
postelegiac, 98, 102, 110, 121

postcolonial, 2, 4, 5n7, 11–17, 27, 28, 30, 34–35, 37–38, 46–47, 50–52, 57–58, 58, 58n33, 136, 155–57, 159, 161–62, 164–67, 170, 172–74, 180, 207, 241, 264, 266, 284n20, 285
postcolonial melancholy, 31. *See also* melancholia of the oppressed
postcolonialism, 5, 41
postcontradictory, 43
powerless, 57, 138, 191–92; powerlessness, 22, 70, 73, 180
predicament, 37, 52, 80, 153, 163, 285; melancholic, 191–92
protest, 1–2, 4, 10–14, 41, 87, 104, 112–13, 115, 127, 154, 163n9, 192, 202, 236, 243, 281, 287
pseudo-epiphanic, 78
pseudo-melancholia, 18, 21
psychoaffective, 21, 97, 251; commitment, 75; conditions, 14; convulsions, 141; crisis, 123, 141; differentials, 88, 2 82; disarray and disorder, 140; discourse, 153; disengagements, 157; dispositions, 125; dissidence, 171; dynamics, 6, 27, 88; effects, 190; forcefields, 288; formation, 180; imprint, 155; investitures, 8, 26, 58; investment, 83, 128; irresolution, 110; legacy, 5, 62, 162; materialization, 79; motor forces, 257; operations, 9; playing forcefield, 232; politics of, 192; process, 254; reaction to loss, 255; release, 4; resistances, 192; response, 2, 4, 148, 221; sovereignty, 171; struggle, 192; swerve, 21, 22; temporalities, 96, 188, 287, 290
psyche, 13–14, 17, 32, 36, 119, 143, 148, 185, 189, 240, 247, 250, 252, 258, 277, 282, 299
psychoanalysis, 1, 5, 6, 8, 18, 27, 39, 41–42, 59n35, 125, 143, 197, 201, 221–22, 233–39, 247–48, 250, 252–55, 261, 267, 274, 277, 281, 283
psychological, 4, 10, 12, 94, 110, 167, 222, 260

qaṣīda (poem), 54, 117; *Qaṣīdat Balqīs*, 99, 101, 117

Rabin, Yitzhak, 22
radicalisation de l'islam (radicalization of Islam), 249
radicalization, 42, 47, 248, 250–52, 264
recognition, 4, 25, 52, 95, 171, 191, 217, 280, 284n20, 287; demand for, 32; dignity of, 49, 56, 64, 189, 250
reenact, 12–13, 26, 69, 79, 90, 112
reenactment, 14–15, 21, 49, 51, 55, 78, 102, 129, 168, 174, 213

revolt, 3, 14, 17, 20, 36, 97, 117, 121, 141, 189n45, 145, 243, 283, 286
revolutionary, 7, 19, 38, 46, 53, 56, 113, 124, 126–29, 131–33, 138–39, 145, 152, 162, 173–74, 178, 190, 237; post-, 40; quasi-, 35
revolution(s), 4, 10, 39, 134, 236, 281–82
revolutionism, 3
regression, 9, 37, 56, 73, 93n6, 147, 247; psycho-pathological, 257; quasi-pathological, 8
regressive, 4, 7, 9, 28–89, 31, 73, 125, 232–33, 240, 245, 255–56, 284, 289
remainder, 9, 143, 214, 263
rithā' (elegy, mourning), 21. See also elegy

sacrifice, 30, 50, 90, 125, 138, 151, 260–61; auto, 251; self-, 22, 199, 208, 257, 277, 280n8, 281, 287; selfless, 24, 31–32. See also martyrdom
Salafi, 7; Salafist, 161, 242
Salafism, 236, 240, 248
salvation, 9, 260; collective, 24, 33; individual, 24, 33
Samson option/parable, 215, 228, 278
settler colonial/colonialism, 3–5, 8, 10, 15, 19, 20, 23, 25–26, 30–31, 33, 36–37, 39, 40, 46–47, 55, 72, 76, 78, 81, 88, 127, 130, 188n43, 190, 192–93, 201, 203, 207–8, 212, 216–18, 222, 229, 232, 265, 288, 289n27
shahāda, 199, 208, 214n36. See also martyrdom
shahīd, 216, 278–80, 287. See also martyr
shame, 2, 3, 6, 8, 12, 30, 52, 60, 65, 98, 187, 220, 230; postcolonial, 4, 253. See also colonial
solidarity, 3, 24–27, 30, 32, 37, 72, 171, 179, 183, 187, 192, 284–85
sovereignty, 6, 22, 42, 52, 60, 68, 72, 171, 193, 203, 208, 216, 223, 224, 270. See also nationalism
steadfast/steadfastness, 9, 24, 88, 118, 156, 193, 199, 256, 265
subjectivity, 42, 56, 60, 68, 93n6, 100–1, 109, 192, 236, 243, 246, 262, 264; Arab, 5, 281; decolonial, 26; impasse of, 42, 264; postcolonial, 46
sublimation, 4; desublimation, 5
Sufi/Sufism, 14, 130, 143, 145–53, 155, 265, 267, 271
suicidal, 19, 42, 59, 199, 201, 215–16, 221; act, 22, 226; protest, 11, 41, 282; resistance, 209
suicide, 2–3, 3n4, 5, 10–11, 18–19, 28, 41–42, 55–56, 59, 67, 76, 104, 117, 126, 199, 222, 222n50, 228; bombers, 205n18, 206–7, 215n37, 280; bombing, 2, 41, 76, 203, 206–8, 215–16, 220n48; martyr, 213–14, 225–26; martyrdom, 22, 207, 209, 214, 226–27, 250, 260; mission, 210; protest, 41, 192, 207; resistance, 208–9, 214–16, 222
suicide protestaire, 282
sumūd (steadfastness), 24, 27, 199. See also steadfast
surmusulman, 42, 245–48, 252–58, 260–62, 265–66
symptom, 8, 10, 12, 15–16, 21n43, 28, 30, 40, 42–43, 62, 68, 75, 138–39, 151, 153, 167, 170, 177, 187, 198, 232, 234, 239, 241, 246, 249, 252–53, 257, 286
symptomatic, 6, 27, 31, 63, 150, 187–88, 270
symptomology, 10, 17
swerve, 16, 21–23, 32–33, 77, 179, 283–84, 283–87, 289

theopathological, 245, 275
Tito, 133
tradition, 6, 9, 21, 35, 40–42, 97, 113, 125, 161–62, 167, 169, 175, 182, 234, 265, 247n40
transgenerational, 3, 12, 52, 154, 176, 283$8$, 184n37
trauma, 6, 12, 28, 49, 50, 55–56, 81, 171, 185, 187, 189, 190, 222, 245, 258, 283
traumatic, 5, 6, 8, 240, 245, 283; posttraumatic, 188
traumatize/traumatization, 6, 7, 11, 50
"travelling theory," 18
turāth, 6. See also tradition

uncanny, 12, 24–25, 81, 200
unsettlement as in "empathic unsettlement," 24, 198

virility, 160, 185, 191–92; authentic, 20; excessive, 65; vaunted, 65
voluntary martyrdom, 202, 220–21, 231, 279–80
vulnerability, 11, 32, 57, 59, 109, 177–78, 182, 185, 187, 209, 223–25, 284; fantasy of, 32. See also invulnerability

waṭan (homeland), 74–75

yabqā (to remain), 215; *baqī* (that remains), 23

Zaynab bint Jaḥsh (cousin and the seventh wife of Muhammad), 62
Zaytouna Mosque, 163–64

Nouri Gana is Professor of Comparative Literature and Near Eastern Languages and Cultures at the University of California, Los Angeles. He is the author of *Signifying Loss: Toward a Poetics of Narrative Mourning* (2011) and editor of *The Making of the Tunisian Revolution: Contexts, Architects, Prospects* (2013) and *The Edinburgh Companion to the Arab Novel in English: The Politics of Anglo Arab and Arab American Literature and Culture* (2013).

www.ingramcontent.com/pod-product-compliance
Lightning Source LLC
Chambersburg PA
CBHW020353080526
44584CB00014B/1003